Arbitral Awards as Investments

International Arbitration Law Library

VOLUME 39

Editor

Professor Julian D.M. Lew QC has been involved with international arbitration for more than 40 years as counsel, as arbitrator and as an academic. He has held the position of Professor and Head of the School on International Arbitration, Centre for Commercial Law studies, Queen Mary University of London since its creation in 1985. He is now an independent arbitrator at 20 Essex Street, London.

Introduction

Since its first volume published in 1993, this authoritative practitioner-oriented series has published in-depth and analytical works on niche aspects of international arbitration, authored by specialists in the field.

Objective

This authoritative and established series covering in-depth analyses of niche areas appeals to both practitioners and academics.

Frequency

A volume is published whenever an interesting topic presents itself.

The titles published in this series are listed at the end of this volume.

Arbitral Awards as Investments

Treaty Interpretation and the Dynamics of International Investment Law

Maximilian Clasmeier

Published by:
Kluwer Law International B.V.
PO Box 316
2400 AH Alphen aan den Rijn
The Netherlands
Website: www.wklawbusiness.com

Sold and distributed in North, Central and South America by:
Wolters Kluwer Legal & Regulatory U.S.
7201 McKinney Circle
Frederick, MD 21704
United States of America
Email: customer.service@wolterskluwer.com

Sold and distributed in all other countries by:
Turpin Distribution Services Ltd
Stratton Business Park
Pegasus Drive, Biggleswade
Bedfordshire SG18 8TQ
United Kingdom
Email: kluwerlaw@turpin-distribution.com

Printed on acid-free paper.

ISBN 978-90-411-8357-6

e-Book: 978-90-411-8358-3
web-PDF: 978-90-411-8359-0

© 2017 Kluwer Law International BV, The Netherlands

All rights reserved. No part of this publication may be reproduced, stored in a retrieval system, or transmitted in any form or by any means, electronic, mechanical, photocopying, recording, or otherwise, without written permission from the publisher.

Permission to use this content must be obtained from the copyright owner. Please apply to: Permissions Department, Wolters Kluwer Legal & Regulatory U.S., 76 Ninth Avenue, 7th Floor, New York, NY 10011-5201, USA. Website: www.wklawbusiness.com

Printed in the United Kingdom.

D 61

Dissertation zur Erlangung des akademischen Grades eines Doktors der Rechte (Dr. iur.) der Juristischen Fakultät der Heinrich-Heine-Universität Düsseldorf

Erstgutachter: Prof. Dr. R. Alexander Lorz, LL.M. (Harvard)

Zweitgutachter: Prof. Dr. Siegfried H. Elsing, LL.M. (Yale)

Jahr der mündlichen Prüfung: 2016

Meinen Eltern
To my parents

About the Author

Maximilian Clasmeier has studied law at the University of Münster, the University of Barcelona, the National University of Singapore and the University of Düsseldorf. He has completed his legal traineeship at the Higher Regional Court (Oberlandesgericht) Frankfurt, Germany and has gained experience in international arbitration and litigation in Düsseldorf, Frankfurt and Singapore as well as with the World Bank in Washington, DC.

Table of Contents

About the Author	ix
Foreword	xvii
List of Abbreviations	xix
Acknowledgments (in English)	xxi
Acknowledgments (in German)	xxiii
Introduction	1

CHAPTER 1
Treaty Interpretation in Public International Law   5
§1.01 Schools of Thought   5
§1.02 Fragmented Interpretation   6
§1.03 Tools of Treaty Interpretation   7
    [A] The Vienna Convention on the Law of Treaties   7
        [1] The Ordinary Meaning-Rule   8
        [2] The Object and Purpose   10
            [a] The Notion of Effectivity   12
            [b] The Classification of Interpretive Approaches   14
        [3] The Special Meaning-Rule   15
        [4] Subsequent Agreements and Practice   16
        [5] *Travaux Préparatoires*   16
    [B] Precedent in Public International Law   17
§1.04 Challenges in Treaty Interpretation   18
§1.05 Distinguishing Interpretation and Law-Making   19
§1.06 Conclusion   20

Table of Contents

CHAPTER 2
Characteristics of International Investment Law   23
§2.01   Public International Law Roots   23
        [A] The Origin of International Investment Law   23
        [B] The Objectives of Investment Protection   25
§2.02   International Treaties as Sources of International Investment Law   26
        [A] Types of Investment Treaties   26
             [1] Bilateral Investment Treaties   26
             [2] Multilateral Investment Treaties   27
             [3] Free Trade Agreements   28
                  [a] North American Free Trade Agreement   28
                  [b] Association of Southeast Asian Nations   28
                  [c] Additional Free Trade Agreements   29
        [B] Standards of Protection   29
             [1] Fair and Equitable Treatment-Standard   30
             [2] Most Favored Nation-Standard   31
             [3] Full Protection and Security-Standard   32
             [4] Umbrella Clauses   32
             [5] Expropriation   33
§2.03   Investment Contracts as Sources of International Investment Law   34
§2.04   Arbitration in International Investment Law   35
        [A] General Remarks on Arbitration   36
        [B] International Investment Arbitration   38
             [1] Theoretical Basis   38
             [2] Hybrid Process of Arbitration   43
             [3] Particularities of Interpretation   43
                  [a] The Role of Precedent in Investment Arbitration   43
                  [b] Model Investment Treaties   46
                  [c] *Expressio Unius Est Exclusio Alterius*   46
§2.05   International Investment Law in a Crisis of Legitimacy   47
§2.06   Conclusion   50

CHAPTER 3
The Protection of Arbitral Awards in the Global Context of Investment Treaty
Interpretation   53
§3.01   Introduction   53
§3.02   The Traditional Facets of an Investment   56
        [A] Considering Individual Investment Protection Mechanisms   56
             [1] Bilateral and Multilateral Investment Treaties   56
             [2] The ICSID-Convention   58
                  [a] Objective and Subjective Approaches   59
                  [b] The Salini-Test   61
                       [i] From Characteristics to Requirements   61

xii

			[ii]	Five Typical Features	62

            [ii]   Five Typical Features   62
            [iii] The Use Outside of the ICSID Framework   64
      [B]   Conclusion   64
§3.03 The Qualification of Arbitral Awards   65
      [A]   Nature of Arbitral Awards   66
      [B]   Treating Arbitral Awards as Investments   66
            [1]   Autonomous Plain Meaning Approach   66
                   [a]   Value as a Starting Point   67
                   [b]   Limitations Related to Time and Location   68
                   [c]   Concretion by Enumeration   68
            [2]   Awards as Continuations of Original Investments   69
                   [a]   *White Industries v. India*   69
                         [i]   Case Brief and Investment Definition   69
                         [ii]   Tribunal's Conclusion and Analysis   70
                   [b]   *ATA v. Jordan*   73
                         [i]   Case Brief and Investment Definition   73
                         [ii]   Tribunal's Conclusion and Analysis   75
      [C]   Treating Arbitral Awards Like Investments   77
            [1]   *Saipem v. Bangladesh*   77
                   [a]   Case Brief and Investment Definition   77
                   [b]   Tribunal's Conclusion and Analysis   79
            [2]   *Frontier Petroleum Services v. Czech Republic*   81
            [3]   *Romak v. Uzbekistan*   83
      [D]   An Antithesis: *GEA v. Ukraine*   86
            [1]   Case Brief and Investment Definition   86
            [2]   Tribunal's Conclusion and Analysis   87
                   [a]   Interpretive Approach   88
                   [b]   The Analytical Distinction   91
                         [i]   Separability in International Commercial Arbitration 91
                         [ii]   Separability in International Investment Arbitration 92
                         [iii] Separability in Characterizing Arbitral Awards   94
      [E]   Analysis of the Principal Arguments   94
            [1]   The Unity of Investment-Doctrine   95
                   [a]   Overview   95
                   [b]   The Doctrine in Practical Context   99
            [2]   The Role of Previous Arbitral Decisions   102
      [F]   Practical Implications of the Analysis   104
      [G]   Observations Regarding Treaty Interpretation   105
            [1]   Application of the Vienna Convention on the Law of Treaties 105
            [2]   Short Reasoning Beyond Interpretive Canons   107
            [3]   Previous Arbitral Decisions   109
            [4]   Conclusion   110
§3.04 Elements of the Potential Impact on Interpretation   110
      [A]   A Trend of Convergence in International Arbitration   111

Table of Contents

		[1]	Increasing Protection of International Commercial Arbitration	111
			[a] International Commercial Arbitration on the Rise	111
			[b] Protective Tendencies in Public International Law	114
			[c] Approaches of International Investment Law	119
		[2] Self-Protection in International Investment Arbitration		122
		[3] Challenging the Divide in International Arbitration		124
		[4] The Impact on Treaty Interpretation		131
	[B]	The Involvement of Commercial Arbitrators		132
	[C]	The Notion of Pro-investor Bias		135
	[D]	The Role of Purposive Interpretation		137
	[E]	Insufficient Treaty Drafting		140
§3.05	Conclusion			141

CHAPTER 4
Ramifications of Interpretive Insufficiencies — 143
§4.01 Introduction — 143
§4.02 The Continuous Relevance of State Sovereignty — 144
　[A] The Development of the Principle — 144
　[B] Political Facets — 147
　[C] The Interplay with International Treaties — 147
　[D] State Sovereignty and Insufficient Interpretation — 150
　　　[1] The Impact of Arbitral Awards — 151
　　　[2] The Impact of Insufficient Interpretation — 154
　　　　　[a] Reflections on Sovereignty in Rulings by the ICJ — 154
　　　　　[b] Reflections on Sovereignty Elsewhere — 156
　　　[3] Conclusion — 156
§4.03 The Role of Policy Space and Public Interest — 157
　[A] Limiting the Policy Space of States — 158
　[B] Arbitrators as Policy-Makers — 160
§4.04 The Rule of Law — 162
§4.05 The Discrepancy Between Developed and Developing States — 164
　[A] Asymmetric Setting of Protection Standards in Treaties — 165
　[B] Nurturing the Perception of Pro-investor Bias — 166
　[C] The Economics of Flawed Interpretation — 167
§4.06 The Responsibility to Protect — 168
§4.07 Conclusion — 168

CHAPTER 5
Potential Routes to Improved Interpretive Discipline — 171
§5.01 Introduction — 171
§5.02 Compliance with Interpretive Methodology — 172
　[A] Adherence to the Vienna Convention on the Law of Treaties — 172
　[B] Specialized Canons of Interpretation — 173
　　　[1] Deploying the ILC's Guiding Principles — 174

			[a] Investment Treaties as Unilateral Acts	175
			[b] Offers to Arbitrate as Unilateral Acts	177
		[2]	The Role of Previous Arbitral Decisions	180
§5.03	Review of Arbitral Decisions			182
	[A]	Annulment Pursuant to Article 52 ICSID-Convention		183
		[1]	The First Phase of Annulment Decisions	183
		[2]	The Second Phase of Annulment Decisions	183
		[3]	The Third Phase of Annulment Decisions	184
		[4]	Grounds for Annulment in the Context of Interpretation	186
			[a] Manifest Excess of Powers	186
			[b] Failure to State Reasons	187
	[B]	Appellate Review in International Investment Arbitration		190
		[1]	Theoretical Benefits of Appellate Review	191
		[2]	Downsides of Appellate Review	193
		[3]	Bargaining for the Right Route	193
§5.04	The Integration of Preliminary Rulings			194
	[A]	Chances for Improvement		195
	[B]	Designing Preliminary Rulings for Investment Arbitration		196
§5.05	Adjusting Investment Treaties			199
§5.06	Conclusion			202

Conclusion   203

Appendices   207

APPENDIX I
Overview of Arbitral Precedent   209

APPENDIX II
Interpretive Approaches in Arbitral Precedent   213

Bibliography   233

Table of Cases   249

Index   255

Foreword

International investment law and investment arbitration as the primary means to resolve disputes stemming from the former have, especially in Europe, become a focal point of a heated public debate. It is an unfortunate reality that this debate is oftentimes fueled by incomplete or even false information. Therefore, thorough legal analyses within the realm of this dynamic field of public international law are ever more needed. From a political perspective, they provide the starting point for countering improper allegations against the field; from a legal perspective, they must be seen either as an opportunity to improve the functioning of international investment law mechanisms where the criticism hits a point or as assurance that the criticism is unfounded. In any case, however, legal analyses within international investment law as in any other field of law are indispensable for theory and practice alike.

Vital to the operations of any investment tribunal is the determination of a dispute as one arising out of an "investment." Despite its immense importance, tribunals can mostly not avail themselves of a definition of the term that will easily clarify whether or not an investment is really at hand. Rather, it is the interpretation of the underlying treaties that will lead tribunals to the determination. This operation becomes especially challenging where investment and commercial arbitration intersect. When a foreign investor encounters a dispute with another company (e.g., owned by the host state) within the territory of that host state, secures a commercial arbitral award and fails to enforce the latter before the courts as a result of host state interference, the intersection between commercial and investment arbitration is by no means a rare occurrence. If that commercial arbitration award is then protected by the guarantees given by the host state within the framework of an investment treaty or contract, investment arbitration may be an avenue of legal recourse. Once again, however, that recourse can only be successful if the arbitral award may be qualified as an "investment."

This question has so far not been addressed in utmost depth. Therefore, the book at hand constitutes an important contribution to further development of legal analysis in this exciting field. The author analyzes if, and under which circumstances, arbitral tribunals are likely to find arbitral awards to fall under an applicable investment definition and thereby enriches theory and practice of international investment law

Foreword

alike. The book approaches the existing decisions on the matter clearly and concisely, guiding the reader through differences and similarities. It is particularly noteworthy that the author considers the perspectives of both the investor and the host state. The analysis is mindful of the ramifications of possible interpretive insufficiencies and highlights the utterly important consequences of the respondent to an investment arbitration being a sovereign state. The book is thus a strong reminder of the relevance of core public international law principles such as state sovereignty within disputes, regardless of the apparent sophistication of an interpretive question.

Additionally, it does not stop at pointing to certain interpretive insufficiencies. Rather, it seeks reasons for these insufficiencies and carves out potential elements of their impact on treaty interpretation. These may be trends of convergence between international commercial and investment arbitration, tendencies to protect arbitration within public international law and similar progression within international investment law itself. The analysis thereby provides new insights into the broader environment in which international investment arbitration nowadays operates. As a result, the reader receives a balanced perspective on the criticism voiced towards treaty interpretation within international investment arbitration as well as various possible solutions to existing problems.

Besides its contribution to the theoretical context of the public sphere in which international investment arbitration functions, the book appeals especially to practitioners of international arbitration. It assists tribunals and counsel alike as a useful reference in determining if and under which circumstances an arbitral award may be qualified as or like an investment and thereby enjoys protection under investment treaties or contracts. At the same time, it is a similarly useful guide for state actors in the process of treaty negotiations. By stressing the importance of treaty drafting, the possible effects of a particular wording or trends within international investment law in an exemplary manner apart from one single practical issue, it serves as a valuable resource for sovereigns in assessing the effects of their conduct at an early stage.

Prof. Dr. R. Alexander Lorz, LL.M. (Harvard)

List of Abbreviations

ASEAN	Association of Southeast Asian Nations
ASEAN-ANZ-FTA	Association of Southeast Asian Nations, Australia and New Zealand Free Trade Agreement
BIT	Bilateral Investment Treaty
CAFTA-DR	Dominican Republic-Central America-United States Free Trade Agreement
DIS	Deutsche Institution für Schiedsgerichtsbarkeit
ECHR	European Court of Human Rights
ECJ	European Court of Justice
ECT	Energy Charter Treaty
EPA	Environmental Protection Agency
EU	European Union
FCN	Friendship, Commerce and Navigation
FIDIC	International Federation of Consulting Engineers
FTA	Foreign Trade Agreement
GAFTA	Grain and Feed Trade Association
GATS	General Agreement on Trade in Services
ICC	International Chamber of Commerce
ICCA	International Council for Commercial Arbitration
ICISS	International Commission on Intervention and State Sovereignty
ICJ	International Court of Justice
ICSID	International Centre for the Settlement of Investment Disputes
IDA	International Development Association
IFC	International Finance Corporation

List of Abbreviations

LCIA	London Court of International Arbitration
MIGA	Multilateral Investment Guarantee Agency
MIT	Multilateral Investment Treaty
MTBE	Methyl Tert-Butyl Ether
NAFTA	North American Free Trade Agreement
NYC	New York Convention
PCA	Permanent Court of Arbitration
PCIJ	Permanent Court of International Justice
SADC	South African Development Community
SCC	Stockholm Chamber of Commerce
SIAC	Singapore International Arbitration Centre
SORTAMAR	Société Mixte de Transports Maritimes
TFEU	Treaty on the Functioning of the European Union
TRIMS	Trade-Related Investments Measures
TRIPS	Agreement on Trade-Related Aspects of Intellectual Property
UNCITRAL	United Nations Commission on International Trade Law
UNCTAD	United Nations Conference on Trade and Development
VCLT	Vienna Convention on the Law of Treaties
WTO	World Trade Organization

Acknowledgments (in English)

The completion of the present book would not have been possible without the support of numerous people to whom I hereby would like to express my gratitude.

First, I would like to especially thank my parents whose support, encouragement and trust have enabled me to develop personally and professionally. My mother and my father, who has unfortunately passed away much too early, have thereby contributed an invaluable part in allowing me to achieve my goals. Their strength and joie de vivre continue to impress me and are going to provide guidance on my further path in life. This book is dedicated to them.

Likewise, I would like to thank my fiancée who has accompanied me through the natural ups and downs of the writing process with tireless understanding, great patience and tremendous commitment. The many conversations have allowed for a continuous and critical scrutiny of my work and have added some valuable economic perspectives.

Also, I would like to thank my supervisor, Prof. Dr. R. Alexander Lorz, LL.M. (Harvard), who has supported my project from the start with conviction and great interest. His passion for academia, public international and investment law as well as international arbitration, and his commitment as a true mentor in addition to serving as Hessian Minister of Education and Religious Affairs have deeply impressed me and have made the collaboration both enjoyable and enriching.

Lastly, I would like to thank Prof. Dr. Siegfried H. Elsing, LL.M. (Yale) for his opinion on my thesis. Furthermore, I would like to thank Dr. Alexandra Diehl, LL.M. (Suffolk University) for her support and the valuable insights into international arbitration as well as all those who have contributed to the development of this book with suggestions and ideas, especially Dr. Aniruddha Rajput and Jan K. Schäfer, LL.M. (Singapore).

Wiesbaden, July 2016
Maximilian Clasmeier

Acknowledgments (in German)

Die vorliegende Arbeit wäre ohne die Unterstützung zahlreicher Menschen so nicht möglich gewesen. Ihnen möchte ich auf diesem Wege meinen herzlichen Dank aussprechen.

Zunächst gilt mein besonderer Dank meinen Eltern, deren Unterstützung, Zuspruch und Vertrauen in meinen Lebensweg es mir überhaupt ermöglicht haben, mich persönlich und beruflich zu entwickeln. Meine Mutter und mein leider viel zu früh verstorbener Vater haben so einen wesentlichen Teil dazu beigetragen, dass ich meine Ziele erreichen konnte. Ihre Stärke und Lebensfreude beeindrucken mich und werden mir auf meinem weiteren Lebensweg stets ein Vorbild sein. Ihnen, meinen Eltern, widme ich diese Arbeit.

Ebenso danke ich meiner Verlobten, die mich mit unermüdlichem Verständnis, großer Geduld und viel Einsatz durch die natürlichen Höhen und Tiefen des Schreibprozesses begleitet hat. Die zahlreichen Gespräche haben dazu beigetragen, meine Arbeit immer wieder kritisch zu hinterfragen und sie mit einigen wertvollen, ökonomischen Überlegungen zu bereichern.

Mein großer Dank gilt zudem meinem Doktorvater, Herrn Prof. Dr. R. Alexander Lorz, LL.M. (Harvard), der mein Vorhaben von Beginn an mit Überzeugung und großem Interesse unterstützt hat. Seine Leidenschaft für die Lehre und Forschung, das Völker-, Investitionsschutz- und Schiedsverfahrensrecht, sowie sein Arbeitseinsatz als wahrer Mentor bei der Betreuung zusätzlich zu seinem Amt als Hessischer Kultusminister haben mir besonders imponiert und die Zusammenarbeit ebenso angenehm wie lehrreich gemacht.

Schließlich bedanke ich mich auch bei Herrn Prof. Dr. Siegfried H. Elsing, LL.M. (Yale) für die Erstellung des Zweitgutachtens. Weiterhin möchte ich hiermit Frau Dr. Alexandra Diehl, LL.M. (Suffolk University) herzlich für die Unterstützung und die wertvollen Einblicke in das Schiedsverfahrensrecht danken, sowie allen, die mit ihren Anregungen und Vorschlägen ebenso zu der Entwicklung der vorliegenden Arbeit

Acknowledgments (in German)

beigetragen haben, insbesondere Herrn Dr. Aniruddha Rajput und Herrn Jan K. Schäfer, LL.M. (Singapore).

Wiesbaden, im Juli 2016
Maximilian Clasmeier

Introduction

> *What we want is not only that parties submit to arbitration, but that they have confidence in it – that they are convinced of the arbitrators' skill and ability to settle the dispute in an adequate manner.*[1]

Lassa Oppenheim so described the task of fostering arbitration in public international law in 1908. He envisaged arbitration as a means to solve disputes among sovereign states and had in mind peace among nations. These states, he observed, were "already inclined to settle differences by arbitration, provided these differences do not concern their independence, honor, or vital interests."[2] Almost a hundred years later, we still witness arbitration as a means to solve disputes in public international law. Nowadays, however, arbitration frequently occurs between states and private investors. The idea was not entirely new at *Oppenheim's* time. In fact, the Jay Treaty of 1794 already provided for a right of British creditors to arbitrate and marked the beginning of what is now known as investment arbitration.[3] Nevertheless, the phenomenon has become less phenomenal. Investment arbitration has rather developed into a conventional method of dispute resolution in today's globalized economic reality. International investment law is a discipline of public international law and characterized by tremendous dynamics. Despite the powerful forces involved, international investment law rests mostly on international treaties; well-established, classic instruments of public international law. Interpretation brings these international treaties to life in their application to real world scenarios. Black and white texts depend on interpretation to give them color. Or, as *Costas Douzinas* has aptly formulated: "Undoubtedly, the law is interpretation, and interpretation is the life of law."[4]

---

1. *Lassa Oppenheim*, The Science of International Law: Its Task and Method, in: American Journal of International Law 1908, Vol. 2 No. 2, pp. 313-356 (p. 323).
2. *Oppenheim*, note 1, p. 322.
3. *See Christopher Dugan/Don Wallace/Noah Rubins/Borzu Sabahi*, Investor-State Arbitration, 2008, p. 34; *see also William W. Park*, Arbitration of International Business Disputes, 2012, p. 702.
4. *Costas Douzinas*, Law and Justice in Postmodernism, in: Steven Connor (ed.), The Cambridge Companion to Postmodernism, 2004, pp. 196-223 (p. 201).

Treatises on legal methodology often share a reputation of being bleak. Practical readers are likely to perceive them as tedious, mere academic art and occasionally aspire to escape into the abyss that was so evoked by the author. The starting point for making an appealing contribution to legal methodology is thus an ambitious one. Nevertheless, the work to be undertaken here rests on the firm belief that treaty interpretation is as important to public international law as is the sea for the survival of fish. To convey this belief, the dynamics of international investment law, and investment arbitration in particular, serve as an ideal illustration. The field's multiplicity is perhaps unparalleled in public international law and touches upon questions of law, politics and economics: how do we characterize a state's offer to arbitrate with a private foreign investor? Can arbitral tribunals scrutinize issues of public policy? What macroeconomic impact does an arbitral award have on a national budget? Certainly, investment arbitration does not lack pressing issues. The banner of the field is colorful. Consequentially, it has attracted increasingly broad attention over time that has brought about more arbitrations, more scholarship and also more public awareness. It has become more complex and challenging, thus naturally providing more grounds for criticism[5] that has stretched so far as identifying a "legitimacy crisis."[6] The center of attention are decisions by investment arbitrators. They may, for example, deal with a tribunal's jurisdiction, the merits of a dispute or an award's annulment. However, in the end, it is the interpretation of investment treaties that produces these decisions, aiming at providing proper reasoning. Interpretation paints the banner of investment arbitration that is visible to all, supporters and critics. Methodology is thus immensely practical. Treatises on the topic, it may be deduced, should be more appealing, if they are embedded in a practical context.

The present analysis aims to avoid creating an abyss between theory and practice. It will rather attempt to demonstrate the impact of treaty interpretation on states, investors and the field of international investment law by turning to a recent interpretive outcome in arbitral practice that deserves attention on a broad scale: arbitral awards as investments. The implications of such understanding are profound. They relate to the interplay between national courts and investment tribunals, remedies of investors on the international plane and the relationship between commercial and investment arbitration, all affected by the interpretation of investment treaties. So much for the outcomes. The process of reaching them, however, is equally important. *Oppenheim* concurs: arbitration must be conducted in an "adequate manner." The focal point of the analysis is thus the way tribunals have arrived at their conclusions. It will contemplate the adequacy of interpretation in an exemplary fashion and

---

5. See *Stephan W. Schill*, International Investment Law and Comparative Public Law – An Introduction, in: Stephan W. Schill (ed.), International Investment Law and Comparative Public Law, 2010, pp. 3-37 (p. 3).
6. *Muthucumaraswamy Sornarajah*, A Coming Crisis: Expansionary Trends in Investment Treaty Arbitration, in: Karl P. Sauvant (ed.), Appeals Mechanism in International Investment Disputes, 2008, pp. 39-45 (p. 41); see also *Susan D. Franck*, The Legitimacy Crisis in Investment Treaty Arbitration: Privatizing Public International Law Through Inconsistent Decisions, in: Fordham Law Review 2005, Vol. 73, pp. 1521-1625; see also *Charles N. Brower*, A Crisis of Legitimacy, in: The National Law Journal, October 7, 2007; see also *Michael Waibel/Asha Kaushal* et al., The Backlash Against Investment Arbitration, 2010.

integrate the findings into a broader perspective. The present work is thus of interest to theory and practice of investment arbitration alike.

The analysis is founded on a strong belief in the capability of international arbitration in dealing with investment disputes. It is motivated by the will for addressing suspicion against the field in a constructive manner. It is critical, yet conducted with the utmost respect for arbitrators that face increasingly intricate problems and apply themselves to finding solutions. It is aimed at contributing to the sustainability of the field in the interest of all its participants. For these purposes, a number of questions shall provide guidance: what is the foundation of interpretation in public international law and when is it adequately carried out? What are the dynamics of international investment law and how does interpretation affect the field's future? Under which circumstances do arbitral awards constitute investments in arbitral practice? Do these specific results stem from adequately conducted interpretation? How do the findings fit into the more general developments of international investment arbitration? What are the ramifications, if interpretation is not fully adequate? Which factors possibly contribute to inadequacy? How can interpretive insufficiencies be successfully addressed? The answers will reveal that despite an increasing number of challenges, there is profound reason to believe in the capabilities of international investment arbitration. It is adequate treaty interpretation that is best suited to provide stability in a dynamic legal environment such as that of international investment law.

CHAPTER 1
Treaty Interpretation in Public International Law

The interpretation of treaties plays a crucial part in the overall context of public international law. It is the means by which international tribunals and courts not only assess the scope of particular protection, rights or obligations that stem from an international treaty, but also if they have jurisdiction to hear a dispute presented to them. In short, interpretation is the methodological essence of public international law. It serves to produce comprehensible results and to ensure adherence to the fine line between mere interpretation and law-making.[7] It is, more generally speaking, the key to legal reasoning. Before engaging in an analysis of interpretive outcomes, however, it is essential to understand the techniques involved in interpretation. Therefore, this chapter is going to focus on the foundations of interpretation that are most commonly relied on by international courts and tribunals.

§1.01 SCHOOLS OF THOUGHT

The interpretation of international treaties is unfortunately not an exact science. Rather, it has been, and to a certain extent still is, a controversial issue among scholars in public international law.[8] One may nevertheless distinguish three schools of thought in interpretation: the schools of intent, textualism and teleology. The school of intent considers the intentions of the signatories to be the starting point of any interpretation.

---

7. *Matthias Herdegen*, in: Max Planck Encyclopedia of Public International Law (online ed.), available at http://opil.ouplaw.com/home/EPIL (last accessed April 15, 2015), Interpretation in International Law, para. 49.
8. *Martin Ris*, Treaty Interpretation and ICJ Recourse to Travaux Préparatoires: Towards a Proposed Amendment of Articles 31 and 32 of the Vienna Convention on the Law of Treaties, in: Boston College International & Comparative Law Review 1991, Vol. 14 No. 1, pp. 111-136 (p. 111); *Rosalie P. Schaffer*, Current Trends in Treaty Interpretation and the South African Approach, in: Australian Year Book of International Law 1981, Vol. 129, pp. 129-173 (p. 130).

These will then guide the interpreter in giving the treaty a meaning that was so envisaged by the signatories.[9] The school of textualism on the other hand, agrees that the intentions of the parties to a treaty are relevant. However, it only looks at the text of the respective treaty. The understanding is that by erecting a treaty, parties essentially transform their intentions into the written word. It is thus the text of a treaty that must guide the interpreter. The wording of a treaty is then the source and the limit of interpretation.[10] Lastly, the school of teleology focuses on the object and purpose of a particular treaty. By taking into account various sources in a nonhierarchical order,[11] this approach sees the role of interpretation in carving out the objectives of a particular treaty and giving them the utmost effect. These strands have all been fueling the debate on "adequate" interpretation. However, it must be noted that all share a common goal: giving effect to the intentions of the parties. Where they differ is on the applicable procedure in determining these intentions.[12] It may be the examination of actual intentions, a plain analysis of a treaty's text that expresses such or a look at the object and purpose of a treaty derived from various sources that will guide the interpretation. Public international law has, by way of *consuetudo* and *opinio juris* and then by codification, adopted a particular school of thought. Nevertheless, the voices of others have not turned mute and continue to contribute to an indeed quieter, yet still relevant debate.

§1.02 FRAGMENTED INTERPRETATION

The evolution of public international law has led to an immense increase in the variety of issues that are nowadays subjects to international treaties. One may, for example, think of treaties establishing international organizations such as the World Trade Organization (WTO), fostering regional integration such as the Association of Southeast Asian Nations (ASEAN) or the European Union (EU), treaties that outlaw crimes against humanity such as the Convention on the Prevention and Punishment of the Crime of Genocide or those guaranteeing robust business environments such as international investment treaties. The forms and contents of international treaties are manifold. Similarly, international treaties may have different objectives and involve various actors. The question is, if these evident differences have an impact on the way treaties are interpreted. More specifically, it is an intriguing and challenging question to ask, if different treaties call for different methodologies. The rapid growth of public international law in a number of fields during the last decades is described as a

---

9. *Hersch Lauterpacht*, Restrictive Interpretation and the Principle of Effectiveness of Treaties, in: British Yearbook of International Law 1949, Vol. 26, pp. 48-85 (p. 73): "The intention of the parties - express or implied - is the law. Any considerations – of effectiveness or otherwise – which tend to transform the ascertainable intention of the parties into a factor of secondary importance are inimical to the true purpose of interpretation."
10. *Gerald Fitzmaurice*, The Law and Procedure of the International Court of Justice 1951-4, in: British Yearbook of International Law 1957, Vol. 33, pp. 203-293 (pp. 204 et seq.).
11. *Ris*, note 8, p. 115.
12. *Schaffer*, note 8, p. 130.

Chapter 1: Treaty Interpretation in Public International Law §1.03[A]

"fragmentation of international law."[13] This fragmentation, by nature, bears a risk of making public international law less consistent and less coherent. Nevertheless, it is argued that fragmented areas of public international law have already developed particular legal orders, which may require flexible approaches to treaty interpretation.[14] This proposition is thought-provoking and plausible. In the course of this analysis, it may provide a starting point in examining options to tackle problems in the interpretive process that are yet to be revealed. Currently, however, it is existing methodology that should be applied in dealing with the fragmentation of public international law and which already provides a well-established framework.[15]

§1.03 TOOLS OF TREATY INTERPRETATION

[A] The Vienna Convention on the Law of Treaties

International treaties are the basis of most of public international law. The well-established framework of interpretation of treaties in public international law is provided by the Vienna Convention on the Law of Treaties (VCLT), which was adopted in 1969 and is the result of a codification process of rules of customary international law.[16] For example, the tribunal in *Sempra Energy v. Argentina* stated:

> The Tribunal also agrees with the Respondent that the rules for a correct interpretation are those of the Vienna Convention, which are also those that were followed in customary international law.[17]

---

13. *International Law Commission*, Fragmentation of International Law: Difficulties Arising from the Diversification and Expansion of International Law, July 18, 2006, available at http://www.un.org/ga/search/view_doc.asp?symbol=A/CN.4/L.702 (last accessed July 5, 2014).
14. Joseph. H.H. Weiler, The Interpretation of Treaties – A Re-examination, in: European Journal of International Law 2010, Vol. 21 No. 3, p. 507; Joseph. H.H. Weiler, Prolegomena to a Meso-theory of Treaty Interpretation at the Turn of the Century, Interpretation and Judgment in International Law, available at http://iilj.org/courses/documents/2008Colloquium.Session5.Weiler.pdf (last accessed July 5, 2014), p. 23: "What is called for is a differentiated approach to hermeneutics which fits differentiated international legal orders."
15. *International Law Commission*, note 13, para. 11: "The justification for the Commission's work on fragmentation has been in the fact that although fragmentation is inevitable, it is desirable to have a framework through which it may be assessed and managed in a legal-professional way. That framework is provided by the VCLT."
16. See *MTD Equity Sdn. Bhd. and MTD Chile S.A. v. Republic of Chile*, Award, ICSID Case No. ARB/01/7, May 25, 2004, para. 112; *Iurii Bogdanov, Agurdino-Invest Ltd., Argudino-Chimia JSC v. Republic of Moldova*, Award, SCC, September 22, 2005, para. 4.2.4; *Alapli Elektrik B.V. v. Republic of Turkey*, Decision on Annulment, ICSID Case No. ARB/08/13, July 10, 2014, para. 29; see also ICJ, Kasikili/Sedudu Island Case (*Botswana v. Namibia*), Judgment, December 13, 1999, ICJ Reports 1999, pp. 1045-1109, para. 18; see also ICJ, Case Concerning the Territorial Dispute (*Libyan Arab Jamahiriya v. Chad*), Judgment, February 3, 1994, ICJ Reports 1994, pp. 6-42, para. 41; see also ICJ, Case Concerning Oil Platforms (*Islamic Republic of Iran v. United States of America*), Preliminary Objections, Judgment, December 12, 1996, ICJ Reports 1996, pp. 803-821, para. 23; see also ICJ, Case Concerning Maritime Delimitation And Territorial Questions Between Qatar And Bahrain (*Qatar v. Bahrain*), Jurisdiction and Admissibility, Dissenting Opinion of Vice President Schwebel, February 15, 1995, ICJ Reports 1995, pp. 27-39 (p. 28).
17. *Sempra Energy International v. The Argentine Republic*, Decision on Objections to Jurisdiction, ICSID Case No. ARB/02/16, May 11, 2005, para. 141.

The VCLT is in this respect not an optional document, but the mandatory tool of interpretation of international treaties.[18] This follows from the VCLT's character as a customary international law codification. The rules therein contained are, for the most part,[19] those to which no states can object as they represent the lowest common denominator in the international community as to how interpretation should be carried out. In the interest of certainty, it is thus imperative to apply them properly where they are applicable. These rules are sufficient for all purposes of treaties and thus are to be utilized.[20] They apply not only to a treaty in general, but in the context of international investment law, also to an agreement to arbitrate between the parties,[21] as will be outlined in detail at a later stage. The provision most relevant to treaty interpretation is Article 31 VCLT. It applies when respective states are signatories to the VCLT and the treaty at hand was concluded after its adoption. It must be noted, however, that even if a state has not signed the VCLT, it may still accept a tribunal applying it due to its customary international law origin[22] which makes it universally applicable. According to Article 31 section 1 VCLT, tribunals will interpret treaties "in good faith in accordance with the ordinary meaning to be given to the terms of the treaty in their context and in the light of its object and purpose." The interpretation may not be divided into separate parts. Rather, it is one single, integrated operation.[23]

[1]   The Ordinary Meaning-Rule

Article 31 section 1 VCLT envisages the ordinary meaning of a treaty's text as the starting point for determining the scope of its provisions. One must first look at the

---

18. *See ICJ*, Case Concerning The Gabčíkovo-Nagymaros Project (*Hungary v. Slovakia*), Judgment, September 25, 1997, ICJ Reports 1997, pp. 7-84 (p. 38): "The Court has no need to dwell upon the question of the applicability in the present case of the Vienna Convention of 1969 on the Law of Treaties"; *see also Joseph Charles Lemire v. Ukraine*, Award, ICSID Case No. ARB/06/18, March 28, 2011, para. 66: "The BIT must be construed, like any other treaty, in accordance with the principles set forth in the Vienna Convention"; *see also Andrea Saldarriaga*, Investment Awards and the Rules of Interpretation of the Vienna Convention: Making Room for Improvement, in: ICSID Review 2013, Foreign Investment Law Journal, Vol. 28 No. 1, pp. 1-21 (p. 2); *see also Evan J. Criddle*, The Vienna Convention on the Law of Treaties in U.S. Treaty Interpretation, in: Virginia Journal of International Law 2004, Vol. 44 No. 2, pp. 431-500 (pp. 448 et seq.).
19. *See ICJ* (*Hungary v. Slovakia*), note 18, p. 62: "The Vienna Convention is not directly applicable to the 1977 Treaty inasmuch as both States ratified that Convention only after the Treaty's conclusion. Consequently only those rules which are declaratory of customary law are applicable to the 1977 Treaty."
20. *See* with regards to common rules of interpretation in general *William Edward Hall*, A Treatise on International Law, 7th ed. 1917, p. 344:

    Some of these rules are either unsafe in their application or of doubtful applicability; the rules tainted by any shade of doubt, from whatever source it may be derived, are unfit for use in international controversy. Those against which no objection can be urged, and which are probably sufficient for all purposes, may be stated as follows: -.

21. *Zachary Douglas*, The International Law of Investment Claims, 2009, p. 76.
22. *Aguas del Tunari, S.A. v. Republic of Bolivia*, Decision on Respondent's Objections to Jurisdiction, ICSID Case No. ARB/02/3, October 21, 2005, para. 88.
23. *International Law Commission*, Draft Articles on the Law of Treaties with commentaries, in: Yearbook of the International Law Commission 1966, Vol. 2, pp. 219 et seq.

ordinary meaning in the context of the words chosen (*ordinary meaning-rule*). The meaning must be determined objectively and without recourse to subjective intentions of the signatories.[24] The VCLT has therefore adopted a textualist approach. It follows the school of textualism. It is, however, a natural feature of language not to be static, not to have one plain meaning. Therefore, ambiguous terms are the norm. Interpretation then begins, where the ordinary meaning of a text allows these diverging perceptions. This is reflected in Article 31 section 1 VCLT, which sees a necessary correlation between the ordinary meaning and the context of the terms, meaning the terms' position within the treaty, not the context of the treaty's conclusion.[25] The VCLT does not clarify, if the ordinary meaning is to be determined based on the predominant perceptions at the time of the treaty's draft or those at the time of determination by a court or tribunal. There may over time develop severe differences in the way that terms are perceived. This phenomenon is not new in the legal world and has in fact been a matter of great controversy on domestic levels. One may think of the conflictive philosophies regarding the interpretation of the United States Constitution, the understanding of it being a "living constitution,"[26] open to dynamic interpretation, or of its particular terms having a "fixed meaning,"[27] However, in public international law, it nowadays seems to be the common denominator that treaty texts are open for being understood in their contemporary meaning unless the parties to the treaty have expressly provided for them to remain static.[28] Identifying the ordinary meaning of treaty terms therefore involves the determination of their original and contemporary

---

24. *Iran-United States Claims Tribunal*, Decision Concerning the Question of Jurisdiction over Claims of Persons with Dual Nationality, Case No. A/18, April 6, 1984: "It is the 'terms of the treaty in their context and in the light of its object and purpose' with which the Tribunal is to be concerned, not the subjective understanding or intent of either of the Parties."
25. *Hrvatska Elektroprivreda D.D. v. The Republic of Slovenia*, Dissenting Opinion of Jan Paulsson, ICSID Case No. ARB/05/24, June 8, 2009, para. 44:

    The permissible context is the context of the terms of the treaty and not the context of the treaty generally, in the way desired by the "total context" proponents. [...] They seem to ignore that they are allowed to refer only to the context of the terms of the Treaty, i.e. the internal consistency of the text as one whole.

26. *Howard Lee McBain*, The Living Constitution: A Consideration of the Realities and Legends of Our Fundamental Law, 1927.
27. *Antonin Scalia*, Originalism: The Lesser Evil, in: University of Cincinnati Law Review 1989, Vol. 57; with regards to international treaties and the limitations of interpretation by national courts *see also The Amiable Isabella*, 6 Wheat. 1, 19 U.S. 71 (1821):

    [T]o alter, amend, or add to any treaty by inserting any clause, whether small or great, important or trivial, would be on our part an usurpation of power and not an exercise of judicial functions. It would be to make, and not to construe, a treaty. Neither can this Court supply a *casus omissus* in a treaty any more than in a law. We are to find out the intention of the parties by just rules of interpretation applied to the subject matter, and having found that, our duty is to follow it as far as it goes, and to stop where that stops -- whatever may be the imperfections or difficulties which it leaves behind.

28. *Sondre Torp Helmersen*, Evolutive Treaty Interpretation: Legality, Semantics and Distinctions, in: European Journal of Legal Studies 2013, Vol. 6 No. 1, pp. 127-148 (pp. 147 et seq.), who explains that "[e]volution is thus possible even though the rule being invoked is not a formal 'rule' in Article 31.3.c's sense, and even though it is not binding on 'the parties'"; *see also NAFTA*

understanding. The terms of an international treaty are thus dynamic, unless the signatories expressly intended otherwise.

[2] The Object and Purpose

Article 31 section 1 VCLT furthermore envisages recourse to the object and purpose of a treaty. It has been argued that such recourse may only take place, if the ordinary meaning-rule does not deliver an exact result.[29] However, such approach remains mostly theoretical as terms will typically have various meanings. The likelihood of arguments based on the object and purpose of a treaty is thus considerable. Recourse to the object and purpose may confirm the result of applying the ordinary meaning-rule, but it may also go beyond what is contained in the treaty terms. Such approach has potential to cross the line of revising a treaty, which is only permissible, provided that a respective treaty so provides. The VCLT does not envisage such far-reaching effect of the object and purpose.[30] Therefore, it is the treaty's text that serves as a limitation to the analysis of the object and purpose.[31] An interpretation based upon the object and purpose may thus only be given effect, if it complies with at least one of the various meanings of a provision's text. In any case, recourse to the object and purpose forms an inherent part of the interpretive methodology of the VCLT. A mere textual approach is thereby complemented by recourse to a broader analysis. This analysis

---

Panel, Canadian Agricultural Tariffs Case, Final Report of the Panel, NAFTA File No. CDA-95-2008-01, December 2, 1996, paras. 137-138:

> But such explicit language limiting the scope of FTA Article 710 to existing rights and obligations cannot be found. The absence of such wording carries an implication that future rights and obligations were not excluded. [...] In other words, reference to the GATT and agreements negotiated under the GATT must have been a reference to the GATT not as a fixed body of law but as one that was capable of developing.

29. *ICJ*, Competence of the General Assembly for the Admission of a State to the United Nations, Advisory Opinion, March 3, 1950, ICJ Reports 1950, p. 8:

    > The Court considers it necessary to say that the first duty of a tribunal which is called upon to interpret and apply the provisions of a treaty, is to endeavour to give effect to them in their natural and ordinary meaning in the context in which they occur. If the relevant words in their natural and ordinary meaning make sense in their context, that is an end of the matter. If, on the other hand, the words in their natural and ordinary meaning are ambiguous or lead to an unreasonable result, then, and then only, must the Court, by resort to other methods of interpretation, seek to ascertain what the parties really did mean when they used these words. [...] When the Court can give effect to a provision of a treaty by giving to the words used in it their natural and ordinary meaning, it may not interpret the words by seeking to give them some other meaning.

30. *ICJ*, Advisory Opinion on Interpretation of Peace Treaties with Bulgaria, Hungary and Romania, 2nd Phase, July 18, 1950, ICJ Reports 1950, pp. 221-261 (p. 229): "It is the duty of the Court to interpret the Treaties, not to revise them"; *see also ICJ*, Case Concerning Rights of Nationals of the United States of America in Morocco, Judgment, August 27, 1952, ICJ Reports 1952, pp. 176-214 (p. 196).

31. *See* note 23, p. 219: "Properly limited and applied, the maxim does not call for an 'extensive' or 'liberal' interpretation in the sense of an interpretation going beyond what is expressed or necessarily to be implied in the terms of the treaty."

examines the treaty as a whole, the reasons for its conclusion and the possible intentions involved as expressed in the text.

Ideally, these subjective and objective ends of a state's action in concluding a treaty are congruent. Realistically, they regularly diverge.[32] First, this highlights the importance of proper treaty drafting. It must be a state's goal for the treaty to express the underlying intentions for its conclusion and the intended scope of its provisions to the most detailed extent possible. The fewer attention is given to this process, the more interpretive latitude is delegated to international adjudicative bodies. While it is in the interpreter's interest and duty to decide in accordance with its mandate, a less accurately drafted treaty is more likely to produce interpretive outcomes that can be perfectly adequate yet surprising to the involved state. Therefore, states enjoy and bear a significant responsibility in the treaty negotiation process. It allows them to actively shape the interpretive playground of arbitrators and judges. Second, the possible divergence of objective and subjective ends reveals a striking scenario: it is imaginable that a treaty is interpreted in such a way that the result fully departs from the signatories' subjective intentions.[33] It is then equally imaginable how such predicament contributes to the discontent of a state signatory with the international adjudicative process, fueling skepticism that may nowadays be observed particularly in the context of international investment law's legitimacy.

Some see a development of an interpretive approach, which favors the consideration of the purpose of a treaty instead of its mere text, a so-called purposive interpretation.[34] Such development would imply a creeping paradigm shift in customary international law, away from the generally objective approach taken by the VCLT. Whether this trend really does reflect a profound change in public international law or is just a temporary occurrence remains yet to be seen. However, heavy reliance on a treaty's object and purpose is, from a contemporary point of view, not proper treaty interpretation. To the contrary, it disregards the fact that it is the text of a treaty that is the focal point of any interpretation in public international law. The object and purpose of such treaty must then be taken into account in order to either confirm or alter the result. It may, however, not serve to replace the ordinary meaning of treaty terms, as was previously outlined. By no means is such purposive approach in line with the applicable interpretive canon of Article 31 section 1 VCLT, but rather turns it upside

---

32. *See WTO Appellate Body*, United States - Import Prohibition of Certain Shrimp and Shrimp Products, Report of the Appellate Body, WTO Report No. AB-1998-4, October 12, 1998, para. 17: "Furthermore, the Panel failed to recognize that most treaties have no single, undiluted object and purpose but rather a variety of different, and possibly conflicting, objects and purposes."
33. *Ian Sinclair*, The Vienna Convention on the Law of Treaties, 1984, p. 131, who warns of the "risk that the placing of undue emphasis on the 'object and purpose' of a treaty will encourage teleological methods of interpretation [which], in some of its more extreme forms, will even deny the relevance of the intentions of the parties."
34. *Michael Byers*, The Shifting Foundations of International Law: A Decade of Forceful Measures against Iraq, in: European Journal of International Law 2002, Vol. 13 No. 1, pp. 21-41 (pp. 25 et seq.); *see also* similarly *Luigi Crema*, Disappearance and New Sightings of Restrictive Interpretation(s), in: European Journal of International Law 2010, Vol. 21 No. 3, pp. 681-700 (p. 691).

down.[35] For the purpose of this analysis, however, it suffices at this point to bear in mind that Article 31 section 1 VCLT provides for an objective interpretation of a treaty's text in its context and in light of its object and purpose until an interpretive outcome would run contrary to the wraith of the treaty. This wraith is ultimately expressed in the text of the treaty. The plurality of terms provides interpretive options and at the same time limits the possible understanding. Thereby, the drafters of the VCLT sought to prevent an overly extensive interpretation.[36]

[a]   *The Notion of Effectivity*

Public international law places peculiar emphasis on the effectivity of treaties (*effet utile*).[37] The maxim of effectivity is closely connected to the object and purpose of treaties and particularly well known in European law, where it serves the purpose of giving full effect to provisions. Vague treaty terms and an occasionally loose usage of the *effet utile*-argument by the European Court of Justice (ECJ) in interpreting them have shed critical light on the maxim.[38] The criticism relates to the immense powers of the effectivity argument, which may impact interpretive outcomes. An interpretation that only aims for the effectivity of a treaty provision is problematic. It would run the

---

35. *See Iran-United States Claims Tribunal*, The Islamic Republic of Iran v. The United States of America, Decision, Case No. A/18 (DEC 32-A18-FT), April 6, 1984, in: Journal of International Arbitration 1984, Vol. 1 No. 2, pp. 173-183 (p. 177):

    With respect to the additional Iranian argument, the Vienna Convention does not require any demonstration of a "converging will" or of a conscious acceptance by each Party of all implications of the terms to which it has agreed. It is the "terms of the treaty in their context and in the light of its object and purpose" with which the Tribunal is to be concerned, not the subjective understanding or intent of either of the Parties.

    See also Hrvatska Elektroprivreda D.D. v. The Republic of Slovenia, Dissenting Opinion of Jan Paulsson, note 25, para. 41: "It is important to see precisely how the majority I regret to say, appear to turn the VCLT on its head."
36. *Mark Eugen Villiger*, Commentary on the 1969 Vienna Convention on the Law of Treaties, 2009, p. 428.
37. ICJ, Dissenting Opinion on ICJ, Interpretation of Peace Treaties with Bulgaria, Hungary and Romania by J.E. Read, 2nd Phase, July 18, 1950, ICJ Reports 1950, pp. 231-247 (p. 235):

    Professor Lauterpacht, in *The Development of International Law by the Permanent Court of International Justice*, made an exhaustive examination of the authorities as they stood at the date of publication, 1934, including most of those which are cited above, and a number of other relevant Judgments and Opinions of the Permanent Court. He records the result of this study at pages 69-70: ".... The work of the Permanent Court has shown that alongside the fundamental principle of interpretation, namely, that effect is to be given to the intention of the parties, full use can be made of another hardly less important principle, namely, that the treaty must remain effective rather than ineffective. *Res magis valeat quam pereat*. It is a major principle, in the light of which the intention of the parties must always be interpreted, even to the extent of disregarding the letter of the instrument and of reading into it something which, on the face of it, it does not contain."
38. *Michael Potacs*, Effet utile als Auslegungsgrundsatz, in: Zeitschrift für Europarecht 2009, No. 4, pp. 465-487 (p. 465).

risk of over-emphasizing one of myriad objects and purposes contained in the treaty. Thus, the "letter" and "spirit" of a treaty serve as corrective measures, limiting an overly broad interpretation that relies solely on the importance of rendering a treaty effective.[39]

In the context of international investment law, arbitral tribunals have interpreted provisions and used the notion of effectivity to a curious extent. In this sense, effective and purposive interpretations intersect. The arbitration in *SGS v. Philippines*[40] concerned two contracts between the claimant, a Swiss company providing certification services to importing states with regards to the quality and quantity of import merchandise and its compliance with national regulations, and the Philippines as respondent. The claimant addressed the arbitral tribunal, seeking payment for services provided under the contracts, arguing a breach of provisions of the bilateral investment treaty (BIT) between Switzerland and the Philippines. The respondent explained that these claims were merely contractual and did not arise out of an investment in the Philippines as required by the BIT. The tribunal then analyzed the BIT in order to determine whether or not the contracts enjoyed protection. It argued:

> The object and purpose of the BIT supports an effective interpretation of Article X(2). The BIT is a treaty for the promotion and reciprocal protection of investments. According to the preamble it is intended "to create and maintain favourable conditions for investments by investors of one Contracting Party in the territory of the other". It is legitimate to resolve uncertainties in its interpretation so as to favour the protection of covered investments.[41]

Therefore, the tribunal interpreted the BIT in such a way that it would be fully effective in light of the intention to provide favorable investment conditions. At no time did it consider other objects of the treaty.[42] In its preamble, the relevant BIT, for example, asserts that it was concluded in recognition of the necessity to promote and protect foreign investments in order to promote the economic prosperity of both states.[43] Such reference would have deserved at least minimal consideration in view of a claim against the Philippines worth approximately USD 140 million that was presented to the tribunal. This kind of decisions indicates that the reliance on objects

---

39. *ICJ*, Advisory Opinion on Interpretation of Peace Treaties with Bulgaria, Hungary and Romania, 2nd Phase, note 30, p. 239, in rejecting the dissenting opinion rendered by Judge Read:

    > The principle of interpretation expressed in the maxim: *Ut res magis valeat quam pereat*, often referred to as the rule of effectiveness, cannot justify the Court in attributing to the provisions for the settlement of disputes in the Peace Treaties a meaning which, as stated above, would be contrary to their letter and spirit.

40. *SGS Société Générale de Surveillance S.A. v. Republic of Philippines*, Decision of the Tribunal on Objections to Jurisdiction, ICSID Case No. ARB/02/6, January 29, 2004.
41. *SGS Société Générale de Surveillance S.A. v. Republic of Philippines*, note 40, para. 116.
42. *Michael Waibel*, International Investment Law and Treaty Interpretation, in: Rainer Hofmann/Christian Tams (eds.), From Clinical Isolation to Systemic Integration, 2011, pp. 29-52 (p. 39).
43. Switzerland-Philippines BIT, March 31, 1997, available at http://investmentpolicyhub.unctad.org/Download/TreatyFile/2174 (last accessed November 5, 2014), Preamble: "reconnaissant la necessity d'encourager et de protéger les investissements estrangers en vie de promouvoir la prospérité économique des deux Etats".

and purposes may be used to deem a treaty effective, favoring the protection of investments without analyzing the full breadth of a treaty's content. The reliance on object and purpose has in the practice of international investment law frequently led to interpretations that give privilege to investors[44] or even deprive underlying and textually expressed intentions of states of their relevance.[45]

[b]   The Classification of Interpretive Approaches

Interpretations are sometimes classified as being of an effective or liberal, rather than a restrictive kind. Arbitral tribunals regularly use such classifications in positioning themselves and in clarifying which school of thought they are going to follow in the course of their decision.[46] However, some tribunals decide to point out that they are not going to follow a particular kind of interpretation.[47] As was rightfully stated though, emphasis should be placed on an adequate interpretation regardless of its categorization.[48] This view was shared by the decision of the tribunal in *Siemens v.*

---

44. *Christoph Schreuer*, Diversity and Harmonization of Treaty Interpretation in Investment Arbitration, in: Malgosia Fitzmaurice/Olufemi Elias/Panos Mercuric (eds.), Treaty Interpretation and the Vienna Convention on the Law of Treaties: 30 Years on, 2010, pp. 129-151 (p. 131), who refers to the arbitration in *Noble Ventures, Inc. v. Romania*, Award, ICSID Case No. ARB/01/11, October 12, 2005, para. 52: "The object and purpose rule also supports such an interpretation. While it is not permissible, *as is* too often done regarding BITs, to interpret clauses exclusively in favor of investors, here such an interpretation is justified."
45. *Plama Consortium Ltd. v. Republic of Bulgaria*, Decision on Jurisdiction, ICSID Case No. ARB/03/24, February 8, 2005, para. 193:

    Here, the Tribunal is mindful of Sir Ian Sinclair's warning of the 'risk that the placing of undue emphasis on the object and purpose' of a treaty will encourage teleological methods of interpretation [which], in some of its more extreme forms, will even deny the relevance of the intentions of the parties'.

    see also note 33.
46. For a restrictive approach *see Noble Ventures, Inc. v. Romania*, note 44, para. 82:

    In consequence, as with any other exception to established general rules of law, the identification of a provision as an 'umbrella clause' can as a consequence proceed only from a strict, if not indeed restrictive, interpretation of its terms and, more generally, in accordance with the well known customary rules codified under Article 31 of the Vienna Convention of the Law of Treaties (1969).

    For an effective approach *see Suez, Sociedad General de Agues de Barcelona S.A., Vivendi Universal S.A. and AWG Group Ltd. v. The Argentine Republic*, Decision on Jurisdiction, ICSID Case No. ARB/03/19, August 3, 2006, para. 60:

    Similarly, Argentina contends that the Tribunal should interpret the most favored nation clauses strictly because such an approach would restrict the principle of res inter alios acta, so as to limit the effects of the treaty to the parties. The Tribunal cannot follow this argument.

47. *Garanti Kola LLP v. Turkmenistan*, Decision on the Objection to Jurisdiction for Lack of Consent, ICSID Case No. ARB/11/20, July 3, 2013, para. 22.
48. *Mondev International Ltd. v. United States of America*, Award, ICSID Case No. ARB(AF)/99/2, October 11, 2002, para. 43; *Rudolf Dolzer/Christoph Schreuer*, Principles of International Investment Law, 2nd ed. 2012, p. 33.

Argentina.[49] The case involved the erection of a migration control and identification system, for which the respondent entered into a contract with the claimant. After a new government had come to power in Argentina, however, it terminated the contract which led the claimant to unsuccessfully address local administrative courts before filing for an investment arbitration. The tribunal expressed its point of view regarding the distinction between restrictive and effective interpretation as follows:

> The Tribunal considers that the Treaty has to be interpreted neither liberally nor restrictively, as neither of these adverbs is part of Article 31(1) of the Vienna Convention.[50]

Interestingly, however, the tribunal then immediately adopted a purposive or effective approach[51] by clarifying that:

> The Tribunal shall be guided by the purpose of the Treaty as expressed in its title and preamble. It is a treaty "to protect" and "to promote" investments. The preamble provides that the parties have agreed to the provisions of the Treaty for the purpose of creating favorable conditions for the investments of nationals or companies of one of the two States in the territory of the other State. Both parties recognize that the promotion and protection of these investments by a treaty may stimulate private economic initiative and increase the well-being of the peoples of both countries. The intention of the parties is clear. It is to create favorable conditions for investments and to stimulate private initiative.[52]

Despite its initial positioning, the tribunal proved that a categorization is not necessarily representative of the actual approach later adopted. Categorization may thus be problematic. The almost philosophical distinction between restrictive and effective interpretation furthermore implies a legal uncertainty and divide in international investment arbitration and, as a consequence, undermines attempts seeking a more consistent interpretation.

[3]   The Special Meaning-Rule

Article 31 section 4 VCLT clarifies that a special meaning shall be given to a term, if it is established that the parties so intended. The immediate difficulty that arises when deploying this special meaning-rule, is determining the characteristics of a "special meaning." Initially, this provision must be demarcated from the ordinary meaning-rule contained in Article 31 section 1 VCLT. In this regard, a meaning of a term will plainly be special, if it is not ordinary. Ordinary is then every meaning that could be derived from an adequate interpretation according to Article 31 sections 1–3 VCLT. The special meaning-rule thus applies, if the meaning that is to be given to a term deviates from the interpretive result of applying Article 31 section 1 VCLT. In this case, Article 31 section

---

49. *Siemens AG v. The Argentine Republic*, Decision on Jurisdiction, ICSID Case No. ARB/02/8, August 3, 2004.
50. *Siemens AG v. The Argentine Republic*, note 49, para. 81.
51. *Waibel*, note 42, p. 40.
52. *Siemens AG v. The Argentine Republic*, note 49, para. 81.

4 VCLT demands proof of the respective mutual intention of the parties. Such proof may be provided by preparatory work or documents relating to the circumstances of the treaty's conclusion. In accordance with the VCLT's focus on the ordinary meaning of treaty texts in their context and in light of object and purpose, it has been explained that internal government statements referring to treaties other than the one applicable do not suffice,[53] setting a prudential standard for invoking Article 31 section 4 VCLT.

[4] Subsequent Agreements and Practice

Article 31 section 3 (a) and (b) VCLT provide that any subsequent agreement regarding the interpretation or practice in the application of the treaty shall be taken into account. Such subsequent agreements constitute the ultimate expression of the parties' will in the interpretive process. Judges or arbitrators must in this context follow the specifications of the parties in interpreting the relevant treaty. Furthermore, it is not uncommon that states issue a joint statement as to the interpretation of a specific provision during pending proceedings, which will then ideally be taken into appropriate account.[54] Subsequent practice, on the other hand, reflects a common understanding on matters of interpretation and is thus implicit. In the boundary dispute between Botswana and Namibia regarding Kasikili/Sedudu Island, the International Court of Justice (ICJ) made detailed references to documents presented to it by the parties that were supposed to display such subsequent practice.[55] Myriad kinds of documents may so complement a particular treaty interpretation in accordance with Article 31 section 3 (a) and (b) VCLT.

[5] Travaux Préparatoires

Apart from the ordinary meaning-rule and interpretation in light of a treaty's object and purpose, Article 32 VCLT provides that recourse may be had to *travaux préparatoires* and the circumstances of a treaty's conclusion where an interpretation is to be confirmed or where such interpretation leaves an ambiguous or obscure or even manifestly absurd or unreasonable result. Article 32 VCLT thus provides a clear limitation to the use of supplementary means of interpretation.[56] *Travaux*

---

53. *El Paso Energy International Company v. The Argentine Republic*, Award, ICSID Case No. ARB/03/15, October 31, 2011, para. 582.
54. *See CME Czech Republic B.V. v. The Czech Republic*, Final Award, UNCITRAL, March 14, 2003, paras. 437 and 504.
55. *ICJ*, Kasikili/Sedudu Island Case (*Botswana v. Namibia*), note 16, paras. 47-80.
56. *See Churchill Mining Plc v. Republic of Indonesia*, Decision on Jurisdiction, ICSID Cases Nos. ARB/12/14 and 12/40, February 24, 2014, para. 180: "As a result, the Tribunal cannot but find that the meaning of 'shall assent' is unclear or ambiguous. Consequently, it will now review any relevant supplementary means of interpretation pursuant to Article 32 VCLT"; *see*, however, a less mindful approach by a tribunal, deploying Art. 32 VCLT without considering the limitation imposed by it in *Metal-Tech Ltd. v. The Republic of Uzbekistan*, Award, ICSID Case No. ARB/10/3, October 4, 2013, para. 145: "[…] To confirm the meaning established pursuant to this rule (among other purposes), one may have recourse to supplementary means of interpretation, which include the circumstances of the treaty's conclusion (Article 32 of the VCLT)" and

préparatoires therefore constitute a secondary source of interpretation. Nevertheless, this should not underestimate the assistance preparatory work is able to provide to interpreters. Depending on their availability and level of detail, they may allow a more precise interpretation of conflicting wordings. Where judges or arbitrators seek to explore the signatories' intentions for concluding a treaty, such *travaux préparatoires* may provide powerful insights. Much like the attention states should dedicate to treaty negotiations, it should be desirable for them to produce detailed supporting documentation. However, in the context of international investment law, this does not regularly seem to be the case.[57] For example, the tribunal in *Aguas del Tunari v. Bolivia* pointed out the scarcity of documentation in an effort to determine the meaning of the term "controlled directly or indirectly" after merely being presented an expert report, a testimony and an oral argument by the parties.[58]

[B] Precedent in Public International Law

Article 59 of the ICJ-Statute explains that the court's judgments have an *inter partes* effect. They bind only the parties to the respective dispute. Article 38 section 1 (d) of the ICJ-Statute furthermore provides that judicial decisions are only subsidiary means of interpretation. Previous decisions in general public international law thus cannot be viewed as forming binding precedent, as is the case with rulings in the common law world. The practice of the ICJ confirms this theoretical foundation. Previous decisions form part of its decision-making process, however, they do not constitute binding rules.[59] Other international courts take similar, sometimes even identical approaches to the matter.[60] Previous decisions are merely subsidiary means, which appears to be common ground among international courts. It will be of particular interest to see then, if international investment tribunals share a similar understanding of previous decisions.

---

    para. 159: "[...] In the Tribunal's view, these other treaties on the same subject matter can be taken into account as supplementary means of interpretation pursuant to Article 32 of the VCLT."
57. *Schreuer*, note 44, p. 138.
58. *Aguas del Tunari, S.A. v. Republic of Bolivia*, Decision on Respondent's Objections to Jurisdiction, ICSID Case No. ARB/02/3, October 21, 2005, paras. 269 and 274:

    The Claimant presented evidence in the form of an expert report and expert testimony from Dr. Nico Shrijver, Professor of Public International Law at the Free University in Amsterdam and a member of the Netherland's Ministry of Foreign Affairs Advisory Committee on International Law Affairs. The Respondent presented evidence in the form of oral argument. Despite such efforts, the Tribunal has before it little evidence of the negotiating history of the BIT. [...] This sparse negotiating history thus offers little additional insight into the meaning of the aspects of the BIT at issue, neither particularly confirming nor contradicting the Tribunal's interpretation.

59. *Gilbert Guillaume*, The Use of Precedent by International Judges and Arbitrators, in: Journal of International Dispute Settlement 2011, Vol. 2 No. 1, pp. 5-23 (p. 12).
60. *Guillaume*, note 59, p. 14.

§1.04 CHALLENGES IN TREATY INTERPRETATION

The process of treaty interpretation has at the beginning of this chapter been depicted as the methodological essence of public international law. The foregoing analysis has revealed that treaty interpretation is sometimes a process on disputed grounds. Conflicting theoretical approaches exist that blur the parting lines, interplay between the applicable methods and provoke calls for more clarity. The same may be said about the terms of international treaties. Breadth and ambiguity often require a high degree of interpretive efforts. As a consequence, a big challenge for international courts and tribunals is the production of predictable results. Predictability fosters confidence. It is not satisfying the parties' expectations what is meant by predictability of the dispute's outcome. Rather, it refers to a well-reasoned application of the canons of interpretation. Where tribunals or courts have properly interpreted treaty provisions and produced judgments that nonetheless spark severe criticism on the legitimacy of public international law, such criticism is without cause. If, however, interpretation has taken place in an unreasonable or incomprehensible manner, criticism is appropriate and necessary.

Another challenge that derives from this situation is the determination of what constitutes an adequate application of the canons of interpretation. Naturally, such evaluation is only feasible on a case-by-case basis. However, it is possible to spotlight general insufficiencies. *Saldarriaga*[61] has, in the context of international investment law, identified a number of problematic issues among which are the partial[62] or nonapplication[63] of the VCLT and the incorrect application of Articles 31 and 32 VCLT. While the former partial or nonapplication of the VCLT is likely to occur only occasionally,[64] the latter incorrect application of it appears to be a more common phenomenon.[65] The above-mentioned observation similarly holds true in the area of international human rights law. The United Nations human rights treaty bodies are empowered to monitor the implementation processes of international human rights obligations and, for that purpose, also to interpret the relevant treaties. Their interpretations also reveal certain methodological weaknesses and inconsistencies, which affect legitimacy and coherence and may cross the line between interpretation and

---

61. *Saldarriaga*, note 18, pp. 7 et seq.
62. *See Jan de Nul N.V. and Dredging International N.V. v. Arab Republic of Egypt*, Award, ICSID Case No. ARB/04/13, November 6, 2008, in which the tribunal only applies the VCLT with regards to the arbitration agreement but no other provisions of the investment treaty.
63. *See Eastern Sugar B.V. (Netherlands) v. The Czech Republic*, Partial Award, UNCITRAL, SCC Case No. 088/2004, March 27, 2007, in which the tribunal does not refer to the VCLT for the purpose of treaty interpretation; *see also Bayview Irrigation District and others v. United Mexican States*, Award, ICSID Case No. ARB(AF), June 19, 2007, in which the tribunal did apply the rules of interpretation, but without reference to the order envisaged by the VCLT.
64. *Schreuer*, note 44, p. 129, who points out that "Tribunals almost invariably start by invoking Article 31 of the Vienna Convention on the Law of Treaties (VCLT) when interpreting treaties."
65. *Saldarriaga*, note 18, pp. 7 et seq.: "The analysis has revealed that the use of the VCLT rules of interpretation by tribunals in the awards is, on various instances, inconsistent, insufficient and even flawed."

law-making.⁶⁶ Similarly, interpretations provided by the WTO's Appellate Body, at times, seem to show a lack of adherence to the methodological canons provided by the VCLT.⁶⁷ However, the VCLT itself is not immaculate and vague in nature. It is therefore at times a demanding task to apply it. Does this mean that the interpretation of international treaties rests on unstable pillars? The answer to this question is not an easy one to provide and likely to differ depending on an individual's particular perspective. The current methodology is, however, by no means insufficient. Its development does require further academic and practical attention.

It is undisputed that theory sometimes does not prove viable in practice. In this regard, compliance with the principles of interpretation as they are contained in the VCLT may be deemed as being too detached from the necessities of modern public international law. However, theoretical approaches on the one hand carve out structures and patterns that allow for a deeper understanding of common practice. On the other hand, they provide guidance and foster a stringent and systematic development of a legal area, which strengthens its users' confidence in it. A disharmonious interaction of theory and practice may thus be partially causal for expressions of discontent with public international law in general and international investment law specifically as will be outlined at a later stage.

§1.05 DISTINGUISHING INTERPRETATION AND LAW-MAKING

In the context of heavy reliance on the object and purpose of a treaty, it has been pointed out that such recourse must not produce an outcome that goes beyond what is expressed in the text. If such care is not exercised, interpretation may turn into law-making. What is not found in the text of a treaty and revealed by proper interpretation, is not an interpretive result. Rather, such results may only occur, if something is added to the text in the process of law-making. That is essentially the rewriting of a treaty. In public international law, law-making in the context of interpretation has always been a matter of controversy.⁶⁸ It has been argued that indeed certain treaties exist that have a law-making character as this new creation of rules going beyond a treaty's text may be in its nature.⁶⁹ Those treaties serve a purpose of establishing new rules and have been characterized as being legislative.⁷⁰ In applying these forms of treaties, law-making is not deemed problematic, provided that it takes place upon firm methodology. What is necessary, however, is to distinguish

---

66. *Kerstin Mechlem*, Treaty Bodies and the Interpretation of Human Rights, in: Vanderbilt Journal of Transnational Law 2009, Vol. 42, pp. 905-947 (pp. 945 et seq.).
67. *Federico Ortino*, Treaty Interpretation and the WTO Appellate Body Report in US-Gambling: A Critique, in: Journal of International Economic Law 2006, Vol. 9 No. 1, pp. 117-148 (p. 30).
68. *Mia Swart*, Judicial Lawmaking at the Ad Hoc Tribunals: The Creative Use of the Sources of International Law and "Adventurous Interpretation," in: Zeitschrift für ausländisches öffentliches Recht und Völkerrecht 2010, Vol. 70 No. 3, pp. 459-486 (p. 460).
69. *Quincy Wright*, Mandates under the League of Nations, 1930, p. 357, describing law-making treaties as those "concluded for the purpose of establishing new rules for the law of nations."
70. *Georges Scelle*, Le Pacte des Nations et sa liaison avec Le Traité de Paix, 1919, p. 49: "Mais à côté d'eux, certains traités présentent un tout autre intérêt de stabilité et de généralité. Ils ont pour but de poser une règle de droit, et sont de véritables actes législatifs."

between these and other treaties. Otherwise, law-making may, on occasion, be applied to treaties that do not envisage such approach. A valuable contribution was made by *Fitzmaurice* in outlining three types of treaties, different in content: first, contractual treaties that are based upon an exchange of rights or benefits, second, interdependent treaties and third, law-making treaties.[71] The latter, he characterizes as "undertakings to conform to certain standards and conditions."[72] The distinction between these law-making or normative treaties and contractual treaties is not always an easy one to make, especially considering the fact that a number of treaties contain elements that may be deemed both, normative and contractual.[73] Nevertheless, even if a treaty is characterized as being normative, this would not explain how the process of law-making, beyond interpretation, is technically carried out utilizing the principles of the VCLT. The textual approach of the VCLT has been outlined above. If normative treaties allow a broader recourse to their object and purpose, it may challenge the interpretive mechanism of the VCLT, which does not make any distinction between normative and contractual treaties. However, this distinction had existed long before the VCLT came into force, and it is thus argued that its drafters considered the VCLT to apply to treaties, regardless of their possible categorization.[74] A possible starting point in using the VCLT to engage in law-making could be Article 31 section 3 (a) and (b), incorporating subsequent agreements and practice. This could open up the interpretive process, allowing an international body to engage in law-making, if the normative character of the respective treaty is thereby determined.

§1.06 CONCLUSION

This chapter has highlighted the predominant role of the interpretive principles contained in the VCLT that apply to the interpretation of international treaties. The VCLT envisages a systematic approach of interpretation that begins by ascertaining the ordinary meaning of a term in its context, before engaging in a broader analysis of it in view of the treaty's object and purpose. At this stage in the interpretive process, courts and tribunals sometimes tend to follow an effective or restrictive path. In order to confirm an interpretation or in case of obscure, ambiguous or even absurd results, recourse to preparatory work is admissible. Furthermore, subsequent agreements or practice may also shed light on the adequacy of an interpretation within the applicability of the VCLT. In addition to these rules, other means of interpretation have been outlined. Unsettled remains their exact relationship with the provisions of the VCLT. Nevertheless, they are frequently applied by courts and tribunals. This makes apparent the importance of sensible interpretations in line with the existing methodological

---

71. *Catherine Brölmann*, Law-Making Treaties: Form and Function in International Law, in: Nordic Journal of International Law 2005, Vol. 74 No. 3, pp. 1-17 (p. 4).
72. *Gerald Fitzmaurice*, Second Reports on the law of treaties, in: Yearbook of the International Law Commission 1957, Vol. 2, pp. 16-70 (p. 31).
73. *Kirsten Schmalenbach*, Preamble, in: Oliver Dörr/Kirsten Schmalenbach (eds.), Vienna Convention on the Law of Treaties: A Commentary, 2012, Art. 2, para. 14.
74. *Sandra L. Bunn-Livingstone*, Juricultural Pluralism vis-à-vis Treaty Law: State Practice and Attitudes, 2002, p. 140.

canons. Decisions that are not traceable in view of the existing interpretive framework or even contrary to it are likely – and rightfully – to be perceived as flawed. An interpretation disregarding the applicable methodology in public international law is thus illegitimate.[75] Interpretations are the products of court or arbitral proceedings. If they go beyond the constraints of interpretive methodology, they consequently bear the risk of producing inadequate results, threatening the existence of public international law from the inside. A cycle of reciprocal consideration or especially reliance on such interpretive outcomes is thus not desirable.

This chapter has at the same time, however, pointed out the existent uncertainty regarding the methodology of treaty interpretation which is a tremendous challenge for public international law. Despite the applicability of the VCLT, it is at times not invoked, invoked on diverging perceptions concerning its systematic order or invoked only partially. This is possibly owed to the nature of public international law itself. Established rules of customary law are not written in stone. *Consuetudo* and *opinio juris* may in fact alter what is currently in existence. The consequence of this openness is frankly a margin for deviations and thus ultimately, uncertainty. That is not to say, however, that treaty interpretation can fully free itself from established methodology. The applicability of the VCLT is well-established and thus common ground in public international law. Courts and tribunals must therefore pay respect to the existing methodology, which is more important than ever as we witness an ever-increasing complexity of the field.

An adequate decision in this regard is then one that reflects attention to and compliance with the existing methodology of interpretation and provides proper reasoning. Interpretations must be traceable. This is best achieved by adherence to the existing canons of the VCLT. The remaining flexibility of the VCLT will in this regard continue to produce interpretations that are based upon its principles but weigh them in differing manners.[76] Despite these differences, however, the VCLT intends to produce interpretations of logic and sense.[77] If an approach attentive to the VCLT is not followed, adequacy will demand an equally traceable exposition of reasons. If such is not provided, a decision is rightfully characterized as "off the rails."[78] However, consistently adequate decisions bear an enormous potential for the development of public international law. It is their quality that will, especially in the context of international investment law, foster confidence in the existing system of investment protection and its mechanisms for dispute resolution. Legitimate awards, in this regard, may shape the framework of investment protection in a way that knows evolutionary interpretations, which nurture the economic benefit of the host state and

---

75. *See Waibel*, note 42, p. 45.
76. *See Michael Waibel*, Uniformity versus Specialisation: A Uniform Regime of Treaty Interpretation?, University of Cambridge, Legal Studies Research Paper Series, Paper No. 54/2013, available at http://papers.ssrn.com/sol3/papers.cfm?abstract_id=2353833 (last accessed September 11, 2014), p. 35.
77. *ILC*, note 23, p. 218; *see also Daniel Patrick O'Connell*, International Law, 1965, p. 272: "These two propositions underlie the so-called 'canons of interpretation', which are no more than logical devices for getting at the real area of treaty operation."
78. *Waibel*, note 76, p. 34.

the investor while paying respect to all the interests involved: those of a merchant and those of a sovereign. Courts and tribunals generally must therefore be vigilant of the interpretive means that exist. As the content of disputes in public international law broadens, the effort to understand, develop and correctly apply the methods of interpretation is imperative for keeping not just public international law in place, but also its fragmented areas such as international investment law, whose dynamics are unparalleled. This and other characteristics make analyses of the field particularly challenging, but similarly exciting.

CHAPTER 2
Characteristics of International Investment Law

§2.01 PUBLIC INTERNATIONAL LAW ROOTS

[A] The Origin of International Investment Law

In history, foreigners have frequently encountered difficulties entering communities. Many were treated as aliens and denied the legal status of the community members.[79] However, commerce necessitated relationships with outsiders. As a result, these outsiders and their home laws were gradually granted acceptance by communities.[80] In his 1758 publication *"Law of Nations,"* Emer de Vattel described a right of foreigners to temporarily enter a foreign country, for business or leisure,[81] or to permanently seek residence.[82] Interestingly, once foreigners were admitted into a state's territory, they were to be regarded as equal to the state's citizens.[83] A violation of their rights was regarded as a violation of the home state's rights,[84] which held particularly true for property.[85] This marked a profound step forward in the protection of foreigners and

---

79. *Andrew Newcombe/Lluís Paradell*, Law and Practice of Investment Treaties – Standards of Treatment, 2009, p. 3.
80. *Edwin M. Borchard*, The Diplomatic Protection of Citizens Abroad or The Law of International Claims, 1916, pp. 3 et seq.
81. *Emer de Vattel*, The Law of Nations, 1758, 2nd ed. 1852 by Joseph Chitty, Book II, § 99.
82. *De Vattel*, note 81, Book I, § 213.
83. *De Vattel*, note 81, Book II, § 104: "The sovereign ought not to grant entrance into his state for the purpose of drawing foreigners into a snare: as soon as he admits them, he engages to protect them as his own subjects, and to afford them perfect security, as far as depends on him."
84. *De Vattel*, note 81, Book II, § 108: "[…] This is at once a violation of the rights of individuals, and of those of the state to which they belong. […]."
85. *De Vattel*, note 81, Book II, § 109: "The property of an individual does not cease to belong to him on account of his being in a foreign country; it still constitutes a part of the aggregate wealth of his nation (§ 81)."

laid the foundation for the emergence of diplomatic protection.[86] States began claiming reparation for violations of their citizens' rights abroad, a procedure that became a common practice in public international law.[87] When one then thinks of public international law in a traditional sense, engaged in border conflicts, war crimes or diplomacy, it may be striking to realize that this area of law nowadays also has a strong impact on economic activity not only between states, but also between states and individuals. As sovereign states, however, have evolved from gunboat diplomacy, so has the law governing their relationships. Consequentially, modern international investment law has further developed from diplomatic protection by way of international treaties. Even at this early stage then, it becomes clear that international investment law has public international law roots.[88] Despite this evolution, it would nevertheless be erroneous to conclude that traditional concepts of public international law therefore no longer apply. The principle of state sovereignty exemplifies this quite clearly: in 1949, *Alejandro Alvarez* stated that "by state sovereignty, we understand the

---

86. Newcombe/Paradell, note 79, p. 4.
87. *See PCIJ*, The Panevezys-Saldutiskis Railway Case (*Estonia v. Lithuania*), Judgment, February 28, 1939, PCIJ Series A./B. No. 76, p. 16:

> This right is necessarily limited to intervention on behalf of its own nationals because, in the absence of a special agreement, it is the bond of nationality between the State and the individual which alone confers upon the State the right of diplomatic protection, and it is as a part of the function of diplomatic protection that the right to take up a claim and to ensure respect for the rules of international law must be envisaged.

88. *ICJ*, Case Concerning Ahmadou Sadio Diallo (*Guinea v. Democratic Republic of Congo*), Preliminary Objections, May 24, 2007, ICJ Reports 2007, pp. 582-618 (p. 614):

> The Court is bound to note that, in contemporary international law, the protection of the rights of companies and the rights of their shareholders, and the settlement of the associated disputes, are essentially governed by bilateral or multilateral agreements for the protection of foreign investments, such as the treaties for the promotion and protection of foreign investments, and the Washington Convention of 18 March 1965 on the Settlement of Investment Disputes between States and Nationals of Other States, which created an International Centre for Settlement of Investment Disputes (ICSID), and also by contracts between States and foreign investors. In that context, the role of diplomatic protection somewhat faded, as in practice recourse is only made to it in rare cases where treaty régimes do not exist or have proved inoperative.

see also Christoph Schreuer, Investment Protection and International Relations, in: August Reinisch/Ursula Kriebaum (eds.), The Law of International Relations – Liber Amicorum Hanspeter Neuhold, 2007, pp. 345-358 (p. 347), who speaks of a "[t]ransfer of investment disputes from the inter-State arena to mixed methods of dispute settlement [...]"; *see also Gabrielle Kaufmann-Kohler*, Non-Disputing State Submissions In Investment Arbitration: Resurgence of Diplomatic Protection, in: Laurence Boisson de Chazournes/Marcelo G. Kohen/Jorge E. Viñuales (eds.), Diplomatic and Judicial Means of Dispute Settlement, 2012, pp. 307-326 (p. 326), who analyzes the consequences of a home state aiding its national in an ongoing arbitration, arguing:

> It would bring back the politicized atmosphere which is the consequence of a direct confrontation between two sovereigns that in the past led to friction between capital-importing and capital-exporting States, and which the investor-State dispute settlement mechanism precisely aims at avoiding (irrespective of which arbitration rules are chosen).

whole body of rights and attributes which a State possesses in its territory, to the exclusion of all other States, and also in its relations with other States. Sovereignty confers upon States and imposes obligations on them."[89] This basic understanding of state sovereignty has been interpreted by the International Commission on Intervention and State Sovereignty (ICISS) in 2001 as encompassing a responsibility towards citizens.[90] This responsibility to protect was already a then hidden sphere of state sovereignty in 1949 as *Alvarez* expressed by referring to states' obligations. However, it was only later due to an evolutionary and interpretive process that state practice and academia carved out a specific responsibility to protect citizens, a development that is rooted in sovereignty. This evolution does not signal the redundancy of state sovereignty in its traditional sense. To the contrary, it highlights the importance of core concepts of public international law that lay the foundation for new and adequate interpretations and developments.

[B] The Objectives of Investment Protection

International investment law is not merely self-serving when it intends to foster benefits for the host state and the investor by way of foreign investments. Capital gains of sovereign nations should ideally go hand in hand with improvements for the public welfare. Although this idyllically painted picture does not always hold true in state practice, it is the theoretical underpinning of the field. Whenever a potential investor seeks to engage in economic activity in a foreign country, he will typically seek a stable and robust legal framework in which his investment – in whatever form it may be made – enjoys security. Possible risks to the investment may lead the investor to diminish the width of his economic activity or even to completely reconsider investing. This situation is unfortunate for the investor and the host state alike. Investors thus commonly turn to commercial risk insurances, the Multilateral Investment Guarantee Agency (MIGA) or the International Finance Corporation (IFC) in order to mitigate risks and secure their economic activities. International investment law, however, has been providing another vital option of growing importance for risk mitigation. It intends to provide a secure investment environment by way of international treaties and the incorporation of dispute resolution mechanisms. Although there has been an

---

89. ICJ, The Corfu Channel Case (*United Kingdom v. Albania*), Separate Opinion of Alejandro Alvarez, April 9, 1949, ICJ Reports 1949, pp. 39-48 (p. 42).
90. *International Commission on Intervention and State Sovereignty*, The Responsibility to Protect, 2001, available at http://responsibilitytoprotect.org/ICISS%20Report.pdf (last accessed September 9, 2014), p. 13, in which the Commission dwells on the modern understanding of state sovereignty as follows:

> Thinking of sovereignty as responsibility, in a way that is being increasingly recognized in state practice, has a threefold significance. First, it implies that the state authorities are responsible for the functions of protecting the safety and lives of citizens and promotion of their welfare. Secondly, it suggests that the national political authorities are responsible to the citizens internally and to the international community through the UN. And thirdly, it means that the agents of state are responsible for their actions; that is to say, they are accountable for their acts of commission and omission.

ongoing debate about the economic effects of the international investment law system, namely whether or not it actually fosters investments, the theoretical purpose of it is just that: providing stability to attract foreign capital inflows for the mutual benefit of the host state and the investor. As this concept is one of basic economic logic, there now exists virtually no disagreement among nations about the importance of investment protection.[91]

§2.02 INTERNATIONAL TREATIES AS SOURCES OF INTERNATIONAL INVESTMENT LAW

In order to promote investment protection, states have entered into an impressive number of international treaties, weaving a dense net that constitutes international investment law. These treaties can generally be divided into three categories:[92] BITs, multilateral investment treaties (MITs) and free trade agreements (FTAs). All share the remarkably simple, yet effective legal idea of signatory states reciprocally granting protection to their citizens' investments within their territory. These kinds of treaties now take on a predominant role in state practice.[93] Protection comes from a number of standards that apply to a respective investment. For this purpose, international treaties most commonly contain most favored nation-clauses, full protection and security-clauses, fair and equitable treatment-clauses, expropriation-clauses and umbrella-clauses. Although states are free to decide how to structure their respective treaty, the majority of them show great similarities as far as their basic setup is concerned.[94]

[A]   Types of Investment Treaties

[1]   Bilateral Investment Treaties

As of the end of the eighteenth century, states began entering into treaties of friendship, commerce and navigation (FCN). As their name suggests, the content of these treaties was broad and mostly not specifically tailored to the needs of investors.[95] The German banker *Hermann-Josef Abs* and the British Attorney General *Lord Shawcross* took a powerful leap forward in the protection of investors abroad. The Abs-Shawcross Draft Convention on Investment Abroad of 1959 laid the foundation for the impressive development of international investment law, as we know it today. In the same year,

---

91. *Schill*, note 5, pp. 3-37 (p. 5).
92. See Mark Mangan, Australia's Investment Treaty Program and Investor-State Arbitration, in: Luke Nottage/Richard Garnett (eds.), International Arbitration in Australia, 2010, pp. 191-218 (p. 192).
93. *Matthias Herdegen*, Völkerrecht, 12th ed. 2013, p. 394.
94. *Stephan W. Schill*, Enhancing International Investment Law's Legitimacy: Conceptual and Methodological Foundations of a New Public Law Approach, in: Virginia Journal of International Law 2011, Vol. 52 No. 1, pp. 57-102 (p. 62), who describes the treaty practice as a "largely uniform system of international investment protection"; *see also* Stephan W. Schill, The Multilateralization of International Investment Law, 2009, p. 16.
95. *See Alexandra Diehl*, Tracing a Success Story or "The Baby Boom of BITs," in: August Reinisch/Christina Knahr (eds.), International Investment Law in Context, 2008, pp. 7-25 (p. 7).

Chapter 2: Characteristics of International Investment Law   §2.02[A]

the history of BITs commenced. Germany and Pakistan entered into an international treaty in which they mutually granted investments made by their citizens' protection within their territories. This innovative legal document sparked a development that currently knows well over 2,500 BITs.[96] While at first, industrialized nations entered into BITs with developing countries, nowadays developing countries also sign such treaties among one another in order to promote their countries as places for investments.[97] These treaties typically contain a legal remedy against adverse state actions. Such investment disputes are typically referred to an international adjudicative body that will consider the merits and later render a decision. Keeping traditional public international law in mind, it does not come as a surprise that this new legal framework has triggered myriad reactions. Where sovereign state actions are scrutinized on the international level, there inevitably occur debates that are challenging but vital to the development of international investment law.

The growing number of BITs that states are signing draws attention to their drafting process. Where they allow for an international adjudicative body to render decisions that may have serious financial consequences, there should be an exceptional care exercised when entering into such agreements. Whether this is actually the case or it proves to be another idyllically painted picture in state practice will remain to be seen throughout the upcoming analysis. What is, however, sufficient to bear in mind at this point, is the central role of BITs in international investment law as well as the importance of their proper drafting and interpretation.

[2]   Multilateral Investment Treaties

While BITs are entered into by two states, MITs bring together a greater number of signatories. Especially those agreements under the auspices of the WTO, the General Agreement on Trade in Services (GATS), the Agreement on Trade-Related Investment Measures (TRIMS) or the Agreement on Trade-Related Aspects of Intellectual Property (TRIPS) are worth mentioning in this context as they contain provisions regarding the treatment of investments. One needs to note, however, that disputes within the WTO are solely settled between states. An individual may not bring a claim against a state based on an alleged violation of one of the above-mentioned agreements.[98]

Also, the Energy Charter Treaty (ECT) constitutes an important MIT with a particular focus on the energy sector. It entered into force in April 1998 and has a twofold mission: on the one hand, energy importing states shall enjoy security regarding their energy supply, while energy exporting states shall enjoy foreign investments. The ECT nowadays is in force for the Member States of the European

---

96. UNCTAD, International Investment Agreements Navigator, available at http://investment policyhub.unctad.org/IIA (last accessed September 9, 2014).
97. *Lauge Skovgaard Poulsen*, The Significance of South-South BITs for The International Investment Regime: A Quantitative Analysis, in: Northwestern Journal of International Law & Business 2010, Vol. 30 No. 1, pp. 101-130 (p. 101).
98. *Jörn Griebel*, Internationales Investitionsrecht, 2008, p. 60.

Union, a number of Eastern European as well as Asian states,[99] providing protection for investments in the energy sector. Its effectiveness was first demonstrated in the dispute *Nykomb v. Latvia*.[100] It arose out of an agreement between SIA Windau, a subsidiary of Nykomb, and Latvenergo – a state enterprise under Latvian law – according to which SIA Windau was obligated to erect a cogeneration plant that was to be purchased by Latvenergo. However, the parties later disagreed on the envisaged purchase price which triggered the initiation of international proceedings by the claimant, which resulted in a decision against the respondent.

[3] Free Trade Agreements

Free trade agreements (FTAs) generally intend to reduce trade barriers and are thus broader in their nature than pure investment treaties. However, many FTAs contain specific provisions with regards to the protection of foreign investments. They are mostly formed among states that share a particular geographic location.

[a] North American Free Trade Agreement

A prominent example is the North American Free Trade Agreement (NAFTA), which entered into force in 1992. Chapter 11 NAFTA is dedicated to the protection of investments. A unique feature of NAFTA is the Free Trade Commission. Should there arise a dispute among the signatory states regarding the interpretation of NAFTA, Article 1131 (2) provides that this Commission is entitled to rule on the interpretation in a binding manner. This mechanism shares similarities with the preliminary rulings procedure that courts of Member States of the European Union may initiate pursuant to Article 267 of the Treaty on the Functioning of the European Union (TFEU). Here, courts may or – in case of an exhaustion of remedies – must seek a decision by the ECJ on how to interpret national law in accordance with the underlying European law instruments, a procedure that will be worth considering during the course of this analysis.

[b] Association of Southeast Asian Nations

Southeast Asia has experienced an immense economic boom in recent years; a region that still has enormous potential for further growth and continues to attract leading corporations from the Western hemisphere. In 1967, the necessity for stable economies has led five Southeast Asian nations to form ASEAN, which currently consists of ten Member States: Brunei, Cambodia, Indonesia, Laos, Malaysia, Myanmar, Philippines, Singapore, Thailand and Viet Nam. In order to create a secure investment environment, ASEAN has agreed on adopting two further documents in 1987: the ASEAN

---

99. *Griebel*, note 98, p. 59.
100. *Nykomb Synergetics Technology Holding AB v. Republic of Latvia*, Award, SCC, December 16, 2003.

Agreement for the Promotion and Protection of Investments, and in 1998, the Framework Agreement on the ASEAN Investment Area that both regulate questions of expropriation, most favored nation-treatment or the settlement of investment disputes.[101]

[c]   Additional Free Trade Agreements

In addition to the ones already introduced, it is worth mentioning that other important FTAs with investment protection regulations exist and continue to be negotiated. For example, this includes the agreement between Australia, New Zealand and ASEAN, the Association of Southeast Asian Nations, Australia and New Zealand Free Trade Agreement (ASEAN-ANZ-FTA) that was signed on February 27, 2009. Furthermore, chapter 10 of the Dominican Republic – Central America – United States Free Trade Agreement (CAFTA-DR)[102] or the Protocol of Colonia that was added to the Mercosur Agreement between Argentina, Brazil, Paraguay and Uruguay in order to regulate the protection of investments are to be named.[103]

All of these international treaties form international investment law. It is safe to predict that the number of these treaties is bound to rise in the near future.[104] States are increasingly going to want to participate in international economic activities. The net of international treaties will thus become more dense. The complexity of international investment law therefore requires continuous academic attention and support.

[B]   Standards of Protection

Once it is found that a particular activity constitutes an investment pursuant to the applicable investment protection instrument, the investor enjoys the breadth of protection standards. Regardless of any categorization, many investment treaties share similar, sometimes even identical provisions as far as their standards of protection are concerned. State parties are free to choose which they would like to incorporate into their treaties. However, state practice has seen a frequent usage of a number of protection standards that have thus become typical in international investment law. For the purpose of this analysis, it suffices to scratch the surface of these individual standards in order to understand their basic contents and nature. A broader discussion

---

101. ASEAN Agreement for the Promotion and Protection of Investments, available at http://investmentpolicyhub.unctad.org/Download/TreatyFile/5109 (last accessed September 7, 2014); Framework Agreement on the ASEAN Investment Area, available at http://www.asean.org/communities/asean-economic-community/item/framework-agreement-on-the-asean-investment-area-2 (last accessed September 7, 2014).
102. Central America - Dominican Republic - United States Free Trade Agreement, available at http://www.sice.oas.org/Trade/CAFTA/CAFTADR_e/CAFTADRin_e.asp (last accessed September 7, 2014).
103. Protocol of Colonia, available at http://www.cvm.gov.br/ingl/inter/mercosul/coloni-e.asp (last accessed September 7, 2014).
104. *August Reinisch*, Internationales Investitionsschutzrecht, in: Christian Tietje (ed.), Internationales Wirtschaftsrecht, 2009, pp. 346-374 (p. 350).

would go beyond the realms of possibility, and a number of publications have done so in an outstanding manner.

The standards of protection serve as legal anchors that grant security to the investor. Where it deems a particular state conduct contrary to the guarantees of the applicable investment treaty, the investor may rely on the standards of protection contained in it to argue a violation of the treaty. Therefore, they represent the material foundation for a successful claim by an investor.[105] They are what arguments in international investment disputes revolve around. Naturally, however, these standards share a broad and general wording that is dependent upon interpretation in each individual case.[106]

[1]   Fair and Equitable Treatment-Standard

The majority of investment treaties nowadays contain a standard that affords to the investor a treatment by the host state that is fair and equitable.[107] This exact wording is vague and imprecise and thus has two practical consequences: first, the fair and equitable treatment-standard is the most relied-upon protection by foreign investors,[108] as virtually any state conduct may theoretically be interpreted as unfair or inequitable. It does not surprise therefore, that the fair and equitable treatment-standard is described as being an "overarching principle"[109] in international investment law. Second, it depends highly on proper interpretive efforts.[110] Tribunals shape the scope and meaning of this standard. In a number of investment disputes, tribunals have given the fair and equitable treatment-standard contours that appear to be commonly accepted in practice. It has been analyzed that this standard typically encompasses protection of the investor's legitimate expectations, protection from hostile treatment, harassment and coercion from government authorities as well as a general obligation for host states to act in good faith.[111]

---

105. *See Ole Spiermann*, Individual Rights, State Interests and the Power to Waive ICSID Jurisdiction under Bilateral Investment Treaties, in: Arbitration International 2004, Vol. 20, pp. 179-212 (p. 183), who refers to the standards of protection as "the archetype of treaties conferring rights on individuals."
106. *See Griebel*, note 98, p. 69, who draws a comparison to the wording of § 242 of the German Civil Code (BGB).
107. *Rudolf Dolzer/Margrete Stevens*, Bilateral Investment Treaties, 1995, p. 58.
108. *Mangan*, note 92, p. 195.
109. *Christoph Schreuer*, Fair and Equitable Treatment (FET): Interactions with other Standards, in: Transnational Dispute Management 2007, Vol. 4 No. 5, pp. 1-26 (p. 26).
110. *See Christina Knahr*, Chapter V: Investment Arbitration – Fair and Equitable Treatment and Its Relationship with Other Treatment Standards, in: Christian Klausegger/Peter Klein (eds.), Austrian Arbitration Yearbook 2009, pp. 493-513 (p. 494).
111. *Christoph Schreuer*, Fair and Equitable Treatment in Arbitral Practice, in: The Journal of World Investment & Trade 2005, Vol. 6 No. 3, pp. 357-386 (p. 386).

[2] *Most Favored Nation-Standard*

Most favored nation-clauses constitute integral parts of a large number of treaties. In short, these clauses intend to guarantee that the respective state parties to a treaty treat one another no less favorable than any other state party they have entered into a treaty with. This has a significant practical consequence: upon entering into another new and more favorable treaty with another state party, the relevant, more favorable provisions are automatically incorporated into the older treaty. By way of this mechanism, investment treaties receive a dynamic element.[112] They do not only remain open to future developments; more importantly, they are self-adapting in the sense that states are not required to re-negotiate previous treaties entered into, if they intend to include a particular provision of a recent treaty into an older one. While this is without doubt a convenient feature, states must also be aware of the fact that by way of most favored nation-clauses, more favorable provisions of a new treaty will become part of an older treaty that does not accord the same favorable treatment, even if the state did not so intend. These clauses then constitute consent to the automatic future adaptation of a treaty. An interesting example of such effect is the application of the most favored nation-clause to the jurisdiction of an international tribunal. In other words: is reliance on the most favored nation-clause sufficient to grant jurisdiction to an international adjudicative body although the directly applicable treaty does not so provide?[113] This dynamic feature of the most favored nation-clause, from a public international law perspective, is not problematic, if it is extracted from the proper application of methodology.[114] It does, however, illustrate the broad practical consequences of its application. Thus, states are to carefully examine the possible effects of using most favored nation-clauses.

---

112. *Alexandra Diehl*, The Core Standard of International Investment Protection – Fair and Equitable Treatment, 2012, p. 73.
113. In case of the applicability of a shorter "cooling off-period" *see Emilio Agustín Maffezini v. The Kingdom of Spain*, Decision of the Tribunal to Objections of Jurisdiction, ICSID Case No. ARB/97/7, January 25, 2000, para. 56, in which the tribunal concluded that "from the above considerations it can be concluded that if a third party treaty contains provisions for the settlement of disputes that are more favorable to the protection of the investor's rights and interests than those in the basic treaty, such provisions may be extended to the beneficiary of the most favored nation clause as they are fully compatible with the *ejusdem generis* principle." and further that "[t]his operation of the most favored nation clause does, however, have some important limits arising from public policy considerations"; *see also Plama Consortium Limited v. Republic of Bulgaria*, Decision on Jurisdiction, ICSID Case No. ARB/03/24, February 8, 2005, para. 223, in which the tribunal in contrast to *Maffezini v. Spain* found that "an MFN provision in a basic treaty does not incorporate by reference dispute settlement provisions in whole or in part set forth in another treaty, unless the MFN provision in the basic treaty leaves no doubt that the Contracting Parties intended to incorporate them."
114. *Andreas R. Ziegler*, Most-Favoured-Nation (MFN) Treatment, in: August Reinisch (ed.), Standards of Investment Protection, 2008, pp. 59-86 (p. 65), who states that this characteristic is in "conformity with the principle that the consent of a State can lead to the creation of new rights as a consequence of a treaty between third States, although it is not a requirement that the contracting States of the later treaty intended the provision also to accord that right to the third State."

[3] Full Protection and Security-Standard

Another standard that is commonly incorporated is that of full protection and security. It primarily intends to shield investments from physical interference by the host state. Whether or not it also encompasses legal interference remains another controversial issue in international investment law. Some tribunals have found this standard to be applicable to merely physical actions, such as that in *Saluka v. Czech Republic*,[115] in which the dispute arose out of the privatization of the Czech banking sector. Others, however, in interpreting the underlying BIT, have found the full protection and security-standard to extend to nonphysical interferences. In *Vivendi v. Argentina*, the tribunal concluded that all measures that may adversely affect the investment may fall under this standard, as the applicable BIT in Article 5 section 1 did not provide otherwise. As a consequence, it simultaneously noted that such treatment may also constitute an unfair and inequitable treatment,[116] carving out a possible overlap with the fair and equitable treatment-standard.[117] The full protection and security-standard creates an obligation for host states to only take measures carefully selected in order to provide a maximum of security to the investment.[118] The broad language of the standard makes the full protection and security-standard difficult to grasp, but it may also encourage claimants to argue in favor of a violation by the host state, taking advantage of the existing uncertainty. Such practical move may be worthwhile whenever it is unclear which position on the interpretive spectrum the tribunal will take, in favor or against an extensive approach.

[4] Umbrella Clauses

Umbrella clauses represent another common feature of investment treaties. They intend to grant an even higher level of protection to an investment by broadening the scope of applicability of the relevant treaty. By way of an umbrella clause, obligations of the host state arising out of a contract with the investor may become obligations under the treaty. In short, contract claims may become treaty claims.[119] The consequences of such transformation are severe, as contractual obligations thereby fall in the domain of public international law, allowing the investor to raise claims before international investment tribunals on the basis of the respective investment treaty. In

---

115. *Saluka Investments BV v. The Czech Republic*, Partial Award, PCA Case, UNCITRAL, March 17, 2006, para. 484, in which the tribunal found that "the practice of arbitral tribunals seems to indicate, however, that the 'full security and protection' clause is not meant to cover just any kind of impairment of an investor's investment, but to protect more specifically the physical integrity of an investment against interference by use of force."
116. *Compañía de Aguas del Aconquija S.A. and Vivendi Universal S.A. v. The Argentine Republic*, Award, ICSID Case No. ARB/97/3, August 20, 2007, para. 7.4.15.
117. *See* George K. Foster, Recovering "Full Protection and Security": The Treaty Standard's Obscure Origins, Forgotten Meaning, and Key Current Significance, in: Vanderbilt Journal of Transnational Law 2012, Vol. 45, pp. 1095-1156 (p. 1156).
118. Giuditta Cordero Moss, Full Protection and Security, in: August Reinisch (ed.), Standards of Investment Protection, 2008, pp. 131-150 (p. 150).
119. *Griebel*, note 98, p. 85.

individual cases, however, it may be a challenging task for tribunals to determine which exact obligation should be transformed. Especially because of the far-reaching impact on a host state's sovereignty,[120] tribunals have indicated that the threshold for presuming a transformation of a contract claim into a treaty claim is a high one and that the wording of the umbrella clause must be clear and specific.[121] This result is supported by the idea that host states will explicitly do so, if they want to allow investors a right of action with regards to contracts.[122]

[5]   Expropriation

An expropriation of an investor's assets by the host state constitutes probably the most apparent form of an interference with a foreign investment. The taking of assets by the host state, known as a direct expropriation, is an action so contrary to the investor's will that it forms the basis of the development of international investment law.[123] Direct expropriations have, however, become relatively unusual. Nowadays, investors are rather confronted with state actions that may fall under so-called indirect expropriations or creeping expropriations. Oftentimes, these cases of indirect expropriations involve licenses which form the basis for the proper use of the investment and, in case of their nonissuance or revocation, may be measures tantamount to a direct expropriation. It is conceivable that the investor is not only never granted but also never refused a license, leaving him in a situation of legal uncertainty.[124] Where a particular investment, however, has from its very first initiation been contrary to a state's public policy and thus not in compliance with domestic laws, but was nevertheless admitted by the host state, it does not constitute an expropriation, if the granting of a license is later denied. In this regard, an investor cannot claim an expropriation as there is no right to an amendment of domestic laws. The state's decision to admit the investment

---

120. *Griebel*, note 98, p. 85.
121. *SGS Société Générale de Surveillance S.A. v. Islamic Republic of Pakistan*, ICSID Case No. ARB/01/13, Decision of the Tribunal on Objections to Jurisdiction, August 6, 2003, para. 173; *see also Consorzio Groupement L.E.S.I.-DIPENTA v. People's Democratic Republic of Algeria*, Award, ICSID Case No. ARB/03/08, January 10, 2005, para. 25, in which the tribunal concluded:

> Il en découle que le consentement n'est pas donné, de manière extensive, pour toutes les créances et les actions qui pourraient être liées à un investissement. Il est nécessaire que les mesures prises reviennent à une violation de l'Accord bilatéral, ce qui signifie en particulier qu'elles soient de nature injustifiée ou discriminatoire, en droit ou en fait. Ce n'est donc pas nécessairement le cas de toute violation d'un contrat.

122. *Jörn Griebel*, Die Einbeziehung von "contract claims" in internationale Investitionsstreitigkeiten über Streitbeilegungsklauseln in Investitionsabkommen, in: Zeitschrift für Schiedsverfahren 2006, pp. 306-311 (p. 311).
123. *Diehl*, note 112, p. 78.
124. *See Biloune and Marine Drive Complex Ltd. v. Ghana Investments Centre and the Government of Ghana*, Award, UNCITRAL, June 30, 1990.

in the first place may rather be a violation of the fair and equitable treatment-standard.[125]

Most importantly, and regardless of the ramifications of individual expropriation scenarios,[126] tribunals generally look at the overall severity of the host states action to determine whether there has been an expropriation or not.[127] If a tribunal answers such question in the affirmative, finding that there has in fact been an expropriation, such act will only be a violation of the underlying treaty or contract, if no compensation is granted to the investor. The issue of compensation and its requirements for being legitimate is yet another highly controversial one. The majority of states choose to provide for prompt, adequate and effective compensation as formulated by former U.S. Secretary of State *Cordell Hull* in 1938, the *Hull-Formula*, as opposed to the *Calvo-Doctrine*. If the investor is granted such compensation, it is thought to balance the loss suffered under the expropriation, re-establishing equilibrium as envisaged by international investment law.

§2.03 INVESTMENT CONTRACTS AS SOURCES OF INTERNATIONAL INVESTMENT LAW

The dynamics of international treaties that authors have referred to as a process of "treatification"[128] sometimes blur the existence of investment contracts. In addition to merely relying on an international treaty between the host state and the home state, an investor will frequently enter into a contract directly with the state itself. This will put the investor in a position in which he will be able to negotiate in accordance with his interests. Complex projects oftentimes call for an opportunity to individualize the legal environment in which the investment activity is conducted. Therefore, it does not surprise that investment contracts mostly do not share similarities in the way that investment treaties do. Their content and set up may vary considerably[129] due to a high level of inherent flexibility; a feature that mere investment treaties do not provide. In this regard, they are preformulated and rigid.

The practice of state entities engaging in contractual activities with private individuals is not a scarce phenomenon. In fact, many legal systems recognize and practice this form of public-private contractual interaction, especially in the area of

---

125. *MTD Equity Sdn. Bhd. and MTD Chile S.A. v. Republic of Chile*, ICSID Case No. ARB/01/7, May 25, 2004, para. 214.
126. *Burkhard Schöbener/Jochen Herbst/Markus Perkams*, Internationales Wirtschaftsrecht, 2010, p. 290.
127. *Schöbener/Herbst/Perkams,* note 126, p. 290, who find three variations in arbitral tribunals' decisions, the first one acting on the assumption that the term "expropriation" must be interpreted broadly, the second one excluding actions that are generally applicable and not investor specific and the third one highlighting the importance of balancing conflicting interests.
128. *Jeswald W. Salacuse,* The Treatification of International Investment Law, in: Law and Business Review of the Americas 2007, Vol. 13, pp. 155-166.
129. *Griebel*, note 98, p. 27, who argues that the variety of investment contracts is as broad as the variety of possible investments: "Investititonsverträge können so vielfältig sein wie der Gegenstand von Investitionen."

energy and commodities.[130] *Alfred Verdross* characterized these contracts as a third category of public international law agreements, *"quasi-völkerrechtliche Verträge."*[131] This form of investment protection is especially crucial to attract foreign investors, if states have not yet entered into any investment treaties, Brazil being the most prominent example. On the other hand, if states are parties to investment treaties, entering into investment contracts creates an individualized foundation for investment activities and provides the investor with an even more secure framework for his economic activity in the host state. Despite its flexible character, an investment contract oftentimes contains two provisions: first, stabilization clauses are intended to shield the investor from changes of the domestic laws of the host state that may have adverse effects on his investment. Second, internationalization clauses deem international law applicable to the contract as opposed to any other domestic law. Determining the law applicable to an investment contract has proved to be a primary matter of controversy. Tribunals' decisions have frequently differed on the issue, opposing the applicability of international law[132] or partially accepting it based on the contract's provisions.[133] Whether this and other debates on investment contracts will continue to be fruitful in the future despite the rapid development of the international treaty network, is not an easy prediction to make. However, for the purpose of this analysis, it is sufficient to bear in mind the general features of investment contracts. These similarly, though not identically, afford to the investor protection of his investment.

§2.04 ARBITRATION IN INTERNATIONAL INVESTMENT LAW

International treaties and investment contracts intend to provide a secure environment for investments by way of setting standards of protection as legal anchors. Not always, however, do host states comply with these standards. Myriad scenarios in practice exist in which investors have been deprived of valuable assets. Although examples of adverse treatment occurring in practice have necessitated the emergence of international investment law, the protection it now affords to investors has not globally resulted in state compliance. Where states interfere with investors' rights, their actions have nowadays perhaps become more subtle than before. Direct expropriations are measures hardly taken anymore, whereas e.g. revocations of licenses or unusual taxations are more common. In this regard, international investment law has two effects: on the one hand, it urges host states to refrain from inadequate takings of assets in all possible forms and thus does gradually foster legal stability. On the other hand,

---

130. *Reinisch*, note 104, p. 353; *see also Muthucumaraswamy Sornarajah*, The International Law on Foreign Investment, 3rd ed. 2010, p. 301, who refers to the frequent usage of investment contracts in the area to some authors terming the phenomenon *lex petrolia*.
131. *Alfred Verdross*, Die Sicherung von ausländischen Privatrechten aus Abkommen zur wirtschaftlichen Entwicklung mit Schiedsklauseln, in: Zeitschrift für ausländisches öffentliches Recht und Völkerrecht 1957/1958, Vol. 18, pp. 635-651 (p. 638).
132. *See ICJ*, Anglo-Iranian Oil Co. Case (*United Kingdom v. Iran*) (Preliminary Objection), Decision, July 22, 1952, ICJ Reports 1951, pp. 93-115 (pp. 111 et seq.).
133. *Rudolf Dolzer*, Libya-Oil Companies Arbitrations, in: Encyclopedia of Public International Law 1997, Vol. 3, pp. 215-218.

it provides investors with increasing options for arguing violations of their rights as it becomes more refined, complex and meaningful. In other words, although the legal environment is becoming more stable, it does not cause disputes to vanish. The refinement of international investment law is instead rather likely to produce a significantly higher number of disputes arising out of it. In an environment of emerging grounds for scrutinizing state conduct, investors are more likely to become claimants. Reliance on judicial mechanisms is an essential indicator for a functioning domestic legal system. Likewise, a rising number of disputes[134] may be a similar indicator for a functioning and successful international investment law system. What is apparent, however, is the importance of effective means to solve investment disputes. For this purpose, international investment law relies on a well-known form of dispute resolution. It is arbitration that allows investors to drop the legal and protective anchors provided by the international law of investments. It is arbitration that makes investors become claimants.

[A] General Remarks on Arbitration

The use of arbitration as a mechanism to resolve disputes dates back as late as Ancient Greece. Poseidon and Hera each raised claims concerning the territory of Argolis, a dispute that was resolved by Inachus, Cephisus and Asterion as arbitrators.[135] International arbitration frequently took place between states, such as the Greek city-states.[136] Commercial arbitration was not any less common: archaeological evidence provides that a private dispute in the Middle East between two neighbors, Tulpunnaya and Killi, concerning the use of water, was resolved by arbitration.[137] We even find commercial arbitration being used by *Homer* in his *Iliad*, depicting a commercial arbitral process in the eighth century B.C.[138] Arbitration thus also took place between commercial parties who would freely choose for their contractual disputes to be

---

134. *See* UNCTAD Report: Recent Developments in Investor-State Dispute Settlement (ISDS) No. 1, May 2013, according to which fifty-eight new investment arbitration cases were filed in 2012, which constitutes the highest number of investment arbitrations filed in one year.
135. *Jackson H. Ralston*, International Arbitration from Athens to Locarno, 1929, p. 153.
136. *Gary B. Born*, International Commercial Arbitration, 2nd ed. 2014, Vol. 1, § 1.01.
137. *Born*, note 136, § 1.01, in referring to *Sophie Lafont*, L'arbitrage en Mésopotamie, Revue de l'arbitrage 2000, Vol. 4, pp. 557-590 (pp. 579 et seq.).
138. *Homer*, Iliad, Book XVIII, translated by Samuel Butler, pp. 497 et seq.:

> Meanwhile the people were gathered in assembly, for there was a quarrel, and two men were wrangling about the blood-money for a man who had been killed, the one saying before the people that he had paid damages in full, and the other that he had not been paid. Each was trying to make his own case good, and the people took sides, each man backing the side that he had taken; but the heralds kept them back, and the elders sate on their seats of stone in a solemn circle, holding the staves which the heralds had put into their hands. Then they rose and each in his turn gave judgement, and there were two talents laid down, to be given to him whose judgement should be deemed the fairest.

brought before an arbitral tribunal.[139] The level of sophistication found in arbitral processes has certainly improved over time. Nevertheless, the fundamentals remain the same. Arbitration requires an explicit waiver of each party's right to address a state court that is contained in the arbitration agreement. The respective dispute then must not be referred to a state court, but only to the arbitral tribunal. This typically consists of one or three arbitrators who will hear the case and reach a decision that will be embodied in an arbitral award that is widely enforceable before national courts in most of the world's states. This concept of alternative dispute resolution is best summarized as follows: "Arbitration, in short, is an effective way of obtaining a final and binding decision on a dispute or series of disputes, without reference to a court of law."[140]

This particular form of alternative dispute resolution continues to attract parties to commercial contracts for obvious reasons: first, parties enjoy great liberty in drafting their individual arbitration agreement which is the vital and determining factor throughout the arbitral process. Therefore, they are free to tailor a future arbitration according to their preferences. The seat of the arbitration, the applicable law, the arbitrators or the language of the proceedings are only a few examples for the possible customization of an arbitration. Where national courts are bound by rigid domestic procedural rules, arbitrations deliver an unrivaled flexibility that is especially attractive to parties to a commercial contract. Second, arbitrations are most commonly held in private and thus constitute a discrete form of dispute resolution. This feature proves to be important where highly confidential information must be protected from being exposed to the public in the best interest of the parties involved. Rather than conducting hearings before a national court that may be accessed by a broad audience, they are typically held in the premises of arbitration institutions such as the London Court of International Arbitration (LCIA), the International Chamber of Commerce (ICC), the Singapore International Arbitration Centre (SIAC), the German Institution for Arbitration (DIS) or the Stockholm Chamber of Commerce (SCC). Third, arbitration still enjoys a reputation of being more cost effective than traditional litigation before state courts. It is, however, being argued that this perception of arbitration is false, and that indeed costs for arbitral proceedings do not always differ greatly from those caused by litigation.[141] Nevertheless, parties still turn to arbitration, seeking a cheaper means of dispute resolution. Fourth, a mechanism for dispute resolution is only as good as its economic outcome. Arbitration enjoys immense popularity especially due to the international enforceability of arbitral awards. The New York Convention (NYC) ensures that international arbitration awards may travel freely across borders and be enforced before all its signatory states' national courts. Currently, 149 states have

---

139. *See Rainer Lukits*, Die private Schiedsgerichtsbarkeit im römischen Recht und heute, in: Zeitschrift für Schiedsverfahren 2013, pp. 269-274 (p. 269), who depicts the complete development of private arbitration in Roman law.
140. *Nigel Blackaby/Constantine Partasides/Alan Redfern/Martin Hunter*, Redfern and Hunter on International Arbitration - Student Version, 2009, p. 2.
141. *See Thomas J. Stipanowich*, Arbitration: The "New Litigation," in: University of Illinois Law Review 2010, No. 1, pp. 1-60 (p. 9).

signed the NYC,[142] including just recently São Tomé and Principe as well as Myanmar. This enforceability feature is likely to be the most relevant factor for international parties in opting for arbitration. They are thereby able to seek enforcement in an unparalleled number of jurisdictions, which may be home to significant assets of their opposing party. Lastly, in an international context, arbitration allows parties to free a dispute from any form of domestic court partiality. It is conceivable that in certain jurisdictions, courts may not act with as much neutrality as they should.[143] Also, parties may feel that litigation before national courts of the respective opposing party may carry an intrinsic bias. Therefore, international arbitration provides an attractive forum of neutrality that is particularly valuable.

Arbitration therefore offers a number of attractive features that keep commercial parties opting for it. This international commercial arbitration has been experiencing an upward trend that is likely to continue as international trade grows.[144] A number of states have recognized this development and continue to create an arbitration-friendly environment. This is typically achieved by reducing the governmental entanglement in the arbitral process, granting flexibility and thus fostering territories as seats of arbitrations.[145] Additionally, this development has become an economic factor of its own: for example, Singapore, Qatar, Malaysia, Turkey or the United Arab Emirates have lately erected dispute resolution institutions for the purpose of profiting from arbitrations themselves[146] as well as demonstrating a willingness to provide a stable framework for business activities.

[B] International Investment Arbitration

[1] Theoretical Basis

The use of arbitration in disputes between states and investors had by no means been uncommon at the time Germany and Pakistan concluded the first BIT. Investment contracts between states and investors had already incorporated arbitration clauses.[147]

---

142. Information taken from http://www.newyorkconvention.org/contracting-states (last accessed September 9, 2014).
143. *See* e.g. World Justice Project (WJP), Rule of Law Index Report 2014, available at http://worldjusticeproject.org/sites/default/files/files/wjp_rule_of_law_index_2014_report.pdf, according to which even within the European Union judicial independence varies considerably.
144. *Born*, note 136, § 1.03.
145. *See Gus van Harten/Martin Loughlin*, Investment Treaty Arbitration as a Species of Global Administrative Law, in: European Journal of International Law 2006, Vol. 17 No. 1, pp. 121-150 (p. 141), who find that "[...] for the purpose of facilitating commerce, most states have decided to limit their involvement with respect to private agreements to arbitrate."; *see also Ronald Wong*, Interim Relief in Aid of International Commercial Arbitration, in: Singapore Academy of Law Journal 2012, pp. 499-532 (p. 532), who refers to Singapore and explains that "[...] the more important key to making Singapore a centre of gravity for international arbitration is the credibility of the legal system and the predictability that its laws provide."
146. *Lord Michael Mustill*, The History of International Commercial Arbitration, in: Lawrence W. Newman/Richard D. Hill (eds.), The Leading Arbitrator's Guide to International Arbitration, 3rd ed. 2014, pp. 3-32 (p. 18).
147. *See Verdross*, note 131, p. 649.

Interestingly, the Pakistan-Germany BIT provided for jurisdiction of the ICJ or, only alternatively, of an arbitral tribunal by request of either party to the treaty, not the investor. It is conceivable that this first BIT was still heavily tinted by the legacy of diplomatic protection that effectively turned a dispute between a host state and an investor into a dispute between a host state and the home state of the investor. Naturally, these state-to-state disputes often have a significant political impetus. Investment treaties that followed started taking a different approach. The establishment of the International Centre for the Settlement of Investment Disputes (ICSID) greatly impacted the development. The Report of the Executive Directors on the ICSID-Convention of 1965 contained a noteworthy explanation:

> Thus, a host State might *in its investment promotion legislation offer to submit* disputes arising out of certain classes of investments to the jurisdiction of the Centre, and *the investor might give his consent by accepting the offer* in writing.[148]

Subsequently, a growing number of BITs incorporated offers of states to arbitrate directly with investors. It appears that the BIT entered into between Indonesia and the Netherlands in 1968 was the first to include a primary referral of investor-state disputes to investor-state arbitration.[149] The importance of diplomatic protection in investment disputes thus declined, as investors became able to directly bring claims against host states. As a result, confrontations between sovereign states were avoided and investment disputes de-politicized.[150] Arbitration turned into the common means to resolve disputes arising in international investment law.

In this context, it is only logical to seek connecting points between commercial and investment arbitration. One might even be tempted to deem them interchangeable terms, actually referring to the same instrument of dispute resolution. In this sense, one could state that arbitration will be arbitration. And indeed, international commercial and investment arbitration do have connecting points and do share certain characteristics.[151] However, despite their similarities, both forms of arbitration each have different theoretical bases. Apart from reasons of mere linguistic clarity, the distinction between international commercial and investment arbitration rests upon the decisive material difference of the two: while commercial arbitration is used between two commercial parties, investment arbitration involves a sovereign state. This peculiarity is the foundation for a number of discussions in international investment law. For example, it is debated if the framework in which an agreement to arbitrate was

---

148. *ICSID*, Report of the Executive Directors on the ICSID Convention, available at http://www.sloarbitration.eu/Portals/0/Arbitrazno-pravo/CRR_English-final.pdf (last accessed September 13, 2014), para. 24.
149. *Newcombe/Paradell*, note 79, p. 44.
150. See *Republic of Ecuador v. United States of America*, Expert Opinion on the Construction of Art. VII of Prof. Christian Tomuschat, UNCITRAL, PCA Case No. 2012-5, April 24, 2012, para. 32: "[...] The BIT aims to depoliticize investment disputes by pushing the home State of the investor back to the sidelines. [...]."
151. *Giuditta Cordero Moss*, Commercial Arbitration and Investment Arbitration: Fertile Soil or False Friends?, in: Christina Binder/Ursula Kriebaum/August Reinisch/Stephan Wittich (eds.), International Investment Law for the 21st Century, Essays in Honour of Christoph Schreuer, 2009, pp. 782-797 (p. 784), who speaks of "striking similarities."

concluded, namely whether it is a treaty or a contract, is relevant in the arbitral process. An international treaty is governed by rules of international law and may be entered into by states. Commercial contracts, however, may be concluded by any party. Distinguishing between the two would thus amount to a differentiation between sovereign and commercial conduct. In the context of umbrella clauses, it has been argued that a distinction between the conduct of a state in its role as a merchant and as a sovereign is necessary:

> However, a basic general distinction can be made between commercial aspects of a dispute and other aspects involving the existence of some form of State interference with the operation of the contract involved.[152]

Also the tribunal in *El Paso v. Argentina* has made this distinction and expressed:

> In this tribunal's view, it is necessary to distinguish the State as a merchant from the State as a sovereign.[153]

However, there is no common definition of which act constitutes a governmental act and which one does not.[154] Also, the abovementioned decisions do not take into account the practical difficulty of clearly distinguishing between commercial (*acta iure gestionis*) and sovereign state conduct (*acta iure imperii*). Instead, there is consensus that commercial and sovereign acts alike can be attributed to a state.[155]

While for the purposes of this analysis one must do without dwelling further upon this example of controversy, it illustrates that the involvement of a sovereign state poses challenges to international investment law and its use of arbitration. It needs to be borne in mind that the distinguishing factor between commercial and investment arbitration is the element of public interest. Where an investment tribunal rules on the conduct of a state, it does so in a public law environment. There is generally not a particular problem, considering that the state in question chose to be subject to the jurisdiction of an arbitral tribunal by way of entering into an international treaty or a contract with the investor itself. However, the willingness to arbitrate in an international treaty is not relatively expressed as in a contract found in commercial arbitration. While in the latter case, the parties to the contract reach an agreement based upon offer and acceptance as soon as the contract is concluded, the offer of a state to arbitrate is only accepted upon filing of a request for arbitration by any investor. It has therefore been described as a "unilateral offer to arbitrate."[156] In contrast to an offer to arbitrate in commercial arbitration, in investment arbitration, it

---

152. *Joy Mining Machinery Limited v. Republic of Egypt*, Award on Jurisdiction, ICSID Case No. ARB/03/11, August 6, 2004, para. 72.
153. *El Paso Energy International Company v. The Argentine Republic*, Decision on Jurisdiction, ICSID Case No. ARB/03/15, April 27, 2006, para. 79.
154. *Noble Ventures, Inc. v. Romania*, Award, ICSID Case No. ARB/01/11, October 12, 2005, para. 82, in which the tribunal found that "the ILC-Draft does not maintain or support such distinction." and furthermore that "there is a widespread consensus in international law, as in particular expressed in the discussions in the ILC regarding attribution, that there is no common understanding in international law of what constitutes a governmental or public act."
155. *Schill*, note 5, p. 325.
156. *Douglas*, note 21, p. 75.

is absolute. Any potential investor may hold the state responsible for its promise and submit a case to the scrutiny of a tribunal.

At this point, one might ask why then there is a need for distinguishing the two types of arbitration. If states waive their sovereignty by way of a treaty or contract, this distinguishing factor may no longer be of significance. Such view, however, would blind out the fact that state sovereignty does not only serve to explain a state's ability to act; it furthermore serves to explain a state's intention to act. Like private parties, states choose to enter into treaties or contracts because they follow specific intentions. Despite a state's general economic interest that naturally affects its conduct towards investors, its actions are mainly rooted in public policy and involve contemplations of general public interest and the state's responsibility towards its population.[157] While commercial arbitration revolves around solving a merely commercial dispute, investment arbitration concerns the evaluation of sovereign, governmental acts. These acts may be based upon specific public concerns, affect myriad matters such as human rights or diplomacy. Therefore, an analysis of state actions within the domain of international investment law takes place on a broader level than that of purely commercial conduct. This particularly deserves utmost respect by those involved in investment arbitration. A state may choose to waive its sovereignty, but it is in interpretation of that waiver that respect for state sovereignty is exercised, serving the purpose of reaching adequate outcomes and at the same time providing the reasoning necessary given the public sphere in which investment arbitration operates.[158] Such respect is found in adherence to appropriate and applicable standards of interpretation in public international law. The element of sovereignty then constitutes a core layer and is the reason why commercial and investment arbitration are of a distinct

---

157. See *International Commission on Intervention and State Sovereignty*, note 90; *see also CME Czech Republic B.V. (The Netherlands) v. The Czech Republic*, Separate Opinion on the Issues at the Quantum Phase of: *CME v. Czech Republic* by Ian Brownlie, UNCITRAL, March 14, 2003, para. 74:

> In this context, it is simply unacceptable to insist that the subject matter is exclusively "commercial" in character or that the interests are, more or less, only those of the investor. Such approach involves setting aside a number of essential elements in the Treaty relation. The first element is the significance of the fact that the Respondent is a sovereign state, which is responsible for the well-being of its people. This is not to confer a privilege on the Czech Republic but only to recognise its special character and responsibilities. The Czech Republic is not a commercial entity.

158. See *Pierre Lalive*, On the Reasoning of International Arbitral Awards, in: Journal of International Dispute Settlement 2010, Vol. 1 No. 1, pp. 55-65 (p. 57):

> Whether or not one is prepared to fully subscribe to that view, one must at least admit that the importance and complexity of the questions raised in Investor-State settlement of disputes and the fact that public interest and the development of the country concerned are involved, "are all dynamics that militate in favour of a very carefully and fully reasoned award," much more so than in what may be considered 'normal' in cases of commercial transactions!

nature.[159] This distinction relates to their respective origins and becomes relevant in a plurality of issues. Nevertheless, a clinical isolation of both would disregard the above-mentioned connecting points. In this context then, international investment law combines public international law with arbitration as a typically commercial means to solve disputes. This interplay in investment arbitration is therefore correctly described by *Schill* as constituting a "hybridization."[160] A correct approach in treating both forms of international arbitration thus lies in understanding interrelations while giving effect to their distinct origins. Arbitration in an international investment law context is the standard mechanism to resolve investment disputes. It is distinct from international commercial arbitration, while both do share certain similarities. It is vital for an accurate understanding to bear in mind the impact of public interest, which allows to appropriately deal with the challenges arising in international investment arbitration. A look at the immense amount of money that can be at stake[161] and must ultimately be borne by national budgets is an ideal illustration: a staggering amount was recently awarded in an investment arbitration under the ECT. In *Yukos v. Russia*,[162] the arbitral

---

159. *See David W. Rivkin*, The Impact of International Arbitration on the Rule of Law - The 2012 Clayton Utz/University of Sydney International Arbitration Lecture, in: Arbitration International 2013, Vol. 29 No. 3, pp. 327-360 (p. 340):

> Investor-state arbitration is of course an entirely different animal than traditional commercial arbitration since these disputes involve sovereign states rather than just private parties. There is simply much more at stake here. In this context, we are concerned not only about certainty but also about legitimacy. We care far more about tribunals "getting it right" because the awards involve public goods and public money.

see also Muthucumaraswamy Sornarajah, The Settlement of Foreign Investment Disputes, 2000, p. 159, who is speaking of "a system of arbitration that is distinct from the two obvious categories and stands in between them, sharing the features of both systems and seldom understood because of the lack of the making sharp distinctions between the three different types."; *see also* p. 161 on which the author explains that "it is an unfortunate facet of many works in the area that they treat these distinct types of arbitration in the same breath, accentuating their similarities and ignoring the fact that their theoretical bases are different."; *see also Stephan W. Schill*, Enhancing International Investment Law's Legitimacy: Conceptual and Methodological Foundations of a New Public Law Approach, in: Virginia Journal of International Law 2011, Vol. 52, pp. 57-102 (p. 75): "International investment arbitration also differs fundamentally from commercial arbitration."; *see also Ruth Teitelbaum*, A Look At The Public Interest In Investment Arbitration: Is It Unique? What Should We Do About It?, in: Berkeley Journal of International Law 2010, Vol. 5, pp. 54-62 (p. 56), who nevertheless points out that "it may be a mistake for the arbitration community to isolate investment treaty arbitration from commercial arbitration, since those involved in the former may learn valuable lessons, good and bad, from what goes on in the latter."

160. *Schill*, note 159, p. 71.
161. *See Occidental Exploration and Production Company v. Republic of Ecuador*, Award, LCIA Case No. UN3467, July 11, 2004, in which the investor was awarded USD 1.17 billion; *see also EDF International S.A., SAUR International S.A. and Leon Participaciones Argentinas S.A. v. Argentine Republic*, Award, ICSID Case No. ARB/03/23, June 11, 2012, in which the claimant was entitled to damages amounting to USD 136 million; or *Deutsche Bank AG v. Democratic Socialist Republic of Sri Lanka*, Award, ICSID Case No. ARB/09/2, October 23, 2012, in which the claimant secured an award amounting to USD 60 million.
162. *Yukos Universal Limited (Isle of Man) v. The Russian Federation*, Final Award, PCA Case No. AA 227, July 18, 2014.

tribunal found the defendant to have violated its international obligations under the treaty and awarded a record sum of USD 50,020,867,798 to the claimant.

[2]   Hybrid Process of Arbitration

The general setup of an arbitration in an international investment law context is generally similar to that of commercial arbitrations. Instead of involving a court in the resolution of a dispute, it is brought before an international arbitral tribunal. These arbitrations may take place on an ad hoc basis, but regularly involve ICSID, which is located in Washington, D.C. and forms part of the World Bank Group. It provides an institutional framework for conducting the arbitration and is based upon the ICSID-Convention of 1963. However, traditional commercial arbitral institutions such as the ICC in Paris have adapted their rules of arbitration to cater to investment disputes.[163] For example, in 2012, Article 1 of the ICC-Rules was modified to include investment disputes: the scope of application was changed from "business disputes" to "disputes." Arbitral institutions have noted the increase in investment cases and reacted in a logical manner. Furthermore, many investment arbitrations take place before tribunals that involve arbitrators who are frequently or mainly involved in traditional commercial arbitrations. This involvement is likely to have an impact on the way the arbitrations are conducted. Commercial arbitrators will especially incorporate similar procedural approaches[164] and thus contribute to the hybridization. They are also highly likely to bring a great deal of experience in the interpretation of contracts to the arbitration and thus can be of significant value to an international investment arbitration.

[3]   Particularities of Interpretation

[a]   The Role of Precedent in Investment Arbitration

In the context of international investment law, the proper role of arbitral decisions is heavily discussed. It has been previously outlined that decisions by international courts or tribunals play a secondary role in the interpretation under public international law. International investment arbitration may have developed a different practical approach. The field does, however, not provide for a binding role of previous decisions. It could thus suffice to state that it simply does not exist and that every tribunal starts anew in interpreting treaty provisions. Such oversimplification would be neither particularly cautious, nor representative of arbitral practice. The consideration of prior decisions allows tribunals to benefit from reasoning that has been developed in similar scenarios, possibly making their own more effective and efficient. It fosters a consistent development of international investment law by facilitating discourse and also permits

---

163. *See Karl-Heinz Böckstiegel*, Commercial and Investment Arbitration: How Different are they Today?, in: Arbitration International 2012, Vol. 28 No. 4, pp. 577-590 (p. 581).
164. *Schill*, note 159, p. 72.

to assess consequences of a particular interpretive approach. In practice then, the consideration of previous arbitral decisions has become almost inevitable despite the inexistence of a rule of binding precedent.[165] In contrast to general public international law, previous decisions of arbitral tribunals are of an immense practical relevance and may profoundly impact the direction of a decision. Rulings by investment tribunals only bind the parties to the dispute. Considering previous decisions in international investment arbitration is thus not mandatory, but rather expedient. It might simply be arbitral consensus, while real reliance on them is not.[166] Based upon consensus, the consideration of prior decisions appears to follow a pattern that is similar to the procedure typically followed by national courts: tribunals generally spot those decisions that are relevant to the dispute at hand. They identify the consequences of both, following and deviating from the reasoning provided in such decisions before reaching their own conclusion and explaining the motivation behind it.[167]

A prominent example of the role of previous decisions in arbitral practice is the dispute in *AES v. Argentina*.[168] The claimant, an American company, invested in eight electricity generation companies and three distribution companies in Argentina. The respondent had agreed on particular tariff calculations and adjustment mechanisms, which it then later allegedly refused to apply. The claimant turned to investment arbitration to have the matter settled before an international tribunal. At that time, the respondent had already been involved in other investment arbitrations that pertained to similar factual backgrounds and identical treaty provisions. It had previously and unsuccessfully raised objections to the jurisdiction of the respective arbitral tribunals. It likewise did so in the dispute with *AES*. Here, the claimant argued that the previous

---

165. *Schreuer*, note 44, p. 139; *see also El Paso Energy International Company v. The Argentine Republic*, Decision on Jurisdiction, ICSID Case No. ARB/03/15, April 27, 2007, para. 39.
166. *See Gabrielle Kaufmann-Kohler*, Arbitral Precedent: Dream, Necessity or Excuse?, in: Arbitration International 2007, Vol. 23 No. 3, pp. 357-378 (p. 368) in referring to the tribunal's decision in *El Paso Energy International Company v. The Argentine Republic*, Decision on Jurisdiction, ICSID Case No. ARB/03/15, April 27, 2006, para. 39:

> ICSID arbitral tribunals are established ad hoc, ... and the present Tribunal knows of no provision, ... establishing an obligation of stare decisis. It is nonetheless a reasonable assumption that international arbitral tribunals, notably those established within the ICSID system, will generally take account of the precedents established by other arbitration organs, especially those set by other international tribunals.

see also Franck Charles Arif v. Republic of Moldova, Award, ICSID Case No. ARB/11/23, April 8, 2013, para. 592, in which the tribunal looked at previous decisions to position its own in the context of common arbitral practice: "The Tribunal is therefore aligning itself to the majority of arbitral decisions [...]."; *see also*, however, *Quiborax S.A., Non Metallic Minerals S.A. and Allan Fosk Kaplún v. Plurinational State of Bolivia*, Decision on Jurisdiction, ICSID Case No. ARB/06/2, December 27, 2012, para. 46: "Arbitrator Stern does not analyze the arbitrator's role in the same manner, as she considers it her duty to decide each case on its own merits, independently of any apparent jurisprudential trend."
167. *Tai-Heng Cheng*, Precedent and Control in Investment Treaty Arbitration, in: Fordham International Law Journal 2006, Vol. 30 No. 4, pp. 1014-1049 (p. 1031).
168. *AES Corporation v. The Argentine Republic*, Decision on Jurisdiction, ICSID Case No. ARB/02/17, April 26, 2005.

decisions might be so persuasive that they could be regarded as constituting precedents binding upon the tribunal of the present case.[169] Argentina, however, replied that:

> Repeating decisions taken in other cases, without making the factual and legal distinctions, may constitute an excess of power and may affect the integrity of the international system for the protection of investments.[170]

Thereby, Argentina relied on the nonexistence of binding arbitral precedent and urged the tribunal to consider the case at hand individually rather than as forming part of a series of other cases. The tribunal concurred with Argentina's argument and stressed the sovereignty of each tribunal in the problem-solving process. However, it also highlighted that previous decisions in similar factual scenarios may be valuable sources to consider in approaching possible solutions to legal problems.[171]

The consideration of previous arbitral decisions is able to shape international investment law. It allows for the development of a more harmonious, predictable and authoritative legal environment and is thus generally desirable. In its most perfect form, such harmony postulates that tribunals mutually accept each others' interpretations, complementing and nurturing them. As was mentioned previously, consistency would greatly benefit from such a concept of binding precedent. Naturally, however, this development would prove problematic, where it blindly led tribunals to adopt unreasonable or inadequate, but at least consistent, reasoning. Tolerating a margin of deviation, revision and correction is thus vital to sustaining a legitimate investment law framework.[172] The downside of this margin is a pursuance of consistency not fully consequent. A salient example of inconsistency is the controversy regarding two parallel international investment arbitrations concerning an investment in a Czech television broadcaster. In *Lauder v. Czech Republic*[173] and *CME v. Czech Republic*,[174] two investment tribunals dealt with the same dispute arising out of a contract termination and reached differing decisions. It is the balancing act between reaching consistent decisions and enabling tribunals to abandon consistency for the sake of adequacy that has been inspiring many to suggest reforms. The call for greater consistency rightfully exists. Nevertheless, it should be added that it will only be beneficial, if the decisions produced are consistently adequate. Arbitral decisions that deviate from others for comprehensible reasons may certainly hinder the emergence of a more consistent international investment law and also make the journey to it more uncomfortable. At the same time, however, they must be looked at as forming an

---

169. *AES Corporation v. The Argentine Republic*, note 168, para. 18.
170. *AES Corporation v. The Argentine Republic*, note 168, para. 22.
171. *AES Corporation v. The Argentine Republic*, note 168, para. 30.
172. *See Irene M. Ten Cate*, The Costs of Consistency: Precedent in Investment Treaty Arbitration, in: Columbia Journal of Transnational Law 2013, Vol. 51, pp. 418-478.
173. *Ronald S. Lauder v. The Czech Republic*, Final Award, UNCITRAL, September 3, 2001.
174. *CME Czech Repubic B.V. (The Netherlands) v. The Czech Republic*, Partial Award, UNCITRAL, September 13, 2001.

important part of a thoughtful and staid process.[175] Simply put, adequacy requires quality.

[b]   Model Investment Treaties

Numerous international investment treaties have come into existence during the last decades. Governments have seen the workload resulting from drafting treaties and thus decided to produce treaties that serve as models or starting points for future negotiations. These model treaties will be more or less detailed,[176] but generally contain those provisions that a respective state deems significant. Where final investment treaties derive from these model treaties, it might be appropriate to consider their value in the interpretive process. One might argue that a deviating provision must receive special attention, as it suggests particular importance to the parties.[177] It seems, however, more suitable to treat references to model treaties much like those to *travaux préparatoires*, namely as a secondary source of interpretation. Therefore, they serve the purpose of confirming an interpretive result. Attributing eminent meaning to them would, as the tribunal in *Siemens v. Argentina* has pointed out, distort the relationship between a template and an actual treaty.[178] It is the treaty that is the final expression of the parties' wills and thus the essential foundation for interpretation which deserves predominant attention.

[c]   Expressio Unius Est Exclusio Alterius

The Latin maxim *expressio unius est exclusio alterius* acts from the assumption that the express mentioning of one subject is the exclusion of another. It is a logical technique[179] used in interpretation, typically for statutes and constitutions.[180] In investment arbitrations, the maxim has frequently been used in interpreting the so-called

---

175. *See Thomas Schultz*, Against Consistency in Investment Arbitration, in: Zachary Douglas/Joost Pauwelyn/Jorge E. Viñuales (eds.), The Foundations of International Investment Law: Bringing Theory into Practice, 2014, pp. 297-316 (p. 298) who argues that: "The pursuit of consistency among decisions only has a very relative value, dependent on what is being made consistent."
176. *See* the 2012 U.S. Model Bilateral Investment Treaty (http://www.state.gov/documents/organization/188371.pdf) and the 2008 German Model Treaty (http://www.italaw.com/sites/default/files/archive/ita1025.pdf).
177. *Siemens AG v. The Argentine Republic*, Decision on Jurisdiction, ICSID Case No. ARB/02/8, August 3, 2004, para. 106, in which the state's argument was, however, rejected by the tribunal:

> The acceptance of a clause from a model text does not invest this clause with either more or less legal force than other clauses which may had been more difficult to negotiate. The end result of the negotiations is an agreed text and the legal significance of each clause is not affected by how arduous was the negotiating path to arrive there.

178. *Siemens AG v. The Argentine Republic*, note 177, para. 106.
179. *Schreuer*, note 44, p. 134.
180. *Clifton Williams*, Expressio Unius Est Exclusio Alterius, in: Marquette Law Review 1931, Vol. 15 No. 4, pp. 191-196 (p. 191).

most favored nation-clause. In the recent dispute *Philip Morris/Abal Hermanos v. Uruguay*, the tribunal ruled on the application of the most favored nation-clause to the dispute settlement provision in the Switzerland-Uruguay BIT[181] of April 22, 1991. As the list of exceptions to the treatment standard did not allude to dispute settlement, the tribunal concluded that it could extend it to such in application of *expressio unius est exclusio alterius*.[182] The principle serves as a logical argument that is regularly deployed. However, this does not happen uniformly. Tribunals have also clearly rejected the maxim and instead pointed out its ineptness.[183] What is problematic, as these tribunals have stressed, is that the inclusion of a term or subject is not necessarily an expression of the parties that others should be excluded. It will very much depend on the circumstances of each individual treaty, whether this maxim shall apply and would produce a reasonable result or not. The value of it has as a consequence been questioned.[184] It suffices, however, to acknowledge its existence and to be aware that the relationship with the interpretive canon framed by the VCLT remains unsettled.[185]

§2.05 INTERNATIONAL INVESTMENT LAW IN A CRISIS OF LEGITIMACY

The development of international commercial arbitration is a success story. Most international contracts nowadays contain an arbitration agreement for the reasons outlined above. One might thus be led to believe that the implementation of arbitration into international investment law would be equally successful. While this assumption is not entirely false, it is neither entirely true. Arbitration in the international investment law context rather presents itself as a double-edged sword. Mainly because international investment arbitrations involve a sovereign state, many discussions in the area are based on exactly this particularity, and the current state of international investment law has been famously described as a "legitimacy crisis."[186] While there may very well be an increasing number of concluded BITs, this depiction of international investment law's current state is fueled by a number of factors. These may be as diverse as the underlying disputes themselves. However, they all contribute their part

---

181. Switzerland-Uruguay BIT, available at http://www.seco.admin.ch/themen/00513/ 00594/04 638/index.html?lang = en&download = NHzLpZig7t,lnp6I0NTU042l2Z6ln1ad1IZn4Z2qZpnO2 Yuq2Z6gpJCEfYR5gmym162dpYbUzd,Gpd6emK2Oz9aGodetmqaN19XI2IdvoaCVZ,s- (last accessed October 7, 2014).
182. *Philip Morris Brands SARL, Philip Morris Products S.A. and Abal Hermanos S.A. v. Oriental Republic of Uruguay*, Decision on Jurisdiction, ICSID Case No. ARB/10/7, July 2, 2013, para. 87; *see also National Grid PLC v. The Argentine Republic*, Decision on Jurisdiction, UNCITRAL, June 20, 2006, para. 82; *see also Waste Management, Inc. v. United Mexican States*, Award, ICSID Case No. ARB/00/3, April 30, 2004, para. 85.
183. *See Enron Corporation and Ponderosa Assets, L.P. v. The Argentine Republic*, Decision on Jurisdiction, ICSID Case No. ARB/01/3, January 14, 2004, para. 46; *see also Siemens AG v. The Argentine Republic*, note 177, para. 140; *see also Pac Rim Cayman LLC v. The Republic of El Salvador*, Decision on the Respondent's Jurisdictional Objections, ICSID Case No. ARB/09/12, June 1, 2012, para. 5.20.
184. *Schreuer*, note 44, p. 134.
185. *Saldarriaga*, note 18, p. 13.
186. *See* note 6.

to the overall perception of the system.[187] Especially in Latin America, there appears to arise a trend of turning backs on the jurisdiction of ICSID and searching for alternative ways of settling investment disputes. Venezuela, Ecuador and Bolivia have chosen to opt out of the ICSID-Convention. Simultaneously, Argentina continues to express its discontent with the system, especially, as it currently faces the largest number of arbitrations brought against any state, and a number of claimants have already been successful in securing awards of significant value. For example, on July 14, 2006 an award was rendered in favor of the claimant in *Azurix v. Argentina*[188] in the amount of USD 165 million. The tribunal concluded that Argentina had failed to accord fair and equitable treatment and full protection and security to Azurix' investment based on the BIT between the United States and Argentina. Azurix entered into a contract with Argentina to provide water and sewage services to the province of Buenos Aires. The city agreed to conduct repairs on the old existing system prior to Azurix' commencement of activity. As such, repairs were never carried out, and Azurix was consequentially unable to provide appropriate water supply. Following complaints by the Province's population, politicians suggested not to pay bills issued by Azurix.

It does not seem unlikely that Argentina will follow the road paved by Venezuela, Ecuador and Bolivia and thus contribute tremendously to criticism expressed towards the international investment arbitration system.[189] This phenomenon is, however, not simply a particularity of Latin America. The Australian Gillard-Government had explained that it would no longer incorporate arbitration clauses into trade agreements;[190] a position that was not adopted by the succeeding Abbott-Government though.[191] Interestingly, the former decision was not based upon Australia being subject to arbitral decisions that it deemed illegitimate. It was more the result of a domestic policy shift.[192] Similarly, state legislators in the United States have composed

---

187. *Schill*, note 5, p. 6.
188. *Azurix Corporation v. The Republic of Argentina*, Award, ICSID Case No. ARB/01/12, July 14, 2006.
189. *William W. Burke-White*, Part IV Chapter 17: The Argentine Financial Crisis: State Liability under BITs and the Legitimacy of the ICSID System, in: *Waibel/Kaushal et al. (eds.)*, note 6, pp. 407-432 (p. 430), who proclaims that "[i]f Argentina were to follow Bolivia's lead and exit the ICSID system, investor-state arbitration would truly face a crisis of confidence."
190. Australian Government, Department of Foreign Affairs and Trade, Gillard Government Trade Policy Statement: Trading our way to more jobs and prosperity, 2011, available at http://blogs.usyd.edu.au/japaneselaw/2011_Gillard%20Govt%20Trade%20Policy%20Statement.pdf(last accessed November 7, 2014) p. 14:

> In the past, Australian Governments have sought the inclusion of investor-state dispute resolution procedures in trade agreements with developing countries at the behest of Australian businesses. The Gillard Government will discontinue this practice. If Australian businesses are concerned about sovereign risk in Australian trading partner countries, they will need to make their own assessments about whether they want to commit to investing in those countries.

191. See http://www.theglobalmail.org/feature/abbott-open-for-business-and-multinational-law suits/700/ (last accessed September 9, 2014).
192. *Jürgen Kurtz*, Australia's Rejection of Investor-State Arbitration: Causation, Omission and Implication, in: ICSID Review 2012, Foreign Investment Law Journal, Vol. 27 No. 1, pp. 1-12 (p. 2).

an open letter[193] in which they explicitly oppose the use of investor-state arbitration in the Trans-Pacific Partnership (TPP), an extended version of the Trans-Pacific Strategic Economic Partnership Agreement (TPSEP) between Australia, Brunei, Chile, Canada, Japan, Malaysia Mexico, New Zealand, Peru, Singapore, the United States and Viet Nam, which is currently being negotiated. This reaction is possibly the aftermath of arbitrations involving the United States that caught special attention by the public. A prominent example of such is the dispute in *Methanex Corporation v. United States*[194] which was based on Chapter 11 of NAFTA. The claimant turned against a ban of the sale and use of a gasoline additive named "MTBE" that was supposed to take effect on December 31, 2002 in the State of California. The ban resulted from California's concern about the quality of its drinking water, as a result of leaking underground fuel storage tanks. Methanol as feedstock for this kind of additive was heavily produced by the claimant, which then was its largest producer. *Methanex* initiated an arbitration on December 3, 1999, claiming compensation in the amount of about USD 970 million and arguing that it was subject to an expropriation, discrimination and denial of a minimum standard of treatment. The tribunal dismissed the case, ruling that it did not have jurisdiction to hear it. The case nevertheless triggered public attention as the State of California's decision to ban MTBE constituted an essential expression of its sovereignty in an attempt to protect its population from health risks, and the arbitration was thus heavily criticized by environmentalists and the U.S. Environmental Protection Agency (EPA).[195]

The factors that trigger discontent with the international law of investments are myriad. However, it appears that some are more pressing and prominent than others, as is outlined by *Stephan Schill*. His analysis finds that the "vagueness of investment treaties" and the "increasing number of conflicting and inconsistent interpretations by arbitral tribunals" contribute heavily to the possible crisis.[196] Furthermore, he explains that the "fragmentation of international investment law" and the "perception of a built-in bias favoring foreign investors" as well as "procedural maxims of arbitration" are among the most common potential problems.[197] What becomes obvious in this regard is the pivotal role of the legal texts that form the foundation of international investment law, namely treaties and contracts, and arbitrations that serve to shed light on them in the contexts of individual disputes. Intertwined with this importance is a twofold responsibility by states to diligently negotiate and draft agreements and by arbitrators to interpret them in full awareness of the practical consequences and adherence to methodology.[198] In 1995, *Jan Paulsson*, in his famous article *Arbitration*

---

193. *See* http://www.citizen.org/documents/State-Legislators-Letter-on-Investor-State-and-TPP.pdf. (last accessed on November 15, 2013).
194. *Methanex Corporation v. United States of America*, Final Award of the Tribunal on Jurisdiction and Merits, UNCITRAL, August 3, 2005.
195. *William W. Park*, Arbitration of International Business Disputes, 2nd ed. 2012, p. 712.
196. *Schill*, note 5, p. 7.
197. *Schill*, note 5, p. 7.
198. *See ConocoPhillips Petrozuata B.V., ConocoPhillips Hamaca B.V. and ConocoPhillips Gulf of Paria B.V. v. Bolivarian Republic of Venezuela*, Dissenting Opinion of Georges Abi-Saab, ICSID Case No. ARB/07/30, March 10, 2014, para. 56:

Without Privity, provided an early glimpse of possible results of excessive conduct in investment arbitration:

> Arbitration without privity is a delicate mechanism. A single incident of an adventurist arbitrator going beyond the proper scope of his jurisdiction in a sensitive case may be sufficient to generate a backlash. But if the mechanism is applied judiciously, it will help fill a void that now exists in the absence of compulsory jurisdiction, and thus contribute to enhancing the legal security of international economic life.[199]

§2.06 CONCLUSION

This chapter has illustrated how international investment law aims to attract foreign capital for the benefit of the investor and the host state alike. What constitutes this legal area is an ever-growing dense net of international treaties and investment contracts that provide standards of protection, which investors may rely on. Its increasing density is bound to make international investment law more complex and challenging, yet at the same time more effective, if it is properly developed. It has become obvious that core concepts of public international law are of great importance to the development. Although the protection of investments may become more stable, it is likely that it will result in a rising number of international disputes. It is thus immensely important that international investment law provides appropriate means to address the caseload. International investment arbitration thus serves as an indispensable feature of today's investment protection regime. As the foundation of the mechanism is found in treaties and contracts, their proper drafting and interpretation is fundamental in allowing investment arbitration to produce adequate outcomes. In order to foster adequacy, it is essential to bear in mind that the involvement of a sovereign state is the feature that sets investment arbitration apart from commercial arbitration. In view of the explicit sovereignty waiver of states, it is imperative to rightfully assess the scope of it. The limits of the waiver constitute the threshold for potential sovereignty claims. The responsibility of states and arbitrators may then be the determining factor of the direction that international investment law is going to head in. In the course of the upcoming analysis, this hypothesis will be tested against a particular interpretive question that

---

> Thus, inherent jurisdiction accrues to any body or organ by the mere fact of it being possessed of the adjudicative function. It brings with it powers as well as duties and responsibilities. [...] These are "to maintain its judicial character," "safeguard its basic judicial function" and be "the guardian of [its] judicial integrity"; in short to ensure and safeguard the efficiency, credibility and integrity of the adjudicative function and the adjudicative character of the organ, whose first and foremost task is to seek the truth and to dispense justice according to law on that basis.

199. *Jan Paulsson*, Arbitration Without Privity, in: ICSID Review 1995, Foreign Investment Law Journal, Vol. 10 No. 2, pp. 232-257 (p. 257).

has arisen in arbitral practice. It will allow making prudent suggestions for strengthening the legitimacy of international investment arbitration, a field that is characterized by strong dynamics.

CHAPTER 3
The Protection of Arbitral Awards in the Global Context of Investment Treaty Interpretation

§3.01 INTRODUCTION

Interpretation is a powerful process. It leads to the adaptability of the terms of international investment treaties and may produce new innovative results. Interpretations may blend in with existing arbitral rulings, modify them or even constitute novelties and, in this regard, be surprising.[200] They are the result of an analytical process with profound practical significance.[201] A number of recent arbitral decisions have dealt with an issue that could fundamentally impact the relationship between commercial and investment arbitration. As it was previously described, investment arbitration is a hybrid of public international law and commercial arbitration. It remains a dispute settlement mechanism deeply rooted in public international law, yet borrowing procedural approaches and oftentimes resting on the experience of commercial arbitrators. The interaction between the two could, however, be undergoing a momentous change. For the purpose of illustration, one may think of a successful international commercial arbitration. The claimant of the dispute receives a final and

---

200. Robert Wisner/Nick Gallus, Nationality Requirements in Investor-State Arbitration, in: The Journal of World Investment and Trade 2004, Vol. 5, pp. 927-945 (p. 927), who refer to surprising and contradicting conclusions reached by arbitral tribunals with regards to the nationality requirement.
201. See Emilio Agustín Maffezini v. The Kingdom of Spain, Decision of the Tribunal on Objections to Jurisdiction, ICSID Case No. ARB/97/7, January 25, 2000, para. 56, in which the tribunal ruled that the MFN-clause extends to dispute settlement mechanisms, allowing for an international arbitration after a six-month cooling-off period as contained in the Chile-Spain BIT, rather than prior eighteen months long proceedings in domestic courts as envisaged by the Argentina-Spain BIT: "In addition to these rules, other means of interpretation have been outlined. Unsettled remains their exact relationship with the provisions of the VCLT. Nevertheless, they are frequently employed by arbitral tribunals."

binding award that is expected to travel freely across state borders into various jurisdictions, being widely enforceable. In an effort to seek such enforcement before a domestic court, in whichever jurisdiction the dispute's respondent may have valuable assets, he is then experiencing difficulties. Perhaps, the proceedings turn out to be lengthy, troublesome or unsuccessful after all. In this scenario, the economic value of the award is at stake and highly likely to be frustrated. The potential loss may have a profound impact and the originally successful claimant may be stunned by the unease of enforcement. What if there could be a second bite at the cherry though? What if an unsuccessful enforcement of an award rendered in the course of a commercial arbitration could trigger an international investment arbitration? What if the unsuccessful claimant could recover the loss suffered by directly addressing the state responsible for judicial measures?

This gate of novelty has been opened by a number of arbitral decisions in the recent years that have been described as "crossover cases."[202] The idea of initiating investment arbitration proceedings against a state that has interfered with the enforcement of an award resulting from a commercial arbitration is highly appealing to commercial stakeholders. Apart from this economic observation, what deserves particular attention is the question of how arbitral tribunals have arrived at the conclusion that such recourse to investment arbitration may be a feasible and, more importantly, permissible option under international investment law. Especially with regards to public international law, permissibility is a particularly interesting issue. The interference of a domestic court with the enforcement of a commercial arbitration award constitutes a sovereign act. During the course of an international investment arbitration, it is then up to the arbitral tribunal to rule on the legality of such act. In other words, arbitrators will judge the measures taken by a sovereign state. This procedure is not new in the sphere of public international law. One may think of the rulings by the ECJ, deciding whether a Member State of the European Union has acted in violation of treaty provisions or similarly, the rulings by the ICJ. In modern public international law, the scrutiny of sovereign state actions is thus generally not problematic. The consent to the respective jurisdiction is in itself a sovereign act and the essential cornerstone of the legitimacy of international rulings. It is what grants authority to produce a lawful decision. It must be borne in mind, however, that consent encompasses the understanding that particular methods of interpretation will be applied in reaching that decision. Article 38 of the ICJ-Statute, for example, enumerates those sources of international law that the court will apply in disputes that are submitted to it. In other words, consent to jurisdiction is also consent to a particular methodology.[203]

---

202. W. Michael Reisman, Investment and Human Rights Tribunals as Court of Last Appeal in International Commercial Arbitration, in: Laurent Lévy/Yves Derains (eds.), Liber Amicorum en l'honneur de Serge Lazareff, 2011, pp. 521-530 (p. 521).
203. See *Garanti Koza LLP v. Turkmenistan*, Dissenting Opinion of Laurence Boisson de Chazournes, ICSID Case No. ARB/11/20, July 3, 2013, para. 8, in which she states that "[w]ell-established principles governing the interpretation of titles of jurisdiction as formulated by the ICJ should guide the interpretation of dispute settlement provisions under the ICSID Convention and BITs."; *see also Hussein Nuaman Soufraki v. United Arab Emirates*, Decision of the Ad Hoc Committee on the Application for Annulment of Mr. Soufraki, ICSID

In the case of arbitral tribunals analyzing the actions of a sovereign state's court, there is no room for criticism, if proper interpretive measures have been taken in the process of it. The consent of the respective state legitimizes the scrutiny by arbitrators.

Where tribunals, however, judge on the legality of domestic court actions on the basis of inadequate methodological approaches, the legitimizing effect of consent dissolves and the risk of crossing the line between interpretation and impermissible law-making ascends. The emergence of new facets of international investment law, such as the here-presented recourse in case of frustrated enforcement efforts is the logical outcome within a dynamic field of law. Once again, it must be remembered that respect for the dividing line between interpretation and law-making is key in ensuring an adequate development. Even if a particular treaty is of a normative nature, law-making may only take place upon a proper application of the respective methodological canons. New legal developments must go hand in hand with an assessment of their interpretive roots. Innovative interpretations are ideally the result of thorough and critical analyses by arbitrators. As such, their willingness to take bold steps in this development of international investment law is to be welcomed. For the sake of strengthening legitimacy, it is at the same time necessary to study these new interpretations, to test them and to take a look at their impacts outside of a single dispute and inside the system of international investment protection as a whole.

The interpretation that possibly provides for a momentous change, a second bite at the cherry, is essentially the treatment of awards resulting from commercial arbitrations as or like investments. Commercial arbitration awards could be understood as constituting an investment in themselves or they could be treated like such. No matter which approach is taken, the practical consequences remain the same. Once a tribunal finds that it is dealing with an investment or any other activity that is to be treated like such, it will apply the entirety of international investment law. Only then may it assume jurisdiction and only then may it apply the substantive principles of investment protection. The doctrine of *Kompetenz-Kompetenz* entitles the arbitral tribunal itself to rule on this important matter. It is in other words the tribunal which rules on whether or not it may hear a case and apply the material provisions of an investment protection instrument. Its decision rests on the interpretation it carries out. If a commercial arbitration award is thereby treated as or like an investment, international investment law could indeed be a promising option for disappointed attempts of enforcement. It is not surprising then that the question of what constitutes an investment is becoming increasingly important.[204] This chapter will embark on a journey to address the aforementioned question in focusing on the protectability of commercial arbitration awards in international investment law. It will attempt to unveil, if and under which circumstances treaty interpretation leads to this innovative outcome. The traditional facets of an investment will be outlined before current lines of

---

Case No. ARB/02/7, June 5, 2007, para. 45: "The relevant provisions of the applicable law are constitutive elements of the Parties' agreement to arbitrate and constitute part of the definition of the tribunal's mandate."

204. *Campbell McLachlan/Laurence Shore/Matthew Weiniger*, International Investment Arbitration – Substantive Principles, 2007, p. 163.

interpretation in investment arbitrations will be taken into account. The analysis intends to provide an insight into a current practical topic of international investment law and the interpretive framework in which it arises. It will illustrate not only the paramount importance of treaty interpretation in theory, but most importantly, the challenges in its application in practice.

§3.02 THE TRADITIONAL FACETS OF AN INVESTMENT

The meaning of the term "investment" is essential to the application of international investment law. It is vital to the question of whether or not a particular arbitral tribunal may assume jurisdiction and if the standards of protection may be deployed. The investment character of an activity is therefore the gateway to enjoying investment protection. If international investment law is to provide a remedy to commercial parties experiencing difficulties in the enforcement of awards, the subsumption under investment definitions is of tremendous importance, which continues to grow as the number of international business activities sees a steady increase.[205] Existing concepts of investment characteristics are oftentimes inconsistent.[206] Despite the difficulty in defining investments, various efforts have been made to contour the term's features, essentially due to mere practical necessity. These efforts are mainly relevant in the context of the respective investment protection mechanisms applicable to the case at hand: bilateral or MITs, FTAs and especially the ICSID-Convention. Nevertheless, findings by tribunals as well as academic work are of general interest in analyses of all existing mechanisms.[207] In this regard, the individual approaches taken by tribunals may be of a complementary nature.

[A] Considering Individual Investment Protection Mechanisms

[1] Bilateral and Multilateral Investment Treaties

The impressive number of existing treaties, aiming at the protection of investments, has already been pointed out. Despite this plurality, however, the majority of them share similar, sometimes identical investment definitions.[208] The BIT between the United Kingdom and Singapore of July 22, 1975, for example, defines investments as follows:

> For the purposes of this Agreement:
>
> (a) "investment" means *every kind of asset* and in particular, though not exclusively, includes:

---

205. See *McLachlan/Shore/Weiniger*, note 204, p. 163.
206. *Christopher F. Dugan/Don Wallace, Jr./Noah Rubins/Borzu Sabahi*, Investor-State Arbitration, 2008, p. 247.
207. *McLachlan/Shore/Weiniger*, note 204, p. 164.
208. See *McLachlan/Shore/Weiniger*, note 204, p. 171.

(i) movable and immovable property and any other property rights such as mortgages, liens or pledges;
(ii) shares, stock and debentures of companies or interests in the property of such companies;
(iii) claims to money or to any performance under contract having a financial value;
(iv) intellectual property rights and goodwill;
(v) business concessions conferred by law or under contract, including concessions to search for, cultivate, extract or exploit natural resources.

What is noteworthy is that the characteristics stated by this treaty are especially broad and in contrast to other investment treaties, namely the U.S. Model Treaty of 2012, which provides for a number of additional features:

"investment" means every asset *that an investor owns or controls, directly or indirectly, that has the characteristics of an investment, including such characteristics as the commitment of capital or other resources, the expectation of gain or profit, or the assumption of risk.* Forms that an investment *may take* include:
(a) an enterprise;
(b) shares, stock, and other forms of equity participation in an enterprise;
(c) bonds, debentures, other debt instruments, and loans;
(d) futures, options, and other derivatives;
(e) turnkey, construction, management, production, concession, revenue-sharing, and other similar contracts;
(f) intellectual property rights;
(g) licenses, authorizations, permits, and similar rights conferred pursuant to domestic law and
(h) other tangible or intangible, movable or immovable property, and related property rights, such as leases, mortgages, liens, and pledges.

The U.S. Model Treaty of 2012 depicts in detail certain characteristics for an activity to fall within the investment definition. Then, it enumerates exemplarily forms that an investment may take. The treaty implements findings by tribunals and thus essentially constitutes a codification of arbitral practice.[209] It indicates the impact interpretations by tribunals may have as well as the interplay of the actors in international investment law. However, even this definition remains broad and leaves room for a similarly broad understanding of investments, which is partially due to the nonexhaustive character of the list provided by the treaty. Article 1139 NAFTA, for example, has taken a different approach. It contains an exhaustive list ("investment means") and additionally a list of forms that do not constitute an investment ("but investment does not mean"). Other investment treaties also rule out investments that have not been made with regards to local laws, such as the Model Treaty of the Republic of Colombia from 2007 ("in accordance with the law of the latter").

---

209. McLachlan/Shore/Weiniger, note 204, p. 172, who explain that the wording is a result of the case law developed by the tribunal's findings in *Fedax N.V. v. The Republic of Venezuela*, Decision of the Tribunal on Objections to Jurisdiction, ICSID Case No. ARB/96/3, July 11, 1997.

Existing investment treaties thus share similar language and structures. They typically depict investments by clarifying that it must be an asset. Under some treaties, such asset must itself meet certain, more distinct criteria. Following exemplary lists may then provide guidance to tribunals in the interpretive process. As these treaties, even in their most detailed form currently in existence, remain vague, it is only to a certain extent the text of the treaty, and more the way in which it is interpreted by a particular tribunal that may shed light on the characteristics of an investment. Such analysis, however, must take place on the foundation that each underlying treaty is individual. When drawing from previous decisions, it is thus imperative to analyze the similarities and differences of the respective treaties. This will ensure appropriate comparing and distinguishing of findings in an attempt to develop structures and patterns.

[2] The ICSID-Convention

A large number of today's existing investment treaties refer disputes to the ICSID. Before an ICSID tribunal may assume jurisdiction, however, Article 25 section 1 of the ICSID-Convention requires that it is presented with:

> any legal dispute arising directly out of an investment.

The understanding of an investment is therefore central to the subject matter jurisdiction of ICSID (*ratione materiae*). Interestingly and in contrast to BITs and MITs previously dealt with, the ICSID-Convention does not provide any defining features of an investment. However, when it was drafted, serious efforts were undertaken but no definition could be agreed upon.[210] The drafters then took into consideration that the necessary consent that a state must give to the jurisdiction of ICSID could serve as a source for defining investments. This may be derived from an agreement between the host state and the investor, the host state's investment legislation and an international treaty.[211] Whenever such consent is given, it was assumed, a definition of the term "investment" within the framework of the respective consent, would almost inevitably have to be included.[212] Current research then comes to the conclusion that the omission of an investment definition was not due to failure, but in fact, an intentional decision by the Convention's drafters to allow for more regulatory space of developing countries in determining which activities they would like to see within ICSID's jurisdiction.[213]

---

210. *See* the detailed analysis of the drafting history by *Christoph Schreuer*, The ICSID Convention – A Commentary, 2nd ed. 2009, Art. 25.
211. *Schreuer*, note 210, Art. 25, para. 378.
212. *Dugan/Wallace/Rubins/Sabahi*, note 206, p. 257.
213. *Julian Davis Mortenson*, The Meaning of "Investment": ICSID's Travaux and the Domain of International Investment Law, in: Harvard International Law Journal 2010, Vol. 51 No. 1, pp. 257-318 (p. 280): "The failure to define 'investment' was not an exasperated throwing of hands in the air; it was an explicit choice that represented categorical adoption of the broad jurisdictional position in exchange for some crucial opt-out provisions aimed at taking the

[a]   Objective and Subjective Approaches

The limited resources provided by the ICSID-Convention regarding the concept of an investment have caused the emergence of a dividing line that is dominating the understanding. On the one hand, it is argued that the above-mentioned freedom implies a subjective approach to the investment concept. As long as an investment character can be derived from the respective underlying consenting instrument, an ICSID tribunal will be able to assume jurisdiction.[214] This freedom, however, is not endless. It has been widely highlighted that not every plainly commercial transaction can be defined as an investment.[215] It is rather necessary to establish that there is some connection to investments from an objective point of view.[216] Consequentially, tribunals have ruled that the investment requirement is objective, and that it must be met in order for an ICSID tribunal to assume jurisdiction.[217] This objective approach[218] to the definition of an investment is the one predominantly taken by tribunals. It has

---

developing countries' concerns into account."; *see also Schreuer*, note 210, Art. 25, para. 123: "[...] it is clear that the parties have much freedom in describing their transactions as an investment [...]."

214. *Lanco International Inc. v. The Argentine Republic*, Preliminary Decision: Jurisdiction of the Arbitral Tribunal, ICSID Case No. ARB/97/6, December 8, 1998, para. 48: "As regards the fact that this dispute arises directly out of an investment, once again where the term 'investment' is not defined in the ICSID Convention, but it is defined in the ARGENTINA-U.S. Treaty which sets the bounds within which we operate in this case."; *Generation Ukraine, Inc. v. Ukraine*, Award, ICSID Case No. ARB/00/9, September 16, 2003, para. 8.2:

> No definition of "investment" is to be found in the ICSID Convention. It is well settled that Contracting Parties may agree upon a more precise definition of "investment" in a separate legal instrument. The Claimant has invoked the jurisdiction of ICSID pursuant to Article VI of the BIT. Hence, the definition contained in Article I(1)(a) of the BIT (set out in full at Paragraph 18.1 below) applies in this reference to ICSID arbitration.

Fraport AG Frankfurt Airport Services Worldwide v. Republic of Philippines, Award, ICSID Case No. ARB/03/25, August 16, 2007, para. 305:

> It is further observed that the boundaries of this Tribunal's jurisdiction are delimited by the arbitration agreement, in the instant case, both the BIT and the Washington Convention. Article 25 of the Washington Convention, which provides, inter alia, parameters of jurisdiction ratione materiae, does not define "investment", leaving it to parties who incorporate ICSID jurisdiction to provide a definition if they wish. In bilateral investment treaties which incorporate an ICSID arbitration option, the word "investment" is a term of art, whose content in each instance is to be determined by the language of the pertinent BIT which serves as a lex specialis with respect to Article 25 of the Washington Convention.

215. *Schreuer*, note 210, Art. 25, para. 122.
216. *See Dugan/Wallace/Rubins/Sabahi*, note 206, p. 258.
217. *Salini Costruttori S.p.A. and Italstrade S.p.A. v. Kingdom of Morocco*, Decision on Jurisdiction, ICSID Case No. ARB/00/4, para. 52: "To the contrary, ICSID case law and legal authors agree that the investment requirement must be respected as an objective condition of the jurisdiction of the Centre."
218. *Malaysia Historical Salvors SDN, BHD v. The Government of Malaysia*, Award on Jurisdiction, ICSID Case No. ARB/05/10, May 17, 2007, para. 54: "It has been considered in *Salini* that the consensus of legal authors and ICSID case law is that the investment requirement under Article 25(1) is an objective condition of the jurisdiction of the Centre."

necessitated a twofold procedure (*double keyhole approach*).[219] First, it needs to be established that the dispute concerns an investment in accordance with the provisions of the ICSID-Convention. The difficulty here lies in the limited resources provided by the ICSID-Convention itself, as was previously described. Second, it needs to be equally established that a particular dispute concerns an investment in accordance with the provisions of the instrument of consent. Substantial interpretation within the constraints of the relevant instrument is thus required for determining the meaning of "investment." This will, due to the common implementation of a definition, provide the tribunal with more interpretive starting points.

The challenging task is to assess the meaning of "investment" within the sole context of the ICSID-Convention. This situation has a practical consequence: although it does not define the term "investment," tribunals are required to test characteristics of the relevant dispute for its compliance with the investment understanding in Article 25 section 1 ICSID-Convention and thereby develop an ever-growing case law. However, it is not entirely discernible how tribunals may conduct these tests, if they are only provided with very limited criteria on what constitutes an investment, namely not every ordinary transaction and that there should be some positive impact on the host state's economy.[220] This suggests that tribunals, in practice, will adopt a negative definition rather than a positive one, expressing what is *not* an investment rather than what is. It must have been evident at the time of the Convention's drafting that the lack of defining terms would necessitate an interpretive foundation for tribunals, which could most likely only have been seen in the treaties or agreements providing for ICSID as a means of dispute resolution. Lastly, an intermediary approach to the investment definition has also been suggested, starting from an objective perspective while giving special consideration to the parties' subjective investment definition.[221]

Regardless of the particular approach taken, practice was able to derive some patterns from cases. In these, tribunals have either not even commented on a particular transaction or thing being an investment, yet considering a dispute to fall within the jurisdiction of ICSID or only briefly touched upon the issue.[222] This has helped shaping the characteristics of an investment pursuant to Article 25 ICSID-Convention. Nevertheless, these findings have been inconsistently handled, weighted and interpreted.

---

219. *Dolzer/Schreuer*, note 48, p. 62.
220. *See Schreuer*, note 210, Art. 25, para. 121, who describes that "[t]herefore, it is arguable that the Convention's object and purpose indicate that there should be some positive impact on development."
221. *Alcoa Minerals of Jamaica, Inc. v. Republic of Jamaica*, Decision on Jurisdiction and Competence, ICSID Case No. ARB/74/2, July 6, 1975: "As regards this second ground, the arbitral tribunal, however, noted that such consent was only a factor of 'great weight'."
222. *See Salini Costruttori S.p.A. and Italstrade S.p.A. v. Kingdom of Morocco*, note 217, para. 52: "The criteria for characterization are, therefore, derived from cases in which the transaction giving rise to the dispute was considered to be an investment without there ever being a real discussion of the issue in almost all the cases."

[b] The Salini-Test

[i] From Characteristics to Requirements

The first ever objection to the jurisdiction of an ICSID tribunal prompted the arbitrators to engage in a broad analysis of the characteristics of investments.[223] In its finding, the tribunal relied on academic effort in carving out those features that are typical to transactions that have already been identified as constituting an investment.[224] These regularly involve a certain duration, a regularity of profit and return, the assumption of risk, a substantial commitment and significance for the host state's development. These criteria are nowadays considered to be an inherent part of Article 25 section 1 ICSID-Convention[225] and originally reflected not a mandatory test, but merely a description of specific facets of an investment.[226] Nevertheless, an interesting development has taken place. The above-mentioned criteria have been utilized in order to test the existence of an investment. In other words, the descriptive features have been converted into mandatory requirements.[227] The term "*Salini*-test" has henceforth been lurking about in international investment law. However, it is questionable whether this strict application of a test that is not evidently compulsory in view of the wording of Article 25 section 1 ICSID-Convention, is a wise approach. It certainly allows tribunals to speed up the process of assuming or declining jurisdiction. The nonexistent normative connection to the ICSID-Convention, however, appears problematic. It purports a restrictive assessment to the cost of individually expressed understandings. As the omission of an investment definition may suggest,[228] the aim of the ICSID-Convention remains the promotion of investments while leaving it to its signatories to determine their characteristics.[229] The transformation of the *Salini*-ruling into a rigid test has been noted and criticized by *Schreuer* himself, who has laid the foundation for distilling the characteristics.[230] Instead of forming part of a mandatory test, his criteria

---

223. *Fedax N.V. v. The Republic of Venezuela*, Decision on Jurisdiction, ICSID Case No. ARB/96/3, July 11, 1997, para. 25: "This is the first ICSID case in which the jurisdiction of the Centre has been objected to on the ground that the underlying transaction does not meet the requirements of an investment under the Convention."
224. *Fedax N.V. v. The Republic of Venezuela*, note 223, para. 43 in referring to *Christoph Schreuer*, Commentary on the ICSID Convention, in: ICSID Review – Foreign Investment Law Journal 1996, Vol. 11 No. 2, pp. 316-492 (p. 372).
225. *Dolzer/Schreuer*, note 48, p. 68.
226. *Schreuer*, note 224, Art. 25, p. 373: "These features should not necessarily be understood as jurisdictional requirements but merely as typical characteristics of investments under the Convention."
227. *Salini Costruttori S.p.A. and Italstrade S.p.A. v. Kingdom of Morocco*, note 217, paras. 52 et seq.
228. See *Mortenson*, note 213, p. 280.
229. *Abaclat and others v. The Argentine Republic*, Decision on Jurisdiction and Admissibility, ICSID Case No. ARB/07/5, August 4, 2011, para. 364: "The Tribunal finds that such a result would be contradictory to the ICSID Convention's aim, which is to encourage private investment while giving the Parties the tools to further define what kind of investment they want to promote."
230. *Schreuer*, note 210, Art. 25, para. 171: "The development in practice from a descriptive list of typical features towards a set of mandatory legal requirements is unfortunate. The First Edition of this Commentary cannot serve as authority for this development."

should remain a valuable source for easing the difficulty of deciding whether or not an investment is at hand.[231] It can be no substitute for a thorough analysis of the parties' expressions of the investment character. It must be in compliance with their individual practice,[232] properly interpreted by tribunals that things or operations are tested with regards to their respective investment quality. If the criteria adopted in *Salini v. Morocco* should therefore really be understood as a test with mandatory requirements is thus at least questionable.[233]

[ii]   Five Typical Features

After analyzing and evaluating the general role of the *Salini*-features, a closer look at them is useful in the context of this analysis. First, an investment is characterized by a certain duration. It is an inherent feature of investments. The general linguistic usage of the term already implies that a merely sporadic transaction is not an investment. Rather, it contains the notion that it is made at a current point in time in order to benefit from its returns at a later stage. Setting a minimum or maximum duration, however, does not seem like a practically necessary move. Nevertheless, it has been pointed out that typical investments generally take place throughout the course of at least two to five years.[234] Such strict understanding fails to acknowledge that the diverse characteristics must not be viewed in isolation from one another. An operation that does not meet a duration of at least two years, may certainly qualify as an investment with regards to, e.g., the commitment or the significance to the host state's economy. A different view would disregard the manifold variants of investments. Consequentially, it has been correctly stated that a rigorous understanding of this feature without

---

231. *Abaclat and others v. The Argentine Republic*, note 229, para. 364: "The Salini criteria may be useful to further describe what characteristics contributions may or should have. They should, however, not serve to create a limit, which the Convention itself nor the Contracting Parties to a specific BIT intended to create."
232. See *Mihaly International Corporation v. Democratic Socialist Republic of Sri Lanka*, Award, ICSID Case No. ARB/00/2, March 15, 2002, para. 33: "Rather the definition was left to be worked out in the subsequent practice of States, thereby preserving its integrity and flexibility and allowing for future progressive development of international law on the topic of investment."; *see also Parkerings-Compagniet AS v. Republic of Lithuania*, Award, ICSID Case No. ARB/05/8, September 11, 2007, paras. 249 et seq., in which the tribunal noted the lack of an investment definition in Art. 25 sec. 1 ICSID-Convention and went on to consider the underlying BIT.
233. See *Ambiente Ufficio S.p.A. v. The Argentine Republic*, Decision on Jurisdiction and Admissibility, ICSID Case No. ARB/08/9, February 8, 2013, para. 480:

> Following Professor Schreuer's approach, the criteria assembled in the Salini test, while not constituting mandatory prerequisites for the jurisdiction of the Centre in the meaning of Art. 25 of the ICSID Convention, may still prove useful, provided that they are treated as guidelines and that they are applied in conjunction and in a flexible manner.

> *see also* the finding in *Deutsche Bank AG v. Democratic Socialist Republic of Sri Lanka*, Award, ICSID Case No. ARB/09/02, October 31, 2012, para. 294.

234. *Salini Costruttori S.p.A. and Italstrade S.p.A. v. Kingdom of Morocco*, note 217, para. 54; *see also Malaysia Historical Salvors SDN, BHD v. The Government of Malaysia*, para. 111.

considering a more global context, e.g. extensions to contracts, is not expedient.[235] Second, a regularity of profit and return is thought to be another characteristic of investments. Once again, the general linguistic usage of the term "investment" almost inevitably implies at least an expectation of a later return. Prospects of monetary loss do not stimulate investment activities. Surprisingly, however, this feature has not been frequently considered in the majority of arbitrations.[236] Third, the assumption of some risk is another criterion that needs to be taken into consideration. Risk may be regarded as a consequence of the duration of the operation, which adds a level of uncertainty to it. It has been a feature heavily relied upon in arbitral practice.[237] The assumed risk must go beyond that of an ordinary contractual relationship.[238] It is in this regard the decisive factor in demarcating an investment from a mere business activity. Fourth, an investment is a commitment that is substantial. This does not necessarily imply a minimum amount of money that must be involved, as such a requirement has specifically not been adopted by the drafters of the ICSID-Convention.[239] However, the financial[240] as well as the human capital or know-how[241] at stake may be valuable indicators in ruling on the substantiality of a respective commitment. Lastly, an investment within the context of the ICSID-Convention is typically characterized by its significance for the host state's development. This feature has been derived from the preamble and its interpretation in view of its object and purpose[242] and can be understood as a peculiar aspect of an investment within the context of the ICSID-Convention. State signatories have thereby expressed their willingness to submit disputes to ICSID arbitration where they deal with operations that have a particular impact on their development. It represents the balance between exposure to international adjudication at the risk of successful claims of compensation and stimulating profitable investments as a return. Development is the signatories' motivation behind the submission. Ultimately then, the development aspect of an investment should receive broad attention,[243] so arbitrators may give consideration to it in the interpretive

---

235. *See Consorzio Groupement L.E.S.I.-DIPENTA v. Republic of Algeria*, Award, ICSID Case No. ARB/03/08, January 10, 2005, p. 20: "On ne peut de toute façon pas se montrer excessivement rigoureux tant l'expérience apprend que des objets du genre de celui qui est en cause justifient souvent des prolongations, sans parler de la durée de la garantie."
236. *Schreuer*, note 210, Art. 25, para. 157.
237. *Noah Rubins*, The Notion of "Investment" in International Investment Arbitration, in: Norbert Horn/Stefan Kröll (eds.), Arbitrating Foreign Investment Disputes, 2004, pp. 283-324 (p. 298).
238. *See Malaysia Historical Salvors SDN, BHD v. The Government of Malaysia*, note 218, para. 112: "While the Claimant may have satisfied the risk characteristic or criterion in a quantitative sense (i.e., that there was inherent risk assumed under the Contract), the quality of the assumed risk was not something which established ICSID practice and jurisprudence would recognize."; *see also Joy Mining Machinery Limited v. The Arab Republic of Egypt*, Award on Jurisdiction, ICSID Case No. ARB/03/11, August 6, 2004, paras. 57 et seq.
239. *Schreuer*, note 210, Art. 25, para. 116.
240. *Liberian Eastern Timber Corp. v. Republic of Liberia*, Decision on Jurisdiction, ICSID Case No. ARB/83/2, October 24, 1984, in: ICSID Reports 1994, Vol. 2, pp. 346 et seq. (p. 350).
241. *Bayindir Insaat Turizm Ticaret VE Sanayi A.S. v. Islamic Republic of Pakistan*, Award on Jurisdiction, ICSID Case No. ARB/03/29, November 14, 2005, para. 131.
242. *Schreuer*, note 210, Art. 25, para. 121.
243. *Dugan/Wallace/Rubins/Sabahi*, note 206, p. 272; *see also Georges R. Delaume*, Convention on the Settlement of Investment Disputes Between States and Nationals of Other States, in: International Lawyer 1966, Vol. 1 No. 1, pp. 64-80 (p. 70).

process, provided that states have implemented it into the text of the applicable BIT. The characteristic has, as a consequence, been frequently considered by arbitral tribunals.[244]

[iii] The Use Outside of the ICSID Framework

The framework around Article 25 section 1 ICSID-Convention provides a relatively dense orientation in defining investments. While it may thus seem appropriate to apply these elements as a test, it must once again be highlighted that such approach is problematic. The urge to find patterns may lead astray and compromise the dedication necessary in interpreting each investment instrument on its own. The tribunal in *Azinian v. Mexico* was quite right when it stated: "Labelling is, however, no substitute for analysis."[245] The present characteristics may give tribunals assurance in their findings. It is not surprising that their applicability outside of the ICSID framework is widely debated.[246] If the aforementioned criteria are in compliance with their origin, of a purely descriptive nature, there generally appears to be no evident issue in applying them outside of the ICSID system. Only the significance of an activity for the host state's development forms an exception. This feature is an inherent part of the preamble of the ICSID-Convention. Where similar wording exists in a respective investment instrument, however, it may undoubtedly be of relevance as well.

[B] **Conclusion**

The foregoing analysis has demonstrated that international investment law does not provide a universally applicable investment definition. The high number of individual investment treaties as well as the inexistence of a definition in the ICSID-Convention makes the process of characterizing activities as investments a mission of immense complexity. There is an evident need for an individual interpretation in view of each underlying investment protection instrument. Such individual interpretation does not imply disregard of previous findings. To the contrary, a more global perspective bears

---

244. See *Joy Mining Machinery Limited v. The Arab Republic of Egypt*, note 238, para. 57; *see also Consortium R.F.C.C. v. Kingdom of Morocco*, Decision on Jurisdiction, ICSID Case No. ARB/00/6, July 16, 2001, para. 65:

> S'agissant enfin de la contribution du marché au développement économique de l'Etat marocain, celle-ci ne peut sérieusement être discutée. La construction des infrastructures relève, dans la plupart des pays, des tâches de l'Etat ou d'autres collectivités publiques. Il ne peut être sérieusement contesté que l'autoroute en cause servira l'intérêt public.

245. *Robert Azinian, Kenneth Davitian, & Ellen Baca v. United Mexican States*, Award, ICSID Case No. ARB(AF)/97/2, November 1, 1999, para. 90.
246. See *White Industries Australia Limited v. The Republic of India*, Award, UNCITRAL, November 30, 2011, para. 7.4.9, although, interestingly, the tribunal did then engage in a detailed analysis of the individual elements.

tremendous potential in shaping the legitimate development of international investment law. An individual interpretation, in this sense, is one that pays respect to the specific facts and the underlying investment protection instrument in each particular case while having due regard to approaches from the outside. State signatories to an investment treaty may each have their individual understanding of an investment as it should be interpreted. However, tribunals may only pay respect to these understandings, if they have objectively found some expression in the treaty. They will be given effect by way of proper methodological approaches, deploying the canons of the VCLT. The individuality of an interpretation does therefore not extend to individual means of interpretation.

The investment definition will inevitably continue to vary where facts and instruments do. It is highly desirable that apart from these variables, inconsistent applications of interpretive canons do not further contribute to the complexity so generated. In this regard, taking into account the differences and similarities of each individual investment dispute and the interpretive outcomes resulting from them will alleviate the decision-making process as a whole. This approach has lastly also helped to find the features highlighted in *Salini v. Morocco*. The wide scope of the term "investment" has been and will continue to pose challenges to investment protection.[247] At the same time, it is precisely this openness that ensures flexibility[248] and facilitates a sustained, legitimate development. This requires a diligent application of the well-established interpretive methods, transparency and clarity.

§3.03 THE QUALIFICATION OF ARBITRAL AWARDS

The protection of commercial arbitration awards within international investment law is dependent upon whether or not they fall in the scope of application of a respective investment protection instrument. This is imaginable in two scenarios: first, a commercial arbitration award could be treated *as* an investment. Second, it could be treated *like* an investment. The practical difference is nonexistent.[249] Hence, the treatment of a commercial arbitration award by a host state may fall within the jurisdiction of an international investment tribunal, if the proper interpretation of the term "investment" so allows. As was already pointed out, this understanding may represent a new

---

247. *See Nova Scotia Power Incorporated (Canada) v. Bolivarian Republic of Venezuela*, Award, ICSID Case No. ARB(AF)/11/1, April 30, 2014, para. 77:

> The Tribunal is of the view that in examining whether or not an investment is present, the definition of "investment" in the BIT cannot be considered self-sufficient. Indeed, one might query if the language attached to "investment" in the BIT can even be properly described as a definition (i.e. a term which offers an exact description of the item in question); this also indicates its limitations.

248. *Dolzer/Schreuer*, note 48, p. 60.
249. *Loukas A. Mistelis*, Award as an Investment: The Value of an Arbitral Award or the Cost of Non-Enforcement, in: ICSID Review 2013, Foreign Investment Law Journal, Vol. 28 No. 1, pp. 1-24 (p. 12): "This functional equivalence is more than sufficient to trigger both State liability and investment protection and, if the factual circumstances are appropriate, provide significant additional support for arbitral awards."

intersection of commercial and investment arbitration with enormous practical potential. Frustrated attempts to enforce a commercial arbitration award may lead to the initiation of an investment arbitration and thus providing an investor with an option for "a second bite at the cherry," broadening the liability of states. The practical significance of such interpretation to the effect that arbitral awards may be granted protection as or like investments is thus considerable.

[A] Nature of Arbitral Awards

Before embarking on an interpretive journey, it may be expedient to briefly bring to mind the general nature of arbitral awards. This nature is intertwined with the nature of arbitration as a whole. One can generally distinguish between four theories concerning the nature of arbitration. The *jurisdictional theory* emphasizes the relationship between the arbitral mechanism and national courts. While arbitration is a means of dispute resolution that intends to offer an alternative to state judiciaries, it is apparent that without their support it would not function. This symbiosis sees arbitrators as resembling judges and their rulings, namely the arbitral awards, as similar to judgments.[250] The *contractual theory*, on the other hand, focuses on the underlying contractual relationship between parties that makes arbitration possible in the first place. In this regard, the arbitral award has been described as being in itself a contract (*agent theory*),[251] but undoubtedly a result of the arbitration agreement.[252] The *hybrid theory* then strikes a balance between the aforementioned approaches. It does acknowledge the contractual nature of arbitration, while at the same time stressing the similarity of the arbitral award to a court judgment.[253] Lastly, the *autonomous theory* attempts to free itself from the classical explanations of arbitration and regards it as a self-sustained system of dispute resolution, tolerated by national laws.[254] Consequentially, an arbitral award is thus neither a contract nor a judgment, but rather a sui generis occurrence.[255]

[B] Treating Arbitral Awards as Investments

[1] Autonomous Plain Meaning Approach

The pivotal question in the context of international investment law remains if an arbitral award may constitute an investment. The answer to this question is dependent on whether or not a respective individual investment treaty allows for such understanding. If one autonomously reflects upon the term "investment" without recourse to

---

250. *Hong-lin Yu*, A Theoretical Overview of the Foundations of International Commercial Arbitration, in: Contemporary Asia Arbitration Journal 2008, Vol. 1, pp. 255-286 (p. 262).
251. *Mistelis*, note 249, p. 5.
252. *Yu*, note 250, p. 272.
253. *Mistelis*, note 249, p. 6.
254. *Mistelis*, note 249, p. 6.
255. *Mistelis*, note 249, p. 6.

particular definitions certain characteristics will come to mind that may provide a first guideline. The VCLT does, however, not envisage an incorporation of subjective perceptions per se. Although the large number of treaties makes the attempt of finding a generally valid answer a fruitless endeavor, a closer look at the typical definitions incorporated will provide a first insight into the functions of deployed wording. An interpretation with regard to the plain meaning of the terms used will then serve as the foundation for a broader analysis of each individual treaty.

[a]   Value as a Starting Point

A large number of treaties begin their definitions by stating that an investment is "every kind of asset."[256] An asset may be understood as anything that is of value and that belongs to someone or something. Regardless of which particular theoretical approach is adopted in explaining the nature of arbitration, it will be consensus that an arbitral award is valuable and thus, based on the ordinary meaning, constitutes an asset. Some treaties add that an investment must be "economic,"[257] "financial"[258] or "connected with the participation in companies and joint ventures."[259] These additions merely substantiate the ordinary meaning of the term "asset" and are thus of purely cosmetic nature. A textual analysis will therefore not struggle to find that an arbitral award is an asset.[260]

---

256. *See* e.g. Greece South Africa BIT, November 19, 1998, available at http://arbitrationlaw.com/files/free_pdfs/greece-south_africa_bit.pdf (last accessed July 4, 2014); Antigua and Barbuda-Germany BIT, July 26, 2000, available at http://www.sice.oas.org/Investment/BITsbyCountry/BITs/ANT_Germany.pdf (last accessed July 4, 2014); Thailand-Bahrain BIT, May 21, 2002, available at http://investmentpolicyhub.unctad.org/Download/TreatyFile/258 (last accessed July 4, 2014); Belize-Taiwan BIT, January 16, 1999, available at http://investmentpolicyhub.unctad.org/Download/TreatyFile/435 (last accessed July 4, 2014).
257. *See* e.g. United Kingdom-Colombia BIT, May 19, 2009, available at http://investmentpolicyhub.unctad.org/Download/TreatyFile/805 (last accessed July 4, 2014); United Kingdom-Bulgaria BIT, December 11, 1995, available at http://investorstatelawguide.com/documents/documents/BIT-0446%20-%20Bulgaria-United%20Kingdom%20BIT%20%281995%29%20%28citation%20and%20source%29.pdf (last accessed April 14, 2015); Mexico-Greece BIT, November 30, 2000, available at http://investmentpolicyhub.unctad.org/Download/TreatyFile/1471 (last accessed July 4, 2014).
258. *See* France-Bulgaria BIT, April 9, 1990, available at http://investmentpolicyhub.unctad.org/Download/TreatyFile/528 (last accessed July 4, 2014).
259. *See* Hungary-Greece BIT, May 26, 1989, available at http://investmentpolicyhub.unctad.org/Download/TreatyFile/1462 (last accessed July 4, 2014).
260. *See* e.g. *ECHR, Kin-Stib and Majiki v. Serbia*, Judgment, Application No. 12312/05, April 20, 2010, para. 84: "Turning to the present case, it is firstly noted that the claim established in the arbitration award undisputedly amounts to a possession within the meaning of Article 1 of Protocol No. 1" which provides that "Every natural or legal person is entitled to the peaceful enjoyment of his [or her] possessions. No one shall be deprived of his [or her] possessions except in the public interest and subject to the conditions provided for by law and by the general principles of international law."

[b]   Limitations Related to Time and Location

The use of participles such as "invested"[261] adds a component to the definition that requires not a sudden occurrence, but rather a relative duration. It implies that there must have been prior activity in the respective territory. This activity typically involves a certain amount of risk and contribution. In other words, under such definition it is not conceivable that a frustrated attempt to enforce an arbitral award would trigger liability under international investment law without such prior activity by the enforcing party in the territory of the state of enforcement. Where the wording of the investment definition poses such limitation, tribunals, before assuming jurisdiction, must therefore establish that there is a link between the arbitral award that is sought to be enforced and prior activity in the state of enforcement.[262] However, participles such as "owned" or "controlled"[263] do not pose a limitation with regards to the qualification of arbitral awards as investments. They simply highlight the element of ownership.

[c]   Concretion by Enumeration

Exhaustive or nonexhaustive lists are typically incorporated into investment treaties and serve to further concretize the investment definition. They provide examples of assets that may be deemed to constitute an investment. One will find these to include "claims to money"[264] or "right to money or to any performance having a financial value, contractual or otherwise."[265] Other investment treaties specifically state which forms of activities or things shall not constitute an investment.[266] Such lists provide an adequate option for states to specifically limit the conduct that may be part of a

---

261. *See* e.g. Croatia-Greece BIT, October 18, 1996, http://investmentpolicyhub.unctad.org/Download/TreatyFile/859 (last accessed July 4, 2014); India-Australia BIT, February 26, 1999, available at http://investmentpolicyhub.unctad.org/Download/TreatyFile/154 (last accessed April 14, 2015); Sweden-Hong Kong BIT, May 27, 1994, available at http://investmentpolicyhub.unctad.org/Download/TreatyFile/1519 (last accessed April 14, 2015).
262. *See Gabrielle Kaufmann-Kohler*, Commercial Arbitration Before International Court and Tribunals – Reviewing Abusive Conduct of Domestic Courts – 2011 American University Washington College of Law Annual Lecture on International Commercial Arbitration, in: Arbitration International 2013, pp. 153-173 (p. 166), who describes this situation as requiring a "territorial nexus between the original investment and the putative respondent state."; *see also William W. Park*, Respecting the New York Convention, in: ICC International Court of Arbitration Bulletin 2007, Vol. 18 No. 2, pp. 65-77 (p. 68).
263. *See* e.g. Australia-Mexico BIT, available at http://arbitrationlaw.com/files/free_pdfs/australia-mexico_bit.pdf (last accessed July 4, 2014); Australia-Laos BIT, April 6, 1994, available at http://dev.arbitration.org/sites/default/files/bit/australia_lao_people's_democratic_republic_english.pdf (last accessed July 4, 2014); Australia-China BIT, July 11, 1988, available at http://investmentpolicyhub.unctad.org/Download/TreatyFile/148 (last accessed April 14, 2015); Turkey-Bangladesh BIT, November 12, 1987, available at http://investmentpolicyhub.unctad.org/Download/TreatyFile/274 (last accessed July 4, 2014).
264. *See* e.g. Austria-Chile BIT, available at http://investmentpolicyhub.unctad.org/Download/TreatyFile/178 (last accessed July 4, 2014).
265. *See* e.g. India-Australia BIT, February 26, 1999, available at http://investmentpolicyhub.unctad.org/Download/TreatyFile/154 (last accessed April 14, 2015).
266. *See* e.g. Canada-Panama BIT, September 12, 1996, available at http://www.bilaterals.org/IMG/pdf/CA-PA_FIPA_1998.pdf (last accessed July 4, 2014).

tribunal's jurisdiction. No investment treaty has yet excluded arbitral awards from the investment definition. This may have multiple reasons. Such understanding is still a relatively recent occurrence and could presumably not have been foreseen at the time of the conclusion of existing treaties. Accordingly, states will most likely not have had the opportunity to react to arbitral developments.

[2] Awards as Continuations of Original Investments

In arbitral practice, an award has been found to constitute a continuation of an original investment. In the course of considering such interpretive outcomes, one must look at the facts that initially gave rise to the dispute. Furthermore, the investment treaty as the legal foundation calls for particular attention as well as the interpretive way the respective tribunals have approached the characterization of arbitral awards. This will provide insights into recent developments in international investment arbitration that may represent growing advancements[267] and help to understand if and how arbitral awards may benefit from the protection of international investment law.

[a] White Industries v. India

[i] Case Brief and Investment Definition

A decision that has advanced into this new territory is the arbitral award in *White Industries v. India*,[268] which is a starting point for the upcoming analysis. Arbitral proceedings were initiated on July 27, 2010 and concerned the treatment of a commercial arbitration award by the Indian judiciary. Following a decision by India in the 1970s to develop its coal industry, India and Australia entered into negotiations about a possible cooperation in this endeavor. The state-owned company Coal India, entrusted with the development of the Indian mining industry, intensified the collaboration and sought to profit from Australian mining experience by way of official visits to Australia throughout which White Industries was heavily involved in the marketing process. Between 1987 and 1989, the relationship became closer as Coal India and White Industries began contractual negotiations about the so-called Piparwar Project. Eventually, the parties entered into a contract for the supply of mining equipment under which White Industries, in return, was to be remunerated in the amount of AUD 206.6 million. This contract included an arbitration agreement, under which all disputes were to be resolved under the ICC Rules of Arbitration. A dispute arose between the two about possibly due bonus payments to White Industries or due penalty payments to Coal India. As a result, on June 28, 1999, White Industries initiated ICC arbitration proceedings, which were held in London. The tribunal rendered an

---

267. *See Richard Kreindler*, Are Tribunals Setting New Limits on Access to International Jurisdiction?, in: ICSID Review 2010, Foreign Investment Law Journal, Vol. 25 No. 1, pp. 37-43 (p. 42), who carefully warns of finding real trends in one or another direction due to individual fact patterns and depicts developments as "maturation."
268. *White Industries Australia Limited v. The Republic of India*, note 246.

award which entitled White Industries to seek compensation from Coal India in the amount of AUD 4.08 million. Coal India then sought to have the award set aside by the High Court of Calcutta on September 6, 2002, while only five days later, White Industries addressed the same court seeking enforcement. What followed was a longsome journey through the Indian judiciary. After the award still had not been enforced, on December 10, 2009, White Industries addressed India to bring to its attention an alleged breach of provisions of the existing BIT between India and Australia by way of judicial actions. United Nations Commission on International Trade Law (UNCITRAL) arbitration proceedings were then initiated by White Industries in Singapore on July 27, 2010. At the time of the arbitral hearing, the Indian Supreme Court had still not set a date for White Industries' appeal and the tribunal *inter alia* was thus faced with the question, whether or not the arbitral award may constitute an investment. The dispute was based on the India-Australia BIT of February 26, 1999, which contains the following definition of investments:

> (c) "investment" means *every kind of asset*, including intellectual property rights, *invested* by an investor of one Contracting Party in the territory of the other Contracting Party in accordance with the laws and investment policies of that Contracting Party, and in particular, though *not exclusively*, includes: [...]
> (iii) *right to money or to any performance having a financial value, contractual or otherwise.*

Like in many BITs, the definition of investments remains very broad, incorporating every kind of asset. However, the definition also provides for some limitations. Such asset must be invested in the territory of the respective state. With regards to the qualification of an arbitral award, this provision proves challenging. From a mere textual approach, it is difficult to see how an arbitral award could be previously invested before it is rendered. Nevertheless, it is a matter of interpretation to allocate its function in a broader context and the object and purpose of the respective BIT. It must in any case be taken into consideration. Lastly, an asset, in order to qualify as an investment, must comply with the laws and investment policies of the host state. A nonexhaustive list then attempts to provide further clarification.

[ii] Tribunal's Conclusion and Analysis

In its decision, the tribunal came to the following conclusion:

> The Tribunal considers that the conclusion expressed by the GEA Tribunal represents an incorrect departure from the developing jurisprudence on the treatment of arbitral awards to the effect that awards made by tribunals arising out of disputes concerning "investments" made by "investors" under BITs represent a *continuation or transformation of the original investment.*[269]

---

269. *White Industries Australia Limited v. The Republic of India*, note 246, para. 7.6.8.

Chapter 3: The Protection of Arbitral Awards in the Global Context   §3.03[B]

And further:

> Accordingly, the Tribunal concludes that rights under the Award *constitute part of White's original investment* (i.e., being a crystallization of its rights under the Contract) and, as such, are subject to such protection as is afforded to investments by the BIT.[270]

This conclusion deserves further attention. First, the tribunal expressed that the award constituted a continuation or transformation of an original investment. In other words, not the award was an investment in itself, but rather the underlying contractual relationship that has given rise to the original arbitration must constitute an investment. Whether the award must thus be regarded as continuing that investment or transforming it was initially left open by the tribunal before deciding that it formed part of the original investment. Second, the tribunal believed to see a developing jurisprudence treating arbitral awards as continuations of original investments. The protection afforded to investments was consequentially deployed by the tribunal which rendered an award in favor of the claimant.

(1) Application of Methodological Canons

The tribunal, before proceeding with the actual characterization of the arbitral award, stated in its award that it was led by what it considered the correct approach in its assessment. It considered that the interpretation must be guided by looking at the plain and ordinary meaning of the wording of the underlying treaty in its context and in the light of its object and purpose.[271] The tribunal did, however, not mention the VCLT. One may argue that India has not signed this Convention and that it was thus simply inapplicable. However, this would disregard the nature of the VCLT as an instrument codifying customary international law.[272] In any case and most importantly, the tribunal was to adequately apply the principles of interpretation as contained in the VCLT regardless of its mentioning. In its award on the question of how to characterize an arbitral award, one does not find any attempt of interpretation. The only recourse to the underlying investment treaty appears in a reference to the claimant's statement, that the award constituted a right to money or to any performance having a financial value, contractual or otherwise. Even if this was considered to be an interpretive effort, it would remain short, as it solely focuses on the text of the treaty.[273] Here, one may argue that the tribunal did not engage in interpretation, as it only needed to consider the contractual relationship as constituting an investment, as it later concluded that an

---

270. *White Industries Australia Limited v. The Republic of India*, note 246, para. 7.6.10.
271. *White Industries Australia Limited v. The Republic of India*, note 246, para. 7.3.2.
272. *Sempra Energy International v. The Argentine Republic*, Decision on Objections to Jurisdiction, ICSID Case No. ARB/02/16, May 11, 2005, para. 141; *see also MTD Equity Sdn. Bhd. and MTD Chile S.A. v. Republic of Chile*, Award, ICSID Case No. ARB/01/7, May 25, 2004, para. 112; *Iurii Bogdanov, Agurdino-Invest Ltd., Argudino-Chimia JSC v. Republic of Moldova*, Award, SCC, September 22, 2005, para. 4.2.4.
273. Patricia Nacimiento/Sven Lange, Case Comment – White Industries Australia Limited v. The Republic of India, in: ICSID Review 2012, Foreign Investment Law Journal, Vol. 27 No. 2, pp. 274-280 (p. 276).

award represents a continuation of such. And indeed did the tribunal here refer to the BIT, indicating that the parties intended that such treaty would be interpreted broadly.[274] Nevertheless, this interpretation remains fully textual and thus lacks recourse to the treaty's object and purpose as part of an integrated interpretive operation. In view of the contentious characterizations of arbitral awards – which the tribunal must have been fully aware of given the emphasis put on previous findings – further analysis at this point was essential. Such would have also revealed that the parties did implicitly highlight the importance of adequate interpretation given its profound practical impact. For example, the preamble of the BIT between India and Australia provides that:

> Considering that investment relations should be promoted and economic cooperation strengthened in accordance with the internationally accepted principles of *mutual respect for sovereignty*, equality, mutual benefit, non-discrimination and mutual confidence.

(2) Reliance on Previous Decisions

Rather than engaging in interpretation, the tribunal consulted previous arbitral findings before it came to the above-mentioned conclusion. It has already been outlined that in drawing from previous decisions, it is essential to analyze the similarities and differences of the respective treaties as well as the facts of each individual case, ensuring appropriate comparing and distinguishing of findings in an attempt to develop structures and patterns. The tribunal in *White Industries v. India* unfortunately did not make such attempt in determining the nature of the arbitration award, but rather enumerated those investment arbitrations that it found to have adopted similar reasoning.[275] This approach also serves to explain the tribunal's emphasis on previous arbitral decisions to the extent that in international investment arbitration, jurisprudence is deemed capable of emerging. Such a doctrine of *stare decisis* does, however, not exist, as was previously pointed out. International investment law allows an adoption of previous decisions at most after careful consideration of the particularities of those cases' fact patterns and treaties.[276] Before reaching its ultimate conclusion, the tribunal sought reassurance by referring to and citing the decision in *Chevron v. United States*, according to which an investment, once established, continues to exist until its

---

274. *White Industries Australia Limited v. The Republic of India*, note 246, para. 7.4.5.
275. *White Industries Australia Limited v. The Republic of India*, note 246, para. 7.6.5.
276. *See also Quiborax S.A., Non Metallic Minerals S.A. and Allan Fosk Kaplún v. Plurinational State of Bolivia*, Decision on Jurisdiction, ICSID Case No. ARB/06/2, December 27, 2012, para. 46:

> The Tribunal considers that it is not bound by previous decisions. At the same time, it is of the opinion that it must pay due consideration to earlier decisions of international tribunals. Specifically, it deems that, subject to compelling contrary grounds, it has a duty to adopt solutions established in a series of consistent cases. It further deems that, subject to the specifics of the Treaty and of the circumstances of the actual case, it has a duty to contribute to the harmonious development of investment law, with a view to meeting the legitimate expectations of the community of States and investors towards the certainty of the rule of law.

ultimate disposal.[277] It is noteworthy though that the United States-Ecuador BIT, as the investment protection mechanism applicable to that dispute, does not pose a limitation on the investment definition in the way that the India-Australia BIT does by requiring that an asset must be "invested." Neither does it contain explicit references to respect for state sovereignty, equality, mutual benefit, nondiscrimination and mutual confidence. Regardless of the final practical impact of these differences, their existence alone already calls for a careful consideration. The tribunal in *Mondev v. United States*, the award relied upon by the tribunal in *Chevron v. United States*, noted that its finding relied on a dispute under NAFTA in order to support its reasoning.[278] Before adopting this view, the tribunal in *Chevron v. United States* clearly explained that it had considered and compared the underlying treaties, namely NAFTA and the United States-Ecuador BIT, without identifying any material difference.[279] This operation thus allowed it to rely on such previous decision. Yet, the tribunal in *White Industries v. India* did not dwell on the possible differences arising out of the applicable investment treaties. Despite the criticism, it must be positively noted that the tribunal paid due respect to India's argument that the criteria of the *Salini*-test must be met. As the case was not one taking place under the auspices of ICSID, the *Salini*-test was actually inapplicable. Nevertheless, the tribunal engaged in an analysis of the argument and applied the test even if only for the purpose of effectuating the argument of the defendant.

[b]   ATA v. Jordan

[i]   Case Brief and Investment Definition

The dispute in *ATA v. Jordan*[280] has put forth another approach in characterizing an arbitral award in the context of investments. It arose out of the annulment of an arbitral award in favor of ATA by the Jordanian courts. ATA, a Turkish construction company, entered into a contract with APC, a Jordanian entity that was controlled by Jordan itself, on May 2, 1998 for the construction of a dike at the Dead Sea. The dike was completed and later filled with water, which caused a part of the dike to collapse. This gave rise to a dispute between the parties as to who was responsible for the deficiency,

---

277. *White Industries Australia Limited v. The Republic of India*, note 246, para. 7.6.9 in reference to *Chevron Corporation and Texaco Petroleum Corporation v. The Republic of Ecuador*, Interim Award, UNCITRAL, December 1, 2008, para. 183.
278. *Mondev International Ltd. v. United States of America*, Award, ICSID Case No. ARB(AF)/99/2, October 11, 2002, para. 80: "In the Tribunal's view, once an investment exists, it remains protected by NAFTA even after the enterprise in question may have failed."
279. *Chevron Corporation and Texaco Petroleum Corporation v. The Republic of Ecuador*, note 277, para. 186: "Nor does the Tribunal see any sufficient difference between NAFTA and the BIT to depart from that reasoning. In the present case, the relevant language of the BIT is at least as broad in scope as the NAFTA provisions relied upon by the *Mondev* tribunal for its 'life-span' theory of investment protection."
280. *ATA Construction, Industrial and Trading Company v. The Hashemite Kingdom of Jordan*, Award, ICSID Case No. ARB/08/2, May 18, 2010.

which led APC to begin arbitration proceedings before the International Federation of Consulting Engineers (FIDIC). ATA brought a counterclaim against APC for compensation still due under the contract. The tribunal rendered an award in favor of ATA, dismissing the liability claim by APC and awarding sums of money to ATA. Later, APC successfully turned to the Jordanian Court of Appeal on October 29, 2003, seeking to have the award set aside under the Jordanian Arbitration Law. An appeal to the Jordanian Court of Cassation by ATA remained unsuccessful after the decision on January 16, 2007. Based upon Article 51 of the Jordanian Arbitration Law of 2001, the ruling of the court caused the extinction of the arbitration agreement between ATA and APC. This situation led ATA to commence ICSID arbitration against Jordan on January 14, 2008 based on the Turkey-Jordan BIT of August 2, 1993, which came into force in Jordan on January 23, 2006 and provides the following investment definition:

> 2. (a) The term "investment", in conformity with the hosting Party's laws and regulations, shall include *every kind of asset* in particular, but not exclusively:
> [...]
> (ii) returns reinvested, claims to money or any other rights to legitimate performance having financial value *related to an investment*.

The investment definition of the BIT is once again of a broad nature. A noteworthy feature of it is, however, the requirement that claims to money or any other rights to legitimate performance having financial value must be "related to an investment." Such "association-clause" can be perceived as making a deliberate distinction between an already existent investment and a related right. One could argue that, if a right must merely be related to or associated with an investment, it will not be part of the investment itself; rather, it could remain distinct and could constitute an investment in and of itself. What is related to an investment, is not equated with the investment itself. On the other hand, it remains analytically problematic how that distinction can be stringently pursued, if there is a clear relation between the investment and a right. In other words, if a right is related to an investment, it will not be fully separate from the investment. One could therefore similarly argue that, if a right is related to an investment, it must be considered as forming part of that overall investment. An association-clause read in isolation may thus be perceived as either isolating an original investment from one only relating to it or as incorporating any such related right into the original investment. The wording of this clause from a mere textual perspective remains ambiguous, which is reflected in the conflicting positions of ATA and the tribunal. The tribunal understands the association-clause in such a way that a claim to money or any other right to legitimate performance is to be considered in separation from the original investment and thus as being distinct.[281] ATA, however, suggested that such right must be viewed as forming part of the original investment.[282]

---

281. *ATA Construction, Industrial and Trading Company v. The Hashemite Kingdom of Jordan*, note 280, para. 112: "Article I(2)(a) of the Turkey-Jordan BIT provides that a 'claim to money' or a 'right to financial performance' is a discrete 'investment,' separate from the investment in the dispute which gave rise to it. [...]."
282. *ATA Construction, Industrial and Trading Company v. The Hashemite Kingdom of Jordan*, note 280, para. 69:

Chapter 3: The Protection of Arbitral Awards in the Global Context §3.03[B]

[ii] Tribunal's Conclusion and Analysis

In its finding, the tribunal firstly noted that it lacked jurisdiction *ratione temporis* over those claims by ATA that related to the annulment of the FIDIC award on October 29, 2003. Nevertheless, it concurrently determined that it did have jurisdiction over those claims that resulted from the decision of the Jordanian Court of Cassation on January 16, 2007 and its consequence in extinguishing the arbitration agreement. The tribunal had to decide whether an investment by ATA was treated by Jordan in violation of the provisions contained in the BIT and thereby needed to analyze the nature of the commercial arbitration award as well as that of the underlying arbitration agreement:

> Now, measured by the standards in Saipem, <u>the Final Award</u> at issue in the present arbitration *would be part of an "entire operation" that qualifies as an investment*. Since the first legal confrontation between the parties over the Final Award occurred prior to the entry into force of the Turkey-Jordan BIT, as previously concluded, the Tribunal cannot claim jurisdiction ratione temporis over any issue concerning the annulment of the Final Award.[283]

In clarifying the lack of jurisdiction over the actual handling of the award, the tribunal took the view that, had the BIT been in force previously, it would have been able to assess whether or not Jordan violated protective provisions of the BIT in handling the award. Nevertheless, the tribunal then turned to the arbitration agreement and came to the following conclusion:

> Given that *the right to arbitration is considered a distinct investment*, it follows that the decision of the Jordanian Court of Cassation extinguishing the Arbitration Agreement between the Claimant and APC, occurring as it did after the entry into force of the BIT, is not barred from the Tribunal's jurisdiction ratione temporis and the Tribunal so finds.[284]

The analysis of the tribunal begins by focusing on the nature of the commercial arbitration award, stating that Article 25 ICSID-Convention does not provide a detailed definition, which left it open to the parties to determine the meaning of investments. A subjective approach was thus adopted without entertaining the existent controversy on the issue. The tribunal then turned to Article 1 section 2 of the BIT, noting a clear distinction between a claim to money and the investment which has given rise to it.

> Moreover, the Claimant's investment includes the Final Award itself, which constitutes a claim to money and a right to legitimate performance having financial value related to an investment, for the purposes of Article I(2)(a)(ii). This is consistent with the principle that investments must be examined holistically and not separated into artificial components. Viewing the investment as a whole, the Claimant's legal and contractual rights under the Contract, as enforced in the underlying arbitration and upheld in the Final Award, cannot be separated from the rest of the Claimant's investment in Jordan.

283. *ATA Construction, Industrial and Trading Company v. The Hashemite Kingdom of Jordan*, note 280, para. 115.
284. *ATA Construction, Industrial and Trading Company v. The Hashemite Kingdom of Jordan*, note 280, para. 120.

One does not find any mentioning of the interpretive approach that was adopted by the arbitrators, nor is there recourse to the VCLT. Instead, the decision refers to a previous ruling by another tribunal before jurisdiction over the annulment of the award is denied. The tribunal subsequently focused on the nature of the arbitration agreement by highlighting the text of Article 1 section 2 of the BIT, concluding that such agreement is a distinct investment and thus falls within its jurisdiction. There is, however, no further interpretation of the underlying investment treaty, which is an unfortunate facet of the decision.[285]

The conclusions do not openly clarify the tribunal's position on the nature of arbitral awards. The subsumption under the ruling provided by *Saipem v. Bangladesh*[286] took place due to the claimant's citation of such in a hypothetical manner, which is expressed by the use of the conditional "would." Furthermore, the tribunal did not analyze the cited decision. Had it intended to adopt the ruling, the tribunal, as it ought to be presumed given the involvement of distinguished arbitrators, would have engaged in further examinations. The reference to such award does therefore, and in contrast to other views,[287] not indicate that the tribunal followed such ruling.

A surprising aspect of the reasoning provided in the award is the lack of clarity in the tribunal's own positioning regarding the investment definition. The tribunal itself highlighted that an investment may consist of a "bundle of rights" that may be "inseparable" or "comparatively free-standing" and thus neither adopted the view that it is to be viewed as an entire operation[288] nor saw them as individual positions. Its statement was in this respect ambivalent. Nevertheless, it came to the above-mentioned conclusion that the right to arbitration constitutes a distinct investment with regards to the wording of the BIT. It remains unclear why the tribunal agreed with the understanding that an investment must be viewed at large, while the relevant BIT – as was found by the tribunal – clearly conflicts. In its conclusion, it aligned its view with the provision of the BIT, noting the distinction between the original investment and rights or claims "related" to it. If the right to arbitrate is characterized as being a distinct investment, it is an inevitable consequence to aspire towards a characterization of an arbitral award that arises out of this right to arbitration as its basis.[289] It was

---

285. *See Kaufmann-Kohler*, note 262, p. 156:

> In contrast, it accepted jurisdiction over the extinguishment claim. Surprisingly, without entering into a separate examination of the requirements of an investment under Article 25 of the Convention on the Settlement of Investment Disputes between States and Nationals of Other States (ICSID Convention), the tribunal considered that the arbitration agreement constituted an 'investment' under the BIT.

286. *Saipem S.p.A. v. The Republic of Bangladesh*, Decision on Jurisdiction and Recommendation on Provisional Measures, ICSID Case No. ARB/05/07, March 21, 2007.
287. *Charles Claypoole*, Recent Developments in the Jurisprudence of Investment Arbitration Tribunals, in: The European and Middle Eastern Arbitration Review 2012, pp. 22-27 (p. 23); *Mistelis*, note 249, p. 15.
288. *ATA Construction, Industrial and Trading Company v. The Hashemite Kingdom of Jordan*, note 280, para. 96.
289. *ATA Construction, Industrial and Trading Company v. The Hashemite Kingdom of Jordan*, note 280, para. 116: "The Arbitration Agreement under the Contract served as the basis for the Final Award in the dispute between the Claimant and APC."

Chapter 3: The Protection of Arbitral Awards in the Global Context   §3.03[C]

previously outlined that the tribunal considered the ruling in *Saipem v. Bangladesh*, but neither concurred nor opposed it. The reticency may be based upon the unique fact pattern of the dispute. The Jordanian courts did handle the actual award and set it aside. Nevertheless, the extinction of the entire arbitration agreement due to the court's decision harkens back to Article 51 of the Jordanian Arbitration Law. The relevant connecting line between the arbitration agreement and the award arising out of it was thus comfortably drawn by way of domestic legislation. Unfortunately, this has allowed the tribunal to solely focus on the underlying arbitration agreement rather than the actual award that was rendered. Following the line of arguments provided by the tribunal, one is nevertheless able to predict the outcome of a respective further interpretation. If the arbitration agreement is understood as a distinct investment, the arbitral award arising out of it, and thus being "related to an investment" itself, will equally be understood as a distinct investment with regard to the underlying BIT.

Not only does this analysis once again support the aforementioned conclusion that the tribunal did not follow the view in *Saipem v. Bangladesh*, but it also illustrates that the tribunal interpreted the association-clause in Article 1 section 2 (a) (ii) BIT as encompassing arbitral awards since the BIT apparently so stipulates. With regard to the ambiguous wording of the association-clause, one might find comfort in a clarification of the tribunal's procedure. The text of the relevant provision ("related to") required the tribunal to establish that an overall investment was existent, and that the relevant arbitration agreement was connected to it. Once it had established such connection, it could proceed taking into account the context of the provision, and find that such arbitration agreement must be considered as being a distinct investment. The tribunal therefore *viewed* the arbitration agreement as related to the investment and then *treated* it as a distinct investment pursuant to the underlying BIT. A subjective approach was thus followed in order to determine the scope of the investment definition. Not only does this become clear from the omission of further analysis of requirements eventually posed by Article 25 section 1 ICSID-Convention, but also more explicitly, in the tribunal's clarification that the ICSID-Convention leaves the definition open to the parties.[290]

[C]   Treating Arbitral Awards Like Investments

[1]   Saipem v. Bangladesh

[a]   Case Brief and Investment Definition

The first and thus most prominent dispute that involved the characterization of arbitral awards is *Saipem v. Bangladesh*.[291] Saipem, an Italian construction company, and Petrobangla, a Bangladeshi oil, gas and mineral state corporation entered into a contract on February 14, 1990 for the erection of a pipeline in the north of Bangladesh

---

290. *ATA Construction, Industrial and Trading Company v. The Hashemite Kingdom of Jordan*, note 280, para. 111.
291. *Saipem S.p.A. v. The Republic of Bangladesh*, note 286.

that would carry gas condensate. The project received funds by the International Development Association (IDA) and was sponsored by the World Bank. The contract envisaged April 30, 1991 as the date of completion. However, the project was significantly delayed due to political turmoil that was directed at it. Thus, the operation was extended by one year and to be completed by April 30, 1992. After the project was completed on June 14, 1992, Petrobangla was to release the remaining half of retention money due under the contract against a warranty bond. This warranty bond was provided by Saipem. A dispute then arose between the parties as to whether or not a letter by Petrobangla constituted a call on the warranty bond as well as Petrobangla's failure to pay the remaining sums allegedly agreed upon and to return the warranty bond. Saipem initiated arbitral proceedings before the ICC on June 7, 1993. Petrobangla attempted to challenge the jurisdiction of the arbitral tribunal, which was later rejected. Consequentially, Petrobangla addressed the First Court of the Subordinate Judge of Dhaka on November 16, 1997, seeking the revocation of the tribunal's jurisdiction. Furthermore, it turned to the High Court of Dhaka on November 17, 1997 in order to have the court stay all further proceedings. On November 17, 1997, the Supreme Court of Bangladesh prevented Saipem from further engaging in the ICC arbitration based on an injunction and then later revoked the authority of the tribunal on April 5, 2000. Nevertheless, the tribunal continued its proceedings and issued an award in favor of Saipem on May 9, 2003. Petrobangla addressed the High Court Division of the Supreme Court of Bangladesh in order to have the award set aside. On April 21, 2004, the court ruled that the rendered award was a nullity and thus nonexistent. Saipem then filed a request for arbitration on October 5, 2004 with ICSID based on the Italy-Bangladesh BIT of September 20, 1994. The tribunal thus had to decide, if the award fell under the definition of investments and was to be afforded the protection under the investment treaty. Article 1 of the Italy-Bangladesh BIT defines investments as follows:

> The term "investment" shall be construed to mean *any kind of property invested* before or after the entry into force of this Agreement by a natural or legal person being a national of one Contracting Party in the territory of the other, in conformity with the laws and regulations of the latter.
>
> Without limiting the generality of the foregoing, the term "investment" comprises:
> [...]
>
>   c) credit for sums of money or any right for pledges or services having an economic value *connected with investments*, as well as reinvested income as defined in paragraph 5 hereafter.

This definition adds some limitations to the consideration of any kind of property as an investment. Namely, it provides that property must have been actually invested, and that this must have taken place in conformity with the laws and regulations of the contracting state. Furthermore, the nonexhaustive list clarifies, much as in the Turkey-Jordan BIT, that any right must be connected with investments. The Italy-Bangladesh BIT therefore combines the association-clause and the requirements of the asset being "invested."

[b] Tribunal's Conclusion and Analysis

The tribunal, analyzing the nature of the ICC award, came to the following conclusion in ruling on the character of the arbitral award:

> This said, the rights embodied in the ICC Award were *not created by the Award*, but *arise out of the Contract*. The ICC Award crystallized the parties' rights and obligations under the original contract. *It can thus be left open whether the Award itself qualifies as an investment, since the contract rights which are crystallized by the Award constitute an investment* within Article 1(1)(c) of the BIT.[292]

The tribunal thereby explicitly refrained from characterizing an arbitral award as an investment under Article 25 section 1 ICSID-Convention[293] and later adopted the same position in view of the relevant BIT.[294] Rather, it explained that the award arose out of the underlying contract and thus took the view that in determining the scope of an investment, the entire operation of it deserved consideration, including a possible award arising out of it.[295] Other than in *ATA v. Jordan*, here, the tribunal did not find the association-clause to separate the original investment and the arbitration agreement arising out of it. In clearly refusing to interpret the award as constituting a distinct investment, the tribunal likewise and implicitly refused to qualify the arbitration agreement as such. An explicit analysis was apparently not deemed necessary, given the tribunal's earlier finding.[296] The approach taken by the arbitrators was thus a rather objective one, acting on the assumption that the ICSID-Convention implies some objective criteria as to determine the existence of an investment.

In referring to the arbitration award as a crystallization of the existing contractual rights, the tribunal expressed that it viewed the award as something different from the original investment. The process of crystallization results in the transformation of an aggregate state. The contractual rights that constitute an investment have thus transformed into a new occurrence.[297] It was highlighted by the tribunal though that

---

292. *Saipem S.p.A. v. The Republic of Bangladesh*, note 286, para. 127.
293. *Saipem S.p.A. v. The Republic of Bangladesh*, note 286, para. 113: "The Tribunal agrees with Bangladesh that the rights arising out of the ICC Award arise only *indirectly* from the investment. Indeed, the opposite view would mean that the Award itself does constitute an investment under Article 25(1) of the ICSID Convention, which the Tribunal is not prepared to accept."
294. *Saipem S.p.A. v. The Republic of Bangladesh*, note 286, para. 122: "In the light of the conclusion reached above according to which Saipem made an investment within the meaning of Article 25 of the ICSID Convention, the Tribunal fails to see how the operation at issue could not be considered as a 'kind of property' protected by the BIT."
295. *Saipem S.p.A. v. The Republic of Bangladesh*, note 286, para. 110: "Finally, the Tribunal wishes to emphasize that for the purpose of determining whether there is an investment under Article 25 of the ICSID Convention, it will consider the entire operation. In the present case, the entire or overall operation includes the Contract, the construction itself, the Retention Money, the warranty and the related ICC Arbitration."
296. *Saipem S.p.A. v. The Republic of Bangladesh*, note 286, para. 128: "Having reached this conclusion, the Tribunal does not need to make a final ruling on Saipem's additional argument that the arbitration agreement contained in the Contract constitutes a 'right of a financial nature accruing by law or by contract' within Article 1(1)(e) of the BIT (Tr. J. II 58:20-23)."
297. *Saipem S.p.A. v. The Republic of Bangladesh*, note 286, para. 113, which supports this understanding as the tribunal itself explains that the rights arising out of the award arise only

this new occurrence remained in close connection with the original investment, as it considered it to still form part of the overall operation that is found to be an investment. According to this reasoning, the arbitral award has an intermediary character. On the one hand, it does not remain part of the original investment. On the other hand, it is the product of a transformation process that has created something new. This new occurrence does not in itself constitute an investment. Rather, it remains closely linked to the underlying contract as its origin which does constitute an investment. As such, the tribunal found Saipem's residual rights under the contract to have been expropriated as the Supreme Court declared the arbitral award a nullity. The award was thus not treated as an investment, but like an investment.

In its decision, the tribunal pointed out that the interpretation of the BIT as well as of the ICSID-Convention was governed by international law. Bangladesh did, however, raise the argument that the use of the terms "any kind of property" as opposed to the use of the word "asset" implied that the BIT must be interpreted according to the law of Bangladesh, as this reference to property is a notion well known under its laws. In dealing with this argument, the tribunal engaged in an analysis of other BITs entered into by Bangladesh and did find the wording of the Italy-Bangladesh BIT to be an exceptional case. Nevertheless, it correctly pointed out the general rule that it was bound to interpret treaties on the basis of international law. First, the tribunal turned to Article 25 ICSID-Convention in order to establish whether an investment is in existence and thus allowing itself to assume jurisdiction under the applicable rules of ICSID. The tribunal then interestingly deployed the *Salini*-criteria in the form of a strict test in order to determine whether or not an investment is at hand. While this approach was criticized by one of the participating arbitrators,[298] the tribunal nevertheless proceeded in applying the respective criteria rigidly and came to the result that Saipem had made an investment in Bangladesh for the purposes of Article 25 section 1 ICSID-Convention.

Second, the tribunal turned to the relevant provision of the BIT and stated that it failed to see how the operation of Saipem could not be considered protected like an investment under the BIT.[299] Despite the broad wording of the BIT, the tribunal proceeded in its decision without further interpretation of the BIT. It essentially synchronized the requirements of the ICSID-Convention with those of the BIT. While the practical result would have remained the same, a more detailed explanation on this issue would have been desirable. Furthermore, the decision then characterizes the ICC

---

indirectly from the investment; *see also Frontier Petroleum Services Ltd. v. The Czech Republic*, Final Award, UNCITRAL, November 12, 2010, para. 231: "This Tribunal accepts that Claimant's original investment consisted of the payments made to MA and Davidová between 18 April 2001 and 14 August 2001, which were transformed into an entitlement to a first secured charge in the Final Award."

298. *Schreuer*, note 210, Art. 25, para. 171: "The development in practice from a descriptive list of typical features towards a set of mandatory legal requirements is unfortunate. The First Edition of this Commentary cannot serve as authority for this development."

299. *Saipem S.p.A. v. The Republic of Bangladesh*, note 286, para. 122: "In the light of the conclusion reached above according to which Saipem made an investment within the meaning of Article 25 of the ICSID Convention, the Tribunal fails to see how the operation at issue could not be considered as a 'kind of property' protected by the BIT."

award as a crystallization of the original investment in the above-mentioned conclusion, but stating that further interpretation is not required as the underlying operation constitutes an investment in either case. Thereby, the tribunal did not have to analyze Saipem's argument that the arbitration agreement may constitute an investment. Concerning the relevance of previous arbitral decisions, the tribunal pointed out that it did not feel bound by them, but nevertheless believed that they deserved due consideration in order to contribute to the harmonious development of international investment law.[300]

In reaching this conclusion and particularly in characterizing in more detail the nature of an arbitration award, the tribunal has made a leap forward into still unexplored territory. The actual interpretive process at times remains intransparent on its face as to the methods applied and the argumentation that is carried out in abstract rather than in connection with the respective treaty provisions. Nevertheless, the tribunal thereby has made a significant contribution to the understanding of arbitral awards. Regardless of individual perceptions, *Saipem v. Bangladesh* has taken a bold step forward that deserves acknowledgment by way of consideration.

[2] **Frontier Petroleum Services v. Czech Republic**

In *Frontier Petroleum Services v. Czech Republic*,[301] the dispute once again arose out of the handling of a commercial arbitration award by state courts. Frontier Petroleum Services, a Canadian company, entered into a joint venture agreement with Moravan-Aeroplanes, a.s., a Czech company, to manufacture aircraft. Frontier Petroleum Services and Moravan-Aeroplanes signed a unanimous shareholder agreement on August 8, 2001. This agreement determined that Frontier Petroleum Services was to finance the purchase of LET, a.s., a Czech state-owned aircraft manufacturing company that had become bankrupt, by Moravan-Aeroplanes. The purchased assets were then supposed to be transferred to Letecké Závody, a.s., a company under the laws of the Czech Republic that was set up for the purpose of carrying out the joint venture. Frontier Petroleum Services later initiated civil and criminal proceedings against Moravan-Aeroplanes after it had allegedly not complied with various provisions of the unanimous shareholder agreement. Also, it successfully obtained an arbitration award against Moravan-Aeroplanes as well as Letecké Závody in arbitral proceedings held in Stockholm. Seeking enforcement, Frontier Petroleum Services turned to the Czech judiciary, which refused recognition and enforcement. Subsequently, it initiated investment arbitration against the Czech Republic before the Permanent Court of Arbitration (PCA) in The Hague based on the Canada-Czech Republic BIT of November 15, 1990. The tribunal was to determine whether Frontier Petroleum Services had made an investment and if there had been measures taken by the Czech courts that affected the investment. Article 1 of the BIT provides the following investment definition:

---

300. *Saipem S.p.A. v. The Republic of Bangladesh*, note 286, para. 67.
301. *Frontier Petroleum Services Ltd. v. The Czech Republic*, note 297.

(a) the term "investment" means *any kind of asset* held or invested either directly, or indirectly through an investor of a third State, by an investor of one Contracting Party in the territory of the other Contracting Party in accordance with the latter's laws and, in particular, through not exclusively, includes:
[...]
(iii) *claims to money, and claims to performance* under contract having financial value;
[...]
Any change in the form of an investment does not affect its character as an investment.

The initial definition of investments is equally broad as the ones that have already been analyzed. A noteworthy feature, however, is the incorporation of a clause, according to which a change in the form of an investment does not affect its character as an investment. This clause may be termed "transformation-clause." It is particularly intriguing for the characterization of arbitral awards. It proved helpful to the tribunal which came to the following conclusion regarding the nature of the arbitral award that was neither recognized nor enforced by the Czech judiciary:

This Tribunal accepts that Claimant's *original investment* consisted of the payments made to MA and Davidová between 18 April 2001 and 14 August 2001, which *were transformed into an entitlement to a first secured charge in the Final Award*. The Tribunal also notes that Article 1(a) of the BIT provides that "[a]ny change in the form of an investment does not affect its character as an investment". Accordingly, by refusing to recognise and enforce the Final Award in its entirety, the Tribunal accepts that Respondent could be said *to have affected the management, use, enjoyment, or disposal by Claimant of what remained of its original investment.*[302]

Much like in *Saipem v. Bangladesh*, which is a case that is relied upon by Frontier Petroleum Services and thus considered in the arbitration,[303] the tribunal considered the arbitral award to constitute a transformation of an original investment. It did, however, not equally describe the transformation process as a crystallization. The tribunal asserted that the award represented a new occurrence that did remain closely connected to the original investment. This analysis was then verified by considering the transformation-clause contained in the BIT. The mere wording of the clause assured the tribunal that both state parties to the BIT have objectively expressed their intentions of extending the protection to transformed versions of original investments. Other than in the Italy-Bangladesh BIT relevant to the dispute in *Saipem v. Bangladesh*, the arbitrators were able to avail themselves of the transformation-clause provided by the Canada-Czech Republic BIT in order to reach their decision. In the award, one does, however, neither find a reference to the provisions of the VCLT, nor is there actual recourse to it. In light of the object and purpose of the treaty, the tribunal could have found that the transformation-clause serves as a vehicle to extend investment protection for the promotion of investments. Such intention may be derived from the BIT's

---

302. *Frontier Petroleum Services Ltd. v. The Czech Republic*, note 297, para. 231.
303. *Frontier Petroleum Services Ltd. v. The Czech Republic*, note 297, para. 225.

Chapter 3: The Protection of Arbitral Awards in the Global Context   §3.03[C]

preamble, according to which the promotion and protection of investments for the purpose of economic cooperation is to be fostered. Recourse to the object and purpose might not have changed the tribunal's finding; however, it would have provided additional authority in line with the applicable VCLT, refining the tribunal's analysis.

[3]   **Romak v. Uzbekistan**

Another prominent case that involves similar issues of interpretation is the dispute in *Romak v. Uzbekistan*.[304] After the dissolution of the Soviet Union, Uzbekistan had an interest in the import of grain into its country. The Swiss cereal trading company Romak S.A. engaged in trade relations with three Uzbek companies, namely Uzkhleboproduct, a state institution responsible for cereal production, supply and distribution, Uzdon, later transformed into a stock corporation, and Odil, a private company specialized in the trading of wheat. Uzkhleboproduct and Odil entered into a supply contract on October 2, 1995 under which Odil agreed to supply 450,000 tons of wheat at a fixed price to Uzkhleboproduct. However, Odil was unable to deliver the full amount. Uzkhleboproduct and Uzdon then entered into a commission agreement, clarifying the involvement of and payments to a foreign company. In the summer of 1996, Romak, Odil, Uzdon and Uzkhleboproduct signed an agreement pursuant to which Romak was to deliver the remaining amount of 50,000 tons of wheat to Uzkhleboproduct. Subsequently, and following a letter of guarantee, Romak, Uzdon and Uzkhleboproduct signed a protocol of intention, aiming at establishing a long-term commercial cooperation between Romak and Uzkhleboproduct. This cooperation was to encompass the supply of recommendations and data to Uzkhleboproduct with regards to the world's grain stocks and preferential treatment of Romak in future wheat imports into Uzbekistan. Romak commenced deliveries and submitted invoices seeking compensation from Uzkhleboproduct. The Chief Consultant of the Office of the President of Uzbekistan noted in return that the supply agreement could not be considered valid and that Romak's performance was not documented. Rather, he referred Romak to Odil. Romak, however, unsuccessfully continued to seek remuneration from Uzkhleboproduct and Uzdon. As a consequence, Romak began arbitral proceedings against Uzdon under the auspices of the Grain and Feed Trade Association (GAFTA) and secured an award in its favor on August 22, 1997. Uzdon appealed the award before GAFTA and also sought to challenge it before the High Court of Justice in London, which was rejected. Romak then turned to the Commercial Court of Tashkent to have the award enforced. Nevertheless, the Uzbek court refused enforcement, a decision later confirmed by the Commercial Court of Tashkent on November 24, 2000. Romak then initiated arbitral proceedings against Uzbekistan under the UNCITRAL rules before the PCA in The Hague on the basis of the Switzerland-Uzbekistan BIT of April 16, 1993. In dispute, among other issues, was the question of whether or not

---

304. *Romak S.A. (Switzerland) v. The Republic of Uzbekistan*, Award, PCA Case No. AA280, November 26, 2009.

Romak had made an investment in Uzbekistan. Article 1 section 2 of the BIT provides as follows:

> (2) Le terme «investissements» englobe *toutes les catégories d'avoirs* et en particulier:
> [...]
> (c) les créances monétaires et droits à toute prestation ayant une valeur économique.

The definition of investments is thus broader than in other treaties previously analyzed. There is no limitation to assets having to be "invested" or that they must have been invested in accordance with domestic laws. Neither does one find an association- or transformation-clause. Once again, the tribunal was faced with the pivotal question of how to characterize an arbitral award. In order for the Uzbek judiciary's actions to constitute a violation of treaty provisions, they had to concern the award as an asset falling under the definition of investments provided by the BIT. The tribunal came to the following conclusion:

> On the basis of the allegations made and the evidence produced by the Parties in the present arbitration, the Arbitral Tribunal has come to the conclusion that the *GAFTA Award is so inextricably linked to the Romak Supply Agreement* that any determination as to whether Romak holds and investment under the BIT cannot be made *without reference to the entire economic transaction* that is the subject of these arbitral proceedings. The *GAFTA Award merely constitutes the embodiment of Romak's contractual rights* (as determined by the GAFTA Arbitral Tribunal) stemming from the wheat supply transaction entered into by Romak. *If the underlying transaction is not an investment within the meaning of the BIT, the mere embodiment or crystallization of rights arising thereunder in an arbitral award cannot transform it into an investment.*[305]

This conclusion was later adopted in the above-mentioned dispute *White Industries v. India*.[306] The present award does, however, allow a deeper insight into the interpretive approach that was taken by the tribunal in coming to its conclusion. Essentially, the tribunal highlighted the continuous character of the arbitral award in that it is an embodiment of contractual rights. If those rights constitute an investment, the award would consequentially constitute a continuation of such. The tribunal's approach is supported by the broad definition provided by the BIT. It was thus crucial for the tribunal to distinguish between mere commercial transactions and investments.

The tribunal rightfully began its analysis by invoking the VCLT. Although Uzbekistan only acceded to it on July 12, 1995 and the applicable BIT was concluded on April 16, 1993, the VCLT still remains applicable based upon its customary international law origin. This was highlighted by the tribunal by way of reference to decisions by the ICJ. It then continued to cite Articles 31 and 32 VCLT before establishing that it was guided by the ordinary-meaning-rule as well as the context and object and purpose of the BIT. In dispute was particularly the role of the nonexhaustive list of possible investments. Romak argued that the definition of investments ("toutes

---

305. *Romak S.A. (Switzerland) v. The Republic of Uzbekistan*, note 304, para. 211.
306. *White Industries Australia Limited v. The Republic of India*, note 246.

les catégories d'avoirs") is an especially broad one and that, with regard to the wording in the list ("les créances monétaires et droits à toute prestation ayant une valeur économique"), an arbitral award would constitute an investment. In this regard, Romak sought a literal approach from the tribunal.[307] Uzbekistan, on the other hand, countered that the enumeration may only be seen in connection with an already-existing investment and may thus not establish jurisdiction in an isolated manner.[308] The tribunal clarifies that the literal approach envisaged by Romak is to be repudiated, as:

> such literal application of the terms of the BIT effectively ignores the second sentence of Article 31(1) of the Vienna Convention, which requires the interpreter to take into account, together with the "ordinary meaning" of the terms of the treaty, their context and the object and purpose of the treaty.[309]

Thereby, the tribunal clearly acted in compliance with the provisions of Article 31 VCLT. Furthermore, it highlighted that such a literal approach would essentially elevate international investment arbitration to a new level, establishing a new instance for reviewing the judiciaries' treatment of arbitral awards.[310] In reference to the VCLT and the object and purpose of the BIT, the tribunal stated that the meaning of investments still remains "ambiguous or obscure," and that it must therefore carve out a more contoured understanding of the term.[311] Assistance was then sought in recourse to previous arbitral findings, which the tribunal thoroughly analyzed. It explained that it was not bound to follow or cite previous arbitral decisions, although the claimant and respondent alike have made various references to such. Unlike other tribunals,[312] it did not find itself to be entrusted with the task of making a contribution to the harmonious development of arbitral jurisprudence. It rather intended to use previous decisions in order to extract rules of law in order to explain its own reasoning.[313] As a consequence, one finds the tribunal resorting to the interpretive canons of the VCLT in its attempt to colorize the investment definition. The tribunal then concluded that an investment, for the purposes of the Switzerland-Uzbekistan BIT, involved a contribution over a certain period of time involving some risk, which it derived from the use of the words "territory" and "returns" throughout the BIT. These characteristics, according to the tribunal, form an inherent part of the term "investment" regardless of which arbitral mechanism is used to solve a dispute.[314] After providing this concretion, the arbitrators turned to the question of whether or not the award could constitute an investment. Due to the tribunal's perception of not being entrusted with making a contribution to arbitral jurisprudence, it placed emphasis on the individual facts of the dispute. As

---

307. *Romak S.A. (Switzerland) v. The Republic of Uzbekistan*, note 304, para. 178.
308. *Romak S.A. (Switzerland) v. The Republic of Uzbekistan*, note 304, para. 175.
309. *Romak S.A. (Switzerland) v. The Republic of Uzbekistan*, note 304, para. 181.
310. *Romak S.A. (Switzerland) v. The Republic of Uzbekistan*, note 304, para. 186.
311. *Romak S.A. (Switzerland) v. The Republic of Uzbekistan*, note 304, paras. 189 et seq.
312. See *East Kalimantan v. PT Kaltim Prima Coal and others*, Award on Jurisdiction, ICSID Case No. ARB/07/3, December 28, 2009, para. 160; *AES Corporation v. The Argentine Republic*, Decision on Jurisdiction, ICSID Case No. ARB/02/17, April 26, 2005, para. 30.
313. *Romak S.A. (Switzerland) v. The Republic of Uzbekistan*, note 304, para. 171.
314. *Romak S.A. (Switzerland) v. The Republic of Uzbekistan*, note 304, paras. 180 and 207.

cited above, it found the award to be linked to the underlying economic transaction that had given rise to the arbitration in the first place. In the course of its further analysis, the tribunal did not find the transactions between Romak and Uzbekistan to constitute an investment and therefore neither found the award to be a continuation of such. Jurisdiction was negated and Romak thus did not succeed in its effort to seek compensation from Uzbekistan.

[D] An Antithesis: *GEA v. Ukraine*

After all relevant cases have been examined that in some form support the understanding of arbitral awards as or like investments, it is necessary, especially for the sake of a balanced contemplation, to turn the attention to the opposite side of the spectrum. This will reveal that the findings in previous decisions are by no means uncontroversial. This is best illustrated by considering an arbitral decision that will pave the way for carving out valuable counter-arguments to the existing reasoning. The relevant decision is *GEA v. Ukraine*.[315]

[1] Case Brief and Investment Definition

The German company Klöckner & Co. AG entered into an agreement with the Ukranian *kombinat* Oriana on December 13, 1995. Such *kombinat* has a corporate structure that is characterized by the centralization of multiple businesses that share a similar or identical line of production. The agreement involved the delivery of 200,000 tons of naphtha fuel that was to be converted by Oriana. The rights of Klöckner & Co. AG later merged into GEA due to a series of corporate restructurings. For the sake of simplicity, any company that was later merged into GEA will be referred to as GEA. After an inspector, entrusted with the supervision of the plant of Oriana, was shot in his knee, investigations revealed that Oriana had not produced as much as it should have under the agreement. This shortage led to consultations between representatives of the companies involved as well as between the German and Ukrainian government. Simultaneously, bankruptcy proceedings were initiated against Oriana. Following the consultations, Oriana signed a settlement agreement, admitting the shortage in its delivery. The agreement contained an arbitration clause, referring any dispute arising out of it to a tribunal operating under the ICC Rules. Later, Oriana entered into another agreement with a company that was later merged into GEA, pursuant to which it agreed to pay a minimum amount of USD 27.6 million to GEA. Once again, the agreement contained a similar arbitration clause. As full payment could not be obtained from Oriana, GEA commenced arbitral proceedings in Vienna on June 27, 2001 which resulted in an award rendered on November 25, 2002 in favor of GEA in the amount of USD 30.4 million. GEA turned to the Ukranian judiciary to have the award recognized and enforced against Oriana. However, on November 30, 2005 the Superior Commercial Court of Ukraine dismissed a cassation complaint and ultimately rejected an appeal

---

315. *GEA Group Aktiengesellschaft v. Ukraine*, Award, ICSID Case No. ARB/08/16, March 31, 2011.

by GEA. As a consequence, on October 24, 2008, GEA initiated arbitral proceedings with ICSID against Ukraine, claiming that it had made an investment in Ukraine in the form of capital loans to Oriana and that Ukraine violated the underlying Germany-Ukraine BIT of February 15, 1993. Article 1 of the BIT provides the following investment definition:

> For purposes of this agreement
> 1) the term "investments" means *assets of any kind*, in particular
>   a) movable and immovable property and other rights in rem such as mortgages and security interests;
>   b) equity interests and other stakes in companies;
>   c) claims to funds used to create material or immaterial values and claims to performances having such value;
>   d) intellectual property rights such as, in particular, copyrights, patents, utility models, industrial designs and models, trademarks, trade names, company and business secrets, technological processes, know-how and goodwill;
>   e) rights to the exercise of an economic activity including rights to the search for and the exploration, extraction and utilisation of natural resources on the basis of statutory provisions or granted under an agreement concluded in accordance with such statutory provisions.
>   *Any change to the form in which assets are invested shall not affect their nature as investments.*

The definition of investments contained therein is in line with those definitions found in BITs that were previously analyzed. It remains broad ("assets of any kind") and includes a nonexhaustive list of possible investments. A noteworthy feature of it is once again the incorporation of a transformation-clause.

[2] Tribunal's Conclusion and Analysis

GEA addressed the tribunal, claiming that the dispute at hand would refer to three alleged forms of investments: first, the initial conversion contract, second, the settlement and repayment agreements and third, the ICC award. The tribunal found the conversion contract to fall within the investment definition of both, the BIT and Article 25 section 1 ICSID-Convention, and thus saw an investment made by GEA in Ukraine. In contrast to this finding, the tribunal then turned to the settlement and repayment agreements and concluded that both did not constitute investments under the BIT or Article 25 section 1 ICSID-Convention. With regard to the ICC award, the decision contains the following result:

> Whether tested against the criteria of Article 1 of the BIT or Article 25 of the ICSID Convention, the ICC Award – in and of itself – *cannot constitute an "investment"*. Properly analysed, it is a legal instrument, which provides for the disposition of rights and obligations arising out of the Settlement Agreement and Repayment Agreement (neither of which was itself an "investment" – see 154 – 157 above).[316]

---

316. *GEA Group Aktiengesellschaft v. Ukraine*, note 315, para. 161.

And further:

> Even if – arguendo – the Settlement Agreement and Repayment Agreement could somehow be characterised as "investments", or the *ICC Award could be characterised as directly arising out of the Conversion Contract or the Products*, the Tribunal considers that the fact that the *Award rules upon rights and obligations arising out of an investment does not equate the Award with the investment itself.* In the Tribunal's view, the two *remain analytically distinct*, and the Award itself involves no contribution to, or relevant economic activity within, Ukraine such as to fall – itself – within the scope of Article 1(1) of the BIT or (if needed) Article 25 of the ICSID Convention. For the same reason, the Settlement Agreement and Repayment Agreement, as well as the Award, cannot be considered as falling within the terminal proviso of Article 1 of the BIT ("Any change to the form in which assets are invested shall not affect their nature as investments").[317]

Recalling the findings that were previously examined, the conclusion by the tribunal is surprising. It is clearly highlighted that, even if the award would directly arise out of the overall investment, this would not equate the award with the investment itself. Then, the tribunal interestingly stated that the award and the investment remained "analytically distinct." This outcome deserves special attention, as it raises an entirely new perspective regarding the qualification of arbitral awards.

[a]   Interpretive Approach

The arbitral award rendered by the tribunal does not contain a reference to the VCLT. This makes it especially difficult to assess which interpretive methods the tribunal has applied in order to arrive at its conclusion. Once again, the dispute raises the question, if Article 25 section 1 ICSID-Convention requires an objective approach in defining investments or if this is left to the parties by way of their individual BIT. GEA naturally instructed the tribunal to only refer to the BIT and thus to adopt a subjective investment definition, trying to avoid the application of the *double keyhole approach*. Ukraine, on the other hand, suggested that Article 25 section 1 ICSID-Convention contains objective criteria that are to be met regardless of the relevant BIT provisions. The tribunal engaged in a broader analysis of the divide between both positions. It referred to previous cases in describing the objective criteria that have been considered as forming part of the ICSID-Convention[318] as well as to a supposedly inherent meaning regardless of the applicable arbitration mechanism.[319] Furthermore, it cited a prominent finding,

---

317. *GEA Group Aktiengesellschaft v. Ukraine*, note 315, para. 162.
318. *GEA Group Aktiengesellschaft v. Ukraine*, note 315, paras. 139 and 140 in referring to *Patrick Mitchell v. The Democratic Republic of Congo*, Decision on the Application for Annulment of the Award, ICSID Case No. ARB/99/7, November 1, 2006, para. 31 as well as *Phoenix Action, Ltd. v. The Czech Republic*, Award, ICSID Case No. ARB/06/5, April 15, 2009, para. 96.
319. *GEA Group Aktiengesellschaft v. Ukraine*, note 315, para. 141: "However, it is not so much the term 'investment' in the ICSID Convention than the term 'investment' *per se* that is often considered as having an objective meaning in itself, whether it is mentioned in the ICSID Convention or in a BIT.", referring to *Romak S.A. (Switzerland) v. The Republic of Uzbekistan*, note 304, paras. 180 and 207.

Chapter 3: The Protection of Arbitral Awards in the Global Context   §3.03[D]

supporting a subjective approach in determining the characteristics of investments.[320] However, the tribunal then noted that the controversy was one that did not have to be resolved for the purpose of the present dispute as all approaches lead to an identical result. Whether tested against objective criteria of investment derived from Article 25 section 1 ICSID-Convention or subjective ones based upon agreement, the tribunal found an investment by the claimant. Nevertheless, the arbitrators pointed out that they had considered both positions thoroughly out of "an abundance of caution."[321] Hereby, the tribunal implicitly expressed its awareness of how significant the outcome of an investment arbitration may be. Nevertheless, omitting a clarification on the divide between objective and subjective approaches was a move that was later criticized as a failure to make a contribution to resolving the ongoing issue.[322]

The decision then makes an interesting and noteworthy observation. In finding that the conversion contract constitutes an investment in terms of the BIT, the tribunal explicitly stated that an investment operation must be viewed in its broader context and relies on the transformation-clause as evident support.[323] The award, at least with regard to the conversion contract, was based upon the unity of investments, taking into account the broad scope of most investment operations. In the following, also under Article 25 section 1 ICSID-Convention, the conversion contract was found to be an investment as it did not fail to fulfill the objective requirements of providing a contribution over some time and involving some risk. In contrast to this conclusion, the tribunal then turned to the settlement and repayment agreements and highlighted that both do not constitute investments under the BIT as well as under Article 25 section 1 ICSID-Convention:

> As legal acts they are *not the same as the investment* in Ukraine itself.[324]

GEA argued that the settlement agreement confirmed that it held valid claims against Oriana, while the repayment agreement quantified these claims. Ukraine responded by emphasizing that neither agreement created rights, a position the tribunal agrees with.[325] Because these agreements constitute legal acts and based upon the understanding that they did not create any rights but rather determined transactional modalities, the tribunal did not further consider the unity of investments. Then, the focus shifted to the ICC award and its qualification as an investment, as claimed by GEA. In its refusal to accept such understanding, the tribunal explained that neither the BIT nor Article 25 section 1 ICSID-Convention would allow for an arbitral award in and of itself to constitute an investment. As far as Article 25 section 1 ICSID-Convention is concerned, this finding complies with that of the tribunal in *Saipem v. Bangladesh*. The

---

320. *GEA Group Aktiengesellschaft v. Ukraine*, note 315, para. 142 in reference to *Biwater Gauff (Tanzania) Ltd. v. United Republic of Tanzania*, Award, ICSID Case No. ARB/05/22, July 24, 2008, paras. 312-316.
321. *GEA Group Aktiengesellschaft v. Ukraine*, note 315, para. 143.
322. Joshua Fellenbaum, GEA v. Ukraine and the Battle of Treaty Interpretation Principles Over the Salini Test, in: Arbitration International 2011, Vol. 27 No. 2, pp. 249-266 (p. 266).
323. *GEA Group Aktiengesellschaft v. Ukraine*, note 315, para. 149.
324. *GEA Group Aktiengesellschaft v. Ukraine*, note 315, para. 157.
325. *GEA Group Aktiengesellschaft v. Ukraine*, note 315, para. 156.

award, however, does not grant deeper insights into which interpretive measures have led to this conclusion. This is an unfortunate facet, especially as the tribunal itself describes its conducted analysis as "proper."[326]

A fundamental difference between the decision at hand and that in *Saipem v. Bangladesh* lies in the assessment of the relationship between an award and the underlying original investment. The tribunal in *Saipem v. Bangladesh* refrained from definitely deciding, whether the award would qualify as an investment under the BIT due to the finding that the award crystallized rights of the contract that qualified as an investment. As a consequence, the award was treated not as an investment, but like an investment. Considering the tribunal's emphasis on viewing the investment in its entirety, this outcome is a logical consequence. Likewise, the tribunal in *GEA v. Ukraine* departed from the same understanding, although only to a much more limited extent. Equating the award with the investment is an approach that the tribunal was explicitly not prepared to accept. However, it highlighted an analytical distinction that must be made between the award and the investment. This determination embodies the core difference between the decisions and significantly challenges previous findings. The ICC award was not viewed as forming part of the entire operation that may qualify as an investment. Once again, one does not find further information on what grounds the tribunal was drawing this clear distinguishing line. Perhaps, it deemed the analytical distinction to have been obvious. Interestingly, it relied on the transformation-clause to support its finding that the award did not fall under the definition of an investment. This suggests that the tribunal did not find an arbitral award to be a change in the form in which assets are invested. Alternatively, another principle may have dominated the analysis. This principle must have been of such major importance that it sufficed to trump the transformation-clause. In awareness of its distinctive finding, the tribunal directly addressed the decision in *Saipem v. Bangladesh*, explaining its difficulty in following the argumentation therein provided by the arbitrators.[327] The reasoning of the tribunal in *GEA v. Ukraine* poses some challenging and intriguing points to the previous principal arguments that were put forward in treating arbitral awards as or like investments. Regardless of whether or not its approach is followed or rejected,[328] the decision contributes much to the controversy. Most pressing, though, is the question of what has led the tribunal to see a clear analytical distinction between the original investment and the award.

---

326. *GEA Group Aktiengesellschaft v. Ukraine*, note 315, para. 161.
327. *GEA Group Aktiengesellschaft v. Ukraine*, note 315, para. 163:

> It may be noted that in the Decision on Jurisdiction in Saipem S.p.A. v. The People's Republic of Bangladesh (a case heavily relied upon by the Claimant), the Tribunal made statements that are difficult to reconcile, *i.e.*, that the ICC arbitration is part of the investment (under the heading: "Has Saipem made an investment under Article 25 of the ICSID Convention?"); that the ICC award is not part of the investment (under the heading "Does the dispute arise directly out of the Investment?"); and that it is unnecessary to decide whether the ICC award is part of the investment (under the heading "Jurisdictional objections under the BIT").

328. *See* e.g. *White Industries Australia Limited v. Republic of India*, note 246, para. 7.6.8:

[b] The Analytical Distinction

The clear distinction between the investment and the award is unfortunately not further elaborated upon by the tribunal. Nevertheless, some information may be derived from the approach. First, viewing an investment in its entirety does not necessarily apply to an award that has arisen out of an investment. Second, an award was not considered to constitute a change in the form of an investment. Third, in light of the tribunal's finding on the settlement and repayment agreement, legal acts are considered to be distinct from investments. These considerations mark the pillars of the tribunal's reasoning. In order to counter the continuous reliance on viewing investments in their entirety as was previously done by other tribunals, another equally important principle must have led the analysis. The tribunal pointed out that legal acts may be viewed in isolation from an underlying investment activity.[329] Furthermore, an arbitral award was characterized as a legal instrument.[330] This distinction between the arbitral award and the underlying business activity brings to mind a principle that is well established in international commercial arbitration. It reminds of the doctrine of separability.

[i] Separability in International Commercial Arbitration

The doctrine of separability is a classic feature of international commercial arbitration. It acts on the assumption that a contract must be viewed in separation from an agreement to arbitrate. Its French name, "l'autonomie de la clause compromissoire," may in this regard be more illustrative. It is not so much a principle of theoretical logic[331] than of practical necessity. The doctrine's *raison d'être* mostly shines when put into practical context: typically, an agreement to arbitrate will form part of a commercial contract, which will refer all disputes arising out of it to arbitration. One may then imagine a dispute concerning the invalidity of such contract. While the contract envisages to grant jurisdiction to an arbitral tribunal, the alleged invalidity of the contract could encompass the arbitration agreement as well. As a consequence, the dispute could no longer be referred to arbitration, but rather to a domestic court. These circumstances lead to a paradox. In this scenario of conflict, recourse to arbitration may

---

The Tribunal considers that the conclusion expressed by the GEA Tribunal represents an incorrect departure from the developing jurisprudence on the treatment of arbitral awards to the effect that awards made by tribunals arising out of disputes concerning "investments" made by "investors" under BITs represent a continuation or transformation of the original investment.

329. *GEA Group Aktiengesellschaft v. Ukraine*, note 315, para. 157.
330. *GEA Group Aktiengesellschaft v. Ukraine*, note 315, para. 161: "Properly analyzed, it (the award) is a legal instrument [...]".
331. George A. Berman, The "Gateway" Problem in International Commercial Arbitration, in: The Yale Journal of International Law 2012, Vol. 37, pp. 1-50 (p. 23): "Accordingly, separability's distinction between the main contract and the arbitration clause, while far from logically compelling, exerts a strong intuitive appeal."

be particularly important.[332] However, no tribunal would be able to derive jurisdiction from an arbitration agreement that forms part of a contract that is invalid. At this point, it is the doctrine of separability that steps in to draw a theoretical distinction between the two with an immensely powerful practical impact. The autonomous arbitration clause will survive the invalidity or termination of the contract and thus allow a tribunal to rule on its own jurisdiction and eventually conduct arbitral proceedings. The doctrine originates from interpreting the arbitration agreement as an agreement on its own, intending to submit all disputes to an arbitral tribunal, including one about the possible invalidity of a contract.[333] The decision to opt for arbitration is a powerful one and thereby receives broad protection. The doctrine of separability is said to foster parties' confidence in international arbitration as a proper means to resolve disputes.[334] It is broadly applied[335] and has been codified in a number of arbitration rules.[336]

[ii]   Separability in International Investment Arbitration

Regardless of the doctrine of separability being applicable in international commercial arbitration, its theoretical approach to the arbitration agreement is only adoptable for the purpose of the current analysis, if it has somehow found its way into international investment arbitration as well. In the context of analyzing Articles 32 and 41 ICSID-

---

332. *Alan Redfern/Martin Hunter*, Law and Practice of International Commercial Arbitration, 4th ed. 2004, p. 162.
333. *Stephen Schwebel*, International Arbitration: Three Salient Problems, 1987, p. 3.
334. *Berman*, note 331, p. 22.
335. *See Harbour Assurance Co. Ltd. v. Kansa General International Insurance Co. Ltd.*, (1992) 1 Lloyd's L.Rep. 81; *see also Prima Paint Corp. v. Flood & Conklin Mfg. Co.*, 388 U.S. 395 (1967).
336. *See* Art. 23 sec. 1 UNCITRAL Arbitration Rules (2010):

> The arbitral tribunal shall have the power to rule on its own jurisdiction, including any objections with respect to the existence or validity of the arbitration agreement. For that purpose, an arbitration clause that forms part of a contract shall be treated as an agreement independent of the other terms of the contract. A decision by the arbitral tribunal that the contract is null shall not entail automatically the invalidity of the arbitration clause.

> *see also* Art. 25 sec. 2 SIAC Rules (2013):

> The Tribunal shall have the power to rule on its own jurisdiction, including any objections with respect to the existence, termination or validity of the arbitration agreement. For that purpose, an arbitration agreement which forms part of a contract shall be treated as an agreement independent of the other terms of the contract. A decision by the Tribunal that the contract is null and void shall not entail *ipso jure* the invalidity of the arbitration agreement.

> *see also* Art. 23 sec. 1 DIFC-LCIA Rules (2008):

> The Arbitral Tribunal shall have the power to rule on its own jurisdiction, including any objection to the initial or continuing existence, validity or effectiveness of the Arbitration Agreement. For that purpose, an arbitration clause which forms or was intended to form part of another agreement shall be treated as an arbitration agreement independent of that other agreement. A decision by the Arbitral Tribunal that such other agreement is non-existent, invalid or ineffective shall not entail ipso jure the non-existence, invalidity or ineffectiveness of the arbitration clause.

Convention and their stipulation that arbitral tribunals shall be entitled to rule on their own jurisdiction, it has been explained that the doctrine of separability must constitute one not just applicable in commercial, but also in investment arbitration.[337] However, one must be aware of a difference: while the arbitration agreement in commercial arbitration is usually found in a contract, in investment arbitration, it is based upon acceptance of a unilateral offer to arbitrate by the state contained in the relevant BIT. The doctrine therefore applies in distinguishing between the arbitration agreement and the underlying investment and its legality or validity.[338] Reassurance for the applicability may be sought in considering an alleged use of corruption in the process of establishing the investment. In most applicable laws, corruption will be sufficient ground for declaring agreements void or illegal, even violating international public policy.[339] Investment tribunals, in absence of the separability doctrine, would then be forced to decline jurisdiction even when illegality is only suspected. If an investment is illegal, it may not be a protected investment under a BIT or the ICSID-Convention and thus none granting jurisdiction to an arbitral tribunal. However, it is then the doctrine of separability that allows tribunals to make a contribution in battling illegal conduct.[340] This is illustrated by selected investment arbitrations: for example, the dispute in *Methanex v. United States*[341] involved the arbitral tribunal making findings on alleged corruption for the purpose of assessing whether it had jurisdiction or not.[342] Furthermore, in *World Duty Free v. Kenya*,[343] an ICSID tribunal dismissed expropriation claims, stating that they were based upon illegality. Without the doctrine of separability, such ruling would not have been admissible. From that, it follows that the doctrine of separability is indeed applicable in international investment arbitration.[344]

---

337. *Schreuer*, note 210, Art. 25, para. 622.
338. *Richard Kreindler*, Competence-Competence in the Faces of Illegality in Contracts and Arbitration Agreements, 2013, p. 248.
339. ICC Case No. 1110 of 1963, in: Arbitration International 1994, Vol. 20 No. 3, pp. 282-294, para. 148:

> After weighing all the evidence I am convinced that a case such as this, involving such gross violation of good morals and international public policy, can have no countenance in any court either in the Argentine or in France, or, for that matter, in any other civilised country, nor in any arbitral tribunal. Thus, jurisdiction must be declined in this case. It follows from the foregoing, that in concluding that I have no jurisdiction, guidance has been sought from general principles denying arbitrators to entertain disputes of this nature rather than from any national rules on arbitrability. Parties who ally themselves in an enterprise of the present nature must realise that they have forfeited any right to ask for assistance of the machinery of justice (national courts or arbitral tribunals) in settling their disputes.

340. *Rashna Bhojwani*, Deterring Global Bribery: Where Public and Private Enforcement Collide, in: Columbia Law Review 2012, Vol. 112 No. 66, pp. 66-111 (p. 79).
341. *Methanex Corporation v. United States*, Final Award of the Tribunal on Jurisdiction and Merits, UNCITRAL, August 7, 2002.
342. *Bhojwani*, note 340, pp. 78 et seq.
343. *World Duty Free Company Limited v. The Republic of Kenya*, Award, ICSID Case No. ARB/00/7, October 4, 2006.
344. See *Zachary Douglas*, The Plea of Illegality in Investment Treaty Arbitration, in: ICSID Review 2014, Vol. 29 No. 1, pp. 1-32 (p. 3); *see also Siemens v. Argentina*, Decision on Jurisdiction, ICSID Case No. ARB/02/8, August 3, 2004, para. 46, in which Argentina argues in favor of the

[iii] Separability in Characterizing Arbitral Awards

After it is established that the doctrine of separability applies in the context of international investment arbitration, its possible impact on the reasoning of the tribunal is still unclear. It is conceivable that the analytical distinction between the investment and the arbitral award rests upon the doctrine. In comparing both, the settlement and the repayment agreement, to the arbitral award,[345] the tribunal could have indicated that it views the latter as just another agreement in itself. This result would be in line with the above-mentioned *agent theory* in the qualification of arbitral awards. The theory stipulates that arbitrators serve as the agents of the parties that have given them authority by way of the arbitration agreement. The resulting arbitral award is considered to be a contract in itself that was formed by the agents on behalf of the respective parties.[346] This perception has a long tradition and deems the arbitral award to form an entirety with the arbitration agreement:

> Une décision arbitrale, rendue en pays étranger, est-celle autre chose qu'un contrat? N'est-elle pas la conséquence du compromis, par suites duquel les arbitres l'ont rendue? Ne se lie-t-elle pas essentiellement à ce compromis? Ne fait-elle pas, avec ce compromis, *un seul et même corps*?[347]

Assuming that the tribunal acts upon this theoretical basis, it consequentially does not find the arbitral award to fall within the protection of the ICSID-Convention or the BIT.[348] The investment and the arbitration agreement are thus really analytically distinct. This distinction must then extend to the arbitral award as arising out of the arbitration agreement and forming a contract in itself. Likewise, the transformation-clause remains inapplicable due to the understanding that an arbitral award cannot constitute an investment and neither be a change in the form in which assets are invested.[349] Unfortunately, the decision does not provide further insights that would allow testing this hypothesis. In any case, however, the ruling here falls short of a full-fledged analysis. Its analytical distinction between the investment and the award is not as obvious as possibly presumed by the tribunal.

[E] **Analysis of the Principal Arguments**

The foregoing analysis of recent investment arbitrations has shed more light on the question, whether arbitral awards may fall under investment definitions and thus be protected by the provisions of a relevant investment treaty. For the purpose of finding structures and patterns, a mere examination of individual awards does, however, not suffice. Rather, it is imperative to further analyze the principal arguments that are

---

doctrine of separability; *see also Plama Consortium Limited v. Republic of Bulgaria*, Decision on Jurisdiction, ICSID Case No. ARB/03/24, February 8, 2005, para. 212.
345. *GEA Group Aktiengesellschaft v. Ukraine*, note 315, para. 162.
346. *Yu*, note 250, p. 272.
347. *Philippe Antoine Merlin*, Recueil Alphabétique de Question de Droit 1829, Vol. 9, p. 145.
348. *GEA Group Aktiengesellschaft v. Ukraine*, note 315, para. 162.
349. *GEA Group Aktiengesellschaft v. Ukraine*, note 315, para. 162.

frequently put forward in the process of interpretation. This will not only allow a careful assessment of the adequacy of the interpretive approaches taken, but also provide insights into possible strengths and weaknesses of interpretation in international investment law. Nevertheless, patterns and structures must be carefully viewed in close connection with the underlying investment treaties.[350]

[1] The Unity of Investment-Doctrine

[a] Overview

The majority of arbitral awards that were discussed share a fundamental starting point. Tribunals stress the perception that an investment may not be viewed in isolation and then separated into individual parts, but rather must be examined in a broader sense.[351] In other words, tribunals emanate from the assumption of the unity of an investment. This principle postulates the understanding that an investment, by nature, consists not of one single, but rather of a number of operations that constitute the investment as a whole. It intends to take into account the economic reality that investments often comprise various contracts, relationships or parties. This unity of investment-doctrine plays an important part in the determination of whether or not a dispute arises directly out of an investment for the purpose of establishing jurisdiction under Article 25 section 1 ICSID-Convention as well as under BITs.[352] It is primarily used to find a relation between an investment and a dispute. This does, however, not directly apply to the question of whether or not a particular operation forms part of an investment.[353] That is a different question. If a dispute thus arises out of a transaction which is in itself not an investment, an ICSID tribunal will still have jurisdiction to hear the case, if that transaction forms part of an overall investment seen as a unity.[354] Such transaction, out of which a dispute arises, must form an "integral part" of that

---

350. *See Schreuer*, note 210, Art. 25, para. 144.
351. *See White Industries Australia Limited v. The Republic of India*, note 246, para. 7.6.8; *see also ATA Construction, Industrial and Trading Company v. The Hashemite Kingdom of Jordan*, note 280, para. 115; *see also Saipem S.p.A. v. The Republic of Bangladesh*, note 286, para. 110; *see also Romak S.A. (Switzerland) v. The Republic of Uzbekistan*, note 304, para. 211.
352. A similar principle exists under NAFTA ("life span-theory"), which places more emphasis on the timely interrelation of various operations for the purpose of determining the scope of an investment; *see Mondev International Ltd. v. United States of America*, note 278, para. 81:

> The shareholders even in an unsuccessful enterprise retain interests in the enterprise arising from their commitment of capital and other resources, and the intent of NAFTA is evidently to provide protection of investments throughout their life-span, i.e., "with respect to the establishment, acquisition, expansion, management, conduct, operation, and sale or other disposition of investments."

353. *Schreuer*, note 210, Art. 25, para. 88.
354. *Fedax N.V. v. The Republic of Venezuela*, Decision of the Tribunal on Objections to Jurisdiction, ICSID Case No. ARB/96/3, July 11, 1997, para. 24:

> It is apparent that the term "directly" relates in this Article to the "dispute" and not to the "investment." It follows that jurisdiction can exist even in respect of investments that are not direct, so long as the dispute arises directly from such transaction. This

investment.[355] One may make a case in suggesting that the unity of investment-doctrine shall be equally applied to the relationship of respective transactions and an underlying investment. Apart from its original function of seeking a link between an investment and a dispute, it could then be utilized to seek a link between particular transactions and an existing investment.

A relatively early case before ICSID, *SOABI v. Senegal*,[356] concerned the qualification of three agreements between the parties regarding the erection of low-cost housing in Senegal. The Establishment Agreement, concerning the construction of a factory for the production of concrete, was the only such agreement containing an arbitration clause, giving jurisdiction to an ICSID tribunal. The arbitrators determined that jurisdiction was limited to those disputes that would arise out of the agreement itself. However, a dispute arose out of the actual construction process of the houses. Senegal argued that any ICSID tribunal would be barred from assuming jurisdiction as the dispute clearly did not arise out of the Establishment Agreement, containing the arbitration clause. The tribunal dealt with the argument and expressed its understanding of the parties' intentions, stating that all agreements were linked for the purpose of the entire project.[357] In so reasoning, it thus took a practical position and was satisfied with an apparent interrelationship between the relevant agreements, together forming an investment. In another arbitration *CSOB v. Slovakia*,[358] the tribunal took a slightly more narrow approach. The dispute concerned a consolidation agreement between CSOB and Slovakia which provided for the assignment of nonperforming receivables by CSOB to two companies that were founded for the purpose of collecting. A loan given to one of the companies was secured by Slovakia. After a repayment of the loan failed, CSOB initiated arbitral proceedings with ICSID. The arbitration clause was contained in the consolidation agreement. Slovakia then argued that the tribunal lacked jurisdiction as the dispute did not arise directly out of the loan. The tribunal

> interpretation is also consistent with the broad reach that the term 'investment' must be given in light of the negotiating history of the Convention.

355. *Ceskoslovenska Obchodni Banka, A.S. v. The Slovak Republic*, Decision of the Tribunal on Objections to Jurisdiction, ICSID Case No. ARB/97/4, May 24, 1999, para. 72.
356. *Société Ouest Africaine des Bétons Industriels v. The Republic of Senegal*, Jurisdictional Decision, ICSID Case No. ARB/82/1, February 25, 1988, in: ICSID Review 1991, Vol. 6 No. 2, pp. 119-124.
357. *Société Ouest Africaine des Bétons Industriels v. The Republic of Senegal*, note 356, p. 123:

> There is not the slightest doubt about the intention of the parties. It was not their intention to execute two independent projects but to carry out a single project consisting of two closely related parts, one of them being the technical pre-condition for the implementation of the other and would therefore have come first.

> and further that the:

> [t]ribunal has reached the conclusion that the agreements between the parties (other than the Establishment Agreement) regarding the construction of the factory and the construction of 15,000 houses are implicitly embraced by the Establishment Agreement and that the disputes related to their execution or to the rights and obligations arising thereunder fall within the scope of the Title VI of the Establishment Agreement.

358. *Ceskoslovenska Obchodni Banka, A.S. v. The Slovak Republic*, note 355.

clarified that it had to look at whether or not the relevant obligation forms an integral part of an underlying investment.[359] However, it explicitly pointed out that this must not lead to a general incorporation of any transaction into the domain of an investment.[360] By referring to a sufficient link between transactions and an investment, both decisions indicate that the requirements for establishing a connection are not different from those of the unity of investment-doctrine in its traditional application. This indication is further supported by the finding of the tribunal in the first ever ICSID arbitration, namely *Holiday Inns v. Morocco*.[361] The Moroccan government in the 1960s considered an expansion of its tourism industry and sought to benefit from the experience of the Holiday Inns Group, an American company well established in the hotel industry. On December 5, 1966, a final agreement was concluded between Holiday Inns and Occidental Petroleum Corporation, which was to be supplemented throughout the development. After commencement of the project, the pressure of political turmoil and new ministers in Morocco caused the renegotiation of the contract. Especially the complex financing structure of the project triggered significant differences between the parties. Negotiations remained unsuccessful, and subsequently, Holiday Inns filed a request for arbitration with ICSID on December 22, 1971. Morocco essentially argued that an ICSID tribunal would not have jurisdiction over the dispute, as it arose out of loan agreements that did not contain an arbitration clause, but rather a choice of forum in favor of the Moroccan judiciary. The arbitral tribunal, however, rejected such argument and came to the conclusion that the unity of investment-doctrine, a principle that inspired the ICSID-Convention, clarifies the composition of an investment encompassing a number of individual operations.[362] It may therefore be concluded that in fact, the unity of investment-doctrine primarily applies in the context of determining whether a dispute arises directly out of an

---

359. *Ceskoslovenska Obchodni Banka, A.S. v. The Slovak Republic*, note 355, para. 75.
360. *Ceskoslovenska Obchodni Banka, A.S. v. The Slovak Republic*, Decision of the Tribunal on Respondent's Further and Partial Objection to Jurisdiction, ICSID Case No. ARB/97/4, December 1, 2000, para. 28:

> This does not mean, however, that the Tribunal thereby automatically acquires jurisdiction with regard to each agreement concluded to implement the wider investment operation. Other requirements have to be met for such jurisdiction to be established. That is, the fact that the agreement to arbitrate referred to in the First Decision must be construed in good faith does not necessarily mean that the interpretation of the consent of the parties under Article 25 (1) of the ICSID Convention must in each case be deemed to extend to any and all agreements comprising the entire transaction.

361. *Holiday Inns v. Kingdom of Morocco*, Decision on Jurisdiction, ICSID Case, May 12, 1974, in: Pierre Lalive, The First World Bank Arbitration (Holiday Inns v. Morocco) – Some Legal Problems, in: British Yearbook of International Law 1980, Vol. 51 No. 1, pp. 123-161.
362. *Holiday Inns v. Kingdom of Morocco*, note 361, p. 159:

> It is well known, and it is being particularly shown in the present case, that investment is accomplished by a number of juridical acts of all sorts. It would not be consonant either with economic reality or with the intention of the parties to consider each of these acts in complete isolation from the others. It is particularly important to ascertain which is the act which is the basis of the investment and which entails as measures of execution the other acts which have been concluded in order to carry it out.

investment and, secondarily, in establishing a connection between a transaction and an overall investment. In other words, the doctrine is applied in ascertaining the existence of an investment within the ICSID structure[363] and outside of it.[364]

The unity of investment-doctrine has in practice received some limitations. In addition to the cautious approach taken in *CSOB v. Slovakia* requiring a transaction to form an integral part of an investment, other decisions have similarly added more contours. For example, it has been pointed out that a distinction must be made between those obligations and rights of an individual that form part of general law and those that are created in the context of an investment agreement.[365] It was, however, rightly commented that a limitation to pure investment agreements with host states is an approach that fails to include other investment protection mechanisms and is thus too narrow.[366] Lastly, the application of the unity of investment-doctrine does not necessarily imply that the investment will be uniformly protected.[367] In other words,

---

363. See *Enron Corporation and Ponderosa Assets, L.P. v. The Argentine Republic*, Decision on Jurisdiction, ICSID Case No. ARB/01/3, January 14, 2004, para. 70: "The Tribunal notes in this context that an investment is indeed a complex process including various arrangements, such as contracts, licences and other agreements leading to the materialization of such investment, a process in turn governed by the Treaty."; see also *Klöckner v. The Republic of Cameroon*, Award, ICSID Case No. ARB/81/2, October 21, 1983, in: ICSID Reports Vol. 2, p. 3: "[The Tribunal] has jurisdiction to rule both on the claim and the counterclaim, while taking into account the Establishment Agreement which, together with the Protocol of Agreement and the Supply Contract, constitutes an indivisible whole."; see also *Saipem S.p.A. v. The Republic of Bangladesh*, note 286, para. 110: "Finally, the Tribunal wishes to emphasize that for the purpose of determining whether there is an investment under Article 25 of the ICSID Convention, it will consider the entire operation."; see also *PSEG v. Republic of Turkey*, Award, ICSID Case No. ARB/02/5, January 19, 2007, paras. 114 et seq.

364. *Chevron Corporation and Texaco Petroleum Corporation v. The Republic of Ecuador*, Third Interim Award on Jurisdiction and Admissibility, UNCITRAL, PCA Case No. 2009-23, February 27, 2012, para. 4.16: "An investment can undergo several successive phases not chronologically coterminous with a concession agreement or concession."; see also *Romak S.A. (Switzerland) v. The Republic of Uzbekistan*, note 304, para. 211:

> On the basis of the allegations made and the evidence produced by the Parties in the present arbitration, the Arbitral Tribunal has come to the conclusion that the GAFTA Award is so inextricably linked to the Romak Supply Agreement that any determination as to whether Romak holds an investment under the BIT cannot be made without reference to the entire economic transaction that is the subject of these arbitral proceedings.

directly referring to the ICSID case *Holiday Inns v. Kingdom of Morocco*, note 361.

365. *AMCO v. Republic of Indonesia*, Resubmitted Case – Decision on Jurisdiction, ICSID Case No. ARB/81/1, May 10, 1988, in: ICSID Review – Foreign Investment Law Journal 1988, pp. 166-190 (p. 187); see also *Joy Mining Machinery Ltd. v. The Arab Republic of Egypt*, Award on Jurisdiction, ICSID Case No. ARB/03/11, para. 44, in which the tribunal does not view a mere bank guarantee to constitute part of an underlying investment: "The Tribunal is not persuaded by this argument either. Even if a claim to return of performance and related guarantees has a financial value it cannot amount to recharacterizing as an investment dispute a dispute which in essence concerns a contingent liability."

366. Schreuer, note 210, Art. 25, para. 98.

367. *Duke Energy International Peru Investments No. 1, Ltd. v. Republic of Peru*, Decision on Jurisdiction, ICSID Case No. ARB/03/28, February 1, 2006, para. 133: "In other words, in the peculiar circumstances of this case (successive agreements for the protection of the investment), the unity of the investment does not necessarily imply the unity of the protection of the

although a transaction may be found to form part of the overall investment, it may still be excluded from the protection that a respective investment protection mechanism provides.

[b]   *The Doctrine in Practical Context*

The unity of investment-doctrine is thus not a principle that tribunals may deploy as they see fit to perpetually establish that a transaction is covered by their jurisdiction. It applies, if the parties have not abrogated it in some form,[368] its requirements are fulfilled and other fundamental principles do not conflict. Otherwise, the applicability of the unity of investment-doctrine may be challenged. In other words, it depends on the practical context, especially the individual constitution of the relevant investment protection instrument. An interesting starting point in this analysis is once again the incorporation of an association-clause into the investment definition of BITs. This clause, as was previously outlined, is typically characterized by an ambiguous wording. While it allows for the treatment of a claim to money or any right to specific performance to be treated as a distinct investment, it nevertheless requires that there be a relation to an overall investment.

The tribunal in *ATA v. Jordan*[369] took this feature into account. The decision highlights that the dispute over the annulment of the award is inseparable from the original dispute that has given rise to the award in the first place.[370] The unity of investment-doctrine was thus applied. However, the arbitrators noted that an analysis must be performed in light of the text, context and object and purpose of the applicable rule.[371] Consequentially, the tribunal came to the conclusion that, after consideration of the association-clause, a right to arbitration, and ultimately an arbitral award, must and would have to be treated as a distinct investment.[372] The association-clause thus has the ability to limit the application of the unity of investment-doctrine. This approach appears very much in line with the finding of the tribunal in *Duke Energy v. Peru*[373] that was touched upon above.

---

   investment."; *see also Kreindler*, note 267, p. 41, who argues in the context of bad faith that the characterization as an investment does not equate to the protection of that investment.
368. See *Schreuer*, note 210, Art. 25, para. 565, in reference to W. Michael Tupmann, Case Studies in the Jurisdiction of the International Centre for Settlement of Investment Disputes, in: International and Comparative Law Quarterly 1986, Vol. 35 No. 4, pp. 813-838 (p. 834).
369. *ATA Construction, Industrial and Trading Company v. The Hashemite Kingdom of Jordan*, note 280.
370. *ATA Construction, Industrial and Trading Company v. The Hashemite Kingdom of Jordan*, note 280, para. 103: "In consequence, it seems to the Tribunal that the dispute over the annulment of the Final Award *per se* (as opposed to the extinguishment of the Arbitration Agreement) is really indistinguishable from the original dispute and, hence, like its progenitor, arose prior to the entry into force of the Turkey-Jordan BIT [...]".
371. *ATA Construction, Industrial and Trading Company v. The Hashemite Kingdom of Jordan*, note 280, para. 102.
372. *ATA Construction, Industrial and Trading Company v. The Hashemite Kingdom of Jordan*, note 280, para. 117.
373. *Duke Energy International Peru Investments No. 1, Ltd. v. Republic of Peru*, note 367.

The ability to limit the application of the unity of investment-doctrine does, however, not imply that this always actually takes place. In order to illustrate this point, further recourse to the decision in *Saipem v. Bangladesh*[374] is useful. Article 1 c) of the applicable BIT equally contained an association-clause ("connected with investments"). Nevertheless, the tribunal explicitly refused to accept that an arbitral award constitutes an investment.[375] The immediate question that arises then is how such differing conclusions can be reached despite a similar wording of the relevant BITs and the applicability of the ICSID-Convention. One must turn to the similarly differing perceptions of the tribunals in how investments are defined. While the tribunal in *ATA v. Jordan*[376] clearly followed a subjective approach in that the BIT defines investments, the tribunal in *Saipem v. Bangladesh*[377] did not. Its finding was based upon Article 25 section 1 ICSID-Convention and thus one of an objective kind, which is further supported by the use of the *Salini*-test. This analysis leads to an interesting result. On the one hand, under a subjective approach, an arbitral award may constitute an investment under the BIT and thereby under the ICSID-Convention, if the BIT so permits. The unity of investment-doctrine may thus be abrogated by provisions of the BIT, affecting not only its applicability within the treaty, but also within the ICSID-Convention. On the other hand, under an objective approach, an arbitral award may constitute an investment under the BIT but not under the ICSID-Convention. The abrogation of the unity of investment-doctrine by way of an association-clause does therefore not affect the definition under the ICSID-Convention. In essence, it is then the initial interpretive approach that may predetermine whether an arbitral award, in the context of the unity of investment-doctrine, may be considered as constituting an investment in itself.

Furthermore, the unity of investment-doctrine may be influenced by the incorporation of a transformation-clause into BITs. Typically, two variations are known: first, one will find a transformation-clause of a very broad nature such as in the Canada-Czech Republic BIT of November 15, 1990:[378]

---

374. *Saipem S.p.A. v. The Republic of Bangladesh*, note 286.
375. *Saipem S.p.A. v. The Republic of Bangladesh*, note 286, para. 113: "Indeed, the opposite view would mean that the Award itself does constitute an investment under Article 25(1) of the ICSID Convention, which the Tribunal is not prepared to accept."
376. *ATA Construction, Industrial and Trading Company v. The Hashemite Kingdom of Jordan*, note 280, para. 111.
377. *Saipem S.p.A. v. The Republic of Bangladesh*, note 286.
378. *See also* e.g. Canada-El Salvador BIT, May 31, 1999, available at http://investmentpolicyhub.unctad.org/Download/TreatyFile/613 (last accessed July 4, 2014); Canada-Costa Rica BIT, March 18, 1998, available at http://www.bilaterals.org/IMG/pdf/CA-CR_FIPA_1999.pdf (last accessed July 4, 2014); Canada-Argentina BIT, November 5, 1991, available at http://www.bilaterals.org/IMG/pdf/CA-AR_FIPA_1993_old_model_.pdf (last accessed July 4, 2014); Canada-Croatia BIT, February 3, 1997, available at http://investmentpolicyhub.unctad.org/IIA/country/35/treaty/780 (last accessed July 4, 2014); Canada-Thailand BIT, January 17, 1997, available at http://www.bilaterals.org/IMG/pdf/CA-TH_FIPA_1998.pdf (last accessed July 4, 2014); Canada-Philippines BIT, November 5, 1995, available at http://www.bilaterals.org/IMG/pdf/CA-PH_FIPA_1996.pdf (last accessed July 4, 2014); India-Poland BIT, October 7, 1996, available at http://investmentpolicyhub.unctad.org/Download/TreatyFile/1587 (last accessed July 4, 2014); Jordan-United States BIT, July 2, 1997, available at http://www.state.gov/documents/organization/43565.pdf (last accessed July 4, 2014).

Chapter 3: The Protection of Arbitral Awards in the Global Context §3.03[E]

> Any change in the form of an investment does not affect its character as an investment.

This clause specifically postulates that an investment may change its form, without having an impact on its characterization as such. In other words, as long as an original investment has existed, its transformation even into something new does not deprive it of its investment quality. In analyzing a particular transaction, it will thus be sufficient for tribunals to establish that an investment exists or has existed and that the transaction in question is somehow related to it. This broad protection is in line with the BIT's object and purpose of fully protecting foreign investments in order to stimulate business according to its preamble. Furthermore, it is in line with the context of the BIT's determination of having more favorable subsequent protection regimes apply equally. It is thus an expression of the parties' intentions to fully apply the unity of investment-doctrine even to the extent that an original investment or a right stemming from it transforms into something new. Second, one will find a transformation-clause that is more limited such as in the Germany-Ukraine BIT of February 15, 1993:

> Any change to the form in which assets are invested shall not affect their nature as investments.

This form of the transformation-clause is not as direct. On its face, it merely clarifies that a change to the form in which assets are invested does not have an impact on their nature as investments. Problematic is the term "are invested," which allows a twofold understanding of the clause. On the one hand, it may be perceived as applying to investments only in their dynamic establishment, the creation of the investment. On the other hand, it may be perceived as applying also to its static existence, even after the investment has been fully created and is now simply being carried out. The question is therefore, whether the investment nature only remains unaffected, if the change in form occurs during or even beyond the creation of the investment.

It has been explained that practically, an investment is not a single operation, but a process. If one understood the wording of the transformation-clause in the former sense, it could disperse such process. It would ultimately lead to the conclusion that the transformation-clause only applies to changes within the investment process, before such investment may be considered complete and established. As an illustration, one may think of a company erecting and running an independent factory in a host country before, much later, engaging in a joint venture with a local entity. In this scenario, the understanding that the transformation-clause would only apply to the original investment operation until it has been established, would thus rule out changes at a later point in time. Changes to the form in which assets are invested after the original erection could then affect the nature as investments. Once the investment is established, the transformation-clause would no longer apply. This conception is by far more limiting on the applicability of the transformation-clause than its alternative, which extends such applicability to an investment that is later simply being operated. However, the former understanding deprives the transformation-clause of its object and purpose. Such transformation-clause intends to take into account the economic reality of investments, adjusting and developing. Investments naturally are an ongoing process, whose natural events can hardly be divided into a phase of establishment and operation. The former limited approach is in this sense misleading and does not reflect business reality. Therefore, the transformation-clause must also apply to the static existence of assets that were once invested and are now merely being operated. This result is supported by the broad determination that "any change" will remain irrelevant. Therefore, despite the curious wording, the transformation-clause in both variations is an expression of the full applicability of the unity of investment-doctrine.

The tribunal in *GEA v. Ukraine*[379] appears to have seen the unity of investment-doctrine in conflict with the doctrine of separability. The tribunal here seemed to have resolved the issue by ruling in favor of the latter. The unity of investment-doctrine, according to the tribunal, did therefore not extend to agreements to arbitrate and awards resulting out of them. It was considered inferior to the doctrine of separability. The practical side is equally intriguing. Under this assumption, arbitral awards may generally not enjoy protection in international investment law. The tribunal might in this sense be opposing the idea of providing a second bite at the cherry. It might be rejecting the idea that investment arbitration may serve to compensate a claimant for losses suffered due to a frustrated enforcement attempt of a commercial arbitration award altogether. The decision of the tribunal is thus to be perceived as an implicit but powerful plea for adherence to the different theoretical bases of commercial and investment arbitration in their practical application.

[2] The Role of Previous Arbitral Decisions

The analysis of arbitral awards has furthermore revealed that the consideration of previous decisions for the characterization of arbitral awards as investments is an important aspect. At the same time, however, consideration takes place on differing theoretical understandings of the role of previous decisions. Before immerging in a more differentiated observation, it is adequate to recall the general role of previous arbitral decisions in international investment law. No formal doctrine of *stare decisis* exists. Despite this inexistence, practice indicates that previous arbitral decisions are heavily considered and even relied upon. Regarding the characterization of arbitral awards as investments, *Saipem v. Bangladesh* has laid a significant part of the foundation for subsequent interpretations. In its decision on jurisdiction[380] and its award,[381] the tribunal even dedicated two paragraphs to its positioning on alleged arbitral precedent. Not only does this take into account the parties' reliance on previous decisions, but it also provides an immediate orientation for the sake of clarity. The tribunal expressed its position as follows:

> The Tribunal considers that it is *not bound* by previous decisions. At the same time, it is of the opinion that it must pay due *consideration* to earlier decisions of

---

379. *GEA Group Aktiengesellschaft v. Ukraine*, note 315.
380. *Saipem S.p.A. v. The Republic of Bangladesh*, note 286.
381. *Saipem S.p.A. v. The Republic of Bangladesh*, Award, ICSID Case No. ARB/05/7, June 30, 2009.

international tribunals. It believes that, subject to compelling contrary grounds, it has *a duty to adopt solutions* established in a series of consistent cases. It also believes that, *subject to the specifics of a given treaty and of the circumstances of the actual case*, it has a duty to seek to *contribute to the harmonious development of investment* law and thereby to meet the legitimate expectations of the community of States and investors towards certainty of the *rule of law*.[382]

One notices the clarification that a doctrine of *stare decisis* does not exist in international investment law. However, the tribunal pointed out that it sought to contribute to the harmonious development of the field, respecting the specific treaty provisions and facts of individual cases. Interestingly, it furthermore highlighted that such an approach may contribute to the rule of law. With regards to *White Industries v. India*, it has been elaborated that the tribunal solely relied on what it believed to be arbitral precedent in finding that an arbitral award is part of an investment. This is especially reflected in the finding that there exists a "developing jurisprudence" in the protection of arbitral awards by way of considering them to be continuations or transformations of investments. Especially the decisions in *Saipem v. Bangladesh* and *Chevron v. Ecuador* were at the core of the tribunal's decision, however, without distinguishing underlying treaties or fact patterns. In *ATA v. Jordan*, reference was made to *Saipem v. Bangladesh* as the claimant heavily relied upon its ruling. The tribunal acknowledged the reference, analyzed it, but then engaged in examining the BIT as the normative basis of the dispute. Previous decisions therefore were not a key element in the tribunal's finding. Lastly, the tribunal in *Romak v. Uzbekistan* took on a different and clear position. It did not find itself bound by previous decisions, nor did it consider them to be a source of international law. The tribunal did not consider itself entrusted with making a contribution to the development of international investment law.[383] In short, the tribunal positioned itself as follows:

> This is not to say that the Arbitral Tribunal will simply ignore awards rendered by distinguished arbitrators. The Arbitral Tribunal may and will examine them, not for the purposes of extracting from them rules of law, but as a means to provide context to the Parties' allegations and arguments, and as to explain succinctly the Arbitral Tribunal's own reasoning.[384]

The analysis of the characterization of arbitral awards thus finds significant differences in the way that previous arbitral decisions are considered. While some tribunals may merely acknowledge their existence, others utilize them as their analytical origin. Under these circumstances, it is conceivable that future tribunals will render awards under heavy reliance on alleged precedent. The scenario may lead to different results and the characterization of arbitral awards may consequentially continue to be a controversial issue in view of critical commentary that is yet to be examined.

---

382. *Saipem S.p.A. v. The Republic of Bangladesh*, note 286, para. 67.
383. *Romak S.A. (Switzerland) v. The Republic of Uzbekistan*, note 246, para. 171.
384. *Romak S.A. (Switzerland) v. The Republic of Uzbekistan*, note 246, para. 171.

[F] Practical Implications of the Analysis

In their characterization of arbitral awards and ultimately in determining whether or not they may be interpreted as investments, tribunals have taken diverse approaches and equally produced diverse outcomes. The practically relevant question is, however, if and under which circumstances the handling of an arbitral award by domestic courts may give rise to a successful claim in investment arbitration. This is dependent upon whether or not an arbitral award may be treated as or like an investment that deserves such protection. The results suggest a certain tendency. Five out of six arbitral decisions qualified the award as a part of an original investment and thus treated it as an investment or like an investment. The existence of a general possibility of an arbitral award being protected by international investment law may therefore be carefully acknowledged. That is, however, not to say that in each case, based upon an individual fact pattern and legal basis, that possibility will turn into a successful claim.

First, respective investment definitions in a BIT must be of a broad nature. Considering the typical breadth of most such definitions, this will most likely not prove to be a significant hurdle for interpretive efforts. The second observation of the analysis concerns the fact patterns. In all decisions, they share the common feature that the respective claimants had previously engaged in business activity of some form in the territory of the state that later became the respondent in the investment arbitration. It is only if that state's judiciary has taken actions, that a possible second bite at the cherry is feasible.[385] This is due to the reliance on the unity of investment-doctrine, requiring such territorial link.[386] As the autonomous plain meaning approach has foreshadowed and the later review of individual treaties and fact patterns supported, an arbitral award cannot be qualified as an investment without any further connection to other economic activity. The mere, possibly insufficient, handling of an award in any jurisdiction does therefore not activate the protective mechanisms of an existing BIT. The third observation relates to the use of transformation-clauses. It has been pointed out that – despite their variations – such clauses are an expression of the full applicability of the unity of investment-doctrine. They allow tribunals to distill from a treaty's text the intention of both parties to give full effect to that principle. The incorporation of a transformation-clause may thus ease the characterization of arbitral awards as or like investments. It is to be noted, however, that in only two out of the six analyzed decisions did the underlying BIT provide for such clause and in only one of them did the tribunal rely on it in finding that the arbitral award must be treated like an investment.[387] In the other, the tribunal contrarily found it to rebut the assumption that an arbitral award may be treated as or like an investment.[388] Consequentially, it is at this point too early to state that the transformation-clause practically has a determining impact on a tribunal's decision. One has to be content with the discovery that its use may at least abet the qualification of arbitral awards as or like investments. The fourth

---

385. *Kaufmann-Kohler*, note 262, p. 166.
386. *Park*, note 262, p. 68.
387. *Frontier Petroleum Services Ltd. v. The Czech Republic*, note 297, para. 231.
388. *GEA Group Aktiengesellschaft v. Ukraine*, note 315, para. 162.

observation refers to the implementation of association-clauses into BITs. Once again, in two out of the six analyzed decisions the arbitrators availed themselves of such clauses. Both found that an award should be treated as or like an investment. While this does certainly not suffice to form a clear indication, the use of an association-clause has so far at least not hindered the interpretation. Both clauses are therefore not a definite requirement. One may conclude that in practice, the following factors may facilitate the protection of arbitral awards within international investment law:

- Relatively broad investment definitions.
- Prior economic activity of the future claimant in the territory of the respondent, to which the award may be linked.
- Incorporation of a transformation-clause.
- Incorporation of an association-clause.

Naturally, these factors remain merely indicative. Whether or not tribunals will in the future increasingly see arbitral awards as somehow protected within the ambit of international investment law is still not easy to predict. The fact patterns of the analyzed disputes were highly specific. To date, recourse to international investment arbitration in case of frustrated enforcement attempts in international commercial arbitration is thus still an exceptional option. The dynamics of international investment law may, in the future, prove that conclusion wrong. It is necessary though that any development will be based upon an adequate application of methodology.

[G] Observations Regarding Treaty Interpretation

The analysis concerning the characterization of arbitral awards has focused on six specific arbitral decisions. It has shed more light on the prerequisites for deploying the protection of international investment law over arbitral awards. While it is certainly one aim to add to this practically intriguing matter, the relevance of the analysis is not limited to making a direct contribution to arbitral practice. It is furthermore an objective to link the study to existing research on the interpretation in international investment arbitration and thereby imbedding it into a broader scholarly framework. This will allow to determine if the observations of the present work are specific to the characterization of arbitral awards or if they are possibly representative of a more global phenomenon.

[1] Application of the Vienna Convention on the Law of Treaties

The first observation concerns the relevance of the VCLT and its principles of treaty interpretation that were derived from customary international law. Only one out of six decisions, *Romak v. Uzbekistan*,[389] explicitly mentions and applies the VCLT with care

---

389. *Romak S.A. (Switzerland) v. The Republic of Uzbekistan*, note 246.

and adherence. *Saipem v. Bangladesh* refers to "international law,"[390] while the remaining ones make no reference to the applicable VCLT. Rather, they either remain mute[391] concerning the ways the relevant BIT or the ICSID-Convention have been approached for the purpose of interpretation or do not follow their intended course of action in compliance with the VCLT.[392] On the specific issue of interpretation regarding arbitral awards, they focus on the ordinary meaning in its context and in light of the provisions' object and purpose. This is especially noteworthy in the case of *White Industries v. India*,[393] which contains the most direct and recent leap into characterizing an arbitral award as part of an investment, but is merely based on the ordinary meaning-rule.[394] In other words, only one-third of the decisions on the characterization of arbitral awards was explicitly based upon the existent and applicable methodology of treaty interpretation. Considering the importance of a fungible procedure to interpretation and the compulsory nature of the VCLT as was expressed in the second chapter, this result is surprising.

The possible breadth of one's individual analysis is naturally limited. This realization is discomforting and wise alike; discomforting, because one is tempted to find globally valid patterns beyond limitations; wise, because this temptation is likely to lead astray. In the context of international arbitral awards and their reasoning, *Pierre Lalive* has in this sense referred to a famous quote in English poetry: "To generalise is to be an idiot!"[395] The beauty of scholarship, however, lies in the interaction with peers. And so, in an attempt to avoid idiocy, the results of the present analysis must be put in perspective. In her most current note,[396] *Andrea Saldarriaga* has randomly looked at thirty arbitral awards under various arbitral set ups such as ICSID, ICC or UNCITRAL and their use of the VCLT. She identifies a number of issues that deserve close attention. Two-thirds of the awards examined make references to the VCLT, while those that do not, neither explain their interpretive approach.[397] She finds that

---

390. *Saipem S.p.A. v. The Republic of Bangladesh*, note 286, para. 82: "However, in the absence of any indication that the contracting states intended to refer to 'property' as a notion of Bangladeshi law, the Tribunal cannot depart from the general rule that treaties are to be interpreted by reference to international law."
391. *GEA Group Aktiengesellschaft v. Ukraine*, note 315; *see also ATA Construction, Industrial and Trading Company v. The Hashemite Kingdom of Jordan*, note 280; *see also Frontier Petroleum Services Ltd. v. The Czech Republic*, note 297.
392. *White Industries Australia Limited v. Republic of India*, note 246, para. 7.3.2 in correctly stating: "The correct approach to be adopted by the Tribunal in assessing whether an 'investment' has been made is to consider the plain and ordinary meaning of the words used in the BIT in their context and in light of its object and purpose and to determine whether the matters relied on by White satisfy the definition employed in the BIT.", but on the characterization of arbitral awards simply concluding: "The Tribunal concludes that this latter statement (the award being part of the original investment) more accurately describes the status of the Award," without further interpretation of the BIT.
393. *White Industries Australia Limited v. Republic of India*, note 246.
394. *Nacimiento/Lange*, note 273, p. 276.
395. *Lalive*, note 158, p. 55.
396. *Saldarriaga*, note 18.
397. *Saldarriaga*, note 18, p. 8; *see also David Minnotte and Robert Lewis v. Republic of Poland*, Award, ICSID Case No. ARB(AF)/10/1, May 16, 2014, para. 121: "For the purposes of establishing the jurisdiction of the Tribunal and the admissibility of the claims, it is sufficient

the VCLT is sometimes only partially or even incorrectly applied.[398] Some tribunals appear to use the principles of interpretation only for a limited number of issues while they do not use them on others.[399] Furthermore, the core problem of an incorrect application appears to be that the order of Articles 31 and 32 VCLT is not respected.[400] A similar study has been conducted by *Ole Fauchald*,[401] specifically analyzing the reasoning of ICSID tribunals in 98 cases. He finds that 35 decisions refer to the relevant articles on interpretation of the VCLT, while only in 20 decisions they are actually applied. The study comes to the impressive conclusion that only in exceptional cases the VCLT was really integrated into tribunals' analyses beyond generalizing references.[402] Also, it finds that mostly, tribunals followed an objective approach to treaty interpretation.[403] The object and purpose of the relevant BITs was looked at in about half of the 98 decisions, however, while mostly not indicating how the respective object and purpose was derived.[404]

The existent decisions on the characterization of arbitral awards as investments and their reasoning, as examined in the course of this analysis, reflect the findings of the above-mentioned studies. The inconsistent adherence to interpretive canons of the VCLT thus seems to be not only a fractional issue within the limits of a particular problem in international investment law, but in fact, part of a broader issue.[405]

[2] *Short Reasoning Beyond Interpretive Canons*

The discovery that the applicable canons of the VCLT are not complied with in a majority of arbitral decisions is problematic. At the same time, one would find at least some comfort – albeit being of a cold character – in finding that beyond these canons, decisions are thoroughly reasoned. The first question is, however, how reasoning and interpretation relate to one another. Does thorough interpretation mean that a decision is thoroughly reasoned? Can an interpretation be in compliance with the VCLT yet poorly reasoned? Reasoning may in this sense be an overarching principle to which the proper application of interpretive principles belongs. The second question is then, which threshold is to apply in deeming reasoning thorough. In turning to the first of the two questions, one might find a starting point in Article 48 section 3 ICSID-Convention.

---

that there was a real investment." The tribunal did, however, not dwell on whether or not this investment would fall under the definition of the applicable BIT, neither did it mention the principles of the VCLT.
398. *Saldarriaga*, note 18, pp. 8 et seq.
399. *Saldarriaga*, note 18, p. 8.
400. *Saldarriaga*, note 18, p. 8.
401. *Ole Kristian Fauchald*, The Legal Reasoning of ICSID Tribunals – An Empirical Analysis, in: The European Journal of International Law 2008, Vol. 19 No. 2, pp. 301-364.
402. *Fauchald*, note 401, p. 314.
403. *Fauchald*, note 401, p. 316.
404. *Fauchald*, note 401, pp. 322 et seq.
405. See also *Michael Waibel*, International Investment Law and Treaty Interpretation, in: Rainer Hofmann/Christian Tams (eds.), From Clinical Isolation to Systemic Integration, 2011, pp. 29-52 (p. 29): "Perhaps as by-product of their cavalier attitude to treaty interpretation, many investment awards do not offer models of careful treaty interpretation for international lawyers working in other areas."

It provides that an award, generally, must state the reasons on which it is based. The award embodies the decision of the arbitral tribunal. The interpretation of an applicable BIT is then a fundamental element, as it forms the entire basis on which the arbitration rests. This logic will equally apply to arbitrations outside of the ICSID framework. Interpretation thus forms part of reasoning. The VCLT intends to guide interpreters in finding solutions of logic and sense. Therefore, respective interpretation based on its principles is a key to providing adequate reasoning and increases the likelihood of a well-traceable decision. In turning to the second question, recourse to the ICSID-Convention is once again helpful. Article 52 section 1 (e) describes a failure of an award to state the reasons it is based on as a ground for annulment. This indicates the caution that must be exercised in the determination of the sensible threshold. International arbitration's success is also rooted in its finality, the fact that – in contrast to most domestic legal systems – further recourse to higher instances is very limited. Consequentially, Article 52 ICSID-Convention does not provide for an appeals mechanism, but rather envisages the possibility of an annulment in only a very limited number of situations.[406] If every improper application of interpretive canons would amount to a failure to provide reasoning, Article 52 section 1 (e) ICSID-Convention would provide for a de facto opportunity of appeal and thus run the risk of impairing the attractiveness of arbitration within the ICSID framework.[407] Therefore, an all too loose standard in examining the reasoning of arbitral decisions may prove problematic. At the same time, a mere application of the relevant interpretive canons without substantial and sensible explanation should not automatically protect a tribunal's decision from a possible annulment procedure. It has been examined that generally, ad hoc committees have adopted an either low or high standard in determining the requirements of proper reasoning.[408] The current analysis does not necessitate making a decision for or against a particular approach. What is of more relevance is the interpretive imperative that derives from the debate. In his dissenting opinion on the annulment decision in *Lucchetti v. Peru*,[409] *Sir Frank Berman*, he has formulated it quite appropriately:

> But to suppose that the Tribunal must have applied the proper rules of treaty interpretation is not, to my way of thinking, the end of the matter. The real question, as I have suggested above, is *whether they adequately explained what they were doing in the interpretative process, and did so specifically with the very particular care needed from a Tribunal* proposing, on the basis of the interpretative outcome, to decline jurisdiction altogether. And the only way to answer that question, given that the Tribunal (somewhat surprisingly, I think) did neglect to

---

406. *Christoph Schreuer*, From ICSID Annulment to Appeal – Half Way Down the Slippery Slope, in: Eduardo Valencia-Ospina/Pierre Bodeau-Livinec (eds.), The Law and Practice of International Courts and Tribunals 2010, Vol. 10, pp. 211-225 (p. 212).
407. See *Lalive*, note 158, p. 59.
408. *Tai-Heng Cheng*, What's Reasonable Depends on Who's Asking, in: Baltic Yearbook of International Law 2008, pp. 1-28 (p. 4) in reviewing the publication Guillermo Aguilar Alvarez/W. Michael Reisman (eds.), The Reasons Requirement in International Arbitration: Critical Case Studies, 2008.
409. *Industria Nacional de Alimientos S.A., and Indalsa Perú S.A. v. The Republic of Peru*, Decision on Annulment, ICSID Case No. ARB/03/4, September 5, 2007.

tell us what they were doing, is to look to what the Tribunal actually did as evidence of what rules they were applying.[410]

This statement clearly indicates that any investment tribunal's decision – not only within the ICSID framework – must meet certain standards of reasoning in the way that it is adequate and careful.[411] The issuance of decisions that provide improper reasoning is highly unfortunate, much like the inconsistent application of the VCLT itself. In their attempts to characterize arbitral awards, the decisions that were previously analyzed must thus have been adequately explained. Whether or not this was really the case is certainly yet another question, whose answer depends on the individual threshold for being poorly reasoned that is applied. It may therefore suffice to indicate that *GEA v. Ukraine*[412] and *White Industries v. India*[413] are probably susceptible to profound criticism in this regard – the former due to its nebulously formulated – that is not to say incorrect – separation of awards from investments, the latter due to its noninterpretation and sole dependence upon previous arbitral decisions.

[3]   Previous Arbitral Decisions

The observation that previous arbitral decisions are of significant importance to a large number of the examined decisions may appear as one within the limited parameters of a single detailed interpretive issue in international investment law; but in fact, it precisely mirrors the problematic stance of previous arbitral decisions within the field's global ambit. For the purpose of analyzing the principal arguments in the tribunals' findings, one is bound to be content with the identification that a tribunal's view on arbitral precedent does not necessarily imply a particular interpretive result. It may, however, indicate its line of argumentation and decreased emphasis on treaty interpretation. Heavy reliance on arbitral precedent may cause a failure to recognize the importance of treaty interpretation. This bears the danger of shifting methodology into an unbalanced and illegitimate position. After all, it is the applicability of interpretive canons that is enshrined in the VCLT. Reliance on alleged arbitral precedent, on the other hand, is not. It is therefore necessary to draw a fine line between the consideration of previous decisions and the reliance on them. While the importance of well-reasoned and adequate awards can hardly be underestimated, they should not serve to deprive treaty interpretation of its primary role in international investment arbitration. The value of those previous decisions is then to add a layer of support to interpretive outcomes.[414] One must have confidence in the scholarly and practical attentiveness concerning arbitral awards, which serves to identify those that rightfully

---

410. *Industria Nacional de Alimientos S.A., and Indalsa Perú S.A. v. The Republic of Peru*, note 409, Dissenting Opinion of Sir Frank Berman, August 13, 2007, para. 6.
411. *Lalive*, note 158, pp. 60 et seq.
412. *GEA Group Aktiengesellschaft v. Ukraine*, note 315.
413. *White Industries Australia Limited v. Republic of India*, note 246.
414. *See Kaufmann-Kohler*, note 166, (p. 372), who describes that tribunals pay great attention to the applicable treaty in context with the individual fact patterns, while beyond these, certain principles appear to emerge from previous decisions.

receive or should receive attention and others that do or should not.[415] Nevertheless, that attention must be paid carefully and in observance of those facts or treaty provisions that make each investment dispute one characterized by uniqueness: "Labelling is, however, no substitute for analysis."[416]

[4] Conclusion

It has become evident that the process of interpretation in determining the character of arbitral awards and eventually treating them as or like investments is not immaculate. Moreover, this observation reflects a common problem in many international investment arbitrations today. The analysis of how tribunals have characterized arbitral awards and which methodological canons they have applied therefore fully integrates into a highly important global issue in international investment law. The defective application of the VCLT, reliance on alleged arbitral precedent and insufficient general reasoning indicate that voices calling for improvement are not without cause, but deserve amplification. A number of propositions for improvement exist. Their assessment, however, first requires a closer look at possible reasons for the insufficiencies.

§3.04 ELEMENTS OF THE POTENTIAL IMPACT ON INTERPRETATION

This analysis has already used idyllic scenes of a perfect international investment law. Cold reality, however, is that a system created and maintained by fallible beings is not immune from erring.[417] Nevertheless, this conclusion is all the less dissatisfactory, realizing that errors bear potential for improvement. This coincides with the natural human curiosity, the urge of finding answers to the questions we encounter. *Aristotle* came to a basic metaphysical discovery in this regard: "All men by nature desire to know."[418] On this foundation, it is of particular interest to understand, if certain causes

---

415. *See Jan Paulsson*, International Arbitration and the Generation of Legal Norms: Treaty Arbitration and International Law, in: Albert Jan van den Berg (ed.), International Arbitration 2006: Back to Basics?, ICCA Congress Series Vol. 13, pp. 879-889 (p. 880):

> The Corpus of decided cases in the field of international investment arbitration is of recent vintage, but it has come into existence with remarkable speed. Its legal status as a source of law is in theory equal to that of other types of international courts or tribunals. In practice, it will also doubtless turn out to be subject to the same Darwinian imperative: the unfit will perish.

> *see also Lucy Reed*, The De Facto Precedent Regime in Investment Arbitration: A Case for Proactive Case Management, in: ICSID Review 2010, Foreign Investment Law Journal, Vol. 25 No. 1, pp. 95-103 (p. 99), calling the development a "primordial soup"; *see also Romak S.A. (Switzerland) v. The Republic of Uzbekistan*, note 304, para. 171: "It is for the legal doctrine as reflected in articles and books, and not for arbitrators in their awards, to set forth, promote or criticize general views regarding trends in, and the desired evolution of, investment law."

416. *Robert Azinian, Kenneth Davitian, & Ellen Baca v. United Mexican States*, Award, ICSID Case No. ARB/(AF)97/2, November 1, 1999, para. 90.
417. In referring to international commercial arbitration *see Kaufmann-Kohler*, note 262, p. 172.
418. *Aristotle*, Metaphysics, Book I, Part 1.

exist that have a potential impact on the way investment treaties are being interpreted. This may also allow further insights into the possible consequences of interpretive shortcomings and, lastly, suggest routes to improvement.

[A] A Trend of Convergence in International Arbitration

The shortcomings in the interpretive process could possibly be traced back to an evolutionary development that might be on its way in international arbitration as a whole: a possible convergence of commercial and investment arbitration. The first layer of this development could be a possible trend of providing broader protection to commercial arbitration by way of domestic state conduct. The second layer could be a similarly broader protection within public international law. The third layer could be an enhancement of investment arbitration towards domestic courts that derives from investment tribunals themselves. Lastly, the fourth layer could be a strengthening of international investment arbitration from its inside. The result of such developments could be that commercial and investment arbitration may be growing closer together. In this regard, it was previously referred to a possible fundamental impact on the relationship between the two, which deserves closer attention. The focus is on the question of whether or not such trend could or does impact the process of treaty interpretation. Providing answers is a challenging task. If both forms of international arbitration are in fact growing closer, it is not automatically a matter of concern. It does require, however, that the development takes place on the foundation of proper interpretation. Otherwise, the risk of blurring the delicate parting line between commercial and investment arbitration that originates from their distinctive theoretical bases may be right around the corner. Given the criticism directed towards international investment law, such scenario is not desirable.

[1] *Increasing Protection of International Commercial Arbitration*

[a] *International Commercial Arbitration on the Rise*

In the first chapter, it was outlined that international commercial arbitration is nowadays the leading means of dispute resolution in international commercial contracts. The erection of new arbitration centers around the globe, the adaptation of arbitral rules and domestic legislation indicate this quite clearly. Likewise, the history of the UNCITRAL Model Law illustrates early efforts in further promoting and harmonizing rules of international commercial arbitration. It was as early as 1933, when experts of the League of Nations commenced works on a unified arbitration law. The efforts, in collaboration with the ICC and the International Council of Commercial Arbitration (ICCA), led to an adoption of the UNCITRAL Model Law in 1985[419] and

---

419. *Gabriele Hußlein-Stich*, Das UNCITRAL-Modellgesetz über die internationale Handelsschiedsgerichtsbarkeit, 1990, pp. 2 et seq.

thereby created a unified document that has ever since served as a powerful source for states to modernize and adapt their domestic arbitration laws. States have recognized that providing a stable legal environment may foster their importance in the international arbitration arena.[420] This has caused many of them to minimize their entanglement in the arbitral process.[421] For reasons of flexibility, enforceability, confidentiality and, at times, cost efficiency, arbitration enjoys immense popularity in the commercial world. An upward trend is likely to continue, while simultaneously, these trends by nature are not forever homogeneous, but rather occur in phases.[422] International arbitration practices around the globe are thus kept busy, and arbitrators receive continued appreciation for their services. Key factor in this development is undoubtedly the NYC, ensuring the enforceability and binding nature of foreign arbitral awards before domestic courts.[423] The way a respective state judiciary perceives its own role in the arbitral process and the way it handles arbitral awards may be an indicator of a state's overall attitude towards arbitration.

A prominent example is the dispute that arose between Kahara Bodas, a company under the laws of the Cayman Islands and owned by two major American energy distributors, and Pertamina, the national oil and gas company of Indonesia. Both companies entered into contracts under which Kahara Bodas was to engage in an energy project in West Java, Indonesia. In view of the Asian financial crisis around 1997, the project was later brought to a hold by Indonesia. Subsequently, arbitral proceedings were initiated in Geneva, Switzerland and resulted in an award rendered in favor of Kahara Bodas, which sought to have the award enforced in the United States, Canada, Hong Kong and Singapore.[424] Pertamina opposed the enforcement proceedings in the United States arguing that a violation of public policy had occurred, the arbitration had been conducted contrary to the agreement to arbitrate and that its due process rights had been violated.[425] The United States District Court for the

---

420. *Wong*, note 145, p. 532; *see also Hailegabriel G. Feyissa*, The Role of Ethiopian Courts in Commercial Arbitration, in: Mizan Law Review 2010, Vol. 4 No. 2, pp. 297-333 (p. 333).
421. *Van Harten/Loughlin*, note 145, p. 141; *see also* United Nations Commission on International Trade (UNCITRAL), Model Law on International Commercial Arbitration, Explanatory Notes on the 1985 Model Law, p. 15:

> Recent amendments to arbitration laws reveal a trend in favour of limiting and clearly defining court involvement in international commercial arbitration. This is justified in view of the fact that the parties to an arbitration agreement make a conscious decision to exclude court jurisdiction and prefer the finality and expediency of the arbitral process.

422. *Sornarajah*, note 159, p. 159: "These swings in the pendulum are discernible within all systems of international commercial arbitration. No observer of the area should present its principles as if they were writ in stone, good for all time."
423. *Ge Liu*, UNCITRAL Model Law v. Chinese Law and Practice: A Discussion on Interim Measures of Protection, in: Albert Jan van den Berg (ed.), New Horizons in International Commercial Arbitration and Beyond, 2005, pp. 278-283 (p. 278).
424. *Noah Rubins*, The Enforcement and Annulment of International Arbitration Awards in Indonesia, in: American University International Law Review 2005, Vol. 20 No. 2, pp. 359-401 (p. 378).
425. *Rubins*, note 424, p. 378.

Southern District of Texas did not follow the arguments put forward by Pertamina, enforcing the award in highlighting the so-called *pro-enforcement bias* of the NYC.[426] Pertamina then successfully turned to the Indonesian judiciary seeking to have the award set aside, while courts in New York, Texas, Canada, Hong Kong and Singapore – all of them being major jurisdictions considered to be favorable locations for arbitration – all granted Kahara Bodas the right to further proceed in executing the award.[427] This dispute indicates the differences in states' perceptions of arbitration and the enormous practical consequences arising out of them. Another dispute that may serve to illustrate the representativeness of judgments is that in *Bharat Aluminium v. Kaiser Aluminium*.[428] In a previous dispute, *Bhatia International v. Bulk Trading*,[429] the Supreme Court ruled on the application of the Indian Arbitration and Conciliation Act of 1996 to arbitrations whose seat was outside of Indian territory. In its first decision, the court affirmed the applicability and thus allowed for further court intervention in the arbitral process to take place. This decision was, however, later reconsidered by the same court. Finally, the Indian judiciary's approach to the dispute changed in moving from significant judicial entanglement to a more arbitration-friendly attitude. The judgment might in this sense even imply a generally more arbitration-friendly approach of Indian courts.

Naturally, commercial arbitrators themselves contribute to the protection of the arbitration process. This is always apparent, when a state judiciary interferes with such on various occasions. A prominent example is the dispute *Himpurna v. Indonesia*.[430] Himpurna entered into an energy sales contract with an Indonesian state electricity company to explore and develop geothermal resources. Two power plants were supposed to be built in Indonesia, the power of which was to be sold to the state electricity company. Due to the economic crisis in 1997, the company failed to purchase the supplied energy. In an UNCITRAL arbitration pursuant to the underlying contract, the tribunal awarded damages to Himpurna. The state-owned company refused payment, which caused Himpurna to revive the proceedings, seeking for Indonesia to ensure payments by its company. On June 4, 1999, Himpurna received notice of a lawsuit in the Central District Court of Jakarta seeking enjoinment of the arbitral proceedings. The court, on July 22, 1999, issued an injunction ordering to suspend all further arbitral proceedings. A fine of USD 1 million was imposed for every day in breach of the order. The arbitral tribunal consequentially ordered an additional hearing in The Hague between September 22 and 23, 1999. It concluded that compliance with the court order would imply an inferior role of an arbitral tribunal, which the

---

426. *Kahara Bodas Co. v. Pertambangan*, 190 F.Supp.2d 936 (2001), para. 945.
427. *Rubins*, note 424, p. 382.
428. *Bharat Aluminium Co. v. Kaiser Aluminium Technical Services, Inc.*, Judgment, Civil Appeal No. 7019 (2005).
429. *Bhatia International v. Bulk Trading S.A.*, Judgment, Civil Appeal No. 6527 (2001).
430. *Himpurna California Energy Ltd. (Bermuda) v. Republic of Indonesia*, UNCITRAL, Interim Award, September 26, 1999.

parties had mandated to rule upon the dispute.[431] Furthermore, it found the actions by the Indonesia court to constitute a denial of justice.[432]

Cases like these are, of course, of an exemplary nature. However, many more similar decisions exist in various jurisdictions. What they share is an indication that jurisdictions are turning towards an arbitration-friendly approach that was previously only existent in traditional arbitration territory such as the United States, England, France or Switzerland. Such movements coincide with efforts to modernize arbitration laws and the erection of arbitration centers. It seems to be a relatively safe claim that international commercial arbitration is experiencing an upward trend in many jurisdictions that are increasingly opening up for international commerce. As much of commercial arbitration is in fact international, it is furthermore safe to state that this trend is of a global nature[433] and so perceived around the world, regardless of whether or not one particular jurisdiction chooses to accede to it. The upward trend of international commercial arbitration consists of increasing protection of the arbitral process by domestic efforts. It is conceivable that states increasingly watch these developments in order to determine their own position on the spectrum, fostering or restricting arbitration. International commercial arbitration is in this sense a truly global phenomenon in that it might even bring about competition among states as to the attractiveness for arbitration and ultimately international commerce. As regulatory powers of a state do not extend beyond its territory, advancements must take place on a domestic level. For the purpose of studying the protection of international commercial arbitration as a whole, a look beyond state borders into the international sphere is thus both necessary and promising.

[b]   *Protective Tendencies in Public International Law*

If international commercial arbitration is increasingly subject to more protection in domestic legal systems, this development may be reflected in general public international law as well. It must not be forgotten that the attractiveness of commercial arbitration profits greatly from the above-mentioned NYC, a document of public international law. As commercial arbitration is contractual, the protection of it is lastly a matter of protecting contractual rights. A very early case concerning such

---

431. *Himpurna California Energy Ltd. (Bermuda) v. Republic of Indonesia*, note 430, para. 176:

> This contention would necessarily imply that the Arbitral Tribunal must defer to the decision of the Jakarta Court. In other words, it does not content itself with denying that the Arbitral Tribunal has a higher authority than the national court with respect to the dispute with which the Parties entrusted the arbitrators; it even rejects the equality of the Arbitral Tribunal and reduces it to an inferior role.

432. *Himpurna California Energy Ltd. (Bermuda) v. Republic of Indonesia*, note 430, para. 184.
433. *See* Munir Maniruzzaman, Modernisation of International Arbitration Law in the Age of Globalisation: A Bangladesh Perspective, in: International Company and Commercial Law Review 2004, No. 5, pp. 132-137 (p. 132), who refers to it as a "global phenomenon."

protection[434] is that of *United States v. Venezuela*,[435] better known as the *Rudloff* case. Here, the United States Commissioner in 1903 stated that a taking of contractual rights is as much of a wrongdoing as the taking of tangible property and thus argued in favor of an equal protection of both.[436] Thereby, it was established that diplomatic protection, the previously applicable method of investment protection, could extend to protecting contractual rights.[437] The case highlights public international law's general willingness to shield intangible forms of property from unlawful interference, a foundation that is essential in sustaining the value of international commercial arbitration. Turning to the specific issue of protecting commercial arbitration awards, another case is of great relevance that was brought before the Permanent Court of International Justice (PCIJ) in 1939. It involved the Belgian company Société Commerciale de Belgique and Greece. Both entered into a contract that was concluded for the erection of a railway. The financial resources for covering the costs of the project were to be acquired by Greece by way of issuing bonds. As Greece later defaulted in paying back the loan granted by Société Commerciale de Belgique, an arbitration was initiated, resulting in an award in favor of the claimant. Greece refused to pay the amounts due under the award, which led Société Commerciale de Belgique to address the Belgian government, seeking diplomatic protection. Belgium turned to the PCIJ seeking clarification that Greece was in breach of its obligations. In its judgment, the tribunal cautiously approached the issue and concluded that an arbitral award may neither be set aside nor annulled in absence of a special mandate in view of the arbitration agreement, deeming the award final and binding.[438] It thereby highlighted the importance of an agreement to arbitrate and thus the parties' intentions as the essence of the entire arbitral process. As a consequence, the ICJ is therefore nowadays also not entitled to function as a review mechanism for ICSID awards.[439]

These decisions came about alongside efforts to further codify the protectability of commercial arbitration as a whole. The Geneva Protocol[440] of 1923 marks a cornerstone in this regard. It was signed at a meeting of the League of Nations and

---

434. Stephen Fietta/James Upcher, Public International Law, Investment Treaties and Commercial Arbitration: an Emerging System of Complementarity? in: Arbitration International 2013, Vol. 29 No. 2, pp. 187-221 (p. 190).
435. *US-Venezuela Mixed Claims Commission*, Rudloff case (interlocutory) (*United States of America v. Venezuela*), Reports of International Arbitral Awards 1903, Vol. IX, pp. 244-255 (p. 250).
436. *United States of America v. Venezuela*, note 435, p. 250.
437. *Fietta/Upcher*, note 434, p. 190.
438. *PCIJ*, Société Commerciale de Bélgique *(Belgium v. Greece)*, Judgment, June 15, 1939, PCIJ Series A/B No. 78, para. 57:

> It should however be added that, since the arbitral awards to which these submissions relate are, according to the arbitration clause under which they were made, "final and without appeal", and since the Court has received no mandate from the Parties in regard to them, it can neither confirm nor annul them either wholly or in part.

439. *Schreuer*, note 210, Art. 53, para. 23.
440. Geneva Protocol (1923) on Arbitration Clauses Signed at a Meeting of the Assembly of the League of Nations Held on the Twenty-Fourth Day of September, Nineteen-Hundred and

provided for recognizing the validity of private agreements to arbitrate. Furthermore, it provided for the international enforcement of arbitral awards. These provisions, however, only related to the territory in which the award was made. The scope of the protocol was therefore still rather limited. With this twofold objective, it was nevertheless the first international agreement dealing with the promotion of commercial arbitration.[441] Shortly after, the Geneva Convention of 1927 made a step forward in extending the protection of commercial arbitration insofar, as arbitral awards were now to be executed in the territories of all signatory states. These early documents paved the road for the possibly most important document of international arbitration to date. The NYC of 1958 simplified and improved the execution of arbitration, be it agreements to arbitrate or the recognition and enforcement of arbitral awards.[442] After a study conducted in 1950 by the Commission on International Commercial Arbitration on the initiative of *Sir Edwin S. Herbert*, finding that the Geneva Convention of 1927 did no longer meet the requirements of international trade, the ICC in 1953 submitted its Draft Convention to the United Nations.[443] A second draft was produced that was more conservative and laid the foundation for an international conference held in New York, which ultimately led to the adoption of the NYC on June 10, 1958.[444] The text was now more liberal than the United Nations' second draft and thus more in line with the propositions submitted by the ICC.[445] It might be that this practical orientation is one reason for the great success of the NYC. Public international law has thus, from a very early stage, been involved in fostering the use of commercial arbitration as an effective means of dispute resolution.

The development in public international law does, however, not end there. The protection of commercial arbitration has received an additional facet in the context of international human rights law. The European Court of Human Rights (ECHR) has been at the forefront of this development. The very foundation of its jurisprudence is the European Convention on Human Rights of 1953. Based upon this document was the dispute in *Stan Greek Refineries and Stratis Andreadis v. Greece*.[446] On July 22, 1972, the claimant entered into a contract with the Greek state for the construction of an oil refinery near Athens. The state was to purchase land for the erection of the refinery. However, the land was later returned to the previous owner. Following a police order, the construction came to a halt. The claimant had already entered into various supply agreements with other companies. This led him to initiate compensation proceedings in the Athens Court of First Instance against the state, which opposed

---

Twenty-Three, available at https://treaties.un.org/doc/Publication/MTDSG/Volume%20II/LON/PARTII-6.en.pdf (last accessed April 16, 2015).

441. *Redfern/Hunter*, note 332, p. 68.
442. *Redfern/Hunter*, note 332, p. 69.
443. Report and Preliminary Draft Convention adopted by the Committee on International Commercial Arbitration at its meeting of March 13, 1953, The ICC International Court of Arbitration Bulletin 1998, Vol. 9 No. 1.
444. *Emmanuel Gaillard/John Savage*, Fouchard Gaillard Goldman on International Commercial Arbitration, 1999, p. 122.
445. *Gaillard/Savage*, note 444, p. 122.
446. ECHR, *Stan Greek Refineries and Stratis Andreadis v. Greece*, Judgment, Application No. 13427/87, December 9, 1994.

Chapter 3: The Protection of Arbitral Awards in the Global Context §3.04[A]

the assumption of jurisdiction of the court, as the relevant contract contained an arbitration clause. The court dismissed the objection on the ground that the clause only referred to disputes arising out of performance, not however, nonperformance. After the state had initiated arbitral proceedings on June 12, 1980, the tribunal came to the conclusion that the arbitration agreement did grant it jurisdiction and found both parties responsible for the losses on a 70/30 basis. Furthermore, the tribunal found that the state was unlawfully retaining a check that belonged to the claimant. The arbitration award passed various instances of the Greek judiciary before it was ultimately pronounced void by the Court of Cassation on April 11, 1990. The ECHR analyzed the facts in view of Article 1 of Protocol No. 1 to the European Convention on Human Rights and came to the following conclusion:

> The Court finds that there was *an interference with the applicants' right of property* as guaranteed by Article 1 of Protocol No. 1 (P1-1). Paragraph 2 of Article 12 of Law no. 1701/1987 declared the arbitration award void and unenforceable.[447]

And further:

> It follows that it was impossible for the applicants to secure enforcement of an arbitration award having final effect and under which the State was required to pay them specified sums in respect of expenditure that they had incurred in seeking to fulfil their contractual obligations or even for them to take further action to recover the sums in question through the courts. In conclusion, there was an *interference with the applicants' property right*.[448]

The ECHR ordered Greece to pay the full amount that was due under the arbitral award. The case thus marks a significant step forward in the protection of commercial arbitration rights under public international law that formed the basis for further decisions with similar outcomes.[449] In *Regent Company v. Ukraine*,[450] the dispute concerned a contract on the processing of raw materials between COM and Oriana. After Oriana had failed to deliver, arbitral proceedings were initiated by COM, which resulted in an award rendered in its favor on December 23, 1998. After a longsome and unsuccessful attempt in enforcing the award against Oriana, COM finally turned to the European of Human Rights. It argued that the failure to allow for a timely enforcement of the arbitral award was contrary to the protections of the European Convention on Human Rights. The court referred to previous findings:

> The Court also notes that it has consistently held that a "claim" can only constitute a "possession" within the meaning of Article 1 of Protocol No. 1 if it is sufficiently established to be enforceable.[451]

---

447. ECHR, *Stan Greek Refineries and Stratis Andreadis v. Greece*, note 446, para. 66.
448. ECHR, *Stan Greek Refineries and Stratis Andreadis v. Greece*, note 446, para. 67.
449. *Fietta/Upcher*, note 434, p. 210.
450. ECHR, *Regent Company v. Ukraine*, Final Judgment, Application No. 773/03, April 3, 2008.
451. *Regent Company v. Ukraine*, note 450, para. 61.

It concluded:

> There has therefore been a *violation of Article 1 of Protocol No. 1*.[452]

Lastly, another case that is interesting to consider in this context is that of *Kin-Stib and Majkic v. Serbia*.[453] The dispute arose out of a contract between Kin-Stib, a Congolese company, and Generalexport, a Yugoslav state-owned company for the construction of a casino in Belgrade. After the casino had been erected, it encountered financial difficulties which forced the business to discontinue the operations. Kin-Stib brought the matter before an arbitral tribunal in 1996 on various grounds, which partially ruled in favor of it. The award envisaged the retaking of possession of the casino by Kin-Stib, which Generalexport did not comply with. Consequentially, enforcement proceedings were initiated, and a Yugoslav court awarded compensation for the nonoperation of the casino to Kin-Stib. However, the Serbian government later granted the license to run the casino to another party.[454] After only partially successful enforcement attempts, Kin-Stib claimed a violation of the European Convention on Human Rights before the ECHR. The court, in reliance on previous case law, held the following:

> Turning to the present case, it is firstly noted that the claim established in the arbitration award undisputedly amounts to a possession within the meaning of Article 1 of Protocol No. 1.[455]

And further:

> In view of the above, the Serbian authorities have thus clearly not taken the *necessary measures to fully enforce the arbitration award* in question and have not provided any convincing reasons for that failure. Accordingly, there has been *a violation of Article 1 of Protocol No. 1*.[456]

This look at existing jurisprudence and codifications in public international law first, highlights that commercial arbitration has always been a matter of significance and received increasing attention. Second, the protectability of commercial arbitrations[457] is fully established and especially, arbitral awards as the outcome of the arbitral process enjoy broad attention under public international law.[458] Third, during the course of the last century, this protection has gained more momentum. This development within public international law indicates a trend of continuous strengthening of parties' rights arising out of arbitral awards.

---

452. *Regent Company v. Ukraine*, note 450, para. 62.
453. ECHR, *Kin-Stib and Majkic v. Serbia*, Final Judgment, Application No. 12312/05, April 20, 2010.
454. Yaruslau Kryvoi, Introductory Note to European Court of Human Rights: Kin-Stib & Majkic v. Serbia, in: International Legal Materials 2010, Vol. 49, pp. 1181-1194 (p. 1181).
455. ECHR, *Kin-Stib and Majkic v. Serbia*, note 453, para. 84.
456. ECHR, *Kin-Stib and Majkic v. Serbia*, note 453, para. 85.
457. *See also* concerning the protection of an international investment arbitration from a domestic court's antisuit-injunction *British Carribbean Bank Limited v. The Attorney General of Belize*, Judgment, Carribbean Court of Justice Appeal No. CV 001 of 2013, June 25, 2013.
458. *See* Sabine Konrad/Marcus Birch, Non-Enforcement of Arbitral Awards: Only a Pyrrhic Victory?, in: Transnational Dispute Management 2010, Vol. 1, pp. 1-9 (p. 8).

[c] Approaches of International Investment Law

International investment law possibly allows the broadest insights into the protection of commercial arbitration. The foregoing analysis on the qualification of arbitral awards as or like investments has elaborated on the access to investment arbitration. It was analyzed that under certain – albeit limited – conditions, tribunals have indeed allowed for international investment arbitration to be an option of recourse in case of a frustrated attempt in enforcing an arbitral award. From a more general perspective, *Saipem v. Bangladesh*[459] has laid a remarkable foundation for investors possibly finding host states liable for disrupting the arbitral process.[460] This option is certainly a strong indicator of a protective attitude towards the commercial arbitration process in international investment arbitration. It is, however, not the only one. Apart from matters of access to investment arbitration, a brief look at tribunals' approaches on the merits – which the *Saipem* case equally contributes to – is similarly fruitful. Has the tribunal found that it is dealing with an investment and an investor, the claimant generally has two options in arguing a violation of his rights under a BIT, if the host state has allegedly interfered with the arbitral process: claiming a violation of the fair and equitable treatment-standard, particularly a denial of justice, and claiming an expropriation.[461] It has been pointed out that originally, investment tribunals were less willing to grant protection from abusive court conduct. The *Martini*-arbitration[462] represents one of the few early instances, in which an investment tribunal has ruled on the matter.[463] Martini & Co., an Italian company, had entered into a concession agreement with the government of Venezuela in 1898, under which it was allowed to exploit coal mines and operate a railway. Due to the civil war in Venezuela, the company's operations came to a halt and it successfully obtained an award before the Italy-Venezuela Mixed Claims Commission. However, the Venezuelan Court of Cassation later cancelled the concession agreement, after the Procurator General of Caracas so requested. Diplomatic efforts then led Italy and Venezuela to submit the matter to an international tribunal in 1930. It analyzed the court's actions and found that Venezuela thereby committed a denial of justice.[464] The case has broken ground for broader protection which appears to be undergoing an evolution in favor of investors.[465]

---

459. *Saipem S.p.A. v. The Republic of Bangladesh,* note 286.
460. *Giulia Carbone*, Interference of the Court of the Seat with International Arbitration, The Symposium, in: Journal of Dispute Resolution 2012, No. 1 Art. 9, pp. 217-244 (p. 243): "Turning to the second question, Saipem is a landmark decision since it gives new hope to investors, holding that States could be considered liable under international law for the wrongful conduct of their courts hindering the arbitral proceedings."
461. *Carbone*, note 460, p. 241.
462. *Italy v. Venezuela*, Award, May 3, 1930, in: American Journal of International Law 1931, Vol. 25, pp. 554-592.
463. *Borzu Sabahi*, Compensation and Restitution in Investor-State Arbitration – Principles and Practice, 2011, p. 75.
464. *Sabahi*, note 463, pp. 74 et seq.
465. *Carbone*, note 460, p. 239; *see also Stephen Schwebel*, Anti-Suit Injunctions in International Arbitration – An Overview, in: Emmanuel Gaillard (ed.), Anti-Suit Injunctions in International Arbitration, 2005, pp. 5-16 (pp. 12 et seq.): "But when a domestic court, an organ of the State in the eyes of international law, blocks access to arbitration through issuance of an anti-suit

For the purpose of illustration, a look at two exemplary decisions and their approaches is of great relevance. The first dispute depicts the willingness of the tribunal to grant the claimant the broadest protection possible from all sorts of interferences by local courts. The decision is one of the landmark cases in international investment arbitration, *Chevron v. Ecuador*.[466] As it is a matter of impossibility to provide details on the entire scope of this momentous dispute within the limits of this analysis, it must suffice to recall its basic fact pattern. The Lago Agrio oil field in Ecuador had been heavily used for oil production, particularly by the oil companies Texaco and Chevron. Upon multiple ecological problems arising out of the operations, Ecuador held both liable and obtained a multibillion dollar judgment against them from an Ecuadorian court. The main issues of the dispute that are of most relevance here, however, concern the diversion of oil revenue by Ecuador in the 1980s that led to contractual disputes. These were brought before Ecuadorian courts and took approximately fifteen years to be adjudicated.[467] The arbitral tribunal was able to avail itself of a useful clause in Article 2 section 7 of the United States-Ecuador BIT of August 27, 1993:

> Each Party shall provide effective means of asserting claims and enforcing rights with respect to investment, investment agreements, and investment authorizations.

The arbitrators took this clause into broad consideration and interpreted it as providing a *lex specialis* to the public international law standard of denial of justice. This approach allowed for a less demanding test to be applied in order to evaluate whether or not a breach of the BIT had occurred.[468] The analysis also provided a comfortable starting point for the decisions in *Saipem v. Bangladesh*[469] as well as *White Industries v. India*,[470] which applied the ruling to a court interference with commercial arbitration.[471] The tribunal in *Chevron v. Ecuador* held as follows:

> Additionally, within *the lex specialis of Article II(7)*, the Tribunal finds no requirement that evidence be shown "of the host State's extreme interference in the judicial proceedings" in order to breach the BIT as had been initially argued by the Respondent (R V, ¶340). [...] The Tribunal reiterates that the standard under Article II(7) is one of "effectiveness" which applies to a variety of State conduct that has an *effect on the ability of an investor to assert claims or enforce rights*. [...] The Tribunal therefore finds that, while instances of governmental interference may be relevant to the analysis under Article II(7), *the provision is applicable to the*

---

injunction, that too constitutes a denial of justice for which the State of which the court is part (whether or not the judicial branch be independent) is internationally responsible."

466. *Chevron Corporation and Texaco Petroleum Corporation v. The Republic of Ecuador*, Partial Award on the Merits, UNCITRAL, PCA Case No. 34877, March 30, 2010.
467. Michael D. Goldhaber, The Rise of Arbitral Power Over Domestic Courts, in: Stanford Journal of Complex Litigation 2013, Vol. 1 No. 2, pp. 373-416 (p. 389).
468. *Chevron Corporation and Texaco Petroleum Corporation v. The Republic of Ecuador*, note 466, para. 244.
469. *Saipem S.p.A. v. The Republic of Bangladesh*, note 286.
470. *White Industries Australia Limited v. Republic of India*, note 246.
471. Goldhaber, note 467, p. 390.

Claimants' claims for undue delay and manifestly unjust decisions even if no such interference is shown.[472]

The second dispute dwells in more detail on the protection of arbitration under international investment law. It is the decision of the tribunal in *DLP v. Yemen*.[473] DLP, a construction company formed under the laws of the Sultanate of Oman, had entered into contracts for the development of road connections in Yemen, which began in 1997. The contractual relationship brought about differences in the payment obligations which resulted in arbitral proceedings on June 26, 2004. On August 9, 2004, the tribunal rendered its award and found that DLP was entitled to receive further payments by Yemen. The government of Yemen then sought to have the award set aside on September 22, 2004. Furthermore, DLP was addressed by Yemen in an attempt to settle the dispute. Although the offer to settle was economically disadvantageous compared to the existing award, DLP finally agreed to signing a settlement agreement before complaining about harassment, threat and theft that had led to the agreement. On August 2, 2005, DLP turned to ICSID and filed a request for arbitration. In taking a strong position, protecting arbitration in general, the tribunal found in favor of DLP and awarded the amount already due under the commercial arbitration award:

> As a matter of essence, arbitral proceedings have a final and binding character. Both parties chose arbitrators whom they trust. In consequence, they waive the right to challenge the arbitral tribunal's decision, except for extraordinary circumstances. *It is therefore contrary to the spirit of arbitration to constrain a party to negotiate in order to obtain a reduction of the amount effectively owed, when an arbitral tribunal has issued a definitive award.*[474]

Both cases illustrate that the protection of jurisdictional rights in general[475] and especially those related to commercial arbitration is a relevant matter within international investment law. At the same time, however, the number of disputes dealing with possible violations is still limited. Nevertheless, it has been pointed out that international tribunals are at least increasingly willing to look at domestic court rulings[476] and also to protect commercial agreements to arbitrate.[477] The requirements for a successful claim on the merits are still high, which might be a reason for the limited number of cases in this regard.[478] However, the treatment of arbitral awards as or like investments might have sparked a development of further protection of the rights arising out of commercial arbitration in international investment law.

---

472. *Chevron Corporation and Texaco Petroleum Corporation v. The Republic of Ecuador*, note 466, para. 248.
473. *Desert Line Projects LLC v. The Republic of Yemen*, Award, ICSID Case No. ARB/05/17, February 6, 2008.
474. *Desert Line Projects LLC v. The Republic of Yemen*, note 473, para. 177.
475. Carbone, note 460, p. 239.
476. Goldhaber, note 467, p. 374.
477. Fietta/Upcher, note 434, p. 217.
478. Richard Garnett, National Court Intervention in Arbitration as an Investment Treaty Claim, in: International and Comparative Law Quarterly 2011, Vol. 60, pp. 485-498 (p. 490).

[2] Self-Protection in International Investment Arbitration

Yet another point of interest is the way in which investment tribunals understand their position and that of international investment arbitration in relation to domestic courts. Especially with regards to a possible development of protecting international investment arbitration from the inside, a few selected cases should be considered. The first one is *SGS v. Pakistan*.[479] SGS had entered into a contract with Pakistan in 1994, offering to aid in the country's customs revenue collection. The contract contained an arbitration clause that referred all disputes to arbitration in Islamabad. A dispute arose out of Pakistan's cancellation of the contract, which allegedly constituted a violation of the agreement between the parties. Pakistan then filed for arbitration, which SGS objected to. Despite its objection, SGS filed a counterclaim and also commenced ICSID arbitration. Pakistan objected to such initiation as the dispute was, in its opinion, plainly contractual. On July 3, 2002, the Supreme Court of Pakistan issued an order, prohibiting SGS to further proceed with the ICSID arbitration and referring the dispute solely to commercial arbitration as allegedly envisaged by the contract. The ICSID tribunal later issued a procedural order, in which it took a strong stand in protecting international investment arbitration:

> It is essential for the proper operation of both the BIT and the ICSID Convention that *the right of access to international adjudication be maintained*. In the Tribunal's view, it has *a duty to protect this right* of access and should exercise such powers as are vested in it under Article 47 of the ICSID Convention in furtherance of that duty.[480]

This order exemplifies a matter that has been raised in a number of investment arbitrations. It concerns an ICSID tribunal's authority to issue recommendations towards domestic courts as envisaged by Article 47 ICSID-Convention.[481] The wording in this provision is clear. It provides for an ICSID tribunal's authority to make mere recommendations. However, tribunals have interpreted it as also granting the authority to issue orders.[482] This elevation of an investment tribunal's position represents the

---

479. *SGS Société Générale de Surveillance SA v. Islamic Republic of Pakistan*, Procedural Order No. 2, ICSID Case No. ARB/01/13, October 16, 2002.
480. *SGS Société Générale de Surveillance SA v. Islamic Republic of Pakistan*, note 479, p. 300.
481. Article 47 ICSID-Convention provides as follows: "Except as the parties otherwise agree, the Tribunal may, if it considers that the circumstances so require, recommend any provisional measures which should be taken to preserve the respective rights of either party."
482. *Emilio Agustín Maffezini v. Kingdom of Spain*, Procedural Order No. 2, ICSID Case No. ARB/97/7, October 28, 1999, para. 9: "Accordingly, for the purposes of this Order, the Tribunal deems the word 'recommend' to be of equivalent value as the word 'order'"; *see also Victor Pey Casado and Fundación Presidente Allende v. The Republic of Chile*, Decision on Provisional Matters, ICSID Case No. ARB/98/2, September 25, 2001, para. 26:

> De lo anterior se concluye que las medidas provisionales tienen, particular y especialmente, como objeto preservar y proteger la eficacia de la decisión a dictarse sobre el fondo del asunto y, por lo tanto, evitar que se perjudique la ejecución del laudo, o impedir que una de las partes, por acción u omisión, atente, de manera unilateral, contra los derechos eventuales de la parte contraria.

regularly challenging interplay between arbitration and domestic courts. The use of *antisuit injunctions* issued by investment tribunals is most illustrative in this regard. These are traditionally orders that are directed at parties, attempting to prevent them from involving domestic courts. Both parties to the dispute have chosen to opt for a resolution outside of the typical judicial framework. In the context of international investment arbitration, however, these orders have been transformed and directed at states.[483] In addition to the keen move of attributing to recommendations the power of orders came the practical consequence that such orders have been interpreted to constitute binding law,[484] which is now found to be well established in international investment arbitration.[485] Interestingly, this interpretive development has taken place despite it being contrary to the legislative history of the ICSID-Convention.[486] This approach of investment tribunals once again highlights that frequently, they are taking powerful steps in securing or even improving the effectivity of investment arbitration.

Apart from *antisuit injunctions*, one finds a similarly interesting internal support of international investment arbitration in the context of so-called *fork in the road*-clauses. These are contained in a number of BITs and aim to make a decision of an investor to address either a domestic court or an arbitral tribunal in resolving the dispute final and binding. In other words, they require investors to make a final decision between litigation and arbitration. This should then limit jurisdiction of investment tribunals, if an investor has previously engaged in litigation concerning the dispute. However, *fork in the road*-clauses appear to have had no effect on limiting the assumption of jurisdiction by tribunals in arbitral practice.[487] Tribunals have almost consistently held that they are only barred from jurisdiction, if the investor has invoked the same provisions before a domestic court than it seeks to invoke before the arbitral tribunal, namely those of the relevant BIT.[488] While this analysis is certainly far from

---

see also City Oriente Limited v. The Republic of Ecuador and Empresa Estatal Petróleos de Ecuador, Decision on Provisional Measures, ICSID Case No. ARB/06/21, November 19, 2007, paras. 83 et seq.; *see also Perenco Ecuador Ltd. v. The Republic of Ecuador and Empresa Estatal Petróleos de Ecuador*, Decision on Provisional Matters, ICSID Case No. ARB/08/6, May 8, 2009, para. 74: "It is now generally accepted that provisional measures are tantamount to orders, and are binding on the party to which they are directed [...]."
483. Goldhaber, note 467, pp. 378 and 383, who points to the *Chevron v. Ecuador* dispute as one that clearly is directed at suspending domestic courts from taking actions: "Of more central concern to this Article, the state's formal absence from the enjoined litigation makes *Chevron v. Ecuador* the purest example of an arbitral attempt to suspend judicial action."
484. Goldhaber, note 467, p. 380.
485. *Tokio Tokelés v. Ukraine*, Procedural Order No. 1, ICSID Case No. ARB/02/18, July 1, 2003, para. 4.
486. Schreuer, note 210, Art. 47, para. 16.
487. Christoph Schreuer, Interaction of International Tribunals and Domestic Courts, in: Arthur W. Rovine (ed.), Contemporary Issues in International Arbitration and Mediation: The Fordham Papers 2010, pp. 71-94 (p. 79).
488. *See Pan American Energy LLC and BP Argentina Explorations Company v. The Argentine Republic*, Decision on Preliminary Objections, ICSID Case No. ARB/03/13, July 27, 2006, para. 157; *see also Toto Costruzioni Generali S.p.A. v. The Republic of Lebanon*, Decision on Jurisdiction, ICSID Case No. ARB/07/12, September 11, 2009, paras. 213-217; *see also Champion Trading Company, Ameritrade International, Inc., James T. Wahba, John B. Wahba, Timothy T.Wahba v. Arab Republic of Egypt*, Decision on Jurisdiction, ICSID Case No.

being complete, it does indicate that frequently, investment tribunals are confident in protecting or even strengthening their powers towards domestic courts. This applies especially, when domestic courts seek to interfere with the arbitral process.[489]

The foregoing observations regarding international arbitration as a whole provide tendencies that are of interest in the context of treaty interpretation. First, international commercial arbitration is experiencing an upward trend in a number of jurisdictions. The willingness of a respective state to promote, foster and protect arbitration as a means of dispute resolution is reflected by a number of factors, such as individual arbitration laws, the erection and maintenance of arbitration centers or the reduced entanglement of the judiciary in the arbitral process. Many states are continuously taking actions to become more arbitration-friendly, a development that is not taking place in isolation, but on a global, sometimes even competitive level. Second, public international law in general has in the past and continues in the present, to promote and protect commercial arbitration. The NYC serves as the most prominent example of that observation that is accompanied by references to international court judgments, protecting the arbitral process. Third, the protection of international commercial arbitration within international investment law appears to be an increasing trend. Fourth, international investment law is strengthened from inside by way of investment arbitration. Nevertheless, while these results are intended to shed light on the direction in which international arbitration is heading, they should not lead to the conclusion that both, commercial and investment arbitration are developing identically.[490]

[3]   *Challenging the Divide in International Arbitration*

It has become evident that international arbitration is dynamic. What is of particular interest in the context of these dynamics are the ramifications for the relationship between international commercial and investment arbitration. The hybrid nature of international investment arbitration has been previously described. However, the increasing protection of international commercial arbitration in international investment arbitration and public international law in general could signal a growing nexus.[491] The arbitral decisions that have been subject to the foregoing analysis, treating commercial arbitration awards as or like investments, indicate a respective interconnection of the two. Simultaneously, they are based on some interpretive insufficiencies that might prove troublesome in the development. International investment arbitration may serve as a forum for frustrated attempts of conducting

---

ARB/02/9, October 21, 2003, para. 3.4.3; *see*, however, contrarily *Pantechniki S.A. Contractors & Engineers (Greece) v. The Republic of Albania*, Award, ICSID Case No. ARB/07/21, July 30, 2009, paras. 53-67.

489.   *Schreuer*, note 487, p. 93.
490.   *See Böckstiegel*, note 163, pp. 589 et seq., who points to existing differences in the implementation of commercial arbitration and the necessary improvements in a number of jurisdictions as well as investment arbitration and its future.
491.   *See Fietta/Upcher*, note 434, pp. 220 et seq.

commercial arbitration. However, is this really part of a more global trend, in which commercial and investment arbitration are in the process of converging?[492]

Arbitral theory might be a starting point in addressing the question. If one were to hypothetically assume that such trend is emerging, the blurring of the theoretical distinction between commercial and investment arbitration might have severe consequences for international arbitration as a whole.[493] From commercial arbitration's point of view, possessing a mechanism to address frustrated arbitral efforts is certainly desirable. However, it is not investment arbitration that can generally serve as an instrument of legal recourse. As intriguing as the protective treatment of commercial arbitration awards may be, it remains an option demanding a fact pattern and legal prerequisites that are highly specific. After all, international investment law envisages the protection of investors, not of commercial arbitration per se. The fact that both protections may at times interlace should not lead astray. Interpretive insufficiencies in the existing decisions that establish the interconnections signal the difficulty of the development. Stretching the realm of investment arbitration by way of, at times, inadequate methodology for the purpose of strengthening commercial arbitration may significantly destabilize the entire mechanism.[494] The development of international commercial arbitration may in the future see new possibilities blossoming that could strengthen the protection of its participants.[495] International investment arbitration, however, is not an appropriate forum for generally providing such service.[496] At the same time, categorically opposing the option of investment arbitration providing a method of recourse would be erroneous. Reliance on investment arbitration in the event of a frustrated commercial arbitration process is a reality, possibly a soaring one.

---

492. See *Garnett*, note 178, p. 198:

> What is clear after Saipem, though, is that the realm of investor-state arbitration has now expanded beyond the context of State repudiation of arbitration agreements to embrace a much wider sphere of state conduct in relation to arbitrations. The formerly "parallel universes" of international commercial arbitration and investor-state arbitration are now coming into closer interaction.

> see also *Mistelis*, note 249, p. 24: "Linking the destiny of commercial arbitration outcomes with foreign investment protection and investment treaty arbitration is indeed an intriguing proposition with consequences which are not yet easy to ascertain fully."

493. *Sornarajah*, note 422, p. 161: "It is an unfortunate facet of many works in the area that they treat these distinct types of arbitration in the same breath, accentuating their similarities and ignoring the fact that their theoretical bases are different." and further: "the failure to understand the element of sovereignty has led to many problems in the area."
494. *Paulsson*, note 199, p. 257: "Arbitration without privity is a delicate mechanism. A single incident of an adventurist arbitrator going beyond the proper scope of his jurisdiction in a sensitive case may be sufficient to generate a backlash."
495. See *William W. Park*, Convention Violations and Investment Claims, in: Arbitration International 2013, Vol. 29 No. 2, pp. 175-186 (p. 186): "Only time will tell whether the international legal order will evolve to accord new mechanisms to promote respect for the New York Convention."
496. See *Kaufmann-Kohler*, note 262, p. 172: "As a result, the idea that a party dissatisfied with any domestic court decision would have automatic access to an international court or tribunal must be dismissed."

Unfortunately, the relationship between law and such realities is anything but a matter of clarity. In an attempt to escape the mythological fate of Pandora, further analysis on this rather philosophical issue shall be omitted. However, if the law is described as having to reflect reality,[497] there is force in the argument. A practical need of investment arbitration, supporting commercial arbitration, may necessitate the field's adaptation. Generally opposing the option may thus partially deprive international investment law of its functionality. If it is derivable by way of properly applying existing methodology, its existence is well deserved. The truth then, as it frequently is the case, lies somewhere in the middle. Assuming that both arbitral mechanisms are converging, the development must come to a halt where the theoretical bases are blurred and weakened. This is achieved by strict adherence to methodological canons: acknowledging and respecting the existent limits of both forms of arbitration while similarly accepting that, subject to individual fact patterns, they may intersect.

The examination of a possible convergence in practice must continue with an immediate letdown. It is that the question will remain unanswered in a clear affirmative or negation. The cause is not unwillingness to do so, but the impossibility of the venture. The number of disputes that exist is still too limited to provide a full-fledged determination. Therefore, meek steps are appropriate.[498] The first such step is a look at the state of international arbitration as it currently stands. The theoretical bases of commercial and investment arbitration are different and thus do not permit the blurring of the two. Nevertheless, we do witness that both forms of arbitration may intersect in practice. Postulating that both constitute legal orders, their overlapping may be the result of the fluidity of the arbitral universe.[499] These intersections are still fractional and thus not sufficient to really speak of a global trend. In practice, a convergence of commercial and investment arbitration may indeed be taking place. Apart from the qualification of arbitral awards, we have seen that international investment tribunals have already taken bold steps in protecting commercial arbitration. This protection is, however, only one form of possible convergence. Such development might be similarly visible in considering further issues of a growing interrelationship. Not because of elliptical stretching of realms, but by way of continuous discovery. The first additional intersection may lie in the consideration of the NYC, an international treaty designed for facilitating and strengthening the attractiveness of commercial arbitration, within international investment arbitration. State judiciaries have been found to act contrary to essential provisions of the NYC. A forum of

---

497. *Jan Paulsson*, The Idea of Arbitration, 2013, p. 75: "Law must ultimately be founded in social reality, Romano reasoned." in referring to *Santi Romano*, L'ordinamento giuridico, 1918.
498. *See Kaufmann-Kohler*, note 262, p. 172, who wisely highlights that "[t]he cases are still modest in number, and it remains to be seen whether they signal the emergence of a permanent phenomenon."
499. *See Jan Paulsson*, Arbitration in Three Dimensions, LSE Law, Society and Economy Working Papers 2/2010, available at http://www.lse.ac.uk/collections/law/wps/WPS2010-02_Paulsson.pdf (last accessed September 11, 2014), p. 26, who describes the fluid universe of arbitration and the efforts in finding a theoretical concept for the phenomenon: "The fluid legal order in which arbitration operates undoubtedly works in practice, but, as the old joke asks: will it work in theory?"

international adjudication on the matter is, however, not existent.[500] The question is then, if such remedy could be provided by international investment arbitration.[501]

An interesting dispute to consider in this regard is one that has only become public after the rendered award was challenged in a domestic court. Duke Investments Limited, a company under the laws of Cyprus, had successfully secured an LCIA arbitral award in a commercial dispute against Kaliningrad. It sought to have the award enforced in Lithuania. The local courts enforced the award against Kaliningrad, which owned a building on Lithuanian territory. Kaliningrad then invoked the BIT between Russia and Lithuania to argue that an expropriation had taken place when the Lithuanian courts froze its asset. In contrast to the cases previously analyzed, here, the claimant turned against the enforcement of the award rather than its nonenforcement. The tribunal thus faced a challenging task. The enforcement of the LCIA award was based upon the principles enshrined in the NYC, including the finality of respective court decisions. The relevant BIT provided for jurisdiction of the tribunal in case there was an investment and possibly a violation of the standards of protection of that investment treaty. The dilemma is obvious: assuming jurisdiction, given this factual and legal pattern, would have represented a challenge to the finality of a court's decision pursuant to the NYC. Not assuming jurisdiction would have possibly disregarded the mandate of the applicable BIT. At this point, commercial and investment arbitration clearly intersected. The tribunal ruled that the provisions of the NYC must prevail and therefore declined jurisdiction;[502] a decision that did not remain uncriticized.[503]

A second additional intersection lies in the interpretation of umbrella clauses contained in BITs. Recalling the brief introduction to these clauses, it is essentially their potential of transforming contract claims into treaty claims that is of interest here. Where a private party has entered into a contract with a state-owned entity, this contract will typically envisage a means of dispute resolution. This will either be litigation or commercial arbitration. In an investment contract or BIT, this will typically

---

500. *Park*, note 495, pp. 178 et seq.
501. *Garnett*, note 478, p. 497: "In particular, could an investment treaty breach ever be found where a court has purported to apply provisions of an international instrument such as the New York Convention or the Model Law but done so in an arguably unreasonable manner?"
502. *Kaliningrad (Fédération de Russie) v. La République de Lituanie*, Arrêt du Cour D'Appel de Paris, 09/19535, November 18, 2010, p. 3; *see also Böckstiegel*, note 163, p. 584:

> But we concluded that it was the clear intention and result of the New York Convention that no further appeals should be available against court decisions recognizing and enforcing a foreign arbitral award other than those expressly mentioned in the Convention itself. Accepting such court decisions as possible expropriations under a BIT would be in conflict with that intention and result and even an examination on the merits would open Pandora's Box for such a further and unwarranted appeal mechanism against such court decisions. In so far as thereby a conflict arises between the BIT and the Convention, by using the tools of interpretation of public international law on conflicts between treaties, we came to the conclusion that the New York Convention must prevail over the BIT. Therefore, we refused to accept our jurisdiction under the BIT.

503. *Kaufmann-Kohler*, note 262, p. 164: "There is an obvious difficulty with this reasoning. Indeed, by adopting this view, the tribunal failed to exercise its jurisdiction under the BIT."

be investment arbitration.[504] An umbrella clause may then elevate a claim that arises out of a commercial contract to a claim arising out of the applicable investment instrument. Instead of pursuing a claim using the mechanism provided for by the contract, an investor may choose to rely on investment arbitration and on the umbrella clause. Its interpretation therefore has the potential of directly affecting the relationship between the chosen methods of dispute resolution in the contract, commercial arbitration and investment arbitration. Both forms of arbitration may, given a respective interpretation, be available to the investor. It does not come as a surprise that such approach has been a matter of controversy in recent years. The first investment arbitration addressing this issue[505] was that of *SGS v. Pakistan*,[506] whose factual pattern was previously outlined. Both parties argued about their contractual obligations, which led SGS to file for arbitration on October 12, 2001. One of its arguments was that Pakistan had violated the umbrella clause, as it is essentially its purpose to transform claims under a contract into claims under a treaty.[507] The arbitrators did not follow the argument, but rather reached the following, interesting conclusion:

> Considering the widely accepted principle with which we started, namely, that under general international law, a violation of a contract entered into by a State with an investor of another State, is not, by itself, a violation of international law, and considering further that the legal consequences that the Claimant would have us attribute to Article 11 of the BIT are so far-reaching in scope, and so automatic and unqualified and sweeping in their operation, so *burdensome in their potential impact* upon a Contracting Party, we believe that *clear and convincing evidence must be adduced* by the Claimant. Clear and convincing evidence of what? Clear and convincing evidence that such was indeed *the shared intent* of the Contracting Parties to the Swiss-Pakistan Investment Protection Treaty in incorporating Article 11 in the BIT. We do not find such evidence in the text itself of Article 11. We have

---

504. *El Paso Energy International Company v. The Argentine Republic*, Decision on Jurisdiction, ICSID Case No. ARB/03/15, April 27, 2006, para. 77:

    > In both cases, it is more than likely that the foreign investor will have managed to insert a dispute settlement mechanism into the contract; usually, in a purely commercial contract, that mechanism will be commercial arbitration or the national courts, while in an investment agreement it will generally be an international arbitration mechanism such as that of ICSID.

505. *David Foster*, Umbrella Clauses – a Retreat from the Philippines?, in: International Arbitration Law Review 2006, Vol. 100, pp. 100-108 (p. 100).
506. *SGS Société Générale de Surveillance SA v. Islamic Republic of Pakistan*, note 479.
507. *SGS Société Générale de Surveillance SA v. Islamic Republic of Pakistan*, Decision of the Tribunal on Objections to Jurisdiction, ICSID Case No. ARB/01/13, August 6, 2003, para. 99:

    > Article 11 of the Treaty is characterized by the Claimant as an "umbrella clause which says that each time you violate a provision of the contract, ..., you also violate norms of international law, you violate the treaty by the same token." Counsel later elaborated on this characterization of Article 11 as follows: ...I myself prefer to call it a mirror effect clause, because in fact it is a mirror effect which it creates. You have a violation of the contract, and the Treaty says, as if you had a mirror, that this violation will also be susceptible to being characterized as a violation of the Treaty. So the same facts, the same breach will be a violation of the contract in itself, and a violation of the Treaty.

not been pointed to any other evidence of the putative common intent of the Contracting Parties by the Claimant.[508]

And further:

A third consequence would be that an investor may, at will, nullify any freely negotiated dispute settlement clause in a State contract. On the reading of Article 11 urged by the Claimant, the benefits of the dispute settlement provisions of a contract with a State also a party to a BIT, would flow only to the investor. For that investor could always defeat the State's invocation of the contractually specified forum, and render any mutually agreed procedure of dispute settlement, other than BIT-specified ICSID arbitration, a dead-letter, at the investor's choice. The investor would remain free to go to arbitration either under the contract or under the BIT. But the State party to the contract would be effectively *precluded from proceeding to the arbitral forum specified in the contract unless the investor was minded to agree*.[509]

Following this decision, another dispute arose that similarly dealt with the interpretation of the umbrella clause. In *SGS v. Philippines*, the claimant sought payments from the respondent allegedly due under a contract between them. In following the same line of arguments concerning the umbrella clause, SGS attempted to elevate the contract claim to a treaty claim. The tribunal ruled as follows:

To summarize, for present purposes Article X(2) includes commitments or obligations arising under contracts entered into by the host State.[510]

Naturally, these conflicting decisions have given rise to a heated debate on both approaches.[511] In their aftermath, they have been considered by other tribunals and triggered intriguing analyses. One example that is especially relevant in the context of this endeavor of spotting intersections between commercial and investment arbitration is the dispute in *Eureko v. Poland*.[512] The claimant had purchased shares in a leading governmental insurance group in Poland. This company was to be privatized by way of a public offering, which also constituted a contractual condition between the claimant and the respondent. However, the insurance group's privatization did not end up taking place, which led Eureko to initiate arbitral proceedings on February 11, 2003.[513] In analyzing the umbrella clause, the tribunal considered both approaches and chose to follow the one in *SGS v. Philippines*.[514] However, the most interesting facet of

---

508. *SGS Société Générale de Surveillance SA v. Islamic Republic of Pakistan*, note 507, para. 167.
509. *SGS Société Générale de Surveillance SA v. Islamic Republic of Pakistan*, note 507, para. 168.
510. *SGS Société Générale de Surveillance SA v. Republic of the Philippines*, Decision of the Tribunal on Objections to Jurisdiction, ICSID Case No. ARB/02/6, January 29, 2004, para. 127.
511. *Foster*, note 505, p. 100.
512. *Eureko B.V. v. Republic of Poland*, Partial Award, UNCITRAL, August 19, 2005.
513. *See Newcombe/Paradell*, note 79, p. 97.
514. *Eureko B.V. v. Republic of Poland*, note 512, para. 257:

> This Tribunal finds the foregoing analysis of the Tribunal in SGS v. the Republic of the Philippines, a Tribunal which had among its distinguished members Professor Crawford, cogent and convincing. While having the greatest respect for the distinguished members of the Tribunal in SGS v. the Islamic Republic of Pakistan, it is constrained to say that it finds its analysis of the umbrella clause less convincing.

the dispute is not so much the actual decision, but more so the dissenting opinion that was delivered by *Jerzy Rajski*, in which he opposed the tribunal's interpretation of the umbrella clause and wisely pointed to the intersection between commercial and investment arbitration:

> It is worth of note that by opening a wide door to foreign parties to commercial contracts concluded with a State-owned company *to switch their contractual disputes from normal jurisdiction of international commercial arbitration tribunals or state courts to BIT Tribunals, the majority of this Tribunal has created a potentially dangerous precedent capable of producing negative effects on the further development of foreign capital participation in privatizations of State-owned companies.* At the same time, this decision may lead to undermine the fundamental principles upon which both national and international laws on contracts have been based: equal legal protection of all parties to commercial contracts irrespective of their nationality. The Tribunal's decision may lead *to create a privileged class of foreign parties to commercial contract who may easily transform their contractual disputes with State-owned companies into BIT disputes. This way, jurisdiction clauses agreed by the parties submitting all contractual disputes between the parties to an international arbitration tribunal or a state court may be easily frustrated by a foreign contracting party.*[515]

This opinion highlights not only the link between both forms of arbitration, it also examines the consequences of the existing approaches. It has not ended the debate on the matter, but certainly contributed greatly to emphasizing its importance. Henceforth, tribunals have continued to take differing steps in either supporting[516] or rejecting[517] the decision in *SGS v. Philippines*. The matter is thus rather unlikely to be settled any time soon. Nevertheless, the intersection in this regard is highly illustrative. Most interestingly, however, it provides a test for an observation that was made earlier. International commercial arbitration has experienced an upward trend that shows in an increasing protection by domestic policies, public international law and international investment arbitration. While investment tribunals have frequently stepped in to balance frustrated commercial arbitrations, the umbrella clause bears the potential of transforming complementarity of investment and commercial arbitration into competition between the two.

Whether or not there is indeed a global trend to the effect that commercial and investment arbitration are gradually converging remains a question that is still impossible to answer in a straightforward manner. The initial warning of this result at

---

515. *Eureko B.V. v. Republic of Poland,* Dissenting Opinion, UNCITRAL, August 19, 2005, para. 11.
516. *Noble Ventures, Inc. v. Romania,* Award, ICSID Case No. ARB/01/11, October 12, 2005, para. 54:

> In other words, two States may include in a bilateral investment treaty a provision to the effect that, in the interest of achieving the objects and goals of the treaty, the host State may incur international responsibility by reason of a breach of its contractual obligations towards the private investor of the other Party, the breach of contract being thus 'internationalized', i.e. assimilated to a breach of the treaty.

517. *El Paso Energy International Company v. The Argentine Republic,* note 504, para. 77 in directly opposing the reasoning of the *Noble Ventures* tribunal: "In this Tribunal's opinion, this is not a good reason, and it can explain why."

the beginning should now ease the disappointment. The analysis has firstly revealed that the interpretation of commercial arbitration awards as or like investments is not the only intersection between commercial and investment arbitration. The handling of the NYC within international investment law, as well as the impact of umbrella clauses, constitute similar points of contact. It is conceivable that in the future, more investors will follow the approach of seeking protection of their commercial arbitration rights by way of investment arbitration. The interplay between the two may thus gain further momentum. It was rightly concluded that such development would challenge the current understanding of the finality of commercial arbitrations and the fragmentation of international dispute settlement.[518] The dynamics that have previously caused the evolution of public international law have not vanished. Rather, they continue to shape the legal reality in which we live.[519] As long as attention to theoretical bases, methodology and care are practiced, the development bears potential of satisfactory results. After all, the evolution from gunboat to table talk diplomacy equally derived from dynamics.

[4] *The Impact on Treaty Interpretation*

The dynamics in international arbitration may impact treaty interpretation as the methodological essence of investment protection. At this point, it is necessary to recall the apparent flaws that were discovered in a number of interpretive approaches, not only in the qualification of commercial arbitration awards, but also in international investment arbitration as a whole. These are limited or no adherence to the principles of the VCLT, generally insufficient reasoning of awards and the implication of an existing doctrine of precedent. In more general terms, such approaches do not meet the requirements of proper interpretation within international investment law. Due to its public international law roots, the standards are high. They descend from the involvement of public interest and the repercussions arbitral awards may have on the development of a state and its population,[520] elements distinguishing investment from

---

518. *Kaufmann-Kohler*, note 262, pp. 1152 et seq.
519. *Pierre-Marie Dupuy*, L'Unité de l'ordre juridique international - Cours général de droit international public 2000, p. 478:

> La Cour international de Justice s'y replierait sur le traitement de questions pour ainsi dire traditionelles du droit international, comme celles relatives a l'attribution de territoires contestés our à leur délimitation, cependant que les jurisdictions plus récentes, pénales, ou spécialisées dans le droit de la mer ou du commerce, se saisiraient chaque fois un peu plus de 'droit qui bouge' et manifeste la dynamique de l'ordre juridique international.

520. *Lalive*, note 158, p. 57:

> Whether or not one is prepared to fully subscribe to that view, one must at least admit that the importance and complexity of the questions raised in Investor-State settlement of disputes and the fact that public interest and the development of the country concerned are involved, "are all dynamics that militate in favour of a very carefully and fully reasoned award", much more so than in what may be considered "normal" in cases of commercial transactions!

commercial arbitration. In this context, it may therefore be stated that a tribunal's unacceptable approach in investment arbitration may still be perceived as acceptable in commercial arbitration. This observation reveals differing understandings of legitimacy, which reflect the equally differing bases of both forms of international arbitration. In this sense, theory meets practice. Furthermore, it provokes the suggestion that intersections impact the way investment treaties are being interpreted.[521] Whether or not this holds true is subject to a closer look at arguments that have been put forward in criticizing the outcomes of international investment arbitrations.

[B] The Involvement of Commercial Arbitrators

One of the most prominent arguments is that the involvement of commercial arbitrators in international investment arbitrations causes problematic, even flawed outcomes. The issue has moved beyond the realm of legal studies and received attention from broader audiences.[522] Critical voices allude to the background of tribunals and their apparent struggling with public international law and especially their alleged (in)ability to apply the relevant interpretive canons.[523] Others take a more moderate approach in pointing to the differences between public and private lawyers while highlighting the mostly beneficial symbiosis within dispute resolution regimes.[524] Nevertheless, the field of investment arbitration is described as characterized by "a division of epistemic communities along different lines," joining the field from public

---

521. See Toby T. Landau QC, Reasons for Reasons: The Tribunal's Duty in Investor-State Arbitration, in: Albert Jan van den Berg (ed.), ICCA Congress Series,Vol. 14, 2009, pp. 187-205 (p. 202): "[...] in the drafting of their awards, it is imperative that Investor-State tribunals cast off the 'commercial arbitration' conception of their role; consider their task afresh; and develop a tendency towards elaboration."
522. See e.g. International Institute for Sustainable Development, Arbitrators' Role in the Recent Investment Arbitration Boom, March 25, 2013, available at http://www.iisd.org/itn/2013/03/25/arbitrators-role-in-the-recent-investment-arbitration-boom/ (last accessed on September 3, 2014); Andreas Zielcke, Sieg über das Gesetz, Süddeutsche Zeitung, May 3, 2014, available at http://www.sueddeutsche.de/politik/transatlantisches-freihandelsabkommen-ttip-sieg-ueber-das-gesetz-1.1948221 (last accessed September 3, 2014).
523. Anthea Roberts, Power and Persuasion in Investment Treaty Interpretation: The Dual Role of States, in: The American Journal of International Law 2010, Vol. 104, pp. 179-225 (p. 207):

> Arbitrators on investment tribunals are not selected solely by the treaty parties and many have a background primarily in international commercial arbitration rather than public international law. These factors may make these arbitrators less familiar with or concerned about public international law interpretive approaches, such as the relevance of subsequent agreements and practices of treaty parties.

> see also Muthucumaraswamy Sornarajah, A Coming Crisis: Expansionary Trends in Investment Treaty Arbitration in: Karl P. Sauvant (ed.), Appeals Mechanism in International Investment Disputes, 2008, pp. 42: "Hence, they tend to lean toward commercial solutions based on commercial prudence and give little concern to the predicament of a State faced with fashioning policy in the context of circumstances that may have undergone changes."

524. Schill, note 5, p. 11.

international law and private commercial law.[525] This division is said to be visible, not in an inability to apply the relevant methodology, but in generally differing approaches to interpretation. While public international lawyers appear to use the VCLT as the interpretive guideline, commercial arbitration lawyers apparently tend to act from a contract-driven perspective.[526] Additionally, the idea that the group of arbitrators active in investment arbitrations should remain "an elite core"[527] is perceived as similarly troubling.[528] At this point, the involvement of commercial arbitrators could ultimately serve to explain the flawed interpretation in investment arbitration with regards to the principles envisaged by the VCLT. Such general assumption would, however, fail to take into account the complexity of the issue. A more structured analysis is advisable to properly assess the impacts of arbitrators from a commercial background in investment arbitrations. Reducing the debate to fractional issues is equally flawed as deficient interpretations, whose impact on international investment law have sparked the debate in the first place.

The involvement of commercial arbitration professionals has resulted from the hybrid nature of investment treaty arbitration. It has been pointed out that the field has availed itself of many procedural rules of commercial arbitration. International investment law, so it is argued, has thus been "commercialized."[529] Such terminology should not mislead. It implies that a public international law phenomenon has changed its nature. Rather, it was commercially influenced, but retained its origin – the real essence of "hybridization."[530] The fundamental idea of arbitrators with a commercial background engaging in investment disputes cannot, in principle, be false. Familiarity with procedural patterns rather is an asset and enrichment to the process. Experience with the interplay of procedural rules may increase an arbitration's efficiency and provide a strong overall framework. For example, interaction with domestic courts at the seat of the arbitration may profit from prior experience in litigation. From a procedural point of view, the involvement of commercial arbitrators does therefore not pose particular problems.

A different issue is the understanding of the overall function of investment arbitration. Commercial arbitrations exemplify the resolution of disputes *inter partes*. The tribunal's service is delivered based on the understanding that it is the parties to

---

525. *Stephan W. Schill*, W(h)ither Fragmentation? On the Literature and Sociology of International Investment Law, in: The European Journal of International Law 2011, Vol. 22 No. 3, pp. 875-908 (p. 888).
526. *Stephan W. Schill*, Public or Private Dispute Settlement? Clash in Investment Treaty Arbitration and its Impact on the Role of the Arbitrator, in: Todd Weiler/Freya Baetens (eds.), New Directions in International Economic Law: In Memoriam Thomas Wälde 2011, pp. 23-43 (p. 24).
527. *Jan Paulsson*, Ethics, Elitism, Eligibility, in: Journal of International Arbitration 1997, Vol. 14 No. 4, pp. 13-21 (p. 19).
528. *David Schneiderman*, Judicial Politics and International Investment Arbitration: Seeking an Explanation for Conflicting Outcomes, in: Northwestern Journal of International Law & Business 2010, Vol. 30 No. 2, pp. 1-33 (p. 14).
529. *Schill*, note 525, p. 888.
530. *Schill*, note 159, p. 71.

which responsibility is owed.[531] This perception does not suffice in the public international law environment of investment arbitration, emphasizing the difference between a dispute of commercial parties and between a commercial party and a state. An arbitrator's service thus does not merely have an impact on a company's accounts. It may severely affect state budgets and thus ultimately their capacity to act on a domestic level. The repercussions for state populations, particularly in developing countries, which are frequently respondents in investment arbitrations, may be tremendous. Furthermore, it may affect the practical implementation of future policy changes not just by the respective state, but also by other observers. The publicity of the decisions thereby functions as a multiplier for the international community. Further distinguishing features have been excellently outlined elsewhere.[532] The significance for this analysis rests in the practical consequences of them. It must at this point therefore suffice to summarize that investment arbitrations are essentially public order disputes, whose global significance exceeds that of commercial arbitrations. The consequence of this difference must, however, not be a call for exclusion of commercial arbitrators. Not only would such rationale deny the ability to get acquainted with new fields, it would also deprive investment arbitrations of significant expertise. A call for strict respect for the differing bases of both forms of arbitration is thus more appropriate. A solid foundation in public international law is indispensable. However, not by background, but by careful familiarization and application is such respect for particularities properly exercised. Otherwise, public international lawyers, without profound experience in the evaluation of commercial transactions,[533] would have to face similar criticism. Consequentially, investment arbitration would soon encounter serious difficulties in filling the seats on international tribunals. A fruitful overall collaboration is

---

531. *See ConocoPhillips Petrozuata B.V., ConocoPhillips Hamaca B.V. and ConocoPhillips Gulf of Paria B.V. v. Bolivarian Republic of Venezuela,* Dissenting Opinion of Georges Abi-Saab, ICSID Case No. ARB/07/30, March 10, 2014, para. 56:

> Thus, inherent jurisdiction accrues to any body or organ by the mere fact of it being possessed of the adjudicative function. It brings with it powers as well as duties and responsibilities. [...] These are "to maintain its judicial character", "safeguard its basic judicial function" and be "the guardian of [its] judicial integrity"; in short to ensure and safeguard the efficiency, credibility and integrity of the adjudicative function and the adjudicative character of the organ, whose first and foremost task is to seek the truth and to dispense justice according to law on that basis.

532. *Schill,* note 526; *see also van Harten/Loughlin,* note 145; *see also International Thunderbird Gaming Corporation v. The United Mexican States,* Separate Opinion of Thomas W. Wälde, UNCITRAL, December 1, 2005, paras. 4, 12:

> My disagreement is based on a different weight which needs to be accorded to this principle in the particular context of an investment promotion and protection treaty which protects interests different from those involved in an ordinary commercial relationship involving two equal private parties. [...] Investment arbitration is fundamentally different from international commercial arbitration. It governs the situation of a foreign investor exposed to the sovereignty, the regulatory, administrative and other governmental powers of a state.

533. *See Hans van Houtte/Maurizio Brunetti,* Investment Arbitration – Ten Areas of Caution for Commercial Arbitrators, in: Arbitration International 2013, Vol. 29 No. 4, pp. 553-574 (p. 554).

thus advisable.[534] For the purpose of treaty interpretation, this demands compliance with the interpretive methodology of public international law.

The criticism concerning its application by commercial arbitrators, however, does not appear to be groundless.[535] This is not due to inability, but possibly due to a particular mindset.[536] The continuous trends of protecting commercial arbitration may be contributing. Absent empirical evaluation, however, this remains speculative. Viable propositions for improvement are helpful. One of them, in all modesty, may be a broader consideration of an inherent feature of investment disputes: the public sphere. In the interest of strengthening the legitimacy of arbitral decisions and thus ultimately that of international investment law, the multiplying character of publicity bears significant potential that should be taken advantage of. The increasing academic attention to the field is an invaluable asset. In a public forum of scholarship it fosters analyses, evaluation and dialogue. The awareness of growing critical interest in the work of investment tribunals may thereby prompt greater awareness of the public international law implications and consequentially, greater adherence to its methodological imperative.

[C] The Notion of Pro-investor Bias

A point that is closely related to the involvement of commercial arbitrators is the alleged existence of bias in international investment arbitration that is believed to favor investor interests over state interests. It is argued that bias is actually in existence and, alternatively, that it may only be perceived to exist due to the entire adjudicative

---

534. *See Schill*, note 524, p. 12: "Furthermore, neither a pure international law understanding nor a pure commercial law understanding of investor-state dispute resolution are sufficient in themselves to comprehend the specific characteristics of international investment law."

535. *Jan Paulsson*, Avoiding Unintended Consequences, in: Karl P. Sauvant (ed.), Appeals Mechanism in International Investment Disputes, 2008, pp. 241-265 (pp. 262 et seq.):

> Some excellent commercial arbitrators seem to have insufficient grounding in public international law. Apart from their unfamiliarity with important recurring issues, they fail to perceive that they are no longer referees in a match which concerns only the participants. Investment arbitrations generate constant public interest. Awards tend immediately to fall into the public domain and contribute to the broad emerging normative tapestry. It may be a serious mistake to perceive one's duty as selecting which of two parties' arguments are better. Even if there is a clear winner, its arguments are not necessarily correct; often they are not. This requires discernment and hard study, lest the arbitral tribunal lend its authority to propositions which may be intuitively convenient in the particular, but are unsound in the general. Commercial lawyers venturing into finely balanced matters of public international law may also be tempted, perhaps by an excess of self-confidence, to deliver themselves of a broad general exposition with the intent of clearing up a troubling issue, presuming hubristically, as it were, to do the world a favour by accounting for their brief foray into this new area. This often leads to trouble.

536. *Schill*, note 525, p. 889; *see also Thomas W. Wälde*, The Specific Nature of Investment Arbitration, in: Philippe Kahn/Thomas W. Wälde (eds.), New Aspects of International Investment Law 2007, pp. 42-120 (p. 43): "The paradigms of commercial arbitration are deeply ingrained in the mind of most or all participants in the investment arbitration process."

process.[537] The first argument alludes to the economic interest of an arbitrator that may lead him or her to rule in favor of investors, which are the ones that initiate investment arbitrations in the first place.[538] Without their belief in the economic advantage of the system, fostered by successful claims, business for investment arbitrators could vanish. As a consequence, it is argued that interpretation may be or may seem to be driven not by impartiality but by bias.[539] This perception goes beyond mere criticism of abilities to recognize the differences between commercial and investment arbitration and the application of the relevant methodology. It touches upon political stances that contribute mostly to a debate outside of the practical application of norms. This shows in attempts to isolate investment arbitrators as individuals merely interested in upholding their reputation and thereby generating business.[540] It is implied that an accusatory tone from investment lawyers towards critics is rooted in the general existence of criticism towards the field.[541] Rather, such accusations are actually directed at those who fall short of exercising their criticism constructively.[542] Therefore, in a modest attempt to pursue that constructiveness, the argument on existing bias might be enriched by raising another point. The support of the involvement of commercial arbitrators gains further momentum in this context of economic bias. Certainly, sitting as arbitrators in investment disputes is not a gratuitous activity. However, arbitrators that are heavily engaged in commercial disputes are not dependent upon business from investment arbitration. The argument on existing bias of arbitrators, based on economic interest, is thus one that should relate to all possible tribunal members, not only those with a commercial law background.

The second argument alludes to structural problems of investment arbitration that may create the impression of promoting bias. Especially the appointment powers of the predominant institutions are questioned. For example, the ICC or SCC are

---

537. *Gus van Harten*, Part IV Chapter 18: Perceived Bias in Investment Treaty Arbitration, in: Waibel/Kaushal et al. (eds.), note 6, pp. 433-453 (p. 437).
538. *Muthucumaraswamy Sornarajah*, Power and Justice in Foreign Investment Arbitration, in: Journal of International Arbitration 1997, Vol. 14, pp. 103-140 (p. 118): "Arbitrators, persons, whom the world is led to believe, are of high eminence, go to bat for the big boys, simply because they will not get any further lucrative business if they do not decide in the only 'right' way that ensures their continuance in business."; *see also van Harten*, note 537, p. 444.
539. *Van Harten*, note 537, p. 445.
540. *Schneiderman*, note 528, p. 28: "The heightened level of intemperate discourse suggests that international investment lawyers feel real anxiety that their symbolic authority is under threat."
541. *Schneiderman*, note 528, p. 28: "The leading investment lawyer and arbitrator Paulsson, for instance, characterizes as 'shrill voices'—'true believers' who float 'propaganda', 'producing much rhetoric but less informed judgment'—those who take issue with investment rules' operating precepts."
542. *Jan Paulsson*, Denial of Justice in International Law, 2005, p. 233:

> The neonationalist currents seem most persuasive to those who are attracted by sensational allegations of conspiracies against the public interest, and are disinclined to make an effort to grasp the more complex themes of international rules and economic cooperation. [...] The open-minded search for policies that contribute to long-term benefits for the community as a whole - national, regional, international - is the nutrient of a healthy democratic diet. Not so propaganda, whose authors pursue an ultimate revealed truth, and care little about the means of advancing their cause.

essentially commercial institutions that are tailored to the needs of investors, bringing about a perception of pro-investor bias.[543] Likewise, ICSID is thought to be similarly problematic as its setup, namely the appointing authority being vested in an international official chosen by the administration of the United States,[544] also impedes an assumption of complete neutrality.[545] However, the argument is closely connected to the first one. Only under the assumption that arbitrators are biased, may the appointment of these arbitrators be problematic. That is not to say that the argument is invalid. Rather, it does require broad attention that would go beyond the possible scope of the present analysis. The notion of pro-investor bias deserves consideration as it serves to spark vital debates. Nevertheless, the majority of academic efforts should focus predominantly on normative issues that have the potential of easing the perception of bias.

[D] The Role of Purposive Interpretation

During the depiction of interpretation in international investment law, it was indicated that one may at times witness an increasing reliance on the purpose of investment treaties and their particular provisions. Article 31 section 1 VCLT, however, provides that it is the text of a treaty that is the starting point of any interpretation in public international law and the limitation on any further interpretive results. The context and the object and purpose of such treaty must be taken into account in a single interpretive operation.[546] This consideration may then either confirm or alter the result found solely in the treaty's terms. Giving effect to an interpretation that goes beyond the text is, however, not admissible.[547] In this sense, the object and purpose of a treaty may not serve to replace the ordinary meaning of treaty terms. This would equate to similarly inadmissible revision of the treaty.[548] The object and purpose of an applicable BIT are typically formulated in a preamble. This usually includes references to the fostering of investments, economic development and mutual benefit. Purposive interpretation may therefore work in two extreme directions: it may overly emphasize the objects of states to enter into an investment treaty and similarly such objects of investors. In either case does such interpretive approach collide with the provisions of the VCLT. It is conceivable that the alleged bias of arbitrators or a general misapplication of the VCLT show, or occur respectively, in deploying this form of purposive interpretation.

---

543. *Van Harten*, note 537, pp. 443 et seq.
544. *Van Harten*, note 537, p. 442.
545. *Van Harten*, note 537, p. 442.
546. *ILC*, Draft Articles on the Law of Treaties with commentaries, in: Yearbook of the International Law Commission 1966, Vol. 2, pp. 219 et seq.
547. *ILC*, note 546, p. 219: "Properly limited and applied, the maxim does not call for an 'extensive' or 'liberal' interpretation in the sense of an interpretation going beyond what is expressed or necessarily to be implied in the terms of the treaty."
548. *ICJ*, Advisory Opinion on Interpretation of Peace Treaties with Bulgaria, Hungary and Romania, 2nd Phase, July 18, 1950, ICJ Reports 1950, pp. 221-261 (p. 229): "It is the duty of the Court to interpret the Treaties, not to revise them."; *see also ICJ*, Case Concerning Rights of Nationals of the United States of America in Morocco, Judgment, August 27, 1952, ICJ Reports 1952, pp. 176-214 (p. 196).

Purposive interpretation has been a matter of concern in arbitral practice. Tribunals have explicitly adopted a purposive approach.[549] Furthermore, it has led to disagreement over whether or not a tribunal's interpretation was overly purposive and thus resulted in separate opinions. One example is the dispute in *Suez & Vivendi v. Argentina*, which resulted from the privatization of water distribution and waste water management in Buenos Aires. In analyzing the fair and equitable treatment-standard under Article 4 of the Spain-Argentina BIT of October 3, 1991, the tribunal found the element of "legitimate expectations" to be part of the protection.[550] In his separate opinion, arbitrator *Pedro Nikken* explained that the tribunal did not indicate how the object and purpose of the BIT could introduce a legitimate expectation standard in view of the text.[551] He highlighted that such approach was inadmissible, given the methodology in public international law.[552] Another example is found in the dispute *HEP v. Slovenia*. It concerned the ownership and operation of a major power plant, Krško NPP. The tribunal highlighted in its approach to interpretation that an object or purpose may serve as a predetermination of how the text of a treaty is to be perceived.[553] This was heavily criticized by arbitrator *Jan Paulsson* in his dissenting opinion. He pointed out that the tribunal acted contrary to the principles of the VCLT[554] and thereby ignored the

---

549. *Siemens AG v. The Argentine Republic*, note 344, para. 81: "The Tribunal shall be guided by the purpose of the Treaty as expressed in its title and preamble."; *see also Noble Ventures, Inc. v. Romania*, Award, ICSID Case No. ARB/01/11, October 12, 2005, para. 52; *see also Ronald S. Lauder v. The Czech Republic*, Final Award, UNCITRAL, September 3, 2001, para. 292.
550. *Suez, Sociedad General de Aguas de Barcelona S.A., Vivendi Universal S.A. and AWG Group Ltd. v. The Argentine Republic*, Decision on Liability, ICSID Case No. ARB/03/19, July 30, 2010, paras. 224 et seq.
551. *Suez, Sociedad General de Aguas de Barcelona S.A., Vivendi Universal S.A. and AWG Group Ltd. v. The Argentine Republic*, Decision on Liability – Separate Opinion of Pedro Nikken, ICSID Case No. ARB/03/19, July 30, 2010, para. 21:

    In my opinion, within the reasoning of the Decision, [...], there is an important link missing, because it does not explain why the object and purpose of the BITs can authorize the introduction therein of the concept of legitimate expectations of investors, which does not appear in any way, shape or form in the terms of the treaty according to its ordinary meaning.

552. *Suez, Sociedad General de Aguas de Barcelona S.A., Vivendi Universal S.A. and AWG Group Ltd. v. The Argentine Republic*, note 551, para. 21:

    In interpreting an international treaty, the primary object of interpretation is to elucidate the meaning of the terms of the treaty so that when doing so in the light of its object and purpose the interpreter should not give these terms a meaning that is clearly outside their normal meaning, without any evidence that the intention of the Parties was to give a special meaning to the terms of the treaty (VCLT, Art. 31.4).

553. *Hrvatska Elektroprivreda D.D. v. The Republic of Slovenia*, Decision on the Treaty Interpretation Issue, ICSID Case No. ARB/05/24, June 12, 2009, para. 176: "No greater or lesser force resides in a term by virtue of the relative magnitude of the clarity with which it has been (or has not been) written."
554. *Hrvatska Elektroprivreda D.D. v. The Republic of Slovenia*, Individual Opinion of Jan Paulsson, ICSID Case No. ARB/05/24, June 8, 2009, para. 41: "It is important to see precisely how the majority, I regret to say, appear to turn the VCLT on its head.", in criticizing the use of Art. 32 VCLT despite a result that was neither ambiguous or obscure nor manifestly absurd. *See also*

important limits a treaty may set for the assumption of jurisdiction by international tribunals.[555]

The assumption that alleged bias is expressed through this form of interpretation is confirmed by the finding that indeed, the placement of inadmissible emphasis on the object and purpose often results in a positive outcome for investors, as was previously highlighted.[556] It does therefore not surprise that by an incorrect application of the VCLT, resulting in favorable outcomes for investors, the matter is extended by a political dimension,[557] which is contrary to the original goal of international investment arbitration. It is interesting here to recall the analytical results of those decisions that characterized arbitral awards. None of the decisions involved such purposive interpretation. Rather than relying too heavily on object and purpose, the tribunals, almost uniformly, did not consider them. The only decision doing so, *Romak v. Uzbekistan*, also contains a far-sighted analysis on the consequences of merely following a textual approach, without further recourse to object and purpose, namely deeming an arbitral award to constitute an investment:

> Second, the mechanical application of the categories found in Article 1(2) would create, de facto, a *new instance of review of State court decisions concerning the enforcement of arbitral awards.* Under the scenario advocated by Romak, any award rendered in favor of a national of a Contracting Party (even one rendered in a purely commercial arbitration procedure) would be considered a "claim to money" or, arguably – as pleaded by Romak – a "right given by decision of the authority." The refusal or failure of the host State's courts to enforce such an award would therefore arguably *provide sufficient grounds for a de novo review – under a different international instrument and on grounds different from those that would normally apply –* of the State courts' decision not to enforce an award.[558]

It is this creation of a de facto review mechanism in international arbitration that led the tribunal to deploy the object and purpose of the BIT:

> Based on the above considerations, Romak's proposed literal construction of Article 1(2) of the BIT *is untenable as a matter of international law.* The Arbitral Tribunal must *therefore explore the meaning* of the word "investments" contained in the introductory paragraph of that Article.[559]

> the careful approach of the tribunal in: *Hulley Enterprises Limited (Cyprus) v. The Russian Federation*, Final Award, PCA Case No. AA 226, July 18, 2014, para. 1415:
>
> > In any event, the Tribunal, having found that the interpretation of Article 21 of the ECT according to the general rule of interpretation under Article 31 of the VCLT results in a meaning that is neither ambiguous nor obscure and does not lead to a result which is manifestly absurd or unreasonable, does not need to call in aid any other rule of interpretation.

555. *Hrvatska Elektroprivreda D.D. v. The Republic of Slovenia*, note 554, para. 44: "As far as I can discern, the Majority's Decision proceeds in ignorance of this fundamental and much-discussed constraint on the freedom of international judges and arbitrators to interpret treaties."
556. Schreuer, note 44, p. 131.
557. See Waibel, note 405, p. 40: "The risk is a re-politicization of investment disputes and, in the long-run, losing support among state parties."
558. *Romak S.A. (Switzerland) v. The Republic of Uzbekistan*, note 304, para. 186.
559. *Romak S.A. (Switzerland) v. The Republic of Uzbekistan*, note 304, para. 188.

This consideration indicates that two problematic extremes are existent: interpretations that place excessive emphasis on the object and purpose and those that do not take them into account. In the context of the above-mentioned trends of increasingly protecting commercial arbitration, this finding might trigger further, mostly political, criticism. Namely – and utilizing language by those that do not fear entering the political arena – it could give rise to "sensational allegations of conspiracies"[560] to the effect that arbitrators purposely omit recourse to objects and purposes, if the interpretive outcome results in an intersection between commercial and investment arbitration creating "lucrative business" which "ensures their continuance in business."[561] Those that observe the political part of the battle in comfort, though not any less passionately, mainly distill that the existence of purposive interpretation in both extremes is a trailblazer for deficient interpretation.

[E] Insufficient Treaty Drafting

Lastly, the practice of treaty drafting deserves attention. The interpretation by arbitrators rests upon the text of the treaties that have been concluded by states. The text delivers material for the application of the arbitrator's interpretive toolbox and is thus the foundation of determining whether or not a tribunal may assume jurisdiction and a state has violated its obligations. Proper treaty drafting is therefore essential to ensure that the interests of a respective state may be fully taken into consideration. Only if they can be derived from the treaty by way of properly applying the interpretive methodology, tribunals can give effect to them. The process of treaty drafting may thus be characterized as a safeguard for state interests. States, by way of treaty drafting, may calibrate the scope of their sovereignty waiver as well as the protection offered to the respective foreign investors. It is apparent that both ends conflict and require compromise. States must determine the adequate balance between the creation of a favorable investment environment and the protection of their own interests. In particular, these considerations include potential economic gain from improving the investment climate by way of a treaty and consequences for domestic decision-making processes and possible future investment disputes. It is argued that no clear evidence exists, indicating a correlation between investment treaty programs and economic growth.[562]

---

560. *Paulsson*, note 542, p. 233.
561. *Sornarajah*, note 538, p. 118.
562. *Mary Hallward-Driemeier*, Do Bilateral Investment Treaties Attract FDI? – Only a bit...and they could bite, World Bank Policy Research Paper 2003, No. 3121, available at http://elibrary.worldbank.org/doi/pdf/10.1596/1813-9450-3121 (last accessed September 11, 2014), p. 22:

> Analyzing twenty years of bilateral FDI flows from the OECD to developing countries finds little evidence that BITs have stimulated additional investment. Those countries with weak domestic institutions, including protection of property, have not gotten significant additional benefits; a BIT has not acted as a substitute for broader domestic reform. Rather, those countries that are reforming and already have reasonably strong domestic institutions are most likely to gain from ratifying a treaty. That BITs act as more of a complement than a substitute for domestic institutions means that those that are benefiting from them are arguably the least in need of a BIT to signal the quality of their property rights.

However, despite this argument, states remain sovereign in their decision to negotiate and sign investment treaties based upon a proper risk assessment. Once such decision is made, the actual drafting process is of eminent importance. Nevertheless, treaties, at times, still appear to be negotiated, drafted and signed without giving the necessary amount of thorough consideration to their implications.[563] The result may be overly broad language that requires exceptional interpretive efforts by tribunals, which might at a later point in time lead to results that are heavily criticized by the respondent states. Therefore, the quality of an investment treaty may directly affect the outcome of an investment arbitration. It is imperative that states understand their responsibility in the process and act with great care in negotiating and drafting treaties.

§3.05 CONCLUSION

The protection of commercial arbitration awards by way of international investment arbitration is an important contemporary topic. It has become evident that, under certain conditions, investors may successfully seek compensation from states that have interfered with the process of enforcing a commercial arbitral award. The result is a growing interconnection between commercial and investment arbitration in practice. This development, however, is challenging, as the theoretical bases of both types are distinct. Adherence to methodological canons is thus crucial in ensuring that the differences between both forms of arbitration are respected. Problems to effectuate the element of public interest in investment arbitration have led to criticism that has developed into an alleged "legitimacy crisis."[564] The analysis has pointed to a number of interpretive insufficiencies that have arisen in the qualification of arbitral awards. Furthermore, it has been highlighted that these shortcomings are not exclusive to a particular practical question. Rather, the problem of interpretive insufficiencies is more global and shows in, at times, defective application of the VCLT, reliance on alleged arbitral precedent and insufficient general reasoning. Possible explanations for this scenario are manifold. They range from a growing protection of international commercial arbitration in public international law to an alleged bias and insufficient treaty drafting. While certainly not every award in investment arbitration is flawed, international investment law's need for professionalism, competence and fairness requires analysis of interpretive approaches. It is in the interest of everyone involved that a critical discourse is taking place. Therefore, it is imperative to now turn to the ramifications of interpretive insufficiencies to facilitate a proper assessment of routes to greater interpretive discipline.

---

see similarly *Andrew T. Guzman*, Why LDCs Sign Treaties That Hurt Them: Explaining the Popularity of Bilateral Investment Treaties, in: Virginia Journal of International Law 1997, Vol. 38, pp. 639-688 (p. 688): "Although BITs improve the efficiency of foreign investment, they may not increase the welfare of developing countries."
563. *Dolzer/Schreuer*, note 48, p. 8.
564. *Sornarajah*, note 523, p. 41.

CHAPTER 4
Ramifications of Interpretive Insufficiencies

§4.01 INTRODUCTION

The previous chapter has depicted interpretive insufficiencies in the approaches taken by investment tribunals in qualifying arbitral awards. It has also pointed out that such insufficiencies are not exclusive to a single interpretive question, but rather occur throughout international investment law in general. Therefore, it is both, theoretically and practically relevant to understand the ramifications that result from the problem. These ramifications may, at first sight, constitute a merely methodological matter of treaty interpretation. However, such isolated approach would not pay due respect to the practical relevance of interpretation. Methodology creates outcomes with serious consequences for the participants to an investment arbitration. Deficiencies in its application therefore spark negative sentiments.[565] The increasing public attention and criticism directed at the current state of international investment law serves as evidence. Frequently, such criticism takes place in the abstract or is without recourse to possible points of contact to legal questions. In other words, it remains political. Nevertheless, the political sphere of interpretive deficiencies deserves to be taken seriously.

In the course of this chapter, however, the focus lies on legal questions posed by public international law. A number of remarkable publications have already contributed greatly to steering the legitimacy debate on international investment law into a normative direction. What still deserves broader attention, though, is the relationship between interpretive flaws and general public international law. Here, particularly state sovereignty is of relevance, an argument that is susceptible to a broad range of perceptions.[566] However, any serious interest in the improvement of international

---

565. *Waibel*, note 405, p. 40: "The risk is a re-politicization of investment disputes and, in the long-run, losing support among state parties."
566. *See Todd Weiler*, The Interpretation of International Investment Law: Equality, Discrimination and Minimum Standards of Treatment in Historical Context, 2013, p. 8, in describing traditional

investment law must encompass the consideration of all possible solutions. The upcoming analysis will carve out scenarios in which state sovereignty is not only relevant, but also perhaps even touched upon. It will focus on the contemporary facets of the principle and lead to the realization that state sovereignty is not an outdated concept. It remains the core of public international law that deserves continuous attention. States, by entering into myriad obligations in public international law, have undoubtedly shaded the light of sovereignty. However, invisibility does not imply inexistence. In fact, as public international law, and international investment law in particular, becomes more complex and dynamic, traditional concepts are the stable pillars necessary for the development to be a successful one. In this sense, the principle of state sovereignty is always relevant.

§4.02 THE CONTINUOUS RELEVANCE OF STATE SOVEREIGNTY

[A] The Development of the Principle

The first elaboration on state sovereignty is found in *Six Livres de la République*, a book written by *Jean Bodin* in 1576. The St. Bartholomew Day Massacre of 1572, directed against the French Huguenots, inspired *Bodin* to reflect upon the role of government. In his publication, he referred to sovereignty as follows:

> La SOUVERAINETÉ est la puissance absolue & perpétuelle d'une République.[567]

He tried to identify the scope of governmental power and the role of the king as the highest authority.[568] The political and social instability of the time called for a sense of order that *Bodin* found in the establishment of a hierarchy. At its top, he placed the sovereign, controlling the ecclesiastical order, the military and the common people.[569] He sought to structure authority and thereby to promote a reliable, predictable and safe societal environment. His idea of the principle of sovereignty thus contributed to the function of the state in exercising control.[570] This power of a state is described by him as being "absolute," an attribute that deserves further attention. On its face, the term implies that no limitations may be placed on a government's power. However, *Bodin* himself relativized the term:

---

approaches to the role of sovereignty as static: "In this regard they demonstrate their ultimate belief in the State, and therefore in statism, as the preferred means of achieving societal goals - whether acting individually (within their own, sovereign territorial domains) or collectively (on the international plane)."; *see also El Paso Energy International Company v. The Republic of Argentina*, Legal Opinion of Muthucumaraswamy Sornarajah, ICSID Case No. ARB/03/15, March 5, 2007, para. 96: "No state could have assumed treaty obligations that are so extensively destructive of sovereignty."

567. *Jean Bodin*, Six Livres de la République, 1583, p. 85.
568. *Stéphanie Beaulac*, The Social Power of Bodin's "Sovereignty" and International Law, in: Melbourne Journal of International Law 2003, Vol. 4, pp. 1-28 (p. 25).
569. *Beaulac*, note 568, p. 19.
570. *Winston P. Nagan/Aitza M. Haddad*, Sovereignty in Theory and Practice, in: San Diego International Law Journal 2012, Vol. 13, pp. 429-520 (p. 442).

> Vray est que ces docteurs ne disent point que c'est de puissance absolue: car si nous disons queue celui a puissance absolute, qui n'est point suet aux lois, il ne se trouvera Prince au monde souverain, vu que tous les Princes de la terre sont *sujets aux lois de Dieu, & de nature, & à plusieurs lois humaines communes à tous peuples.*[571]

Bodin thus saw the only limitations on sovereignty in divine law, the law of nature and human law that is common to every people. In this context, one should note that the latter does not describe international law.[572] The principle of state sovereignty has since undergone continuous changes in its contemporary meaning,[573] but never ceased to exist. It experienced further developments through the works of philosophy. Only three years after the Westphalian Peace, in 1651, *Thomas Hobbes* published his famous treatise *Leviathan*. Based on the understanding that the function of a government is to protect its people from one another, he argued that a social contract is the instrument through which power is delegated. The obedience of people is rewarded by way of governmental protection, which may only be effective if the power vested in the state is absolute. A limitation to this absolute exercise of power, according to *Hobbes*, only lies in an individual's right to self-defense.[574] Later on, the existing understanding of state sovereignty was further developed by *John Locke*. In his famous 1689 publication *Two Treatises of Government*, he departed from *Hobbes'* theory of a social contract between individuals. Rather, *Locke* found such contract to exist between the individual and the sovereign. As a consequence, the sovereign could now be held accountable for violations of such contract that occur due to violations of individual rights. *Locke* placed limitations on the exercise of a sovereign's powers. It was in large his work that has contributed greatly to the modern understanding of sovereignty, deriving from the people.[575] His understanding of sovereignty received further adjustments by *Jean-Jacques Rousseau* in the 1763 publication *The Social Contract*. He tied sovereignty to the function of the legislature. By way of a social contract, the actual sovereign, the people, confer upon the legislator the power to exercise sovereignty.[576] Such exercise was now considered to be dependent upon the people's consent,[577] constituting a trade between a limit to individual liberty on the one hand and realization of individual interest through the sovereign on the other. *Rousseau* thereby accentuated the role of the people. It is their consent that empowers the state to act in accordance with their will.

The above-mentioned philosophical approaches largely focus on sovereignty and its internal function. However, for public international law and especially the present analysis, it is the external function of sovereignty that is crucial. When an end was put to the Thirty Years' War in the Roman Empire and the Eighty Years' War between Spain

---

571. *Bodin*, note 567, p. 131.
572. *See Beaulac*, note 568, p. 13; *see* contrarily *Nagan/Haddad*, note 570, p. 441.
573. *Beaulac*, note 568, p. 25.
574. *Nagan/Haddad*, note 570, p. 444.
575. *Hallie Ludsin*, Returning Sovereignty to the People, in: Vanderbilt Journal of Transnational Law 2013, Vol. 46, pp. 97-169 (p. 118).
576. *Ludsin*, note 575, p. 117.
577. *Ludsin*, note 575, p. 118.

and the Dutch Republic, external state sovereignty was exercised. The signing of a number of treaties in Münster and Osnabrück in 1648, the Westphalian Peace, marked the beginning of modern public international law.[578] The most powerful theoretical move towards modern public international law, however, occurred even before the Westphalian Peace or *Leviathan*. It was *Hugo Grotius* who devoted a great deal of his intellectual power to the relations of states. In a remarkably clear manner, *Grotius* dwelled on the consensual origin and global nature of public international law. In his 1625 masterpiece *De Jure Belli ac Pacis*, he provided a first legal framework for warfare between nation-states. He assumed a nation's right to go to war, but focused on providing constraints to the use of force. It was his concept of a just war.[579] In this context, *Grotius* made statements that were fundamental to the emergence of public international law:

> But just as the laws of each state have in view the advantage of that state, so by *mutual consent* it has become possible that certain laws should originate as between all states, or a great many states; and it is apparent that the laws thus originating had in view the advantage, not of particular states, but of the great *society of states*. And this is what is called the *law of nations*, whenever we distinguish that term from the law of nature.[580]

Grotius considered this law of nations as binding.[581] Interestingly, even at this early stage of the law's development, he already considered a treaty as a "more excellent kind of agreement."[582] Furthermore, interpretation of treaties, he argued, must take place in "good faith."[583] His theoretical contribution greatly impacted the practical success of the Westphalian Peace. Similarly, the Congress of Vienna in 1815 benefitted from *Grotius'* work. The French Revolution and the Napoleonic Wars had shaken the European continent and created instability. In an effort to restore peace, ambassadors of sovereign European nations negotiated a number of treaties that were embodied in the Final Act on June 9, 1815. This event represents the understanding of sovereign states being able to negotiate and agree on limitations to their external sovereignty for mutual benefit. This included e.g. the surrender of certain territories or a guarantee for free navigations on a number of major rivers. The power of *Grotius'* ideas had found its solid place in history before a year after the Paris Peace Conference in 1919, the creation of the League of Nations marked a further step towards international cooperation among sovereign states. As a consequence, public international law witnessed the erection of the PCIJ in 1922 as well as of the United Nations in 1945. Today, the principle of state sovereignty remains utterly important. However, it has naturally further evolved and is, in its contemporary sense, understood as the

---

578. *Daud Hassan*, The Rise of the Territorial State and the Treaty of Westphalia, in: Yearbook of New Zealand Jurisprudence 2006, Vol. 9, pp. 62-70 (p. 66).
579. *Nagan/Haddad*, note 570, pp. 445 et seq.
580. *Hugo Grotius*, De Jure Belli ac Pacis, 1625, translated by *Francis W. Kelsey*, De Jure Belli ac Pacis, 1925, p. 15.
581. *Mark W. Janis*, Sovereignty and International Law: Hobbes and Grotius, in: Ronald St. John Macdonald (ed.), Essays in Honour of Wang Tieya, 1993, pp. 391-400 (p. 397).
582. *Grotius*, note 580, pp. 391 et seq.
583. *Grotius*, note 580, p. 409.

people's sovereignty that must be given effect.[584] In this sense, sovereignty is the sovereignty of the people. The role of the state is then to serve as a medium through which sovereignty is exercised.

[B]   Political Facets

An interesting feature of state sovereignty is its political facet. Beyond normative logic, it contains a strong subjective component. It reflects culture, tradition and values. State sovereignty is deeply rooted in national sentiment and thus not a concept of disposability.[585] Sovereignty arguments must thus not be treated as "views of ideologues."[586] Rather, vigilance must be exercised in distinguishing legal from political spheres. A recent example is Argentina's institution of proceedings against the United States before the ICJ regarding possible sovereignty violations following a decision of the Second U.S. Circuit Court of Appeals. The court found Argentina to have acted contrarily to an equal-treatment promise by making payments to its newer, but not its older bondholders.[587] Despite its legal relevance, the claim by *Cristina Fernández de Kirchner*, relying on Argentina's sovereignty, is also a political reaction to the growing international discontent with the country's fiscal discipline. These subjective, political features pose difficulties to the legal relevance of the principle. It is easy to utilize sovereignty as a rhetorical superpower, risking debates in a normless sphere. While these debates may be of immense political value in shaping powerful policy decisions, they are only legally useful where they recur to norms. In order for any sovereignty claim to be legally useful, it must be freed from its political facets and condensed to its legal core. A normative standard must filter sovereignty arguments. This will, especially in the context of international investment law, ensure that sovereignty claims can be assessed in close connection to normative anchors. This will allow the framework of modern public international law to adequately respond to valid legal issues.[588]

[C]   The Interplay with International Treaties

The normative framework of public international law is nowadays largely built on international treaties. In understanding the relevance of state sovereignty in its modern

---

584. W. *Michael Reisman*, Sovereignty and Human Rights in Contemporary International Law, in: The American Journal of International Law 1990, Vol. 84, pp. 866-876 (p. 869).
585. ICJ, Corfu Channel Case *(United Kingdom v. Albania)*, Individual Opinion by Judge Alvarez, April 9, 1949, ICJ Reports 1949, pp. 39-48, p. 43: "Some jurists have proposed to abolish the notion of the sovereignty of States, considering it obsolete. That is an error. This notion has its foundation in national sentiment and in the psychology of the peoples, in fact it is very deeply rooted."
586. *Sornarajah*, note 538, p. 105.
587. ICJ, Press Release, No. 2014/25, August 7, 2014, available at http://www.icj-cij.org/presscom/files/4/18354.pdf (last accessed August 7, 2014).
588. See *Sornarajah*, note 586, p. 105: "What is required to ensure trust in the system of international investment arbitration, which is an inherently useful method of resolving foreign investment disputes, is a cathartic change which will rid the system of its past dominance by unprincipled power and make it dependent on normative standards."

context, it is imperative to examine its interplay with these treaties. The ICJ has dealt with the principle of state sovereignty and shaped certain contours of its modern understanding. At its core is the independent exercise of state functions within a respective territory.[589] It was previously outlined that the prevailing understanding of modern public international law is dominated by *Grotius'* theoretical foundation. He saw mutual consent as a limit to external sovereignty to be embodied in international treaties entered into by sovereign states. Despite an increase in complexity and the use of, at times, highly technical language, the concept has survived and also governs today's system of international investment law. In this sense, one could argue that an international treaty limits a state's sovereignty, because it imposes specific obligations. However, this approach fails to take into account that a state is under no obligation to enter into a treaty. Rather, the conclusion of a treaty constitutes a voluntary act and is as such an exercise of sovereignty. The PCIJ rendered a judgment in 1923 that is particularly explicit and of great practical significance:[590]

> The Court declines to see in the conclusion of any Treaty by which a State undertakes to perform or refrain from performing a particular act an abandonment of its sovereignty. No doubt any convention creating an obligation of this kind places a restriction upon the exercise of the sovereign rights of the State, in the sense that it requires them to be exercised in a certain way. *But the right of entering into international engagements is an attribute of State sovereignty.*[591]

The waiver of sovereignty is thus an exercise of sovereignty in itself. This ruling is significant. It embodies the modern understanding of sovereignty in the context of international treaties. As these lay the foundation for international investment law, the importance of the PCIJ's contribution is significant. Whether or not the rationale also applies to international contracts between a sovereign state and a foreign private entity is a controversial issue.[592] The PCIJ at least only referred to the Treaty of Versailles. Much as sovereignty is not absolute, however, neither is its waiver. An international

---

589. *ICJ*, Corfu Channel Case, note 585, p. 43: "By sovereignty we understand the whole body of rights and attributes which a state possesses in its territory, to the exclusion of all other states, and also in its relations with other states."; *see also* Draft Declaration on Rights and Duties of States, 1949, Art. 1: "Every State has the right to independence and hence to exercise freely, without dictation by any other State, all its legal powers, including the choice of its own form of government."
590. *Jan Paulsson*, The Power of States to make Meaningful Promises to Foreigners, in: Journal of International Dispute Settlement 2010, Vol. 1 No. 2, pp. 341-352 (p. 343): "This is a simple sentence, but it has great weight."
591. *PCIJ*, S.S. Wimbledon Case *(United Kingdom, France, Italy, Japan v. Germany)*, Judgment, August 17, 1923, p. 25, available at http://www.icj-cij.org/pcij/serie_A/A_01/03_Wimbledon_Arret_08_1923.pdf (last accessed on August 12, 2014); *see also Verdross*, note 131, p. 645: "Eine souveräne Gewalt, die diese Befugnis nicht hat, ist aber undenkbar, da es zum Wesen der Souveränität gehört, sich selbst binden zu können."; *see also Holiday Inns v. Kingdom of Morocco*, Decision on Jurisdiction, ICSID Case, May 12, 1974, in: *Lalive*, note 361.
592. *See Jan Paulsson*, Third World Participation in International Investment Arbitration, in: ICSID Review 1987, Foreign Investment Law Journal, Vol. 2 No. 1, pp. 19-65 (p. 46), who implies such elevation of a contract to a treaty; *see also* differently *Muthucumaraswamy Sornarajah*, The Climate of International Arbitration, in: Journal of International Arbitration 1991, Vol. 8 No. 2, pp. 47-86 (p. 54): "It is clear that the use of the dictum in Wimbledon to elevate the foreign investment transaction to a treaty is grossly inappropriate."

treaty always serves a particular purpose for which certain obligations are accepted. In other words, a state, by way of an international treaty, waives sovereignty only to the extent as it is embodied and defined in such treaty.

This may be derived from a simple *argumentum e contrario*: if the positive decision to waive sovereignty constitutes a sovereign act, the negative decision not to do so must be equally sovereign. It is rightly stated that holding a state responsible to its own commitments cannot be a violation of sovereignty.[593] Conversely, holding a state responsible to commitments it did not make must be a violation of sovereignty. However, the question is, if this conclusion properly reflects the reality of modern public international law. Are states really only bound by rules which they have consented to? States are becoming bound by rules that do not originate from their individual will.[594] A prominent example in the context of international investment law is the role of previous arbitral decisions that was already discussed. While these are only valid *inter partes*, their persuasive authority may foster the emergence of new rules that may at times be applied to other disputes. But also in the context of international organizations, this holds true. It has been examined that beyond their express powers, implied powers may be equally exercised due to a practical need for ensuring the realization of the respective ends.[595]

It thus appears like the concept of state sovereignty is in the process of further adapting, much like it has been during the course of its history. It could be argued that continuous and increasing consent by sovereign states to a number of different new rules in various areas, in awareness of the emergence of additional rules not carried by their will, constitutes a more general consent: consent that extends to such evolution of public international law and the rules it produces beyond a specific treaty. The future role of consent, however, is not an undisputed field. For the purpose of this analysis, one must acknowledge that the concept of sovereignty is evolving. States may nowadays be bound by rules that do not originate from their will. The question that still remains unanswered is how this public international law reality may be explained in theory. Nevertheless, in the attempt to detect the ramifications of interpretive deficiencies, finding such answer is not the most pressing issue. Rather, it is essential to understand the consequences for state sovereignty, if a rule or an obligation is created by a flawed application of established methodological principles.

---

593. *Paulsson*, note 590, p. 344.
594. ICJ, Corfu Channel Case, note 585, p. 43: "Today, owing to social interdependence and to the predominance of the general interest, the States are bound by many rules which have not been ordered by their will."
595. ICJ, Advisory Opinion on the Legality of the Threat or Use of Nuclear Weapons, July 8, 1996, ICJ Reports 1996, para. 25:

> The powers conferred on international organizations are normally the subject of an express statement in their constituent instruments. Nevertheless, the necessities of international life may point to the need for organizations, in order to achieve their objectives, to possess subsidiary powers which are not expressly provided for in the basic instruments which govern their activities. It is generally accepted that international organizations can exercise such powers, known as 'implied' powers.

[D] State Sovereignty and Insufficient Interpretation

The agreement of a state to arbitrate constitutes an expression of understanding that interpretation of relevant treaty provisions will be based upon the existing methodology, namely the VCLT.[596] If an international body does not adhere to the canons thereby deemed applicable, that body will go beyond its mandate.[597] In the context of an international investment arbitration this is of particular interest, given the finality and binding character of arbitral awards. These awards may create obligations for a respective state without being subject to appeal. If the award comes into existence under adherence to methodological rules, the obligations are created within the confines of the state's sovereignty waiver. Here, asking if the relevant award violates state sovereignty is rightly characterized as "a bad question";[598] holding a state to its own commitments cannot constitute a violation of state sovereignty, if proper methodological rules are applied.[599] However, the argument that an arbitral award violates state sovereignty is still advanced.[600]

An assessment of the matter may only be carried out by giving the above-mentioned question more accuracy. In the question's former wording, it fails to capture the nuance that is central to the legitimacy of international investment arbitrations. It carries the subtle notion that any investment arbitration poses the inherent risk of a sovereignty violation. The perspective that is thereby taken is misleading. Consent to arbitration generally waives sovereignty, and thus possible claims relating to it after the arbitration was conducted. A valuable first question must therefore abandon such notion and change its initial perspective: is an arbitral award *at all* capable of violating state sovereignty? If the first question can be answered in the affirmative, a second

---

596. *See Garanti Koza LLP v. Turkmenistan*, Dissenting Opinion of Laurence Boisson de Chazournes, ICSID Case No. ARB/11/20, July 3, 2013, para. 8: "(w)ell-established principles governing the interpretation of titles of jurisdiction as formulated by the ICJ should guide the interpretation of dispute settlement provisions under the ICSID Convention and BITs."; *see also Hussein Nuaman Soufraki v. United Arab Emirates*, Decision of the Ad Hoc Committee on the Application for Annulment of Mr. Soufraki, ICSID Case No. ARB/02/7, June 5, 2007, para. 45:

   > Thirdly, one must also consider that a tribunal goes beyond the scope of its power if it does not respect the law applicable to the substance of the arbitration under the ICSID Convention. It is widely recognized in ICSID jurisprudence that failure to apply the applicable law constitutes an excess of power. The relevant provisions of the applicable law are constitutive elements of the Parties' agreement to arbitrate and constitute part of the definition of the tribunal's mandate.

597. *See ICJ*, Case Concerning Delimitation of the Maritime Boundary in the Gulf of Maine Area (*Canada v. United States of America*), Judgment, October 12, 1984, ICJ Reports 1984, pp. 246-352 (p. 266): "The Chamber concludes that, in the task conferred upon it, it must conform to the terms by which the Parties have defined this task. If it did not do so, it would overstep its jurisdiction."
598. *Paulsson*, note 590, p. 344.
599. *Paulsson*, note 590, p. 344.
600. *See Alexander Schilling*, Gesprächskreis "Investitionsrecht und -schiedsgerichtsbarkeit" - achtes Jahrestreffen, in: Zeitschrift für Schiedsverfahren 2013, pp. 106-109 (p. 109): "Allerdings gab Prof. van Aaken zu bedenken, dass auch die Verurteilung zur Zahlung eines hohen Schadensersatzes in die staatliche Souveränität eingreifen kann."

[1] The Impact of Arbitral Awards

In view of the sovereignty argument's recent prominence, an exploration of the first aforementioned question is merited. Considering the ICJ's central role in public international law, it is fruitful to start out by examining relevant rulings and the context in which they were made. Naturally, the jurisdiction of the ICJ is limited due to the narrow prerequisites of Article 36 of the ICJ-Statute. Despite such limitation, the consideration of relevant ICJ-jurisprudence is necessary and instructive in approaching the question at hand. It is of utter importance to note, however, that it is not suggested here that the ICJ may thus function as a general body for the review of arbitral decisions. Such implication would be contrary to reality. The ICSID framework, for example, considers the review of decisions an internal matter that may not be referred to the ICJ. In this sense, the ICSID regime is a self-contained system.[601] The consideration of ICJ rulings rather serves the purpose of deriving general principles. The court, as an international body, according to Article 1 of the ICJ-Statute, is the principal judicial organ of the United Nations and is equally open to those few states that are not yet members of the United Nations. It may therefore be considered as a general court of the international community.[602] It is competent to rule on any question of international law pursuant to Article 36 section 2 (b) of the ICJ-Statute. Article 2 Nr. 1 of the United Nations-Charter points out that the entire organization is based upon the principle of sovereign equality. From this, it follows that the ICJ is generally entrusted with ruling on possible violations of state sovereignty upon consent by respective state parties to do so. In its history, it has carried out this function numerous times.[603] In this sense, the court functions as a safeguard for the principle of state sovereignty.[604] Therefore, one may be tempted to argue that the ICJ has general jurisdiction to hear

---

601. *Schreuer*, note 210, Art. 64, para. 14.
602. Karin Oellers-Frahm, in: Andreas Zimmermann/Christian Tomuschat/Karin Oellers-Frahm/Christian J. Tams (eds.), The Statute of the International Court of Justice - A Commentary, 2nd ed. 2012, Art. 92, para. 29.
603. See ICJ, The Corfu Channel Case (*United Kingdom v. Albania*), Judgment, April 9, 1949, ICJ Reports 1949, pp. 4-169 (p. 35): "But to ensure respect for international law, of which it is the organ, the Court must declare that the action of the British Navy constituted a violation of Albanian sovereignty."; *see also ICJ*, Case Concerning Armed Activities on the Territory of the Congo (*Democratic Republic of the Congo v. Uganda*), Judgment, December 19, 2005, ICJ Reports 2005, pp. 168-283 (p. 227): "In relation to the first of the DRC's final submissions, the Court accordingly concludes that Uganda has violated the sovereignty and also the territorial integrity of the DRC."; *see also ICJ*, Case Concerning Military and Paramilitary Activities in and against Nicaragua (*Nicaragua v. United States of America*), Judgment, June 27, 1986, ICJ Reports 1986, pp. 14-150 (p. 128): "Accordingly, such actions constitute violations of Nicaragua's sovereignty under customary international law."
604. ICJ, (*Nicaragua v. United States of America*), note 603, p. 29, in relying on *PCIJ*, The Mavrommatis Palestine Concessions (*Greece v. United Kingdom*), Judgment, August 30, 1924, Publications of the Permanent Court of International Justice 1924, pp. 4-37 (p. 16): "The Court therefore is at liberty to adopt the principle which it considers best calculated to ensure the administration of justice, most suited to procedure before an international tribunal and most in

claims regarding arbitral awards and their impact on state sovereignty. However, such broad competence would run contrary to the finality and binding nature of international arbitration. The interplay of the ICJ's jurisdiction and the principles of international arbitration are instructive for clarifying the sovereignty impact of arbitral awards. If the ICJ assumed general jurisdiction for claims arising from allegedly improper awards, it would effectively carry out the function of an international review court. Such approach would run contrary to the pillars of international arbitration. If, on the other hand, the ICJ generally declined jurisdiction, it would possibly devitalize its capacity as a safeguard for state sovereignty. This dilemma allows for a conclusion: where the ICJ does assume jurisdiction, in practice, it interferes with the finality and binding character of international arbitration. Only the principle of state sovereignty provides the permissible grounds for such procedure, given the ICJ's above-mentioned dedication to it.

The relationship between principles of international arbitration and jurisdiction of the ICJ has already been subject to analysis by the court. It came to the following conclusions:

> In this respect the Court would emphasize that, as the Parties were both agreed, these proceedings *allege the inexistence and nullity of the Award* rendered by the Arbitration Tribunal and *are not by way of appeal* from it or application for revision of it.[605]

And in a previous ruling:

> Before doing so, the Court will observe that the Award is *not subject to appeal* and that the Court cannot approach the consideration of the objections raised by Nicaragua to the validity of the Award as a Court of Appeal. The Court is *not called upon to pronounce on whether the arbitrator's decision was right or wrong*. These and cognate considerations have no relevance to the function that the Court is called upon to discharge in these proceedings, which is to decide whether *the Award is proved to be a nullity having no effect*.[606]

The ICJ thereby indicates that it recognizes the delicate line between its impermissible functioning as an arbitral appeals mechanism and its role as an international body called upon to rule on whether or not an obligation was created by an award as a question of international law. It rightly sees its duty in determining, if an award is so flawed that it must be deemed a nullity and thus as not creating such obligation for a respective state. This understanding is representative of a more general principle: international tribunals acting beyond their authority cannot coin an international

---

conformity with the fundamental principles of international law."; *see also Mosler/Oellers-Frahm*, note 602, para. 27: "The ICJ is therefore in a better position than any other judicial institution to contribute through its case law to the development of general international law."
605. ICJ, Case Concerning the Arbitral Award of July 31, 1989 (*Guinea-Bissau v. Senegal*), Judgment, November 12, 1991, ICJ Reports 1991, pp. 53-76 (p. 62).
606. ICJ, Case Concerning the Arbitral Award made by the King of Spain on December 23, 1906 (*Honduras v. Nicaragua*), Judgment, November 18, 1960, ICJ Reports 1960, pp. 192-218 (p. 214).

obligation.[607] The principle already existed in Roman law, *arbiter nihil extra compromissum facere potest*, and was adopted in public international law: arbitrators cannot exceed their powers and create obligations that go beyond their mandate.[608] However, it must be noted that there does not appear to be consensus, whether or not such nullity must be so pronounced by a judicial body.[609] The pronouncement of an award's nullity by such judicial body, however, practically only affects the likelihood of a state's actions to comply with the award. In the absence of such explicit nullity ruling, it is conceivable that a defendant state is more likely to follow the arbitral award. It may thereby act according to an alleged international obligation that either did not exist, provided that one does not require an explicit pronouncement by a judicial body, or was not supposed to exist. This scenario is capable of constituting a de facto violation of state sovereignty. It may not be argued that a state in this position voluntarily exercises compliance. Such approach would disregard the nature of public international law that largely does not achieve state actions by way of judicial force, but rather a combination of e.g. political pressure, concerns of reputation or morality. The fact that a respective pronouncement by the ICJ of an award's nullity is dependent upon both states' consent, that will typically be a rare occurrence, makes the matter particularly severe.

Seeing this existing option of recourse to the ICJ is an interesting observation. It further proves and exemplifies the ICJ's role as a safeguard to state sovereignty: first, the ICJ's approach implies that an award may suffer from serious flaws that are so grave that it is null and void. Second, the ICJ assumes jurisdiction to hear such claims in order to eventually pronounce that a state is not under an obligation resulting from such award. Bearing in mind the above-mentioned dedication of the ICJ to the principle of state sovereignty, the underlying protective notion becomes evident. More importantly, the observation encompasses the perpetual relevance of state sovereignty. Certainly, it may be waived and thus create a restriction on the state's authority resulting from it. However, it does not cease to exist in its formal character.[610] Rather,

---

607. W. Michael Reisman, Has the International Court Exceeded its Jurisdiction?, in: American Journal of International Law 1986, Vol. 80, pp. 128-134 (p. 128): "When an international tribunal purports to act beyond the authority granted to it, its acts, like those of any other entity that exceeds its authority, are null and void."; *see* specifically with regards to arbitration W. Michael Reisman, The Breakdown of the Control Mechanism in ICSID Arbitration, in: Duke Law Journal 1989, No. 4, pp. 739-807 (p. 745):

> Conversely, a purported award which is accomplished in ways inconsistent with the shared contractual expectations of the parties is something to which they had not agreed. The arbitrator has exceeded his power or, to use the technical term, committed an exces de pouvoir. If the allegation of such an excess can be sustained, the putative award is null, and may be ignored by the 'losing' party.

608. *ICJ*, Case Concerning the Arbitral Award of July 31, 1989 (*Guinea-Bissau v. Senegal*), Dissenting Opinion of Judge Weeramantry, November 12, 1991, ICJ Reports 1991, pp. 130-174 (p. 157).
609. *See* answering in the affirmative Hersch Lauterpacht, The Development of International Law by the International Court, 1982, p. 329; *see* contrarily the apt analysis by Judge Weeramantry in *ICJ*, note 608, pp. 158 et seq.
610. *See PCIJ*, Lighthouses in Crete and Samos (*France v. Greece*), Judgment, October 8, 1937, Fascicule No. 71, pp. 94-106 (p. 103): "Even though the Sultan had been obliged to accept

it is of continuous relevance and becomes a legal issue, provided that an act goes beyond the confines of the authority limitation. Despite its limited reach, an analysis of ICJ-jurisprudence provides sufficient grounds for addressing the question: is an arbitral award *at all* capable of violating state sovereignty? The answer must be in the affirmative. However, the threshold for a successful claim is high.

[2] The Impact of Insufficient Interpretation

The second question turns to the impact of insufficient interpretation on state sovereignty. A successful sovereignty claim must overcome the high threshold set by the binding and final character of international arbitration. If one were to understand any error of a tribunal as causing an award to be null and void, it would require the involvement of "the perfect arbitrator." A state's consent must rather be understood as tolerating a commonly accepted margin of error. It is in this sense the involvement of "the imperfect arbitrator" that forms the basis of a state party's consent to arbitration. Of relevance to the present analysis is the threshold at which an arbitrator is acting more imperfect than others. In other words, at which point does an arbitrator really exceed his or her authority?[611]

[a] Reflections on Sovereignty in Rulings by the ICJ

The answer to the aforementioned question provides an indicator of sovereignty violations. An excess of authority can certainly not occur, if an error is merely "tolerable."[612] Another look at the ICJ's jurisprudence will shed more light on this crucial issue:

> However, the Court does not have to enquire whether or not the Arbitration Agreement could, with regard to the Tribunal's competence, be interpreted in a number of ways, and if so to consider which would have been preferable. By proceeding in that way the Court would be treating the request as an appeal and not as a recours en nullité. The Court could not act in that way in the present case. It has simply to *ascertain whether by rendering the disputed Award the Tribunal acted in manifest breach of the competence* conferred on it by the Arbitration

---

important restrictions on the exercise of his rights of sovereignty in Crete, that sovereignty had not ceased to belong to him, however it might be qualified from a juridical point of view."

611. *ICJ*, Case Concerning the Arbitral Award of July 31, 1989 (*Guinea-Bissau v. Senegal*), Separate Opinion of Judge Shahabuddeen, November 12, 1991, ICJ Reports 1991, pp. 106-119 (p. 110):

> [W]hen the parties invest an arbitrator, whether expressly or by implication of law, with competence to interpret the compromise, within what limits, if any, are they to be understood as thereby engaging to be bound by an exercise of the competence by the arbitrator which results in a misinterpretation by him of the compromise concerning his powers?

612. *ICJ*, Case Concerning the Arbitral Award of July 31, 1989, note 611, p. 110: "Conceivably, in the larger interests of securing a resolution of their dispute, the Parties might be understood as having undertaken to be bound by decisions made within some tolerable margin of appreciation as to competence in minor matters even though erroneous."

Chapter 4: Ramifications of Interpretive Insufficiencies §4.02[D]

Agreement, either by deciding *in excess of, or by failing to exercise*, its jurisdiction.[613]

Key question to the analysis must thus be, whether or not a tribunal has acted in manifest breach of its competence that is derived from the applicable arbitration agreement. This may be the case when a tribunal exceeds its jurisdiction or does not exercise it, the former here being the central matter of concern. Can flawed interpretation constitute such manifest breach of competence? The ICJ has addressed this issue in a clear and concise manner:

> Such manifest breach might result from, for example, the *failure of the Tribunal properly to apply the relevant rules of interpretation* to the provisions of the Arbitration Agreement which govern its competence. An arbitration agreement (compromise d'arbitrage) is an agreement between States which *must be interpreted in accordance with the general rules of international law governing the interpretation of treaties*.[614]

And concerning the requirement of providing reasons:

> The last ground of nullity raised by Nicaragua is the alleged lack of *inadequacy of reasons* in support of the conclusions arrived at by the arbitrator. However, an examination of the Award shows that it deals in *logical order and in some detail with all relevant considerations that it contains ample reasoning and explanations in support of the conclusions arrived at by the arbitrator*. In the opinion of the Court, this ground is without foundation.[615]

From this, it follows that insufficient interpretation may constitute a manifest breach of the competence of an arbitral tribunal and thus also a violation of state sovereignty.[616] Is insufficient interpretation then capable of constituting a violation of state sovereignty? Once again, the answer to this question must be in the affirmative.

---

613. ICJ, Case Concerning the Arbitral Award of July 31, 1989, note 605, p. 69.
614. ICJ, Case Concerning the Arbitral Award of July 31, 1989, note 605, p. 69.
615. ICJ, Case Concerning the Arbitral Award made by the King of Spain on December 23, 1906, note 606, p. 216; *see also* ICJ, Case Concerning the Arbitral Award of July 31, 1989, note 605, p. 74: "The reasoning mentioned above is, once again, brief but sufficient to enlighten the Parties and the Court as to the reasons that guided the Tribunal."; *see also* ICJ, Case Concerning the Arbitral Award of July 31, 1989 (*Guinea-Bissau v. Senegal*), Dissenting Opinion of Judge Weeramantry, note 608, pp. 164 et seq.
616. *See also Hrvatska Elektroprivreda D.D. v. The Republic of Slovenia*, Dissenting Opinion of Jan Paulsson, ICSID Case No. ARB/05/24, June 8, 2009, para. 41 concerning the correct, meaning textual, application of interpretive canons of the VCLT: "More importantly, it is the bedrock of the international law of treaties, and it is therefore impermissible to ignore it when giving effect to what States understand they do when they sign treaties."; *see also Waibel*, note 565, p. 45: "Such attempt went beyond the legitimate role of arbitrators and risks undoing the treaty bargain concluded by the two state parties."; *see also Radio Corporation of America v. The National Government of the Republic of China*, Decision in the Arbitration Case, April 13, 1935, in: United Nations Reports of International Arbitral Awards, Vol. 3, pp. 1621-1636 (p. 1627): "But as a sovereign government, on principle free in its action for the public interest as it sees it, it cannot be presumed to have accepted such restriction of its freedom of action, unless the acceptance of such restriction can be ascertained distinctly and beyond reasonable doubt."

[b]   Reflections on Sovereignty Elsewhere

The rationale is, however, not exclusive to the rulings by the ICJ. Article 52 of the ICSID-Convention contains similar language. In fact, the provision is based upon Article 35 of the International Law Commission's (ILC's) Model Rules on Arbitral Procedure of 1958, which aimed at creating a permanent review procedure for international arbitral awards conducted by the ICJ.[617] Article 52 ICSID-Convention now allows a party to an ICSID arbitration to request annulment of a rendered award for a number of reasons. These include a tribunal that has manifestly exceeded its powers (b) and an award that has failed to state the reasons on which it is based (e). It is argued that Article 52 of the ICSID-Convention thereby generally balances the principle of finality and the principle of correctness.[618] This view implies that correctness is merely self-serving. Correctness, however, serves the purpose of preventing flawed decisions against state parties that could have serious repercussions. It was previously pointed out that the fundamental difference between commercial and investment arbitration is the element of state sovereignty. While an arbitral award in commercial arbitration affects the financial statement of a company, in investment arbitration it affects the budget of a sovereign state. Depending on amounts owed under an award and financial power, the consequences for a state of an international investment arbitration might be severe and impact an entire population. Concerning the dilemma between finality and correctness, it is conceivable that in its commercial form, international arbitration will place a stronger emphasis on finality, given the needs of a fast-paced business world. In its public form, international arbitration should place a stronger emphasis on correctness.[619] This is essentially paying respect to the principle of state sovereignty.

[3]   Conclusion

The analysis has revealed that insufficient interpretation of an international investment treaty may, in specific circumstances, be understood as being capable of constituting a violation of state sovereignty. The threshold for making a valid sovereignty claim is, however, a high one. It requires such improper interpretation that it constitutes a

---

617. *Schreuer*, note 210, Art. 52, para. 1.
618. *Christoph Schreuer*, The ICSID Convention: A Commentary, in: ICSID Review - Foreign Investment Law Journal 1998, Vol. 13 No. 2, pp. 507-717 (p. 520).
619. *David D. Caron*, Reputation and Reality in the ICSID Annulment Process: Understanding the Distinction between Annulment and Appeal, in: ICSID Review 1992, Vol. 7 No. 1, pp. 21-56 (p. 51): "But given the size of claims and political sensitivity of the disputes that come before ICSID, doesn't it seem equally possible that the correctness of the award is, or should be, also important both to the parties and the international community"; *see also Gabrielle Kaufmann-Kohler*, Interpretive Powers of the Free Trade Commission and the Rule of Law, in: Frédéric Bachand/Emmanuel Gaillard (eds.), IAI series on International Arbitration No. 7 - Fifteen Years of NAFTA Chapter 11 Arbitration, 2011, pp. 175-194 (p. 194): "First, the interpretation itself must be understandable or clear. Otherwise it makes no contribution to predictability and fails the test of promulgation."

manifest breach of competence. In order to properly capture the interplay of interpretation and sovereignty, the final answer therefore necessitates an adjustment: insufficient interpretation as such is generally incapable of constituting a violation of state sovereignty. This answer reflects a general rule. The immense threshold of successful sovereignty claims causes most of them to be unfounded. This answer thus properly respects the cornerstones of international arbitration.

Likewise, it respects the sovereignty of states. If a state's consent to arbitration constitutes a sovereign act, it must be treated with sincerity. What a state intends to be accountable for, it must be held accountable to. Otherwise, a state would be deprived of its "power to make a meaningful promise."[620] However, to every rule there is an exception. Sincere respect for state sovereignty must similarly acknowledge that the process of holding a state accountable to its own commitments is not always immaculate. Excessively insufficient interpretation may see promises a state has never made. The impact of such findings on states may be severe and spark strong sentiments. In the interest of keeping international investment arbitration in place as "an inherently useful method of resolving foreign investment disputes,"[621] sovereignty claims in these exceptional circumstances must not be disregarded. It is in allowing for this exception to exist and sovereignty claims to be heard that the weight of a state's promise to be bound by an arbitral award is treated with sincerity. This too, is not different from relationships between individuals: a man whose promise continues to be misinterpreted will eventually stop promising.[622]

§4.03 THE ROLE OF POLICY SPACE AND PUBLIC INTEREST

Closely connected to the principle of state sovereignty is the ability of a state to shape its own policies.[623] These generally involve an unlimited number of decisions regarding matters of culture, economics or politics.[624] It can be understood as sovereignty's peculiarity. Policy decisions are typically based upon public interest. They may serve myriad purposes such as e.g. water supply, food security or pure business regulation and embody the modern sovereignty understanding of a state existing to serve its people. Here, the term "policy space" is becoming increasingly used in the scholarship surrounding international investment law. It is nevertheless evident that the promises made to foreign investors by way of international investment treaties or contracts may

---

620. *Paulsson*, note 590, p. 343: "The ability to make a binding commitment is part of what makes a state a state. We are talking about the power to make a meaningful promise."
621. *Sornarajah*, note 586, p. 105.
622. *See* similarly *Paulsson*, note 590, p. 343: "[...] a man whose promises mean nothing will have great difficulties in life."
623. *See Lao Holdings N.V. v. The Lao People's Democratic Republic*, Decision on Jurisdiction, ICSID Case No. ARB(AF)/12/6, February 21, 2014, para. 27: "[...] The New Tax Code, as an exercise of its sovereign power, applies to Savan Vegas according to its terms. [...]".
624. *Thomas G. Weiss/Don Hubert*, The Responsibility to Protect: Research, Bibliography, Background: Supplementary Volume to the Report of the International Commission on Intervention and State Sovereignty, 2001, p. 6.

limit a state's freedom in regulation.[625] When a state implements a particular policy, it will be wise to consider the implications for its international commitments.[626] This will help to assess, whether or not a change in policy will give rise to potential compensation claims by foreign investors. It is then up to the state to calculate risks and benefits of a policy operation. In any case, however, the existence of international commitments to protect foreign investors may pose significant challenges to the work of policy-makers. Despite careful governmental considerations, an investor may still initiate arbitral proceedings and thereby bring the state's actions before an international tribunal. At this point, it is the tribunal's scrutiny that rules on the legality of a domestic action on the international level. The interpretation as the methodological essence of international investment law thereby serves as an analytical instrument. Public interest demands particular caution in the instrument's operation.[627] Insufficient interpretation, however unpleasant within the sphere of international commercial arbitration, may have severe ramifications of a larger, public dimension.

[A] Limiting the Policy Space of States

Stating that arbitral awards directly limit the policy space of states is not accurate. By entering into an investment treaty, a respective state has agreed to expose its policy choices to the scrutiny of an international tribunal. It is the arbitrators' function to assess whether or not a particular governmental activity is contrary to the promise

---

625. *See Gus van Harten*, The Public-Private Distinction in the International Arbitration of Individual Claims against the State, in: International and Comparative Corporate Law Quarterly, Vol. 56 No. 2, pp. 371-394 (p. 382): "The stabilization clause thus restricts the policy options available to Chad's Government, and to the people represented by the State of Chad, in relation to the oil project for a substantial period (at least 30 years in this case)."
626. *Jeffery Atik*, Identifying Antidemocratic Outcomes: Authenticity, Self-Sacrifice, and International Trade, in: University of Pennsylvania Journal of International Economic Law 1998, Vol. 19 No. 2, pp. 229-262 (pp. 231 et seq.): "The further implication of this structure is that national lawmakers will learn the bounds on their remaining freedom of action and will prospectively circumscribe legislation that runs counter to international trade norms."
627. *See Czechoslovakia v. Radio Corporation of America*, Arbitration Case, April 1, 1932, in: The American Journal of International Law 1936, Vol. 30, pp. 523 et seq. (p. 531), which acknowledged the particularity of public interest in the case of an investment contract and ruled "that public interests of vital importance would suffer if the agreement should be upheld"; *see also Teco Guatemala Holdings LLC v. The Republic of Guatemala*, Award, ICSID Case No. ARB/10/17, December 19, 2013, para. 490: "The Arbitral Tribunal, in deciding this dispute, is mindful of the deference that international tribunals should pay to a sovereign State's regulatory powers."; *see also CME Czech Republic B.V. (The Netherlands) v. The Czech Republic*, Separate Opinion on the Issues at the Quantum Phase of: CME v. Czech Republic by Ian Brownlie, UNCITRAL, March 14, 2003, para. 74:

> In this context, it is simply unacceptable to insist that the subject matter is exclusively "commercial" in character or that the interests are, more or less, only those of the investor. Such approach involves setting aside a number of essential elements in the Treaty relation. The first element is the significance of the fact that the Respondent is a sovereign state, which is responsible for the well-being of its people. This is not to confer a privilege on the Czech Republic but only to recognise its special character and responsibilities. The Czech Republic is not a commercial entity.

made by the state to an investor.[628] However, such finding is not able to directly limit the state's policy decision. Rather, it imposes an obligation to compensate the investor. A power to adapt the law of the host state is not vested within an arbitral tribunal. Nevertheless, the indirect effect of such arbitral decision is of particular relevance and may be far-reaching. It serves as an indicator for new policies and may factually impact a state's freedom of choice in the future.[629]

This complication of policy-making already poses a limitation on a state's policy space. Given the state's consent to be bound by its international obligations, however, this limitation is an anticipated consequence. It is accepted for the bargain of attracting investments. At the same time, one must bear in mind that in any state with a proper rule of law, policy space is naturally limited by the guarantee of basic rights to the individual. Nevertheless, insufficient treaty interpretation is typically only to a certain extent part of a state's equation, as was previously outlined in the context of state sovereignty. Limitations on policy space, even if imposed by way of proper interpretation of a respective investment treaty, may have significant impacts on a state's decision-making process. Prominent examples include the arbitration in *Methanex v. United States* that was previously referred to, in which the State of California's decision to ban the sale and use of a gasoline additive named "MTBE" for the sake of ensuring water quality was tested. This was, unsuccessfully, claimed to be a violation of its investment protection obligations under NAFTA.[630] Similarly, the Swedish energy company *Vattenfall* has filed a request for arbitration against Germany in 2012 in view of the country's decision to phase out its nuclear power engagement.[631]

If interpretation is carried out improperly, it may not only be legally problematic, but it may also raise serious concerns of state parties. These may lose flexibility in dealing with changing environments[632] and deprive them of the adequate power to protect and serve their populations.[633] Such restrictions are profound and are all the more dissatisfactory if their legal bases are insufficient. Not only does improper interpretation thereby allude to the subjective elements of state sovereignty, namely political sentiments, it may also impair the realization of *Leitmotifs* of the international community in tackling the issues most pressing in a respective state. Had the tribunal in *Methanex v. United States*, for example, found the State of California's ban of "MTBE" to constitute a violation of its investment protection obligations and done so

---

628. *Kaufmann-Kohler*, note 262, (p. 163).
629. See *Stephan W. Schill/Marc Jacob*, Trends in international investment agreements, 2010/2011: The Increasing Complexity of International Investment Law, in: Karl P. Sauvant (ed.), Yearbook on International Law & Policy 2011-2012, 2013, pp. 141-179 (pp. 157 et seq.).
630. *Methanex Corporation v. United States of America*, Final Award, UNCITRAL, August 3, 2005.
631. See also *Vattenfall AB, Vattenfall Europe AG, Vattenfall Europe Generation AG v. Federal Republic of Germany*, Award, ICSID Case No. ARB/09/6, March 11, 2011, in which both parties have reached a settlement concerning Hamburg's decision to impose higher water quality standards as tested against standards of investment protection.
632. *Ilija Mitrev Penusliski*, A Dispute Systems Design Diagnosis of ICSID, in: Waibel/Kaushal et al. (eds.), note 6, pp. 507-536 (p. 520).
633. See similarly *Schill*, note 159, p. 76; see also *William Schreiber*, Realizing the Right to Water in International Investment Law: An Interdisciplinary Approach to BIT Obligations, in: Natural Resources Journal 2008, Vol. 48, pp. 431-478 (p. 476), who describes the difficult task of implementing the right to water; see also *van Houtte/Brunetti*, note 533, p. 559.

by way of improper interpretation, such decision would have, rightly, generated serious criticism towards that particular tribunal or investment protection as a whole. It is furthermore conceivable that any state which, for example, intends to oppose the privatization of water supply in the interest of its population will have largely negative sentiments, if its actions are deemed a violation of investment protection obligations based upon improper interpretation. Particularly in developing countries though, that must predominantly manage to form policies revolving around basic human needs, illegitimate limitations on policy space may have serious consequences[634] that go beyond sentiments and may touch upon the effectivity of those states' functions.

[B] Arbitrators as Policy-Makers

Another dimension that deserves attention is the possible role of arbitrators as active policy-makers. Views diverge on the matter. The exercise of a policy-making power is, on the one hand, categorically rejected[635] and, on the other hand and in its indirect form, implicitly[636] and explicitly[637] confirmed. While the former rejection of policy-making power results from a fundamental analysis of the role of states and international tribunals, the latter confirmation depicts arbitral practice in an effort to contribute to the legitimacy of international investment law. Also, the former statement refers to the shaping of domestic policies, while the latter refers to the shaping of international policies. Once again, arbitral tribunals are called upon to resolve a particular dispute based upon an international treaty,[638] not to shape a state's domestic policies. However, it is conceivable that tribunals do assume such function based upon an insufficient interpretation of the investment treaty's provisions. This has been pointed out in the context of the *Salini*-test. Unless it is explicitly so determined, the investment descriptions should not be transformed into rigid requirements. Otherwise, subjective elements would be introduced into the analysis that practically allows arbitrators to act as policy-makers.[639] If, for example, a "sufficient duration" is required for an activity to

---

634. *See Tai-Heng Cheng*, Power, Authority and International Investment Law, in: American University International Law Review 2005, Vol. 20 No. 3, pp. 465-520 (p. 515).
635. *Paulsson*, note 590, p. 348: "International tribunals do not establish policy. They give effect to international agreements."
636. *Schill*, note 633, p. 85:

> Because arbitral jurisprudence frames the discourse and arguments of later litigants and arbitrators, and constitutes the focal point around which normative expectations of the users of the system develop, arbitrators are in a position to craft, and investors in a position to enforce a body of 'state liability law for foreign investors' that has a deep impact on the exercise of the regulatory powers of states.

637. *Martin Hunter/Gui Conde E. Silva*, Transnational Public Policy and Its Application in Investment Arbitrations, in: The Journal of World Investment 2003, Vol. 4 No. 3, pp. 367-378 (p. 377), deducing a form of "transnational policy" in investment arbitrations.
638. *Kaufmann-Kohler*, note 262, p. 163.
639. *Pantechniki S.A. Contractors & Engineers (Greece) v. The Republic of Albania*, Award, ICSID Case No. ARB/07/21, July 30, 2009, para. 43: "They may introduce elements of subjective judgment on the part of arbitral tribunals (such as 'sufficient' duration or magnitude or contribution to economic development) which (a) transform arbitrators into policy-makers and

Chapter 4: Ramifications of Interpretive Insufficiencies §4.03[B]

be deemed an investment, arbitrators will be free to determine that part of a state's policy on investment protection, at least within the narrow confines of a particular dispute. It may then be stated that arbitrators must not act as direct policy-makers for domestic issues, if they are not empowered with such function. That is not to say, however, that they never do. Inadequate interpretation may in this regard enable arbitrators to assume functions they are not empowered with. The consequence could be a direct deprivation of a state of some of its regulatory powers. This similarly applies to the role of arbitrators in directly shaping international policies.

A related question is whether arbitral tribunals indirectly shape state policies. The foregoing chapters have illustrated how the decisions of arbitral tribunals are becoming increasingly interconnected. The reliance on previous awards provides de facto a valuable source for decision-making processes. Despite the nonexistence of a doctrine of *stare decisis*, parties to investment arbitrations frequently rely on previous findings and bring them to the attention of the tribunal.[640] Similarly, tribunals oftentimes seek comfort in conclusions that confirm their own.[641] The result is a systematization of international investment law by way of arbitral jurisprudence that may create general principles. Their existence may influence states in the process of shaping future investment policies. In this sense, international investment arbitration is thought of as a "mechanism of global governance."[642] It may thus be said that arbitrators, at times, have the power to indirectly affect the policy-making process of states. Here too, the impact of insufficient interpretation of investment treaties may be profound in indirectly steering state policies without a solid legal foundation, namely properly interpreted treaty provisions. The role of policy space and public interest in

---

above all (b) increase unpredictability about the availability of ICSID to settle given disputes." and further para. 45: "But other States may precisely want to benefit from the aggregate investment flows of attracting the small to middle sized businesses which have contributed so notably to the development of economies such as Germany and Italy. This is their policy choice; not that of arbitrators."

640. *See AES Corporation v. The Argentine Republic*, Decision on Jurisdiction, ICSID Case No. ARB/02/17, April 26, 2006, para. 18:

> The argument made by the Claimant on the basis of these decisions, treated more or less as if they were precedents, tends to say that Argentina's objections to the jurisdiction of this Tribunal are moot if not even useless since these tribunals have already determined the answer to be given to identical or similar objections to jurisdiction.

> *see also El Paso Energy International Company v. The Argentine Republic*, Decision on Jurisdiction, ICSID Case No. ARB/03/15, April 27, 2006, para. 39:

> It is, nonetheless, a reasonable assumption that international arbitral tribunals, notably those established within the ICSID system, will generally take account of the precedents established by other arbitration organs, especially those set by other international tribunals. The present Tribunal will follow the same line, especially since both parties, in their written pleadings and oral arguments, have heavily relied on precedent.

641. *Ten Cate*, note 172, p. 443.
642. *Stephan W. Schill*, International Investment Law and Comparative Public Law - An Introduction, in: Stephan W. Schill (ed.), International Investment Law and Comparative Public Law 2009, pp. 3-37 (p. 18).

international investment arbitrations therefore indicates the immense responsibility of arbitrators and also the ramifications, if such is not exercised with the necessary amount of care.

§4.04 THE RULE OF LAW

The rule of law may be understood as the primacy of norms, as opposed to political power.[643] Public international law nowadays has a profound influence on the rule of law and its promotion among states.[644] The ICJ's role in this operation is seen as central.[645] More and more disputes in public international law are resolved by international tribunals, particularly in the context of investment disputes. It is thus merited to ask, what role international investment arbitration plays with regards to the rule of law. Like many matters in international investment law, this one is controversial. However, the idea of arbitration as a mechanism to promote the rule of law is of historic value. The 1899 The Hague Convention aimed at "extending the empire of law" and, pursuant to its Article 20, established the PCA.[646] Nowadays, investment arbitration is seen as having the potential of promoting the rule of law worldwide for investors and countries alike[647] or, contrarily, as adversely affecting it.[648] For the purpose of the present analysis, it suffices to acknowledge the diverging views. The focus, however,

---

643. *Dencho Georgiev*, Politics or Rule of Law: Deconstruction and Legitimacy in International Law, in: European Journal of International Law 1993, Vol. 4, pp. 1-14 (p. 4).
644. *Bruno Simma*, The Contribution of Alfred Verdross to the Theory of International Law, in: European Journal of International Law 1995, pp. 33-54 (pp. 46 et seq.); *see*, however, the critical assessment of *Muthucumaraswamy Sornarajah*, Power and Justice: Third World Resistance in International Law, in: Singapore Year Book of International Law 2006, pp. 19-57 (p. 56):

> It is demonstrable that in the last decade and a half, after the emergence of a single hegemonic power, international law has been set upon a course that has resulted in it being perceived as an instrument of power rather than as a neutral body of rules that applies to the international community through processes of law making in which the whole world shares.

645. *See Hersch Lauterpacht*, The Revision of the Statute of the International Court of Justice, in: Elihu Lauterpacht (ed.), International Law - Collected Papers, Vol. 5, Disputes, War and Neutrality, 2004, pp. 112-183 (p. 118), in which he argues that the ICJ's "[...] original and primary purpose was to decide disputes between States and, by fostering the rule of law among them, to contribute to international peace."
646. 1899 Convention for the Pacific Settlement of International Disputes, Preamble, available at http://avalon.law.yale.edu/19th_century/hague01.asp (last accessed April 18, 2015).
647. *Santiago Montt*, State Liability in Investment Treaty Arbitration, 2012, p. 75; *see also International Thunderbird Gaming Corporation v. The United Mexican States*, Separate Opinion by Thomas Wälde, UNCITRAL, January 26, 2006, para. 13:

> Abuse of governmental powers is not an issue in commercial arbitration, but it is at the core of the good-governance standards embodied in investment protection treaties. The issue is to keep a government from abusing its role as sovereign and regulator after having made commitments of a more formal character (contracts and licenses) or of a less formal character (i.e. the assurances by explicit communication or by meaningful conduct that form the basis of the legitimate expectations principle under Art. 1105 of the NAFTA).

lies on an assessment of the impact arbitral decisions might have on the rule of law, if they are based upon an insufficient application of methodological canons of interpretation.

It is necessary to first consider the relevance of investment treaties with regards to the rule of law. It is evident that international treaties do not reform domestic legal systems. Rather, they embody an international guarantee of certain standards that serve as an orientation for what may internationally be understood as the rule of law. In this sense, it may even be said that investment treaties serve the purpose of promoting that rule of law.[649] Such promotion can take place on the domestic[650] or the international level. A scenario of domestic promotion by way of an arbitral decision may involve an award passing judgment on state actions that are contrary to the promise made by the state to the investor. In aiming to protect itself from future investment claims, the state may subsequently engage in efforts to improve its system of governance.[651] Not only foreign investors, but also the state's population would eventually benefit; possibly another idyllically painted picture of international investment law's functioning.

The scenario implies that a state accepts the decision of the respective tribunal and deems it correct. Even provided that it was reached on a solid methodological foundation, it is questionable, whether states will so react. Provided then that the decision rests on improper interpretation, the likelihood of such reaction will possibly

---

648. *Mark Halle/Luke Erik Peterson*, Investment Provisions in Free Trade Agreements and Investment Treaties - Opportunities and Threats for Developing Countries, 2005, p. 23: "The upshot of this may be to remove significant disputes between foreign investors and Government agencies from the purview of local courts and tribunals.", available at http://www.snap-undp.org/elibrary/Publications/InvestmentProvisions.pdf (last accessed August 6, 2014); *see also Tom Ginsburg*, International Substitutes for Domestic Institutions: Bilateral Treaties and Governance, Illinois Law and Economics Working Paper Series 2006, Working Paper No. LE06-027, p. 28: "Furthermore, the impact of BITs on subsequent governance is ambiguous, and the results here suggest that under some circumstances BITs may lead to lower institutional quality in subsequent years.", available at http://papers.ssrn.com/sol3/papers.cfm?abstract_id=916351 (last accessed August 6, 2014).
649. *Kenneth D. Vandevelde*, Bilateral Investment Treaties: History, Policy and Interpretation, 2010, pp. 2 et seq.: "Promoting the rule of law with respect to foreign investment may be regarded as the primary function of a BIT."; *see also* the problematic suggestion of lowering the standards of protection for developing countries in order to accommodate their capability by *Emily A. Alexander*, Taking Account of Reality: Adopting Contextual Standards for Developing Countries in International Investment Law, in: Virginia Journal of International Law 2008, Vol. 48 No. 4, pp. 815-839 (p. 816).
650. *See* for the purpose of distinguishing between the Complement and Substitute Model on the impact of BITs on domestic rule of law *Benjamin K. Guthrie*, Beyond Investment Protection: An Examination of the Potential Influence of Investment Treaties on Domestic Rule of Law, in: International Law and Politics 2013, Vol. 45, pp. 1151-1200 (pp. 1167 et seq.).
651. *Stephan W. Schill/Benedict Kingsbury*, Investor-State Arbitration as Governance: Fair and Equitable Treatment, Proportionality and the Emerging Global Administrative Law, IILJ Working Paper 2009/6, pp. 16 et seq.:

> These processes, and a general normative seepage as more people become familiar with developments in arbitral jurisprudence and in other areas of international law on similar topics, may have effects for the future on the procedural rights and consideration accorded to foreign investors or indeed to others under national law, and even on the exercise and review of administrative discretion.

decline. In its international dimension, the situation is similar. The rule of law helps to develop global standards of good governance that can serve as a model. Whether they become domestically implemented is, however, not predictable. In any case, it is difficult to see how an arbitral decision may contribute to the national or international rule of law, if the decision itself stems from flawed application of international law. The risk of fluctuating results may create uncertainty in understanding what an international standard of the rule of law really looks like. In its more extreme form, improper interpretations may generate concerns about the entire legitimacy of the system of international investment law. The result may be a counterproductive renunciation of states from efforts to implement an international rule of law standard.[652] This risk must be properly addressed. Otherwise, international investment arbitration may be perceived as impairing the rule of law, while it is actually capable of advancing it.[653]

§4.05 THE DISCREPANCY BETWEEN DEVELOPED AND DEVELOPING STATES

A reality of international investment arbitration is that especially developing countries find themselves in the role of respondents. According to a recent study, the exact number of developing country defendants is at 85% of ICSID-administered investment arbitrations.[654] This figure indicates a discrepancy between developed and developing countries and their roles in international investment arbitration. Reasons for this may be manifold. However, statistics have not gone unnoticed and certainly fueled arguments on the alleged current legitimacy crisis and especially the notion of a perceived systemic bias towards investors from developed countries. This notion rests on a number of arguments.[655] In the context of flawed interpretation, the process of setting investment protection standards and then their application to fact patterns by arbitrators are of particular interest. While the former produces raw material, the latter shapes the final product, that is, the arbitral decision. Interpretation is the methodological

---

652. *Guthrie*, note 650, p. 1197: "In its most extreme form, this dissatisfaction with the BIT regime can lead states to reject it altogether as illegitimate."
653. *See* Charles T. Kotuby Jr./Luke A. Sobotta, Practical Suggestions to Promote the Legitimacy and Vitality of International Investment Arbitration, in: ICSID Review 2013, Vol. 28 No. 2, pp. 1-12 (p. 11); *see also Paulsson*, note 590, p. 349.
654. *Michael Waibel/Yanhui Wu*, Are Arbitrators Political?, available at https://www.researchgate.net/publication/256023521_Are_Arbitrators_Political (last accessed August 7, 2014), p. 27, permission by authors obtained.
655. *See van Harten*, note 537, pp. 432 et seq., in which he analyzes problematic areas of the existing system of investment arbitration for the purpose of enhancing its legitimacy while carefully highlighting that it is not necessarily actual, but rather perceived bias that may cast doubt "on all of the awards and interpretations that emanate from the system," in referring to *Thomas W. Wälde*, International Investment Law: An Overview of Key Concepts and Methodology, in: Transnational Dispute Management 2007 - New Aspects of International Investment Law - 2004 Research Seminar by The Hague Academy of International Law, Vol. 4 No. 4, pp. 1-86 (p. 45), who warns against "an extensive criticism of the integrity and competence of the investment arbitration process and all its participants, including the application of commercial arbitration models to investment arbitration."

essence of this process. If it is carried out insufficiently and to the disadvantage of developing countries, the result is likely to be further allegations of systemic bias.

[A]   Asymmetric Setting of Protection Standards in Treaties

The setting of investment protection standards results primarily from the drafting of investment treaties. Creating model BITs has become a common practice among developed countries. These function as a starting point for treaty negotiations, which are supposed to allow for compromise between the parties as to which standards of protection will be mutually agreed upon. The introduction of model BITs seems to have great force. Profound departures from their provisions are rare.[656] It is, however, at this point not fully traceable how treaty negotiations, particularly between developed and developing states, are and have been carried out. It is argued that the relationship between negotiating states in the early days was not so much characterized by parity,[657] and the influence of a number of states in determining the content of treaties was thereby practically diminished. This position is disputed, especially as today still a large number of countries, developed and developing, continue to enter into BITs.[658] Even in the early days, developing countries showed themselves an interest in the conclusion of BITs.[659] Model treaties, however, are typically drafted by capital-exporting states,[660] although an increasing number of developing states have formulated their own and signed treaties among one another.[661]

The first investment treaty program of the United States in the 1980s was apparently conducted quite fiercely, and it was suggested to develop more variations so that the program could generally find more acceptance.[662] In view of the experiences with investment treaties today, negotiations have not become easier, as is indicated by the ongoing efforts between the United States and China in erecting a BIT.[663] The suggested level playing field of treaty negotiations, however, seems to be, at times,

---

656. *Jeswald W. Salacuse*, The Law of Investment Treaties, 2009, p. 117.
657. *José E. Alvarez*, Remarks, American Society of International Law and Procedure 1992, pp. 550-555 (p. 550): "BIT partners turn to the U.S. BIT with the equivalent of an IMF gun pointed at their heads."
658. *Diehl*, note 112, p. 44.
659. *K. Scott Gudgeon*, United States Bilateral Investment Treaties: Comments on Their Origin, Purposes and General Treatment Standards, in: Berkeley Journal of International Law 1986, Vol. 4 No. 1, pp. 105-135 (p. 133).
660. *See* e.g. the 2012 U.S. Model Bilateral Investment Treaty, available at http://www.state.gov/documents/organization/188371.pdf (last accessed November 7,2014) and the 2008 German Model Treaty, available at http://www.italaw.com/sites/default/files/archive/ita1025.pdf (last accessed November 7, 2014).
661. *Dolzer/Schreuer*, note 48, pp. 8 et seq.
662. *Valerie H. Ruttenberg*, The United States Bilateral Investment Treaty Program: Variations on the Model, in: University of Pennsylvania Journal of International Business Law 1986, Vol. 9 No. 1, pp. 121-143 (p. 143): "The United States has been very forceful in requiring that certain provisions be included in the treaties and, moreover, that they be included as specified by the U.S. For the future success of the BIT program, variations on the Model BIT should be developed so that the treaty program as a whole can find wider acceptance."
663. *David A. Gantz*, Challenges for the United States in Negotiating a BIT with China: Reconciling Reciprocal Investment Protection with Policy Concerns, Arizona Legal Studies: Discussion

distorted by an economic contemplation. One country will typically be the provider of investments while the other will be at the receiving end.[664] This holds true especially with regards to negotiations between developing and developed countries. It is an interesting observation that this asymmetry impacts the negotiation process. Apparently, developing countries tend to favor broad language and exceptions, while developed countries prefer clear obligations.[665] The consequence of vague terms is an increased margin for interpretation. Thus, tribunals are more dependent upon interpretive methodology.

This observation highlights the responsibility of states in the treaty drafting process. Some developing countries' preferences for broad language and exceptions may result from skepticism and a desire to preserve state sovereignty to the largest possible extent. On the other hand, however, the increased interpretive latitude results in the respective international treaties to be more susceptible to interpretive difficulties. As a consequence, criticism of developing countries towards allegedly insufficient interpretations of tribunals may be countered by pointing to vague language of the international treaties that have laid the foundation for those interpretations in the first place. In the interest of legal certainty, developing countries may thus be well advised to opt for more clarity in their international obligations. The more direct restriction on state sovereignty that may result from clearer treaty terms also brings about a decreased exposure to interpretive risks – a tradeoff that may be worth considering.

[B] Nurturing the Perception of Pro-investor Bias

Investment protection standards are also further shaped by the interpretations of arbitrators, who give them contours and color. This has sparked academic debates that revolve around possible harms to developing countries through arbitrators mainly from developed countries.[666] Myriad views exist on the matter: it is argued that some arbitrators per se favor certain outcomes of investment arbitrations and are thus deliberately chosen to serve as tribunal members.[667] In contrast to that, international arbitration and consequentially arbitrators are regarded as being neutral.[668] Furthermore, it is analyzed that certain variables impact arbitrators' approaches to a dispute. This is said to include arbitrators' perceptions of appropriate sovereign control, which is ultimately based upon factors like education or background.[669] Certainly, there is no shortage of viewpoints on the role of arbitrators. Their existence, however, indicates

---

Paper No. 14-03, January 2014, available at http://papers.ssrn.com/sol3/papers.cfm?abstract_id=2383919 (last accessed August 7, 2014), p. 43.
664. *Salacuse*, note 656, pp. 117 et seq.
665. *Salacuse*, note 656, p. 117.
666. *Susan D. Franck*, Development and Outcomes of Investment Arbitration, in: Harvard International Law Journal 2009, Vol. 50, pp. 435-489 (pp. 445 et seq.).
667. *Sornarajah*, note 644, p. 33.
668. *Paulsson*, note 592, p. 20.
669. *Amr A. Shakalany*, Arbitration and the Third World: A Plea for Reassessing Bias under the Scepter of Neoliberalism, in: Harvard International Law Journal 2000, Vol. 41 No. 2, pp. 419-468 (p. 430).

the importance of proper interpretation. The notion of systemic bias against developing countries gains momentum, if methodology is improperly deployed.

The high number of developing countries involved in investment disputes and the perceived great weight of developed countries in the erection of protection standards by way of treaties and interpretations have caused skepticism. It is evident that arbitral decisions resting on an unstable methodological foundation cannot provide a cure. An athlete that does not live up to his potential is at risk of jeopardizing success. The promises of neutrality and de-politization that surrounded the introduction of arbitration as a means to resolve investment disputes may be deemed hollow. What leaves an impression on respondent states might not be the excellence of decision-making, but a perceived bias that has allegedly predetermined the outcome of the arbitration. What is thereby fostered is not the credibility of international investment arbitration, but the belief that it is an instrument of modern western imperialism.[670] It is thus the potential of legal arguments unleashed by the application of proper methodology that may best counter possible discrepancies between developed and developing countries.

[C] The Economics of Flawed Interpretation

What adds more force to the discrepancy debate is an economic perspective on investment arbitration. The costs are exemplarily analyzed in a recent study[671] conducted by the Global Development and Environmental Institute at Tufts University. It finds a cost discrepancy of investment arbitrations between developed and developing countries that is considerable. The average amount of awards that Canada, as an example for a developed country, is liable for accounts for 0.003% of its annual government spending.[672] The average amount of awards that developing countries are liable for, on the other hand, accounts for 0.53% of their annual government spending.[673] This illustrates the economic impact of arbitral decisions and similarly the importance of their proper crafting. The earlier general observation that flawed interpretation causes awards having severe repercussions directly on a developing state's budget and indirectly on its population is thereby no longer a merely legal abstract, but an economic reality. The discrepancy between developing and developed countries in the context of international law is a delicate issue and deserves ongoing attention by all participants in the field.

---

670. *See Muthucumaraswamy Sornarajah*, ICSID Involvement in Asian Foreign Investment Disputes: The AMCO and AAPL Case, in: Ko Swan Sik/J.J.G. Syatauw/M.C.W. Pinto (eds.), Asian Yearbook of International Law 1994, Vol. 4, pp. 69-98 (p. 69), explaining the sentiments of formerly colonized Asian states in the 1960s towards the ICSID Convention and its creation of investment dispute settlement by way of arbitration.
671. *Kevin P. Gallagher/Elen Shrestha*, Investment Treaty Arbitration and Developing Countries: A Re-Appraisal, Global Development and Environment Institute, Working Paper No. 11-01, May 2011, available at http://ase.tufts.edu/gdae/Pubs/wp/11-01TreatyArbitrationReappraisal.pdf (last accessed November 7, 2014).
672. *Gallagher/Shrestha*, note 671, p. 9.
673. *Gallagher/Shrestha*, note 671, p. 9.

§4.06 THE RESPONSIBILITY TO PROTECT

Certainly, it is not only the process of interpretation that can lead to such result but it is primarily the state's conduct towards investors that determines whether or not the initiation of arbitral proceedings is at all feasible. In this regard, states bear responsibility towards investors and for the promises they have made to them, but ultimately also towards their own people. This responsibility urges states to act in compliance with international obligations for the sake of protecting the state's population. International investment law may thereby have added a new nuance to the concept of a state's responsibility to protect that, traditionally, applies to matters of direct physical integrity: it may further encompass responsibility to protect a state's population from grave financial losses. This plays out not only in governmental conduct towards foreign investors. It is similarly relevant in the process of treaty negotiations when states define the obligations they will later possibly be held accountable to. Apparently, however, some governments have not fully weighted the benefits and costs of investment treaties.[674] In order to create a more level playing field, this room for improvement should be recognized and appropriate steps be taken. Arbitrators, on the other hand, must fulfill their duties by responsibly adhering to their jurisdiction. This encompasses, as was previously outlined, also the proper application of interpretive canons.

§4.07 CONCLUSION

This chapter has focused on the ramifications of interpretive insufficiencies. Naturally, the analysis must be limited to selected issues that are of peculiar importance. However, it has, once again, become evident that interpretation is not just an academic art, but rather a practical mechanism producing real and profound outcomes. Policy space, public interest, the rule of law and discrepancies between developed and developing states are concerns of public international law that are heavily affected when this practical mechanism is operated inadequately. The examination of these concerns has furthermore illustrated the relevance of state sovereignty. Policy space describes the state's regulatory freedom and public interest the modern understanding of a state serving its people as the actual sovereign. The rule of law focuses on the exercise of state sovereignty, and the discrepancy between developed and developing countries is really a matter of sovereign equality. These interconnections illustrate that state sovereignty is not an outdated concept, but rather of relevance that is continuous. The fact that states have chosen to limit their sovereignty by way of assuming international obligations cannot be understood as a global surrender. State sovereignty has evolved and formed facets that each describe different aspects of it. Within these facets, states have made deliberate but limited decisions to waive their sovereignty. The complexity and dynamics of modern public international law have undoubtedly complicated the process of identifying the contours of these waivers. Therefore,

---

674. *Gus van Harten*, Five Justifications for Investment Treaties: A Critical Discussion, in: Trade, Law & Development 2010, Vol. 2 No. 1, pp. 19-58 (p. 54).

properly applying interpretive methodology is ever more important. This holds true especially in view of ongoing debates concerning the legitimacy of international investment law. It is conceivable that what we are witnessing is the result of paying too little attention to the early warnings that have surfaced long before the recent boom of investment arbitration.[675] In the absence of adequate interpretation, the ramifications of such must be recognized and the insights utilized.[676] Improvements that properly respond to the insufficiencies help to keep international investment arbitration in place and allow both claimants and respondents alike to benefit from its advantages.[677] It is thus desirable that the trend of growing academic attention to international investment law continues.[678] This will ensure further systematization, dialogue and assurance, advancing an informal mechanism of checks and balances. The future of international investment law is largely dependent upon the field's responsiveness in theory and practice.[679] A judicious application of international investment arbitration is equally in the interest of states and investors. Certainly, it would be illusory to assume that a call to methodological discipline will bring about arbitral perfection. Not only does that assumption stumble upon defining perfection, but it also disregards human fallibility. Realism thus demands a different approach to the matter. What is hereby suggested is a quest for more perfect imperfection.

---

675. *Paulsson*, note 199, p. 257:

> Arbitration without privity is a delicate mechanism. A single incident of an adventurist arbitrator going beyond the proper scope of his jurisdiction in a sensitive case may be sufficient to generate a backlash. But if the mechanism is applied judiciously, it will help fill a void that now exists in the absence of compulsory jurisdiction, and thus contribute to enhancing the legal security of international economic life.

> *see also* more generally *Muthucumaraswamy Sornarajah*, note 592, p. 48: "Yet, even in this area, the fact that a State entity is a party to the transaction does have important consequences."

676. L. *Yves Fortier*, Arbitrating in the Age of Investment Treaty Disputes, in: University of New South Wales Law Journal 2008, Vol. 31 No. 1, pp. 282-291 (p. 282): "'Good arbitration practice' in this context requires that the international arbitration community reflect on and contribute to the development of meaningful responses capable of satisfying public concern over the use of international arbitration to resolve investor-state disputes."
677. *Sornarajah*, note 586, p. 105: "[...] the system of international investment arbitration, which is an inherently useful method of resolving foreign investment disputes [...]."
678. See *Schill*, note 642, p. 10.
679. *See* concerning further inclusion of public interest considerations *Nigel Blackaby*, Public Interest and Investment Treaty Arbitration, in: Albert Jan van den Berg (ed.), International Commercial Arbitration: Important Contemporary Questions, ICCA Congress Series 2002, 2003, pp. 355-365 (p. 355):

> There is a risk of this new child in the world of international arbitration dying in infancy, delicate and overprotected by its parents from exposure to the outside world. The arbitration community should not take the role of the overprotective parents, suffocating its natural development and depriving it of survival skills in the outside world by reciting the mantra of confidentiality. Concrete steps can be taken to everyone's advantage to ensure that investment treaty arbitration matures into a powerful tool for the effective protection of foreign investment and thereby a motor for international commerce, whilst at the same time balancing the legitimate concerns that have been expressed. To do that we need to understand and seek to reconcile competing public interests.

CHAPTER 5
Potential Routes to Improved Interpretive Discipline

§5.01 INTRODUCTION

The future success of international investment law depends largely on the responsiveness of the field. A quest for more perfect imperfection begins by an assessment of potential routes that may foster interpretive discipline in the current system. These routes must pay respect to the field's public law foundation. Specifically, a proper balance between the protection of investors' rights and state sovereignty is vital.[680] The increased academic attention to international investment law has produced many suggestions. The United Nations Conference on Trade and Development (UNCTAD) has identified four major streams of ideas that are currently being debated: maintaining the status quo, disengaging from the international investment arbitration regime, introducing selective adjustments and engaging in systematic reform.[681] The present analysis has indicated that maintaining the status quo in view of surfacing discontent could be a tenuous endeavor. If the system is unable to respond to the needs of its participants, international investment arbitration may eventually be deemed unfit and thereby jeopardize its potential. The same consequence arises, considering a complete disengagement from the international investment arbitration system. The potential of arbitration as a means to resolve investment disputes[682] could be at risk. Investors have found comfort in the increasing number of investment treaties that refer disputes to international arbitration. This means has become today's common feature surrounding the safeguarding of foreign investments. It is conceivable that the disengagement of a

---

680. See Schill, note 5, p. 9.
681. UNCTAD, Reform of the IIA Regime: Four Paths of Action and a Way Forward, in: IIA Issues Note No. 3, June 2014, p. 2, available at http://unctad.org/en/PublicationsLibrary/webdiaepcb2014d6_en.pdf (last accessed on August 14, 2014).
682. Sornarajah, note 644, p. 105: "[...] the system of international investment arbitration, which is an inherently useful method of resolving foreign investment disputes [...]."

state from investment arbitration will trigger concern. In view of other available protection mechanisms, such as contracts or insurance, investors might not be fully deterred from investing. However, concerns of investment security may at least make it all the more attractive to consider alternative locations. In the interest of states and investors, what is hereby advocated is a focus on possible adjustments to or reforms of the existing system of international investment protection. This system is well capable of responding and thereby properly balancing sovereignty and investment protection.[683] The focus of this present analysis lies on treaty interpretation and its role in the current debate on the legitimacy of international investment law. This chapter will therefore focus on potential routes to improvement that directly relate to the process of interpretation. In other words, the goal is to identify which actions may be most appropriate and effective in addressing existing interpretive insufficiencies that more or less frequently surface. These are generally the defective application of the VCLT, reliance on alleged arbitral precedent and insufficient reasoning.

§5.02 COMPLIANCE WITH INTERPRETIVE METHODOLOGY

It has become evident that the qualification of commercial arbitration awards in international investment arbitration has been a challenging task for tribunals. The existing decisions contain interpretive approaches that do not always fully comply with interpretive methodology in public international law. This observation, however, is not limited to a specific question of interpretation, but rather forms part of a more global phenomenon of interpretive insufficiencies in international investment arbitration. Therefore, the first call for improvement relates to more compliance with interpretive methodology. This is at the core of a sustainable development of the field.

[A] Adherence to the Vienna Convention on the Law of Treaties

Compliance with the VCLT is possibly the simplest form of improvement. This instrument already provides a well-established canon of interpretive rules that is based upon customary international law.[684] The inherent flexibility of the VCLT has already been outlined. In this context, it is necessary to point out that deeming an interpretation correct or incorrect is a difficult task and one that should be carried out with great caution. Interpretations must be traceable, which is best achieved by adherence to the

---

683. Schill, note 5, p. 9.
684. *Sempra Energy International v. The Argentine Republic*, Decision on Objections to Jurisdiction, ICSID Case No. ARB/02/16, May 11, 2005, para. 141; *see also MTD Equity Sdn. Bhd. and MTD Chile S.A. v. Republic of Chile*, Award, ICSID Case No. ARB/01/7, May 25, 2004, para. 112; *Iurii Bogdanov, Agurdino-Invest Ltd., Agurdino-Chimia JSC v. Republic of Moldova*, Award, SCC, September 22, 2005, para. 4.2.4; *see also* ICJ, Kasikili/Sedudu Island Case (*Botswana v. Namibia*), Judgment, December 13, 1999, ICJ Reports 1999, pp. 1045-1109, para. 18; *see also* ICJ, Case Concerning the Territorial Dispute (*Libyan Arab Jamahiriya v. Chad*), Judgment, February 3, 1994, ICJ Reports 1994, pp. 6-42, para. 41; *see also* ICJ, Case Concerning Oil Platforms (*Islamic Republic of Iran v. United States of America*), Preliminary Objections, Judgment, December 12, 1996, ICJ Reports 1996, pp. 803-821, para. 23.

existing canons of the VCLT. Then, analyses are at their greatest chance to be logical and make sense.[685] This is a step that requires tribunals in international investment arbitrations to engage in the process of interpretation with care and discipline. Undoubtedly, that is a demanding operation. However, the ability of arbitrators generally to cope with complex and challenging disputes indicates a distinct level of professionalism. This facilitates the exercise of further methodological rigor that is open to suggestions from outside. The common goal is to put the framework of the VCLT to the best possible use in the context of international investment law.[686]

[B]   Specialized Canons of Interpretation

Noncompliance with the principles of the VCLT, it may be argued, is indicative of a need to develop specialized canons of interpretation for international investment law. The debate on different international treaties calling for different interpretive approaches is not new. It does, however, gain momentum in view of the emerging voices of discontent with the existing system of international investment law. The question is, if the field has already developed its own particular methods of treaty interpretation. If not, one might further ask, if such specialized methodology is expedient. One can generally distinguish two schools of thought concerning the diversification of interpretive methodology. The *unity-school* assumes that treaty interpretation is a uniform process.[687] It does not matter, if an international treaty deals with a particular subfield of public international law. The VCLT and its principles are considered "treaty-blind."[688] The *diversity school*, on the other hand, finds that methods of treaty interpretation may change depending on the nature of a respective treaty.[689] However, bearing in mind the relatively flexible character of the VCLT, it is argued that speaking of adaptations rather than changes may be more appropriate.[690] Both positions can draw from previous rulings of the ICJ. The court has described treaty interpretation not

---

685. *See*, for example, *Churchill Mining Plc v. Republic of Indonesia*, Decision on Jurisdiction, ICSID Case Nos. ARB/12/14 and 12/40, February 24, 2014, paras. 148-231.
686. *Saldarriaga*, note 18, p. 19.
687. *See Alexander Orahelashvili*, The Recent Practice on the Principles of Treaty Interpretation, in: Alexander Orahelashvili/Sarah Williams (eds.), 40 Years of the Vienna Convention on the Law of Treaties, 2010, pp. 117-154 (p. 117).
688. *Waibel*, note 76.
689. *Joseph H.H. Weiler*, Prolegomena to a Meso-theory of Treaty Interpretation at the Turn of the Century, IILJ International Legal Theory Colloquium, Interpretation and Judgment in International Law, p. 14: "As I shall argue below, all these differentiations may be relevant to question of hermeneutics, not only in the sense of articulating different rules and different methods which will make outcomes more 'appropriate' and more predictable, but also in helping to cast the very role of interpretation differently."; *see also Jan Klabbers*, Virtuous Interpretation, in: Malgosia Fitzmaurice/Olufemi Elias/Panos Merkouris (eds.), Treaty Interpretation and the Vienna Convention on the Law of Treaties: 30 Years on, 2010, pp. 17-37.
690. *Catherine Brölmann*, Specialized Rules of Treaty Interpretation: International Organizations, in: Duncan B. Hollis (ed.), The Oxford Guide to Treaties, 2012, pp. 507-524 (p. 508 et seq.): "As result, it may be best to approach treaty interpretation in this context, not as a separate regime, but rather as a version of the VCLT framework to which additional or supplementary approaches have emerged in light of the 'special' characteristics that these constitutive instruments possess."

only as a process with general principles,[691] but also allowed for special needs to be taken into account in case of founding treaties of international organizations.[692]

In order to determine, whether international investment law has already developed its own particular interpretive methodology, quantitative data is required. The existing studies, however, are unable to provide such. They simply highlight that the VCLT is not always, but at least frequently referred to.[693] Public international law requires common practice, *consuetudo*, as well as a common understanding of states to be bound, *opinio iuris*, for the validity of a customary rule. Specific nuances of interpretation that are particular to international investment law and commonly practiced are not discernible. It is therefore premature to speak of such in context with interpretive principles in international investment law. Nevertheless, the relevance of public policy in today's investment arbitrations has put forward suggestions to clarify the application of the VCLT.[694] At the suggestion's core is the question, if a specialized interpretive framework is really expedient.

[1] Deploying the ILC's Guiding Principles

In the first arbitration that was based upon a BIT, *Asian Agricultural Products v. Sri Lanka*, the tribunal highlighted the VCLT as its starting point, but then developed its own framework of interpretation.[695] This is interpreted as an illustration for the need to depart from the VCLT in the context of international investment law.[696] In *Andreeva's*

---

691. Spiermann, note 105, p. 184.
692. ICJ, Legality of the Use of Force By a State of Nuclear Weapons in Armed Conflict, Advisory Opinion, July 8, 1996, ICJ Reports 1996, pp. 66-85, para. 19:

> But the constituent instruments of international organizations are also treaties of a particular type; their object is to create new subjects of law endowed with a certain autonomy, to which the parties entrust the task of realizing common goals. Such treaties can raise specific problems of interpretation owing, inter alia, to their character which is conventional and at the same time institutional; the very nature of the organization created, the objectives which have been assigned to it by its founders, the imperatives associated with the effective performance of its functions, as well as its own practice, are all elements which may deserve special attention when the time comes to interpret these constituent treaties.

693. See Saldarriaga, note 18, p. 8, who finds two-thirds of her examined decisions to contain references to the VCLT; *see also Fauchald*, note 401, p. 314, who finds thirty-five out of ninety-eight examined decisions to refer to the VCLT.
694. Saldarriaga, note 18, p. 19.
695. *Asian Agricultural Products Ltd. (AAPL) v. Republic of Sri Lanka*, Final Award, ICSID Case No. ARB/87/3, June 27, 1990, paras. 38 et seq.:

> Therefore, the first task of the Tribunal is to rule on the controversies existing in this respect by indicating what constitutes the true construction of the Treaty's relevant provisions in conformity with the sound universally accepted rules of interpretations as established in practice, adequately formulated by l'institut de Droit International in its General Session in 1956, and as codified in Article 31 in the Vienna Convention on the Law of Treaties.

696. *Yulia Andreeva*, Interpreting Consent to Arbitration as a Unilateral Act of State: A Case Against Conventions, in: Arbitration International 2011, Vol. 27 No. 2, pp. 129-147 (p. 133).

view, the tensions between sovereignty and the promotion of investments can hardly be settled by the objective approach of the VCLT.[697] Rather, she argues that it is more suitable to follow interpretation in accordance with the ILC's principles of interpretation that relate to unilateral acts of states (Guiding Principles).[698] In their Rule 7, the principles provide as follows:

> A unilateral declaration entails obligations for the formulating State only if it is stated in clear and specific terms. *In the case of doubt* as to the scope of the obligations resulting from such a declaration, such obligations must be interpreted in a *restrictive manner*. In interpreting the content of such obligations, weight shall be given first and foremost to the text of the declaration, together with the context and the circumstances in which it was formulated.

The interpretation of specific obligations here generally follows an approach that is similar to Article 31 VCLT. The text serves as a starting point and must be considered in its context and with regard to its object and purpose. However, the interpretive approach differs profoundly in the case of doubt. Here, Rule 7 envisages a restrictive interpretation. This provision is understood as allowing for subjective intent of the state to be taken into account during the interpretation.[699] Bearing in mind the foregoing analysis of the VCLT, this difference is fundamental. Restrictive interpretation is typically a means favorable to states, achieving greater sovereignty protection.[700] It was previously outlined that interpretive insufficiencies may have severe impacts that all relate to the principle of state sovereignty. In this regard, the use of restrictive interpretation could be a powerful safeguard. It is certainly an idea that addresses criticism by a number of states.

[a]   Investment Treaties as Unilateral Acts

However, the real scope of *Andreeva's* suggestion is not entirely clear: does it refer only to a state's offer to arbitrate or to the entire investment treaty including its standards of protection? Her analysis is ambiguous.[701] What she seems to implicitly suggest is a

---

697. Andreeva, note 696, p. 136.
698. *International Law Commission*, Guiding Principles applicable to unilateral declarations of States capable of creating legal obligations, available at http://legal.un.org/ilc/texts/instruments/english/draft%20articles/9_9_2006.pdf (last accessed on August 14, 2014).
699. Andreeva, note 696, p. 136.
700. Schreuer, note 44, p. 132.
701. Andreeva, note 696, p. 140, where the author explains: "These well-established rules of interpretation of unilateral acts of states supply a modern formula for understanding state consent to arbitrate disputes with foreign investors.", p. 146: "These principles are particularly relevant in the context of investment treaty arbitration, at the heart of which lies a state's unilateral promise to arbitrate disputes with all qualified investors, a promise that is confined to a conventional state-to-state treaty model.", but in contrast to that p. 140: "Instead of stretching the out-of-date conventions that existed in 1969, it accommodates the dynamic of a hybrid public-private relationship and responds to the unilateral nature of state obligations codified in investment treaties.", p. 146: "The application of these principles will require us to peel off the onion layers of this model, step out of the conventional bilateral box, and acknowledge the unilateral nature of obligations recorded in a document that formally only has two states parties subscribed to it."

general interpretation of BITs based upon Rule 7 of the ILC's Guiding Principles. This would include a state's offer to arbitrate as well as the substantive protections of a treaty. It would, in its entirety, constitute a unilateral act of a state towards foreign investors. It is the substance, as opposed to the form, of an investment treaty that leads the author to such proposition.[702] The question is, if such distinction is admissible. The ICJ has formerly clarified that international agreements may have a number of different forms.[703] Therefore, even oral agreements may constitute binding international agreements.[704] More specifically, Article 2 section 1 (a) VCLT, as a codification of customary international law, for the purpose of clarifying the scope of application of the VCLT, provides that:

> "Treaty" means an *international agreement* concluded between *States* in *written form* and governed by *international law*, whether embodied in a single instrument or in two or more related instruments and whatever its particular designation.

Treaties are therefore international agreements that fulfill additional requirements. The text of the provision is straightforward. An international agreement between two states that is governed by international law, but is not in writing, is not a treaty for the purpose of applying the VCLT.[705] In this sense, the form of the agreement, if all other requirements are met, is what elevates it to a treaty. When *Andreeva* abandons formalism and turns to the substance of an investment treaty, she finds it to constitute a unilateral obligation of a state towards an investor.[706] This argument marks the pillar for suggesting to abandon the use of the VCLT. The approach, however, conflicts with the considerations that have led to the VCLT in the first place. If an international agreement was reached between two or more states, in writing and was governed by international law, this agreement would constitute a treaty.[707] These characteristics are common to all international investment agreements. The formalism serves the purpose of including generally all agreements that meet the requirements for being treaties within the meaning of the VCLT. *Andreeva* looks to the substance of that treaty to argue that such is essentially a unilateral obligation. This approach is precisely what the VCLT intends to avoid. Furthermore, investment treaties are mutual promises

---

702. *Andreeva*, note 696, p. 133: "But when taken on their terms and substance, as opposed to their form, these treaties represent a code of unilateral obligations undertaken by one state party vis-á-vis private investors of the other state party."
703. ICJ, Case Concerning Maritime Delimitation and Territorial Questions Between Qatar And Bahrain (*Qatar v. Bahrain*), Judgment, July 1, 1994, ICJ Reports 1994, pp. 112-128, para. 23: "The Court would observe, in the first place, that international agreements may take a number of forms and be given a diversity of names."
704. ICJ, Aegean Sea Continental Shelf Case (*Greece v. Turkey*), Judgment, December 19, 1978, ICJ Reports 1978, pp. 3-46, para. 96: "On the question of form, the court needs only to observe that it knows of no rule of international law which might preclude a joint communiqué from constituting an international agreement to submit a dispute to arbitration or judicial settlement."
705. *See International Law Commission*, Draft Articles on the Law of Treaties with commentaries, note 23, p. 188: "Fourthly, the use of the term 'treaty' as a generic term embracing all kinds of international agreements in written form is accepted by the majority of jurists."
706. *Andreeva*, note 696, p. 133.
707. *International Law Commission*, note 705, p. 188: "The term 'treaty' as used in the draft articles, covers only international agreements made between 'two or more states'."

Chapter 5: Potential Routes to Improved Interpretive Discipline §5.02[B]

between states to adhere to a particular standard of protection towards foreign investors. The obligations exist among states, not among investors and states. It is only indirectly that the promises are directed towards investors. The state's consent to arbitrate provides an investor with the possibility of holding that state accountable for violations of treaty obligations, which have directly affected the investor. *Lauterpacht* has in this regard stated the following:

> An apparently unilateral assumption of obligations which *accepts the provisions of an already existing instrument* or which is followed by *acceptance of the party* to which it is addressed constitutes *a treaty obligation*.[708]

Unilateral acts and treaties are thus mutually exclusive. A unilateral act transforms into a treaty obligation upon acceptance of an existing instrument or upon acceptance by the addressee. Following *Andreeva's* suggestion of assuming a unilateral act, an investment treaty in its entirety could no longer be characterized as a treaty. It is then indeed merely a unilateral act. This is a curious result. Not only does the term "bilateral investment treaty" follow a common understanding but the instrument also fulfills all the requirements of being a treaty. Therefore, if *Andreeva* does suggest to apply the Guiding Principles to an investment treaty in its entirety, the approach is inadmissible. A treaty must be interpreted in accordance with the provisions of the VCLT.

[b]   Offers to Arbitrate as Unilateral Acts

The ambiguity of *Andreeva's* argument has caused doubt as to its scope. Treating her own proposition as a unilateral act, the argument will here thus similarly be construed restrictively. What is left is the suggestion to treat a state's consent to arbitration as a unilateral act and thus applying to it the Guiding Principles. The doctrine of separability demands to distinguish between consent to arbitration and the rest of the instrument, in which it is contained. Thus, it is not problematic to take an isolated view on a state's offer to arbitrate. Rather, it is mandatory to do so. And indeed, the state's offer is directed only at a potential investor. *Andreeva* thus correctly describes it as a unilateral act. Her proposition would then be of immense value to arbitral practice, if an arbitration, based upon a unilateral offer to arbitrate, was really "arbitration without privity."[709] However, there is one profound problem with the assertion. A state's offer to arbitrate transforms into an arbitration agreement upon acceptance by an

---

708. *Hersch Lauterpacht*, Law of Treaties, Document A/CN.4/63, in: Yearbook of the International Law Commission 1953, Vol. II, pp. 90-162 (p. 102); *see also International Law Commission*, note 705, p. 188: "Thus a unilateral declaration constitutes a treaty if the party to whom it is directed accepts it or acts upon it."; *see also* p. 103: "Otherwise the principle must be accepted that whenever there exist in fact the elements of an offer and an acceptance thereof - a recorded instrument or succession or combination of recorded instruments - there may fairly be held to exist a treaty. The object of article 2 is to give expression to that principle."
709. *Paulsson*, note 199, pp. 232-257.

investor.[710] What *Paulsson* meant was essentially arbitration that does not require a previous contractual relationship between a state and an investor.[711] The initiation of arbitral proceedings against the state implies acceptance of the offer to arbitrate by the investor.[712] An arbitral tribunal then derives its jurisdiction from an arbitration agreement, not a mere offer to arbitrate. This poses an additional problem: will a state's prior consent to arbitration be understood as a unilateral act even after an arbitration agreement was concluded? A number of tribunals have answered the question in the affirmative, however, without analyzing the effect of an investor's acceptance of the offer to arbitrate.[713] Tribunals have thus looked at a state's consent to arbitrate

---

710. *Muthucumaraswamy Sornarajah*, The Retreat of Neo-Liberalism in Investment Treaty Arbitration, in: Catherine A. Rogers/Roger P. Alford (eds.), The Future of Investment Arbitration, 2009, pp. 273-296 (p. 279):

    The term "arbitration without privity" is a term without substance. There cannot be arbitration without privity. An agreement is central to all types of arbitration. What purports to happen in treaty arbitration is that a unilateral offer of arbitration that is held out by the state is converted into an agreement by its later acceptance by the foreign investor who has a dispute with the state.

    see also Christoph Schreuer, Consent to Arbitration, in: Peter Muchlinski/Federico Ortino/Christoph Schreuer (eds.), The Oxford Handbook on International Investment Law, 2008, pp. 830-867 (p. 837): "Once the arbitration agreement is perfected through the acceptance of the offer contained in the treaty, it remains in existence even if the states parties to the BIT agree to amend or terminate the treaty."; *see also Douglas/Pauwelyn/Viñuales*, note 175, p. 31; *see also Plama Consortium Limited v. Republic of Bulgaria*, Decision on Jurisdiction, ICSID Case No. ARB/03/24, February 8, 2005, para. 198.
711. *Paulsson*, note 709, p. 232.
712. *Generation Ukraine, Inc. v. Ukraine*, Award, ICSID Case No. ARB/00/9, September 16, 2003, para. 12.2: "First, it is firmly established that an investor can accept a State's offer of ICSID arbitration contained in a bilateral investment treaty by instituting ICSID proceedings."; *see also American Manufacturing & Trading, Inc. v. Republic of Zaire*, Award, ICSID Case No. ARB/93/1, February 21, 1997, para. 5.23.
713. *Mobil Corporations, Venezuela Holdings, B.V., Mobil Cerro Negro Holding, Ltd., Mobil Venezolana De Petróleos Holdings, Inc., Mobil Cerro Negro, Ltd., and Mobil Venezolana De Petróleos, Inc. v. Bolivarian Republic of Venezuela*, Decision on Jurisdiction, ICSID Case No. ARB/07/27, June 10, 2010, para. 85:

    Legislation and more generally unilateral acts by which a State consents to ICSID jurisdiction must be considered as standing offers to foreign investors under the ICSID Convention. Those unilateral acts must accordingly be interpreted according to the ICSID Convention itself and to the rules of international law governing unilateral declarations of States.

    see also Cemex Caracas Investments B.V. and Cemex Caracas II Investments B.V. v. Bolivarian Republic of Venezuela, Decision on Jurisdiction, ICSID Case No. ARB/08/15, December 30, 2010, para. 79:

    Unilateral acts by which a State consents to ICSID jurisdiction are standing offers made by a sovereign State to foreign investors under the ICSID Convention. [...] But, whatever may be their form, they must be interpreted according to the ICSID Convention and to the principles of international law governing unilateral declarations of States.

    see also Southern Pacific Properties (Middle East) Ltd. v. Arab Republic of Egypt, Decision on Jurisdiction, ICSID Case No. ARB/84/3, April 14, 1988, para. 61:

Chapter 5: Potential Routes to Improved Interpretive Discipline   §5.02[B]

regardless of its transformation into an arbitration agreement. They have taken an *ex ante* perspective, which allowed them to interpret a respective state's consent as a unilateral act. The basis of this approach may be found in rulings by the ICJ:

> It must seek the interpretation which is in harmony with a natural and reasonable way of reading the text, having *due regard to the intention* of the Government of Iran *at the time when it accepted* the compulsory jurisdiction of the Court.[714]

And in a different case:

> A declaration of acceptance of the compulsory jurisdiction of the Court, whether there are specified limits set to that acceptance or not, is *a unilateral act of State sovereignty*. [...] The regime relating to the interpretation of declarations made under Article 36 of the Statue is *not identical* with that established for the interpretation of treaties by the *Vienna Convention on the Law of Treaties* (ibid., p 293, para. 30). [...] The Court observes that the provisions of that Convention may only apply analogously to the extent compatible with the *sui generis character of the unilateral acceptance* of the Court's jurisdiction.[715]

And further, concerning the consequences for interpretation:

> At the same time, since a declaration under Article 36, paragraph 2, of the Statute, is a *unilaterally drafted instrument*, the Court has not hesitated to place a certain emphasis on *the intention of the depositing State*.[716]

These rulings indicate that unilateral acts by states are to be interpreted with regards to subjective elements from an *ex ante* perspective. It was explicitly referred to these rulings in order to deem a state's consent to the jurisdiction of ICSID a unilateral act.[717] However, it is questionable if the rulings of the ICJ may so easily be transferred and applied to a state's offer to arbitrate. The analyses of the ICJ's rulings relate to a state's declaration of acceptance pursuant to Article 36 section 2 of the ICJ-Statute to

---

> Thus in deciding whether in the circumstances of the present case, law n°43 constitutes consent to the Centre's jurisdiction, the Tribunal will apply general principles of statutory interpretation, taking into consideration, where appropriate, relevant rules of treaty interpretation and principles of international law applicable to unilateral declarations.

714. ICJ, Anglo-Iranian Oil Co. Case (*United Kingdom v. Iran*), Judgment, July 22, 1952, ICJ Reports 1952, pp. 93-115 (p. 104); *see also* implicitly ICJ, Rights of Minorities in Upper Silesia (*Germany v. Poland*), Judgment, April 26, 1928, Publications of the PCIJ 1928, Series A No. 15, pp. 3-47 (p. 22): "The Court's jurisdiction depends on the will of the Parties."; *see also* PCIJ, Phosphates in Morocco (*Italy v. France*), Judgment on Preliminary Objections, June 14, 1938, Publications of the PCIJ 1938, pp. 9-30 (pp. 22 et seq.).
715. ICJ, Fisheries Jurisdiction Case (*Spain v. Canada*), Judgment, December 4, 1998, ICJ Reports 1998, pp. 432-469 (p. 453), para. 46.
716. ICJ, Fisheries Jurisdiction Case (*Spain v. Canada*), note 715, p. 454, para. 48.
717. Mobil Corporations, Venezuela Holdings, B.V., Mobil Cerro Negro Holding, Ltd., Mobil Venezolana De Petróleos Holdings, Inc., Mobil Cerro Negro, Ltd., and Mobil Venezolana De Petróleos, Inc. v. Bolivarian Republic of Venezuela, note 713, 85; *see also* Cemex Caracas Investments B.V. and Cemex Caracas II Investments B.V. v. Bolivarian Republic of Venezuela, note 713, para. 79.

recognize the court's jurisdiction. Provided that proceedings before the ICJ are initiated against a state, its declaration stands as it is. As was previously outlined, however, the initiation of an investment arbitration transforms the state's offer to arbitrate into an arbitration agreement. While the former remains, the latter changes. It is thus questionable, if a declaration of acceptance of the ICJ's jurisdiction and an offer to arbitrate may be treated equally. Given the above-cited depiction of declarations as having a sui generis character, such assumption seems even more troubling. One could argue that both constitute instruments relating to the jurisdiction of an international body.[718] Nevertheless, this would disregard their differing nature. What is presented to an investment tribunal is no longer an offer to arbitrate, but a full arbitration agreement between the state and the investor. As such, it cannot be interpreted as a unilateral act of a state. Rather, one is well advised to consider the general principle stated by *Lauterpacht* above.[719] In this sense, once the investor accepts the offer of the host state to arbitrate, it is a treaty obligation of the host state to be bound by that arbitration agreement with the investor. Therefore, the arbitration agreement is to be treated accordingly. It must be interpreted like any other treaty obligation, according to the principles of treaty interpretation. While *Andreeva's* proposition provides an interesting point of departure for further analysis, it does not so provide adequate legal explanations. The inclusion of subjective elements into the process of investment arbitration is certainly one way to address the criticism. However, the road suggested is an unmade one. Stating that the VCLT is no longer able to cope with the challenges of today's international investment law,[720] disregards its nature as the common denominator of the international community and does not acknowledge the flexibility built into it. The quest for more perfect imperfection must continue.

[2] The Role of Previous Arbitral Decisions

The consideration of previous arbitral decisions is nowadays an almost natural feature of international investment arbitration.[721] It has been pointed out that the status quo does, however, not contain a doctrine of binding precedent. The question at this point

---

718. See implicitly *Renta 4 S.V.S.A., Ahorro Corporación Emergentes F.I., Ahorro Corporación Eurofondo F.I., Rovime Inversiones SICAV S.A., Quasar de Valors SICAV S.A., Oregor de Valores SICAV S.A., GBI 9000 SICAV S.A. v. The Russian Federation*, Award on Preliminary Objections, Separate Opinion of Charles N. Brower, SCC, March 20, 2009, para. 7: "Thus, the International Court of Justice and numerous arbitral tribunals have repeatedly stated that instruments containing a State's consent to submit to the jurisdiction of an international court or tribunal are to be interpreted like any other legal instrument, that is neither restrictively nor liberally, but according to the standards set down in the Vienna Convention.", who yet still comes to the result that consent should be interpreted according to the canons of the VCLT.
719. *Lauterpacht*, note 708, p. 102: "An apparently unilateral assumption of obligations which accepts the provisions of an already existing instrument or which is followed by acceptance of the party to which it is addressed constitutes a treaty obligation."
720. *Andreeva*, note 696, p. 145: "Are the traditional rules of interpretation of state consent still relevant today? Hardly."
721. See *Kaufmann-Kohler*, note 166, p. 368, in referring to the tribunal's decision in *El Paso Energy International Company v. The Argentine Republic*, Decision on Jurisdiction, ICSID Case No. ARB/03/15, April 27, 2006, para. 39:

is then, if such doctrine could assist in achieving greater interpretive discipline. Despite the inexistence of binding precedent, the persuasive authority of previous rulings can already be significant. Tribunals bear tremendous responsibility when rendering awards. Here, the publicity of decisions is an invaluable feature of international investment arbitration. The awareness that an award will be made public and is thereby exposed to practical and academic evaluation will typically motivate particular care in its drafting. In the context of interpretive insufficiencies, it is desirable that only those awards are authoritative that are of high legal quality. Mutual analysis of arbitral awards can insofar serve as a filter. Thus, blind reliance on previous decisions is not admissible. Such reliance would be especially problematic, where it led tribunals to adopt inadequate reasoning. It would serve as a multiplier of poor methodology.[722]

What is therefore necessary is analysis.[723] The existent informal role of previous decisions requires tribunals to explain why they are taken into account and to which extent they will affect their own decisions. If a real doctrine of binding arbitral precedent existed, it would merely invert a tribunal's analytical perspective. Tribunals would have to provide reasons for why they intend to depart from a particular decision, given a similar or equal factual and legal foundation. Interpretive insufficiencies would equally be subject to broad public evaluation. It is difficult to predict, if such evaluation would be carried out more thoroughly, provided the existence of a doctrine of binding precedent. If, however, even defective awards were truly binding upon future tribunals, negative repercussions for the legitimacy of international investment arbitration would soar. Vigilant tribunals would still disapprove, yet, the remaining potential for a multiplication of errors were substantial. The risk of spreading flawed interpretation by way of binding precedent outweighs its unpredictable contribution to interpretive discipline. Therefore, a doctrine of binding precedent in international investment

---

> ICSID arbitral tribunals are established ad hoc, ... and the present Tribunal knows of no provision, ... establishing an obligation of stare decisis. It is nonetheless a reasonable assumption that international arbitral tribunals, notably those established within the ICSID system, will generally take account of the precedents established by other arbitration organs, especially those set by other international tribunals.
>
> see also Franck Charles Arif v. Republic of Moldova, Award, ICSID Case No. ARB/11/23, April 8, 2013, para. 592, in which the tribunal looked at previous decisions to position its own in the context of common arbitral practice: "The Tribunal is therefore aligning itself to the majority of arbitral decisions [...]."; see also, however, Quiborax S.A., Non Metallic Minerals S.A. and Allan Fosk Kaplún v. Plurinational State of Bolivia, Decision on Jurisdiction, ICSID Case No. ARB/06/2, December 27, 2012, para. 46: "Arbitrator Stern does not analyze the arbitrator's role in the same manner, as she considers it her duty to decide each case on its own merits, independently of any apparent jurisprudential trend."

722. See similarly in referring to tribunals' approaches to the fair and equitable treatment standard Schill, note 5, p. 157; see also Van V. Veeder, The Necessary Safeguards of an Appellate System, in: Federico Ortino/Audley Sheppard/Hugo Warner (eds.), International Investment Law – Current Issues, Vol. 1, 2006, pp. 9-11 (p. 9): "But, for the unsuccessful investor, an adverse final award can act as a defect of precedent for other investors facing the same issues."
723. See AES Corporation v. The Argentine Republic, Decision on Jurisdiction, ICSID Case No. ARB/02/17, April 26, 2005, para. 18: "Repeating decisions taken in other cases, without making the factual and legal distinctions, may constitute an excess of power and may affect the integrity of the international system for the protection of investments."

arbitration is out of place. The existing persuasive authority of previous decisions is well established and has proven to be a valuable source of predictability, if not the rule of law.[724] Additionally, the informal role of previous decisions necessitates thorough analysis. It thus assumes a vital role in the process of fostering interpretive discipline. If the Darwinian imperative,[725] survival of the fittest, is to function effectively, natural selection is a prerequisite. The discourse triggered among arbitral tribunals by the existing informality is the safeguard to such selection. Therefore, it is not conceivable that a doctrine of binding precedent could really contribute to achieving greater interpretive discipline. Rather, tribunals could place more emphasis on previous decisions, if the parties actively refer to such throughout their submissions. This could be understood as an indicator that greater authority is given to the findings of other tribunals. Thus, arbitrators could legitimately rule with greater focus on previous decisions.

§5.03 REVIEW OF ARBITRAL DECISIONS

Reviewing arbitral decisions may take place for two purposes: for the legitimacy of the decision-making process and the substantive correctness of the decision. While the former goal is typically achieved by way of an annulment procedure, the latter involves appeals functions. Furthermore, review of arbitral decisions may take place on two levels: the national and international level. National review of arbitral awards is generally admissible based upon the provisions of the NYC, at the place of arbitration or the place of enforcement.[726] However, its application may be limited in the international investment arbitration context. Article 53 section 1 ICSID-Convention declares awards to be final and binding and not subject to any remedy except those provided for in the Convention. Therefore, the ICSID regime is independent of the NYC.[727] International review is more common and also the center of many suggestions concerning possible ways of improving the international investment law framework. Parties to international investment arbitrations are able to avail themselves of the existing annulment procedure pursuant to Article 52 ICSID-Convention. An appeal mechanism does currently not exist. However, the idea is by no means new. Before engaging in an analysis of possibilities for appeal, it is necessary to understand the existing grounds for annulment.

---

724. *Kaufmann-Kohler*, note 721, p. 378.
725. *See Paulsson*, note 415, p. 880:

> The Corpus of decided cases in the field of international investment arbitration is of recent vintage, but it has come into existence with remarkable speed. Its legal status as a source of law is in theory equal to that of other types of international courts or tribunals. In practice, it will also doubtless turn out to be subject to the same Darwinian imperative: the unfit will perish.

726. For a detailed analysis, *see Franck*, note 6, pp. 1548 et seq.
727. *Schreuer*, note 210, Art. 54, para. 4.

[A] Annulment Pursuant to Article 52 ICSID-Convention

Grounds for annulment are set out in Article 52 ICSID-Convention. The Convention's text is open to interpretation, and it is thus not surprising that grounds for annulment have been subject to differing understandings. In fact, the annulment process has evolved over time. This evolution shows in three phases, during which tribunals have taken particular approaches to annulment under the ICSID-Convention. To date, however, the mechanism seems firmly established.

[1] The First Phase of Annulment Decisions

The first phase to be considered is represented by *AMCO v. Indonesia*.[728] The American investor, Amco Asia, had entered the Indonesian market in 1968 for the erection of an apartment and retail complex, following Indonesia's new foreign investment law. After completion of the project, Indonesia revoked the investment license, which led Amco Asia to initiate arbitral proceedings with ICSID. An award was rendered in favor of the claimant, but Indonesia sought annulment of the award. The annulment committee found that the award partially failed to state reasons and that the tribunal had misapplied provisions of Indonesian law. Similar was the dispute in *Klöckner v. Cameroon*.[729] The claimant entered into an agreement with Cameroon to set up a fertilizer factory in the country. After its erection and first operation, the government decided to close the factory, leading the claimant to initiate investment arbitration before an ICSID tribunal. The decision was not satisfactory on Klöckner's side which successfully started annulment proceedings. The decisions were later criticized for crossing the delicate line between annulment and appeal, considering anew the merits of the cases.[730]

[2] The Second Phase of Annulment Decisions

MINE v. Guinea[731] marks the next phase of the evolution. The parties had entered into a contract in 1971 for the creation of a joint venture, named Société Mixte de Transports Maritimes (SOTRAMAR). Intended was the providing of shipping services to buyers of bauxite from Guinea.[732] However, the entity was never properly constructed and the

---

728. *Amco Asia Corporation, Pan American Development Limited and PT Amco Indonesia v. Republic of Indonesia*, Resubmitted Case – Decision on Jurisdiction, ICSID Case No. ARB/81/1, May 10, 1988.
729. *Klöckner v. The Republic of Cameroon*, Decision by the Ad Hoc Committee, ICSID Case No. ARB/81/2, May 3, 1985.
730. Georges R. Delaume, The Finality of Arbitration Involving States: Recent Developments, in: Arbitration International 1989, Vol. 5 No. 1, pp. 21-34 (pp. 30 et seq.); *see also* W. Michael Reisman, The Breakdown of the Control Mechanism in ICSID Arbitration, in: Duke Law Journal 1989, No. 4, pp. 739-807.
731. *Maritime International Nominees Establishment v. Government of Guinea*, Decision on the Application by Guinea for Partial Annulment, ICSID Case No. ARB/84/4, December 14, 1989.
732. Bette E. Shifman, Maritime International Nominees Establishment v. Government of Guinea: Effect on U.S. Jurisdiction of an Agreement by a Foreign Sovereign to Arbitrate before the

dispute taken to an ICSID tribunal. Later, an ad hoc committee analyzed whether the award that resulted from the dispute was so poorly reasoned that it was null and void. It took a restrictive view, distinguishing between the functions of annulment and appeal.[733] Guinea's annulment request was consequentially rejected. The decision further explains that an annulment based upon poor reasoning may only be successful, if it is impossible to follow a tribunal's points.[734] The decision is characterized as one that has "alleviated" the concerns raised after the first generation of annulment cases.[735]

[3]   The Third Phase of Annulment Decisions

The disputes in *Wena v. Egypt*[736] and *Vivendi v. Argentina*[737] represent the third phase of annulment decisions. The former dispute concerned a long-term agreement between the claimant and Egyptian Hotels Company, a company of the Egyptian public sector, to operate hotels in Egypt. The parties later disagreed on the exact scope of obligations contained in the agreements, which resulted in a deterioration of their relationship. The claimant finally turned to investment arbitration, arguing that Egypt had engaged in harassment and thereby deprived Wena of the investment. The tribunal agreed and rendered an award in favor of the claimant. Egypt, however, sought annulment of the award mainly stating that a serious departure from a fundamental rule of procedure had occurred pursuant to Article 52 section 1 (d) ICSID-Convention. The decision reaffirmed the importance of the departure being serious and thus set a high standard for a successful annulment claim.[738] The latter dispute concerned a thirty-year long

---

International Centre for Settlement of Investment Disputes, in: George Washington Journal of International Law and Economics, 1981-1982, pp. 451-470 (p. 453).

733. *Maritime International Nominees Establishment v. Government of Guinea*, note 731, para. 5.08:

> The Committee is of the opinion that the requirement that an award has to be motivated implies that it must enable the reader to follow the reasoning of the Tribunal on points of fact and law. It implies that, and only that. The adequacy of the reasoning is not an appropriate standard of review under paragraph (l)(e), because it almost inevitably draws an ad *hoc* Committee into an examination of the substance of the tribunal's decision, in disregard of the exclusion of the remedy of appeal by Article 53 of the Convention. A Committee might be tempted to annul an award because that examination disclosed a manifestly incorrect application of the law, which, however, is not a ground for annulment.

734. *Maritime International Nominees Establishment v. Government of Guinea*, note 731, para. 5.09.
735. Christoph Schreuer, Three Generations of ICSID Annulment Proceedings, in: Emmanuel Gaillard/Yas Banifatemi (eds.), Annulment of ICSID Awards, 2004, pp. 17-42 (p. 18).
736. *Wena Hotels Limited v. Arab Republic of Egypt*, Decision on the Application by the Arab Republic of Egypt for Annulment of the Arbitral Award dated December 8, 2000, ICSID Case No. ARB/98/4, February 5, 2002.
737. *Compañia de Aguas Del Aconquija S.A. and Vivendi Universal v. The Argentine Republic*, Decision on Annulment, ICSID Case No. ARB/97/3, July 3, 2002.
738. *Wena Hotels Limited v. Arab Republic of Egypt*, note 736, para. 58:

> In order to be a "serious" departure from a fundamental rule of procedure, the violation of such a rule must have caused the Tribunal to reach a result substantially different from what it would have awarded had such a rule been observed. In the words of the

concession contract between the claimant and the Argentine province of Tucumán, following the government's decision to privatize its water and sewage system. The claimant argued that many governmental officials attempted to destroy the concession and initiated ICSID arbitration against Argentina. The tribunal did not find a violation of BIT provisions and thus ruled in favor of the respondent. Vivendi addressed an ad hoc committee, seeking annulment of the decision. In its analysis, the committee highlights the necessary distinction between annulment and appeal.[739] At the same time, it implies that the requirements for a successful annulment must not be overly strict, but just strict enough.[740] It thereby advocates a balanced approach.[741]

It appears that ad hoc committees have fully recognized the importance of properly distinguishing between annulment and appeal. The existing decisions seem rather consistent[742] and largely coherent[743] and, more recently, characterized by a great deal of awareness for the correct functions of annulment.[744] The ICSID framework

---

ad hoc Committee's Decision in the matter of MINE, "the departure must be substantial and be such as to deprive a party of the benefit or protection which the rule was intended to provide."

739. *Compañia de Aguas Del Aconquija S.A. and Vivendi Universal v. The Argentine Republic*, note 737, para. 64: "It bears reiterating that an ad hoc committee is not a court of appeal."
740. *See Compañia de Aguas Del Aconquija S.A. and Vivendi Universal v. The Argentine Republic*, note 737, para. 63:

> No doubt the Committee must take great care to ensure that the reasoning of an arbitral tribunal is clearly understood, and must guard against the annulment of awards for trivial cause. But where a tribunal has "manifestly exceeded its powers" or has committed "a serious departure from a fundamental rule of procedure" - both grounds for annulment under Article 52 of the ICSID Convention and both relied on by Claimants in this proceeding - the matter is by definition not trivial.

741. *See Schreuer*, note 735, p. 18.
742. *MTD Equity Sdn Bhd. & MTD Chile S.A. v. The Republic of Chile*, Decision on Annulment, ICSID Case No. ARB/01/7, March 21, 2007, para. 54:

> Given that (after an uncertain start) successive decisions of ad hoc committees have established with reasonable clarity the extent and limits of the grounds for annulment under Article 52, the Committee believes that "the fundamental justice of the arbitral process" under the Convention is best served by adhering to the established approach.

743. *Aniruddha Rajput*, AES Summit Generation Limited and AES-Tisza Erömü Kft v Hungary - The Scope of ad hoc Committee Review for Manifest Excess of Powers and Failure to State Reasons, in: ICSID Review 2013, Foreign Investment Law Journal, Vol. 28 No. 2, pp. 273-278 (p. 278).
744. *See AES Summit Generation Limited and AES-Tisza Erömü Kft v. Hungary*, Decision of the Ad Hoc Committee on the Application for Annulment, ICSID Case No. ARB/07/22, June 22, 2012, para. 52: "In view of the settled doctrine on this issue, the Committee again emphasises that it will not enter into an assessment of the merits of the dispute, either directly or indirectly."; *see also SGS Société Générale de Surveillance S.A. v. The Republic of Paraguay*, Decision on Annulment, ICSID Case No. ARB/07/29, May 19, 2014, para. 130: "This Committee cannot act as an appeals tribunal and review whether the interpretation of the umbrella clause and the forum-selection clause by the Tribunal were correct."; *see also Alapli Elektrik B.V. v. Republic of Turkey*, Decision on Annulment, ICSID Case No. ARB/08/13, July 10, 2014, paras. 30 et seq.; *see also M.C.I. Power Group L.C. and New Turbine Inc. v. Republic of Ecuador*, Decision on Annulment, ICSID Case No. ARB/03/6, October 19, 2009, para. 24: "The annulment mechanism is not designed to bring about consistency in the interpretation and application of

benefits greatly from such stability. Also, it allows to assess whether or not an appeal mechanism is a feasible option in the system's further development.

[4] Grounds for Annulment in the Context of Interpretation

Article 52 ICSID-Convention sets out in detail the grounds on which an award may be annulled. As far as insufficient interpretation is concerned, Article 52 section 1 (b) and (e) are particularly relevant. They provide that an award may be annulled, if (b) a tribunal has manifestly exceeded its powers or (e) an award fails to state the reasons on which it is based. While it is impossible at this point to engage in a full analysis of all existing decisions, it is helpful to consider those points that may prove helpful in understanding available options of review in case of insufficient interpretations.

[a] Manifest Excess of Powers

Regarding a manifest excess of powers, Article 52 (b) ICSID-Convention, it is interesting that the original proposal of the provision did not include the term "manifestly." It was only upon Germany's insistence that it was incorporated in order to protect the finality of arbitral awards.[745] The threshold for a successful claim was thus raised. It is highlighted that an excess is not simply manifest when it is particularly grave; rather, it is manifest when it is easily visible.[746] This may be a failure to apply the proper law. It has been analyzed that this encompasses the application of an actually inapplicable law, but not an erroneous application of the proper law.[747] As far as interpretation in the context of international investment law is concerned, the applicable law is that of the VCLT. It is thus a matter of great importance to ask, if a failure to apply its canons of interpretations may lead to a successful annulment under Article 52 section 1 (b) ICSID-Convention. Generally, international law forms part of the applicable law in many ways.[748] Therefore, so does the VCLT. It is hard to see why a complete nonapplication of its principles would be anything but a failure to apply the proper law.[749] It must be noted, however, that tribunals may apply these principles without explicitly mentioning the VCLT. This holds particularly true, given its customary

---

international investment law. The responsibility for ensuring consistency in the jurisprudence and for building a coherent body of law rests primarily with the investment tribunals."
745. *Schreuer*, note 618, p. 561.
746. *Schreuer*, note 618, p. 561.
747. *Schreuer*, note 210, Art. 52, para. 210; *see also CMS Gas Transmission Company v. The Argentine Republic*, Decision of the Ad Hoc Committee on the Application for Annulment of the Argentine Republic, ICSID Case No. ARB/01/8, September 25, 2007, para. 49: "It is well established that the ground of manifest excess of powers is not limited to jurisdictional error. A complete failure to apply the law to which a Tribunal is directed by Article 42(1) of the ICSID Convention can also constitute a manifest excess of powers."; *see also Maritime International Nominees Establishment v. Government of Guinea*, note 731, para. 5.04: "Disregard of the applicable rules of law must be distinguished from erroneous application of those rules which, even if manifestly unwarranted, furnishes no ground for annulment."
748. *See Schreuer*, note 210, Art. 52, para. 259.
749. *See Industria Nacional de Alimentos, S.A. and Indalsa Perú, S.A. v. The Republic of Peru*, Decision on Annulment, ICSID Case No. ARB/03/4, September 5, 2007, para. 113.

international law nature. Approaches to possible annulment based on a nonapplication of the VCLT must therefore be exercised with a great deal of caution. However, the distinction between nonapplication and a failure in the application of such rules is apparently subject to a creeping erosion.[750] This would mean that a failure to apply the canons of interpretations properly could already constitute a ground for annulment. Such approach is a bold one. It could potentially blur the line between an annulment and an appeal. The matter therefore calls for a great deal of attention. Future annulment proceedings will show, whether the tendency will turn into a common practice. If this is the case, it will be all the more important for ad hoc committees to adhere to a high threshold before effectively engaging in appeal functions. Such threshold may have been carefully set in *Soufraki v. UAE*:[751]

> Misinterpretation or misapplication of the proper law may, in particular cases, be so gross or egregious as substantially to *amount to failure to apply the proper law*. Such gross and consequential misinterpretation or misapplication of the proper law which *no reasonable person ("bon père de famille") could accept* needs to be distinguished from simple error – even a serious error – in the interpretation of the law which in many national jurisdictions may be the subject of ordinary appeal as distinguished from, e.g., an extraordinary writ of certiorari..[752]

The ad hoc committee thereby equated a grave misapplication with a nonapplication of the proper law. While the approach is certainly analytically problematic, it bears practical truth. Despite the arguable entry into the domain of appeal, the decision nevertheless provides a significant barrier for misapplications being grounds for annulment. The decision is thus considered to strike a right balance between finality and correctness.[753]

[b] Failure to State Reasons

A failure to state reasons pursuant to Article 52 section 1 (e) ICSID-Convention is of similar interest in case of insufficient interpretation. The reasoning requirement is generally uncontested.[754] Where a decision does not provide any reasons, this absence forms an appropriate ground for annulment. Problematic is rather the degree of existent reasoning that would provide grounds for annulment.[755] The approaches of ad hoc committees in determining the sufficient level of reasoning vary. "Reasonably capable of justifying the result"[756] or "enabl(ing) the reader to follow the reasoning of the Tribunal on points of fact and law"[757] are among typical formulations. If a decision

---

750. Schreuer, note 406, p. 217.
751. *Hussein Nuaman Soufraki v. The United Arab Emirates*, Decision of the Ad Hoc Committee on the Application for Annulment of Mr. Soufraki, ICSID Case No. ARB/02/7, June 5, 2007.
752. *Hussein Nuaman Soufraki v. The United Arab Emirates,* note 751, para. 86.
753. Rajput, note 743, p. 277.
754. Schreuer, note 210, Art. 52, para. 338.
755. Schreuer, note 210, Art. 52, para. 344.
756. *Klöckner v. The Republic of Cameroon,* note 729, paras. 138 et seq.
757. *Maritime International Nominees Establishment v. Government of Guinea*, note 731, para. 5.08.; *see also Patrick Mitchell v. The Democratic Republic of Congo*, Decision on the Application

appears incorrect and then falls short of required reasoning, a failure to state reasons may be at hand.[758] Similarly, incomplete or contradictory reasoning may provide grounds for annulment.[759] However, the problem is that the understanding of acceptable reasoning is by nature quite subjective.[760] It may vary depending on who is to evaluate it. Reasoning that one annulment committee deems sufficient, another one might deem insufficient. At the same time, such scrutiny of an award, it may be argued, could already constitute a quality control and thus an appeal function.[761]

Broad consensus exists today that an ad hoc committee is not to evaluate the quality or persuasiveness of reasons.[762] To do otherwise would constitute the exercise of appeal functions. An evaluation of the merits in the context of Article 52 section 1 (e) ICSID-Convention is thus not permissible. In *AES v. Hungary*, this has recently been confirmed, as the committee rejected the argument that frivolous reasons by themselves may constitute sufficient grounds for annulment.[763] The analysis of frivolousness essentially evaluates the quality of reasons. The ad hoc committee therefore rightly rejected the argument.[764] Rather, it has adopted the view that a frivolously reasoned decision may amount to providing no reasons at all.[765] It is obvious that a number of nuanced approaches exist. Nevertheless, all share a few common denominators concerning the qualitative requirements for an arbitral award. These have been

---

for Annulment of the Award, ICSID Case No. ARB/99/7, November 1, 2006, para. 21; *see also Industria Nacional de Alimentos, S.A. and Indalsa Perú, S.A. v. The Republic of Peru*, note 749, para. 127; *CMS Gas Transmission Company v. The Argentine Republic*, note 747, para. 97:

> In these circumstances there is a significant lacuna in the Award, which makes it impossible for the reader to follow the reasoning on this point. It is not the case that answers to the question raised "can be reasonably inferred from the terms used in the decision"; they cannot. Accordingly, the Tribunal's finding on Article II(2)(c) must be annulled for failure to state reasons.

> *see also Caratube International Oil Company LLP v. Republic of Kazakhstan*, Decision on the Annulment Application of Caratube International Oil Company LLP, ICSID Case No. ARB/08/12, February 21, 2014, para. 185: "[...] The Convention requires arbitrators to state reasons for their decisions, but the requirement is satisfied if the reasoning can be followed. [...]."

758. *Schreuer*, note 210, p. 624.
759. *Schreuer*, note 210, pp. 624 et seq.
760. *Schreuer*, note 210, Art. 52, para. 344.
761. *Schreuer*, note 210, Art. 52, para. 344.
762. *Schreuer*, note 210, Art. 52, para. 388; *see also Caratube International Oil Company LLP v. Republic of Kazakhstan*, note 757, para. 185.
763. *AES Summit Generation Limited and AES-Tisza Erömü Kft v. Hungary*, note 744, para. 54: "Finally, for the reasons discussed above, the Committee also takes the view that the giving of frivolous reasons will almost never amount to a failure to state reasons within the meaning of Article 52(1)(e), since this would impermissibly encroach into appellate territory. [...]."
764. *See Rajput*, note 743, p. 277.
765. *AES Summit Generation Limited and AES-Tisza Erömü Kft v. Hungary*, note 744, para. 54: "[...] The better approach is to recognise that reasons which are sufficiently frivolous or absurd in nature would in effect amount to no reasons at all.", relying on *Schreuer*, note 210, Art. 52, para. 344.

Chapter 5: Potential Routes to Improved Interpretive Discipline §5.03[A]

succinctly and carefully derived by the arbitral tribunal in the dispute *Sudan v. Sudan People's Liberation Movement/Army*.[766] Its analysis came to the following conclusion:

> To meet the minimum requirement, an award should contain *sufficient ratiocination* to allow the reader to *understand how the tribunal reached its binding conclusions* (regardless of whether the ratiocination might persuade a disengaged third party that the award is substantively correct). As to the substantive issue, awards may be set aside for failure to state reasons where conclusions are *not supported by any reasons at all*, where the reasoning is *incoherent* or where the reasons provided are *obviously contradictory or frivolous*.[767]

The grounds for a successful annulment pursuant to Article 52 section 1 (e) ICSID-Convention are narrow. Interpretation must thus be seriously insufficient in order to constitute a "failure to state reasons." If interpretive efforts are made throughout an arbitral award and no doubt is left concerning a tribunal's foundation for reaching a certain conclusion, there is no ground for annulment. Therefore, if a tribunal has failed to apply the VCLT fully or partially, an annulment pursuant to Article 52 section 1 (e) ICSID-Convention will only be successful, if no reason was provided at all for a particular result. If the tribunal has solely relied upon doctrines, case law or other standards,[768] its award may certainly lack desirable quality. However, it then still does not fail to state reasons.

Annulment pursuant to Article 52 section 1 ICSID-Convention is certainly an option in case of insufficient interpretation. However, it has become apparent that an arbitral award must suffer from serious defects in order for such annulment to be successful. The mechanism provides a strong and indispensable safeguard to the quality of investment arbitration. Its application though is limited to only the most serious insufficiencies. It is imperative that ad hoc committees uphold the sometimes delicate distinction between annulment and appeal functions. This calls for a great deal of caution. At the same time, their review of awards must be carried out assertively. A mindful application of the annulment process is necessary in order to sort out those awards that potentially pose a threat to the legitimacy of the international investment law framework.[769] The unfit will only perish,[770] if they are clearly marked as such.

---

766. *The Government of Sudan v. Sudan People's Liberation Movement/Army*, Final Award, PCA, July 22, 2009.
767. *The Government of Sudan v. Sudan People's Liberation Movement/Army*, note 766, para. 531.
768. *Industria Nacional de Alimentos, S.A. and Indalsa Perú, S.A. v. The Republic of Peru*, note 749, para. 129:

> The Ad hoc Committee has found above that the Award does not give a full picture of the various elements which should be taken into account for treaty interpretation under the Vienna Convention. However, in order to establish whether it was the dispute from 1997-1998 that continued after the BIT had entered into force, the Tribunal did refer to various standards adopted in international case-law and doctrine and set out the elements which the Tribunal found conclusive. The Committee cannot find in the Tribunal's reasoning any contradiction or lack of precision such as to leave a doubt about the legal or factual elements upon which the Tribunal based its conclusion.

769. *Rajput*, note 743, p. 278.
770. *See Paulsson*, note 725, p. 880.

Thankfully, seriously defective awards are not the rule, but the exception. The most pressing concern of today's international investment law, as was revealed in previous chapters, is the quality of awards. Annulment, however, is not the appropriate mechanism to broadly foster such quality. It remains an exceptional means of review[771] that is intended to filter only the weakest of the weak.

[B] Appellate Review in International Investment Arbitration

Appeal constitutes another possibility of review. Its application is broader and intended to not only filter the weakest, but also the weak. To date, however, Article 53 section 1 ICSID-Convention, for example, provides that no award shall be subject to an appeal. Chapter 11 of NAFTA is silent on the matter. The possibility of qualitative review is dependent upon the particular arbitral framework, in which dispute resolution has taken place.[772] In the context of international trade law, appeal is a more common option of review. The dispute resolution mechanism of the WTO, for example, in Article 17 of the Understanding on Rules and Procedures Governing the Settlement of Disputes (DSU), provides for the existence of an appellate body. Similarly, in 2004, the Olivos Protocol has introduced a Permanent Court of Review into the MERCOSUR dispute settlement framework.[773] Also, the GAFTA Arbitration Rules provide extensively for review of arbitral awards by way of appeal.[774] The use of appellate review in public international law is thus not uncommon. In the context of investment arbitration, however, its popularity seems to be of a volatile nature. Discussions about a possible appeal mechanism have mostly occurred in the context of investment disputes under the auspices of ICSID.[775] In 2004, ICSID itself released a discussion paper suggesting the erection of an appeal body.[776] Nevertheless, the proposition was

---

771. *See CMS Gas Transmission Company v. The Argentine Republic*, Decision of the Ad Hoc Committee on the Application for Annulment of the Argentine Republic, ICSID Case No. ARB/01/8, September 25, 2007, para. 158:

> Throughout its consideration of the Award, the Committee has identified a series of errors and defects. The Award contained manifest errors of law. It suffered from lacunae and elisions. All this has been identified and underlined by the Committee. However the Committee is conscious that it exercises its jurisdiction under a narrow and limited mandate conferred by Article 52 of the ICSID Convention. The scope of this mandate allows annulment as an option only when certain specific conditions exist.

772. *Noemi Gal-Or*, Private Party Direct Access: A Comparison of the NAFTA and the EU Disciplines, in: Boston College International & Comparative Law Review 1998, Vol. 21 No. 1, pp. 1-41 (p. 30).
773. Article 17 sec. 1 Olivos Protocol, available at http://www.sice.oas.org/Trade/MRCSR/olivos/polivos_p.asp (last accessed April 21, 2015).
774. Article 10 et seq. GAFTA No. 125 Arbitration Rules.
775. *Andrea K. Bjorklund*, The Continuing Appeal of Annulment: Lessons from Amco Asia and CME, in: Todd Weiler (ed.), International Investment Law and Arbitration: Leading Cases from the ICSID, NAFTA, Bilateral Treaties and Customary International Law, 2005, pp. 471-522 (p. 512).
776. *ICSID*, Possible Improvements of the Framework for ICSID Arbitration, Discussion Paper, October 22, 2004, available at https://icsid.worldbank.org/ICSID/FrontServlet?requestType=

deemed premature only a year later.[777] Consideration was given particularly to the interplay between the already existent annulment option pursuant to Article 52 ICSID-Convention and a possible appeal mechanism.[778] Now, ten years after ICSID's first leap into the option of appeal, the issue may be ripe for another discussion. This holds particularly true, considering that states themselves have taken measures to accommodate a future appeals mechanism. The 2012 U.S. Model BIT, for example, in its Article 29 section 10 provides as follows:

> In the event that an appellate mechanism for reviewing awards rendered by investor-State dispute settlement tribunals is developed in the future under other institutional arrangements, the Parties shall consider whether awards rendered under Article 34 should be subject to that appellate mechanism.

The driving force behind most calls for an appeals mechanism is typically the desire for greater consistency and correctness.[779] The positive effects on correctness are of most interest in the present context of dealing with interpretive deficits.

[1]   Theoretical Benefits of Appellate Review

The option of appeal would allow to reconsider the merits of a given dispute. In contrast to the annulment process, it would be able to assess the quality of an award. The benefits for interpretive discipline would be twofold: first, the availability of appeal might create an additional incentive for tribunals to properly apply interpretive methodology.[780] Second, additional review would provide a chance to correct insufficiencies before an award becomes final and binding. For example, failures in applying the VCLT may only result in a successful annulment, if no reasons for a particular decision were provided. In case of appeal, interpretations would be subject to a full qualitative analysis. Thereby, defective approaches could be evened out at least to

---

ICSIDPublicationsRH&actionVal = ViewAnnouncePDF&AnnouncementType = archive&AnnounceNo = 14_1.pdf (last accessed August 18, 2014).
777. ICSID, Suggested Changes to the ICSID Rules and Regulations, Working Paper of the ICSID Secretariat, May 12, 2005, para. 4, available at https://icsid.worldbank.org/ICSID/FrontServlet?requestType = ICSIDPublicationsRH&actionVal = ViewAnnouncePDF&AnnouncementType = archive&AnnounceNo = 25_1.pdf (last accessed August 18, 2014).
778. ICSID, note 776, para. 9.
779. Thomas W. Walsh, Substantive Review of ICSID Awards: Is the Desire for Accuracy Sufficient to Compromise Finality?, in: Berkeley Journal of International Law 2006, Vol. 24, pp. 444-462 (p. 458).
780. See Pierre Lalive, Concluding Remarks, in: Emmanuel Gaillard/Yas Banifatemi (eds.), note 741, pp. 297-316 (p. 299): "As an arbitrator, I think it is good and sound to know that you run the risk of having your decision reviewed, corrected or annulled by others; to quote Hans Houtte, it is 'always good' to know about this Sword of Damocles."; see also W. Michael Reisman, The Breakdown of the Control Mechanism in ICSID Arbitration, in: Duke Law Journal 1989, No. 4, pp. 739-807 (p. 807): "Arbitration, like all systems involving delegated and limited powers, cannot operate without systems of control."; see also Anders Nilsson/Oscar Englesson, Inconsistent Awards in Investment Treaty Arbitration: Is An Appeals Court Needed?, in: Journal of International Arbitration 2013, Vol. 30 No. 5, pp. 561-579 (p. 576), who argue differently: "A system with an appellate mechanism would create a two-stage system, with the first instance tribunals seeing themselves as no more than the first round in a dispute that almost inevitably will be finally resolved by another tribunal at a later stage."

some extent.[781] The theoretical result is a higher likelihood of correct outcomes. Bearing in mind the public law implications of international investment arbitration, such increased correctness is of great value. It might strengthen the legitimacy of the system to the benefit of its participants.[782]

A possible appeals mechanism could have a number of different characteristics. The differences may lie especially in the possible scope of its mandate and its setup. It is imaginable that one single appeals body could come into existence for all investment arbitration procedures. As was outlined above, appellate bodies are already in use in some areas. However, such approach is utopian. First, investment arbitration operates on a number of different fragmented foundations such as ICSID, NAFTA, MERCOSUR or CAFTA. The realization of a uniform appeals mechanism for all investment disputes would thus be tremendously challenging, not only politically, but also legally. Rather, appeals mechanisms appear more feasible when integrated into an existing system such as ICSID.[783] Furthermore, an appellate mechanism could take the form of a standing body as well as that of an ad hoc committee. A standing body would be especially attractive to those aiming at greater consistency in arbitral awards, while ad hoc committees might be seen as more independent. Lastly, it is also suggested that, in the context of ICSID, the mandate of annulment committees could be broadened as to encompass appeal functions.[784] Available options are the amendment of Article 52 section 1 ICSID-Convention and an expansive interpretation of the existing provision. However, the former path could easily turn out to be a political impossibility, given that all signatory states would have to agree on the amendment.[785] The latter path would run contrary to the wraith of the ICSID-Convention, as an appeals mechanism was purposely omitted.[786] The possible variations of an appeals mechanism are manifold. What all of them have in common, however, is that they would, in any case, bring about downsides that deserve attention.

---

781. *See Lord Justice Dyson*, The Eversheds Lectures: Finality in Arbitration and Adjudication, in: Arbitration 2000, Vol. 66, pp. 288-298 (p. 288): "[T]he more generous the scope for challenging decisions by appeal or review, the greater the chance of eliminating error."; *see also Bjorklund*, note 775, pp. 515 et seq.; *see also Franck*, note 726, p. 1606.
782. *See Erin E. Gleason*, International Arbitral Appeals: What Are We So Afraid Of?, in: Pepperdine Dispute Resolution Law Journal 2007, Vol. 7 No. 2, pp. 269-293 (p. 272): "The lack of an appellate process has also resulted in a lack of public confidence in international arbitral systems."; *see also Christian J. Tams*, An Appealing Option? - The Debate about an ICSID Appellate Structure, in: Christian Tietje/Gerhard Kraft/Rolf Sethe (eds.), Beiträge zum Transnationalen Wirtschaftsrecht 2006, No. 57, available at http://tietje.jura.uni-halle.de/sites/default/files/altbestand/Heft57.pdf (last accessed April 21, 2015), p. 42: "It may also be that an appeals system would increase the authority of ICSID decisions."
783. *Bjorklund*, note 775, p. 515.
784. *South Centre*, Developments on Discussions for the Improvement of the Framework for ICSID Arbitration and the Participation of Developing Countries, Analytical Note, February 2005, available at http://www.southcentre.int/wpcontent/uploads/2013/07/ AN_INV1_Improvement-of-the-Framework-for-ICSID_EN.pdf (last accessed September 2, 2014), para. 55.
785. *Tams*, note 782, p. 36.
786. *Tams*, note 782, p. 36.; *see also Delaume*, note 730, pp. 22 et seq.

[2] Downsides of Appellate Review

The review of arbitral awards inevitably impairs finality. Especially viewed in its commercial context, arbitration would thereby be deprived of a cornerstone. It is not surprising that particularly commercial parties find this consequence troubling.[787] Finality is the paramount asset of arbitration. It is one aspect that makes it particularly useful not just in its commercial, but also in its public context. States and investors alike have an interest in a definite settlement of investment disputes. The uncertainty caused would require additional resources from the parties. Simply put, review takes time. An appeals mechanism is likely to create significant drawbacks on the speed of investment arbitrations[788] and thereby increase costs.[789] The return is a promise of greater correctness. However, it remains a mere promise and does not automatically bring about improvements.[790] It is the probability of more accurate interpretation that is increased by compromising finality. But if, in theory, an appeals mechanism produced insufficient interpretations, the legitimacy of international investment arbitration would suffer further.[791]

[3] Bargaining for the Right Route

The introduction of an appeals mechanism would be a revolutionary step, particularly within the ICSID framework. It is certainly a possible way of achieving greater interpretive discipline and a possibility to counter insufficiencies. It would allow for broader review of decisions than a mechanism of mere annulment. Its ultimate goal is the fostering of correctness. The potential of an appeals mechanism is thus considerable. However, the flipside is a number of possible drawbacks that might adversely affect the entire process of investment arbitration. Bargaining for the right route to increased interpretive discipline is thus a balancing act. More specifically, it is the right balance between correctness and finality that is at the heart of the debate about whether or not to respectively reform the system. This balance is not easy to strike, and every effort must be exercised with caution and care.[792] It is conceivable that particularly states may have a preference for the correctness of awards.[793] The possibility of greater correctness through appeal comes at a price, namely the interference with finality. Maybe it is just the necessary evil, if arbitration, as an instrument of dispute resolution with a commercial pedigree, is to successfully operate in the public sphere. The crucial question to answer, however, is, if the price is worth paying. *Elihu*

---

787. *Walsh*, note 779, p. 459.
788. *Nilsson/Englesson*, note 780, p. 576.
789. *Walsh*, note 779, pp. 459 et seq.
790. See *Caron*, note 619, p. 54: "Why should we think that a second panel of three arbitrators will yield a better decision than the first panel of three arbitrators?"
791. See *Bjorklund*, note 775, p. 522.
792. See *Bjorklund*, note 775, p. 522.
793. See *Caron*, note 619, p. 50: "In such circumstances, it would appear to me that the international community has a strong interest in every dispute being perceived as being both legitimately produced and substantively correct." See also *Gleason*, note 782, pp. 282 et seq., in referring to a presentation given by *Ignacio Suarez Anzorena* in 2004.

Lauterpacht has aptly formulated his thoughts on the matter, which may provide guidance:

> Arbitration is, however, an important component of the international system and cannot be done away with. We should contemplate the possibility that its value may be enhanced if it is linked to a system of appeal. The choices before us are simple. One alternative is to have no appeals at all – in the sense of review of the merits. (...) Another is that we have the present unregulated and haphazard system – which is developing empirically without any real planning and may not be entirely satisfactory. The third is that we go the whole way and try to establish a proper appeals arrangement. But if we are to do that, how is it to be structured? The solution to this last question is so fraught with difficulties that we may find that, despite its idealistic appeal, it is not a practical alternative.[794]

Certainly, the system described by *Lauterpacht* as "haphazard" has since 1992 greatly advanced. However, the present analysis has revealed that interpretive insufficiencies exist that require attention and actions. Establishing an appeals mechanism is indeed a difficult endeavor. The price for an increased probability of more interpretive discipline is a high one. Compromising the finality of arbitration may have grave consequences that are not fully foreseeable in theory. The principle of trial and error is not an option in an ambit of public interest given the important implications resulting from it. Therefore, despite the obvious need for greater correctness, the price of appeal seems not worth paying.[795]

§5.04 THE INTEGRATION OF PRELIMINARY RULINGS

A powerful suggestion for improving the current process of treaty interpretation has been made by *Gabrielle Kaufmann-Kohler*. She argues that preliminary rulings, similar to those established by Article 267 TFEU could be feasible.[796] The argument is supported especially with regards to greater consistency.[797] However, interpretive discipline may similarly benefit. Article 267 (a) TFEU provides that the ECJ has jurisdiction to give preliminary rulings on the interpretation of treaties. The provision further states that a national court or tribunal may seek a preliminary ruling if it considers that a decision on the question is necessary to enable it to give judgment. Where any such question is raised in a case pending before a court or tribunal of a Member State against whose decisions there is no judicial remedy under national law, the court or tribunal is under an obligation to seek a preliminary ruling. The ECJ will,

---

794. *Elihu Lauterpacht*, Aspects of the Administration of International Justice, 1991, p. 112.
795. *See* similarly *Tams*, note 782, p. 42; *see also* the careful assessment by *Irene M. Ten Cate*, International Arbitration and the Ends of Appellate Review, in: International Law and Politics 2012, Vol. 44, pp. 1109-1204 (p. 1204).
796. *Gabrielle Kaufmann-Kohler*, Annulment of ICSID Awards in Contract and Treaty Arbitrations: Are There Differences?, in: Emmanuel Gaillard/Yas Banifatemi (eds.), note 741, pp. 189-222 (p. 221), who refers to ex Art. 234 TEC, which has been newly implemented as Art. 267 TFEU.
797. *See Christoph Schreuer*, Preliminary Rulings in Investment Arbitration, in: Karl P. Sauvant (ed.), Appeals Mechanism in International Investment Disputes, 2008, pp. 207-212 (p. 211); *see also Gabrielle Kaufmann-Kohler*, In search of transparency and consistency: ICSID reform proposal, in: Transnational Dispute Management 2005, Vol. 2 No. 5, pp. 1-8 (p. 8).

however, not apply the law. Its only function is to answer specific questions of interpretation in the abstract. Before evaluating the potential of such option in international investment arbitration, it is necessary to consider similarities and differences between investment arbitration and the preliminary ruling procedure under European law.

First, the mechanism has public international law roots. It operates for the purpose of achieving uniform interpretations of the international treaties that form the European Union.[798] However, correctness of interpretations is of equal importance to the ECJ.[799] Thus, there is a similar starting point, considering the public sphere in which investment arbitration operates. Second, the mechanism distinguishes between voluntary and mandatory questions to the ECJ, depending on the existence of a further legal remedy against a decision. Due to the finality of investment arbitration, such remedy is not existent. Therefore, the distinction would not result from a need to protect the judicial rights of the parties involved in the dispute. It would only be a fundamental issue in designing the mechanism for investment arbitration to make it most efficient and adequate. Third, in investment arbitration, tribunals, not courts would formulate interpretive questions.

[A]   Chances for Improvement

The potential of preliminary rulings in international investment arbitration is profound. In contrast to the idea of appeal, the formulation of interpretive questions would take place during, not after the arbitration. Finality would remain intact. Furthermore, the arbitrators could determine the questions to be submitted for preliminary ruling and thereby control the extent of outside assistance. This ensures that the competence of the tribunal continues to function as the pivot of the proceedings. Unnecessary frictions of a "two-stage system,"[800] like that of appellate review, could be avoided. The mechanism would ensure the protection of a tribunal's sovereignty,[801] much like it

---

798. *ECJ*, Recommendations to national courts and tribunals in relation to the initiation of preliminary ruling proceedings, 2012/C 338/01, November 6, 2012, available at http://eur-lex.europa.eu/legal-content/EN/TXT/PDF/?uri=CELEX:32012H1106(01)&from=EN (last accessed September 3, 2014), para. 1: "The reference for a preliminary ruling is a fundamental mechanism of European Union law aimed at enabling the courts and tribunals of the Member States to ensure *uniform* (emphasis added) interpretation and application of that law within the European Union."
799. *ECJ*, note 798, para. 13:

> Thus, a national court or tribunal may, in particular when it considers that sufficient guidance is given by the case-law of the Court of Justice, itself decide on the *correct* (emphasis added) interpretation of European Union law and its application to the factual situation before it. However, a reference for a preliminary ruling may prove particularly useful when there is a new question of interpretation of general interest for the uniform application of European Union law, or where the existing case-law does not appear to be applicable to a new set of facts.

800. *Nilsson/Englesson*, note 780, p. 576.
801. *See AES Corporation v. The Argentine Republic*, Decision on Jurisdiction, ICSID Case No. ARB 02/17, April 26, 2005, para. 30:

does for national courts in the context of European law. Preliminary rulings thus function on a much more cooperative[802] basis than systems of review. This is further fostered by a clear separation of duties, that is the interpretation of a treaty provision in the abstract and its later application to the case at hand. The limitation to a specific array of questions also reduces the time necessary for rendering the preliminary ruling. As a result, the mechanism is likely to be more time-efficient than a full review of arbitral decisions. Lastly, the implementation of preliminary rulings also appears easier to realize than appellate review. In the context of ICSID, Article 53 ICSID-Convention could remain as it currently stands.[803] What would be necessary is an amendment of the ICSID Rules of Arbitration[804] that could be conducted by the ICSID Administrative Council. For example, it is imaginable that Chapter 5 "Particular Procedures" be amended to include preliminary rulings.

[B]   Designing Preliminary Rulings for Investment Arbitration

The feasibility of preliminary rulings in investment arbitration is a general matter. More specific, however, is the possible design of such facility. It is argued that a body giving preliminary rulings would have to be of a permanent nature.[805] A permanent body is more likely to produce consistent interpretations. The experience with the ECJ and European law serves as evidence. A given number of experts would be able to concentrate their work on the interpretation of investment treaties and answer questions posed to them in the course of ongoing investment arbitrations. The argument for a permanent body thus particularly holds true, if achieving consistency is the ultimate goal of such mechanism. At the same time, interpretive insufficiencies similarly call for greater correctness. The option of ad hoc committees answering questions on interpretation has not been voiced. If only interpretive correctness is sought, an ad hoc committee may equally contribute. However, the present analysis has highlighted that consistency will only be beneficial, if the decisions produced are not only consistent, but also consistently adequate. Such adequacy depends on interpretive correctness. Therefore, if the introduction of preliminary rulings by way of a permanent body has the potential of addressing both, consistency and correctness, preference should be given to that option.

> Each tribunal remains sovereign and may retain, as it is confirmed by ICSID practice, a different solution for resolving the same problem; but decisions on jurisdiction dealing with the same or very similar issues may at least indicate some lines of reasoning of real interest; this Tribunal may consider them in order to compare its own position with those already adopted by its predecessors and, if it shares the views already expressed by one or more of these tribunals on a specific point of law, it is free to adopt the same solution.

802. *Carl Otto Lenz*, The Role and Mechanism of the Preliminary Ruling Procedure, in: Fordham International Law Journal 1994, Vol. 18 No. 2, pp. 388-409 (p. 390).
803. *Schreuer*, note 797, p. 212.
804. *Tams*, note 782, p. 41.
805. *Schreuer*, note 797, p. 211.

Additionally, seeking preliminary rulings could either be a voluntary or a mandatory procedure. In the former case, arbitral tribunals could address the permanent body as they see fit. This variation would least interfere with the authority of the arbitrators and may prove helpful in resolving disagreements or uncertainties as to the interpretation of a treaty. In the latter case, arbitral tribunals would be obligated to address the permanent body. This immediately raises an important question: what are the preconditions for imposing upon an arbitral tribunal the obligation to seek a preliminary ruling on matters of interpretation? A general obligation would deprive arbitrators of the competence of interpreting investment treaties and thus gravely interfere with their authority. Consequentially, the option is unfeasible. An amendment to the ICSID Arbitration Rules would have to precisely circumscribe the conditions for an obligatory involvement of the permanent body. One option could be a disagreement among the arbitrators as to the proper interpretation of an investment treaty. This, however, implies tribunals that are composed of more than one arbitrator. A single arbitrator could be under an obligation to formulate questions, if he faces uncertainty. However, such approach practically amounts to voluntariness, as the uncertainty is not objectively discernible. Another option would be a request by the parties. This is in line with party autonomy and already forms part of the existing procedures. Currently, a tribunal must, for example, seek mutual consent of the parties pursuant to Rule 36 (b) of the ICSID Arbitration Rules, if it intends to arrange for the examination of a witness or expert other than before the tribunal itself. A practical question is, why the parties would choose to seek a preliminary ruling on interpretation, if they have previously opted for having the dispute resolved by an arbitral tribunal that they deem capable of dealing with all relevant factual and legal issues. A possible obligation of tribunals to address a permanent body for interpretation seems to pose a number of challenges. It might therefore be more feasible to focus on preliminary rulings that are of a voluntary nature. Respect for party autonomy may then call for a prior consultation of the claimant and the defendant to the dispute. Not only would that foster cooperation; it is also a form of arbitral culture that is already being practiced within the ICSID framework.[806]

The produced preliminary ruling of a permanent body for interpretation could then function as a recommendation to the tribunal or even have binding force. In international investment arbitration, such binding rulings once again touch upon the powers of the arbitral tribunal. Giving preliminary rulings mere persuasive authority might first appear ineffective. However, its immense impact is, for example, illustrated by the role of previous arbitral decisions. Despite the inexistence of a doctrine of precedent, previous decisions frequently provide tribunals with comfort in their interpretations. It is therefore questionable, if preliminary rulings on interpretation in investment arbitration must really be binding in order to be effective. In the context of

---

806. *See*, for example, Rule 36 sec. 4 ICSID Arbitration Rules, requiring consultation between the parties and the chairman of the administrative council before he appoints members of the tribunal; *see also* Rule 37 sec. 2 ICSID Arbitration Rules, requiring consultation of the parties before a third party or entity may file a written submission (amicus curiae).

Article 267 TFEU, preliminary rulings of the ECJ are of such binding character to the submitting courts. The courts' acts are attributed to the Member States.[807]

The underlying purpose is a particularity. Preliminary rulings pursuant to Article 267 TFEU have been designed to ensure the full effectuation of European law at the cost of judicial freedom of the national courts. The Member States of the European Union have committed themselves to such effectuation by way of international treaties. Preliminary rulings of the ECJ then further ensure that the judiciaries act according to the promises made in those treaties. As a result, preliminary rulings directly bind the promisors to safeguard compliance with their treaty obligations and to give them full effect. In international investment arbitration, however, the situation is different. Arbitral tribunals are not parties to investment treaties. Their competence derives from the arbitration agreement between the parties. The arbitrators are thus promisors towards the parties of the arbitration. In its most basic form, this encompasses adherence to their duty to act with professionalism, competence and fairness.[808] In a more specific form, it is understood that their promise encompasses the proper application of the relevant law[809] and thus also the law of international treaties. Here

---

807. *See*, for example, Art. 7 of the Articles on Responsibility of States for Internationally Wrongful Acts: "The conduct of an organ of a State or of a person or entity empowered to exercise elements of the governmental authority shall be considered an act of the State under international law if the organ, person or entity acts in that capacity, even if it exceeds its authority or contravenes instructions."; *see also* concerning anti-suit injunctions in international arbitration *Schwebel*, note 465, pp. 12 et seq.: "But when a domestic court, an organ of the State in the eyes of international law, blocks access to arbitration through issuance of an anti-suit injunction, that too constitutes a denial of justice for which the State of which the court is part (whether or not the judicial branch be independent) is internationally responsible."

808. *See*, for example, the mandatory declaration by arbitrators pursuant to Rule 6 sec. 2 ICSID Arbitration Rules:

> I shall judge fairly as between the parties, according to the applicable law, and shall not accept any instruction or compensation with regard to the proceeding from any source except as provided in the Convention on the Settlement of Investment Disputes between States and Nationals of Other States and in the Regulations and Rules made pursuant thereto.
>
> *see also* Art. 14 sec. 1 ICSID Convention:
>
> Persons designated to serve on the Panels shall be persons of high moral character and recognized competence in the fields of law, commerce, industry or finance, who may be relied upon to exercise independent judgment. Competence in the field of law shall be of particular importance in the case of persons on the panel of Arbitrators.

809. *See Garanti Koza LLP v. Turkmenistan*, Dissenting Opinion of Laurence Boisson de Chazournes, ICSID Case No. ARB/11/20, July 3, 2013, para. 8, in which she states that "(w)ell-established principles governing the interpretation of titles of jurisdiction as formulated by the ICJ should guide the interpretation of dispute settlement provisions under the ICSID Convention and BITs."; *see also Hussein Nuaman Soufraki v. United Arab Emirates*, Decision of the Ad Hoc Committee on the Application for Annulment of Mr. Soufraki, ICSID Case No. ARB/02/7, June 5, 2007, para. 45:

> Thirdly, one must also consider that a tribunal goes beyond the scope of its power if it does not respect the law applicable to the substance of the arbitration under the ICSID Convention. It is widely recognized in ICSID jurisprudence that failure to apply the applicable law constitutes an excess of power. The relevant provisions of the applicable

Chapter 5: Potential Routes to Improved Interpretive Discipline   §5.05

then, binding preliminary rulings would safeguard compliance with the arbitrators' obligations towards the parties. Also, if one recognizes investment arbitration's contribution to the rule of law,[810] its positive impact would be similarly supported. While the value of preliminary rulings would generally benefit from a binding nature in investment arbitration, the freedom of an arbitral tribunal would become more narrow. Therefore, the effects of binding preliminary rulings must be assessed against the limitation of investment arbitrators' competence.

Certainly, investment arbitration with preliminary rulings would be less time-efficient than without. Also, the involvement of outside capacity, from a traditional point of view, might appear curious to some tribunals at first. However, reflections upon the option of integrating preliminary rulings into investment arbitration indicate that the chances for improvement outweigh the risks of deterioration. Most convincing is the inherent difference between this and other options of reform: preliminary rulings address the cause, not the symptoms of interpretive insufficiencies. Lastly, the realization of preliminary rulings is dependent upon the political will of states.[811] What is advocated here is further exploration in order to improve the general quality of interpretations in investment arbitration and thereby a contribution to the sustainability of the field.

§5.05 ADJUSTING INVESTMENT TREATIES

Much has been said about systemic adjustments. However, it must not be forgotten that investment treaties are the foundation of international investment law. Where disputes arise, they revolve around the interpretation of treaty provisions. Their text is the focal point of investment arbitrators. There is a simple principle: the broader the text, the more interpretation is required.[812] The present analysis has proved this point

---

law are constitutive elements of the Parties' agreement to arbitrate and constitute part of the definition of the tribunal's mandate.

810. See *Kotuby/Sobotta*, note 653, p. 464; *see also Paulsson*, note 590, p. 349.
811. *August Reinisch*, Proliferation of International Dispute Settlement Mechanisms: The Threat of Fragmentation vs. the Promise of a More Effective System - Some Reflections from the Perspective of Investment Arbitration, in: James Crawford/Alain Pellet/Isabelle Buffard/Stephan Wittich (eds.), International Law Between Universalism and Fragmentation - Festschrift in Honour of Gerhard Hafner, 2008, pp. 107-125 (p. 121).
812. See exemplarily the criticism of the tribunal in *Nova Scotia Power Incorporated (Canada) v. Bolivarian Republic of Venezuela*, Award, ICSID Case No. ARB(AF)/11/1, April 30, 2014, para. 77:

> The Tribunal is of the view that in examining whether or not an investment is present, the definition of "investment" in the BIT cannot be considered self-sufficient. Indeed, one might query if the language attached to 'investment' in the BIT can even be properly described as a definition (i.e. a term which offers an exact description of the item in question); this also indicates its limitations. In ascertaining the ordinary meaning of "investment", the Tribunal must do more than simply look to the list of examples offered in Article I(f) of the BIT.

see also *Anatolie Stati, Gabriel Stati, Ascom Group SA and Terra Raf Trans Traiding Ltd. v. Republic of Kazakhstan*, Award, SCC Arbitration V (116/2010), December 19, 2013, by examining the characterization of commercial arbitral awards as investments. Naturally, the likelihood of insufficiencies increases with a growing need for interpretation. The criticism directed towards international investment arbitration is, to a large extent, based upon the vagueness of treaty terms as well as upon conflicting and inconsistent decisions.[813] At the beginning of the present analysis, however, it was already pointed out that the legitimacy of international investment arbitration does not solely depend upon arbitrators and the institutional framework in which it takes place. Rather, the responsibility is twofold. States too are to exercise utmost diligence in the negotiating and drafting of investment treaties. The textual approach of the VCLT necessitates that states carefully design the terms to ensure that their intentions are embodied in the treaty. Only then may arbitrators give effect to the individual ends behind guarantees of investment protection. Broad language is more likely to produce unexpected results that eventually spark discontent among state parties.

Given the recent criticism, it is highly possible that states will take further actions in adjusting their investment treaty programs.[814] The flexibility to do so is a great asset of international investment law.[815] It is oftentimes ignored when heavy criticism against the field is voiced. What matters most, however, is that states are aware of their ability to actively shape international investment law according to their needs. UNCTAD has pointed out that a number of options in improving investment treaties exist: states may revise existing treaties, for example, by adding more detailed definitions to provisions, replace or consolidate them.[816] Some have already taken respective measures.[817] A good example are the efforts by the Southern African

---

para. 807, in which the tribunal acknowledged that a carefully drafted defintion may render broad interpretations on an issue unnecessary:

> Article 32 VCLT provides that supplementary means of interpretation may only be used in order to confirm the meaning from the terms of the treaty or, if the Art. 31.1 interpretation leaves the meaning ambiguous or obscure or leads to a result which is manifestly absurd or unreasonable. These latter conditions for recourse to supplementary means of interpretation are clearly not fulfilled by the wide and highly detailed above definition of 'investment' in the ECT.

813. *Schill*, note 5, p. 7.
814. *Lucy Reed/Jan Paulsson/Nigel Blackaby*, Guide to ICSID Arbitration, 2004, p. 62.
815. *See* with regards to the U.S. Model BIT *Michael R. Reading*, The Bilateral Investment Treaty in ASEAN: A Comparative Analysis, in: Duke Law Journal 1992, Vol. 42, pp. 679-705 (pp. 681 et seq.); *see also Joshua Boone*, How Developing Countries Can Adapt Current Bilateral Investment Treaties To Provide Benefits To Their Domestic Economies, in: Global Business Law Review 2011, Vol. 1, pp. 187-202 (p. 194): "However, BITs do not need to be simply accepted 'as-is', nor do they need to be scrapped completely."
816. *UNCTAD*, International Investment Policymaking in Transition: Challenges and Opportunities of Treaty Renewal, in: IIA Issues Note No. 4, June 2013, available at http://unctad.org/en/PublicationsLibrary/webdiaepcb2013d9_en.pdf (last accessed on September 7, 2014), p. 2.
817. *See Andrew Newcombe*, Developments in IIA Treaty-Making, in: Armand de Mestral/Céline Lévesque (eds.), Improving International Investment Agreements, 2013, pp. 15-24 (p. 21); *see also* Concerning Model BITs *Hamed El-Kady*, Revision of Model BITs: Salient Features and Global Trends, UNCTAD Training course for economies in transition on a new generation of international investment policies, available at http://investmentpolicyhub.unctad.org/Upload/Documents/DOWNLOAD13-UNCTAD_Revision%20of%20Model%20BITs.pdf (last accessed April 15, 2015).

Development Community (SADC), which was founded in 2012. Fifteen African states have worked together in an effort to create a model BIT that is now publicly accessible.[818] Member States and others may use the document as a template to depart from in modernizing their existing BITs. Similarly, for example, the U.S. Model BIT[819] has been adjusted in 2012, and Canada has added a more detailed provision concerning indirect expropriation to its 2006 BIT with Peru.[820] In 2008, 132 BITs were already renegotiated.[821] It remains to be seen, if the investment disputes examined in detail during this present analysis will also have an impact on future investment treaties. These might exclude certain interpretive results, such as the qualification of commercial arbitral awards as or like investments. States could thereby prevent investment tribunals from scrutinizing judicial actions in handling the enforcement of awards. This specific example, however, illustrates the more general fact that states play an active part in shaping international investment law. The adjustment of investment treaties takes into account the dynamic developments of international investment arbitration during recent years. It shows the responsiveness of the actors and is in the interest of operating a system of international investment law to the satisfaction of its users. The increasing awareness is likely to result in greater care in treaty drafting processes. Improved drafting of BITs as the foundations of international investment arbitrations is therefore a positive development. It has potential to adapt the existing system of investment protection in a way that benefits investors and states alike.[822] A more carefully drafted network of investment treaties will support arbitrators in their interpretations and thereby also mitigate the risk of insufficiencies.

---

818. SADC Model Bilateral Investment Treaty Template with Commentary 2012, available at http://www.iisd.org/itn/wp-content/uploads/2012/10/SADC-Model-BIT-Template-Final.pdf (last accessed November 7, 2014).
819. Available at http://www.ustr.gov/sites/default/files/BIT%20text%20for%20ACIEP%20Meeting.pdf (last accessed September 6, 2014).
820. Canada-Peru BIT, November 14, 2006, whose Annex B.13(1) (c) provides:

> Except in rare circumstances, such as when a measure or series of measures is so severe in the light of its purpose that it cannot be reasonably viewed as having been adopted and applied in good faith, non-discriminatory measures of a Party that are designed and applied to protect legitimate public welfare objectives, such as health, safety and the environment, do not constitute indirect expropriation.

> see also Stephen Clarkson/Stephan Wood, A Perilous Imbalance – The Globalization of Canadian Law and Governance, 2010, p. 103.

821. *UNCTAD*, Recent Developments in International Investment Agreements (2008-June 2009), IIA Monitor No. 3 (2009), available at http://unctad.org/en/Docs/webdiaeia20098_en.pdf (last accessed September 7, 2014), p. 6: "With the completed renegotiation of eight EU BITs, the number of renegotiated BITs reached a total of 132 by the end of 2008 (figure 4). While this is the continuation of an earlier trend at a lower scale, the fact that numerous renegotiations are ongoing suggests an acceleration of this trend in the future."
822. *Boone*, note 815, p. 202: "Developing countries can benefit from FDI so long as they work together to ensure that FDI helps their respective economies. Further, deliberalizing all present BITs to ensure that there is mutual benefit for both investors and states, rather than a unilateral inventor benefit, can do this."

§5.06 CONCLUSION

The quest for more perfect imperfection has revealed that a number of routes are available within international investment law to achieve greater interpretive discipline. It has similarly revealed that some routes are more feasible than others. In particular, the introduction of preliminary rulings has enormous potential. It is a route that deserves further attention as it is fit to strike a healthy balance between the needs of public law implications and the fundamental principles of international arbitration. Similarly, the adjustment of investment treaties is a necessary component of leading investment arbitration to greater interpretive discipline. These routes are likely to strengthen international investment law. Responsible actions by states and arbitrators alike will enhance the quality of investment arbitration. The analysis has illustrated that the field is well equipped to address the criticism by adjustments from its inside.[823] Especially the increasing academic attention to international investment law is a tremendous asset that will frame the developments. These synergies provoke a positive outlook. If the current momentum is utilized effectively and adjustments are carried out with diligence, international investment arbitration will continue to contribute to enhancing the legal framework in which modern economic life operates.[824]

---

823. See *Schill*, note 5, p. 10.
824. See *Paulsson*, note 709, p. 7: "But if the mechanism is applied judiciously, it will help fill a void that now exists in the absence of compulsory jurisdiction, and thus contribute to enhancing the legal security of international economic life."

Conclusion

> *What we want is not only that parties submit to arbitration, but that they have confidence in it - that they are convinced of the arbitrators' skill and ability to settle the dispute in an adequate manner.*[825]

Once again, so did *Lassa Oppenheim* describe the path to fostering arbitration in public international law in 1908. International arbitration has since come a long way. The present analysis has revealed, however, that there is room for improvement in the area of investment arbitration. Nevertheless, it has similarly revealed that the field is fit to face and cope with current and future challenges. It is the goal of this work to contribute to the sustainability of international investment law. For this purpose, a number of questions were posed that have led the analysis. It is not the claim of the answers to provide an ultimate truth. This too, would be disregarding the fallibility of men. They are humble efforts to bring forward the development of the field and to constitute part of its eminently important responsiveness. Fallibility, however, does not make the belief that this work is founded on any less ardent: international arbitration is and continues to be capable of dealing with disputes that arise out of investments. Its potential is fully realized through the quality of arbitral decisions. That quality depends largely on the process of treaty interpretation.

The VCLT constitutes the foundation of interpretation in public international law. Its purpose is to produce decisions of logic and sense. Therefore, if the canons set forth in Article 31 VCLT are not properly applied, the quality of a decision is likely to deteriorate. An adequate decision is one that reflects attention to and compliance with the existing methodology of interpretation and thereby provides proper reasoning. This holds especially true in the context of international investment law. The unparalleled dynamics of the field, triggered by issues of law, politics and economics, require stable pillars. Interpretive methodology provides such stability. However, if it is applied inadequately, the ramifications can be severe.[826] The fundamental principle of state

---

825. *Oppenheim*, note 1, p. 323.
826. *See William W. Burke-White/Andreas von Staden*, Investment Protection in Extraordinary Times: The Interpretation and Application of Non-Precluded Measures Provisions in Bilateral Investment Treaties, in: Virginia Journal of International Law 2008, Vol. 48, pp. 307-410

sovereignty illustrates this clearly. Interpretation in the context of characterizing arbitral awards has proven that insufficiencies in treaty interpretation exist. These are not exclusive to a fractional matter of international investment law, but occur on a more global scale. Therefore, it must be acknowledged that there remains work to be done in decreasing the likelihood of flaws. From the perspective of arbitral practice, it is an interesting observation that arbitral awards have been treated as or like investments. Certain factors appear to facilitate such approach by arbitral tribunals: broad definitions of the term "investment" and prior economic activity of the claimant in the territory of the possible respondent state that a commercial award may be linked to. Additionally, the incorporation of transformation and association-clauses will further increase the chances of a tribunal ruling similarly to those that have decided the disputes herein analyzed. Nevertheless, the implications of these results must not be overstated. The fact patterns of the relevant cases were highly specific. It is thus not conceivable that investment tribunals are, in the future, generally going to provide a second bite at the cherry, given a frustrated attempt to enforce a commercial arbitral award. Under specific circumstances, however, international investment law could indeed be a promising option after frustrated attempts of enforcement.

Despite existing challenges in the interpretive process, international investment law is fit to utilize critical arguments for improvement.[827] Greater adherence to existing methodological canons, the integration of preliminary rulings and adjustments to investment treaties are feasible routes to more interpretive discipline. In essence: it is a twofold responsibility by states and arbitrators[828] alike. Treaty interpretation will continue to paint the flag of investment arbitration and add color to international treaties. Adequately applied, it is the key to further fostering international arbitration in the domain of public international law. It is hoped that the present analysis has, to the best possible extent, avoided bleak elaborations and built a bridge between theory and practice. The synergies of both are vital to the success of international investment arbitration. They are what has been previously termed "responsive." Anyone convinced of a legal field's capabilities must not ignore that the comfort of a belief may be vicious. It may hinder vigilance of developments that occur around that field. Both,

---

(p. 316): "Unfortunately, the tribunals that have addressed NPM clauses to date have often failed to engage in the kind of rigorous treaty interpretation mandated by the Vienna Convention and instead have taken interpretive short-cuts that threaten the very legitimacy of the investor-state arbitration system."

827. Schill, note 5, p. 10; see also Blackaby, note 679, p. 364: "One thing is clear: unless the criticisms of the current system are addressed (either more modestly or in the grand plan), this new child of the arbitration world may be stunted in its growth."

828. See ConocoPhillips Petrozuata B.V., ConocoPhillips Hamaca B.V. and ConocoPhillips Gulf of Paria B.V. v. Bolivarian Republic of Venezuela, Dissenting Opinion of Georges Abi-Saab, ICSID Case No. ARB/07/30, March 10, 2014, para. 56:

> Thus, inherent jurisdiction accrues to any body or organ by the mere fact of it being possessed of the adjudicative function. It brings with it powers as well as duties and responsibilities. [...] These are "to maintain its judicial character", "safeguard its basic judicial function" and be "the guardian of [its] judicial integrity"; in short to ensure and safeguard the efficiency, credibility and integrity of the adjudicative function and the adjudicative character of the organ, whose first and foremost task is to seek the truth and to dispense justice according to law on that basis.

responsiveness and vigilance, are required to accommodate the realities of a dynamic discipline. Together, they will strengthen confidence as envisaged by *Oppenheim* and provide assurance that the belief in international investment arbitration is well founded.

Appendices

Appendix I
Overview of Arbitral Precedent

Appendix I

Date	Case	Mentioning the VCLT	Plain Meaning or Object and Purpose	ICSID - Objective or Subjective Approach	Full Unity of Investment Doctrine	Reliance on Precedent	Association Clause	Transformation Clause	Outcome
30 November 2011 (Award)	White Industries Australia Limited v. The Republic of India	no	plain meaning	n/a	yes	yes	no	no	award as investment
31 March 2011	GEA Group AG v. Ukraine	no	n/a	n/a	no	no	no	yes	award as distinct
12 November 2010 (Final Award)	Frontier Petroleum Services Ltd. v. Czech Republic	no	n/a	n/a	yes	no	no	yes	award like investment

210

Appendix I

Date	Case							
18 May 2010 (Award)	ATA Construction, Industrial and Trading Company v. The Hashemite Kingdom of Jordan	no	n/a	subjective	no	no	yes	no	award as investment
26 November 2009 (Award)	Romak S.A. (Switzerland) v. The Republic of Uzbekistan	yes	object and purpose	n/a	yes	no	no	no	award like investment
30 June 2009 (Award)	Saipem S.p.A. v. The People's Republic of Bangladesh	'international law'	n/a	objective	yes	no	yes	no	award like investment
21 March 2007 (Decision on Jurisdiction)	Saipem S.p.A. v. The People's Republic of Bangladesh	'international law'	n/a	objective	yes	no	yes	no	award like investment

Appendix II
Interpretive Approaches in Arbitral Precedent

Appendix II

Date	Case	Investment Protection Mechanism	Arbitral Setup	Arbitrators	BIT Definition	Findings	Quick Reference
27 February 2012 (Third Interim Award on Jurisdiction and Admissibility)	*Chevron Corporation and Texaco Petroleum Corporation v. The Republic of Ecuador*	USA - Ecuador BIT from 11 May 1997	UNCITRAL, PCA in The Hague	*Dr. Horacio A. Grigera Naón* *Professor Vaughan Lowe* *V.V. Veeder*	'(a) "investment" means every kind of investment in the territory of one Party owned or controlled directly or indirectly by nationals or companies of the other Party, such as equity, debt, and service and investment contracts; and includes: (iii) a claim to money or a claim to performance having economic value, and associated with an investment;'	'To the contrary, it is necessary to treat the 1995 Settlement Agreement as a continuation of the earlier concession agreements, so that it forms part of the overall investment invoked by TexPet.' (p. 112) 'An investment can undergo several successive phases not chronologically coterminous with a concession agreement or concession.' (p. 112) 'The Tribunal has reached this decision on the basis of its interpretation of the BIT's wording, together with the	– continuation – unity of investment – life-span theory – precedent

214

Date	Case	Treaty	Forum	Arbitrators	Provision	Reasoning	Notes
30 November 2011 (Award)	*White Industries Australia Limited v. The Republic of India*	India - Australia BIT from 6 February 1999	UNCITRAL, London	*Charles N. Brower Christopher Lau J. William Rowley*	'(c) "investment" means every kind of asset, including intellectual property rights, invested by an investor of one Contracting Party in the territory of the	facts of this case, both assumed and non-disputed between the Parties. Having made that decision independently, the Tribunal notes, however, that its approach regarding the overall life-span of an investment materially accords with the reasoning of other tribunals in *Commercial Cases Dispute, Saipem v Bangladesh, Mondev v USA, Frontier Petroleum Services v Czech Republic and White Industries v India.*' (p. 114) 'The Tribunal considers that the conclusion expressed by GEA Tribunal represents an incorrect departure from the developing jurisprudence on the	– award part of original investment transformation

215

Appendix II

Date	Case	Investment Protection Mechanism	Arbitral Setup	Arbitrators	BIT Definition	Findings	Quick Reference
					other Contracting Party in accordance with the laws and investment policies of that Contracting Party, and in particular, though not exclusively, includes: (...) (iii) right to money or to any performance having a financial value, contractual or otherwise; (...)'"	treatment of arbitral awards to the effect that awards made by tribunals arising out of disputes concerning 'investments' made by "investors" under BITs represent a continuation or transformation of the original investment.' (pp. 81 et seq.)	
31 March 2011	*GEA Group AG v. Ukraine*	Germany - Ukraine BIT from 15 February 1993	ICSID	*Professor Albert Jan van den Berg Mr Toby Landau QC Professor Brigitte Stern*	'1. umfaßt der Begriff »Kapitalanlagen« Vermögenswerte jeder Art, insbesondere c) Ansprüche auf Geld, das verwendet wurde, um einen materiellen oder immateriellen Wert zu schaffen, oder Ansprüche auf Leistungen, die einen solchen Wert haben; Eine Änderung der Form, in der Vermögenswerte	'The Tribunal agrees again with the Respondent. Whether tested against the criteria of Article 1 of the BIT or Article 25 of the ICSID Convention, the ICC Award – *in and of itself* – cannot constitute an "investment." Properly analysed, it is a legal instrument, which provides for	– rejection of unity of investment – doctrine of separability

216

angelegt werden, läßt ihre Eigenschaft als Kapitalanlage unberührt;'

the disposition of rights and obligations arising out of the Settlement Agreement and Repayment Agreement (neither of which was itself an "investment" – see ¶¶ 154 – 157 above).' (p. 47)

'Even if – *arguendo* – the Settlement Agreement and Repayment Agreement could somehow be characterised as 'investments,' or the ICC Award could be characterised as directly arising out of the Conversion Contract or the Products, the Tribunal considers that the fact that the Award rules upon rights and obligations arising out of an investment does not equate the Award

Appendix II

Date	Case	Investment Protection Mechanism	Arbitral Setup	Arbitrators	BIT Definition	Findings	Quick Reference
						with the investment itself. In the Tribunal's view, the two remain analytically distinct, and the Award itself involves no contribution to, or relevant economic activity within, Ukraine such as to fall – *itself* – within the scope of Article 1(1) of the BIT or (if needed) Article 25 of the ICSID Convention.' (p. 47) 'It may be noted that in the Decision on Jurisdiction in *Saipem S.p.A. v. The People's Republic of Bangladesh* (a case heavily relied upon by the Claimant), the Tribunal made statements that are	

218

difficult to reconcile, *i.e.*, that the ICC arbitration is part of the investment (under the heading: "Has Saipem made an investment under Article 25 of the ICSID Convention?"); that the ICC award is not part of the investment (under the heading "Does the dispute arise directly out of the Investment?"); and that it is unnecessary to decide whether the ICC award is part of the investment (under the heading "Jurisdictional objections under the BIT").' (p. 47 et seq.)

Appendix II

Date	Case	Investment Protection Mechanism	Arbitral Setup	Arbitrators	BIT Definition	Findings	Quick Reference
12 November 2010 (Final Award)	*Frontier Petroleum Services Ltd. v. Czech Republic*	Canada - Czech Republic BIT from 15 November 1990	UNCITRAL, PCA in The Hague	*David A.R. Williams* *Henri Alvarez* *Christoph Schreuer*	'(a) the term "investment" means any kind of asset held or invested either directly, or indirectly through an investor of a third State, by an investor of one Contracting Party in the territory of the other Contracting Party in accordance with the latter's laws and, in particular, through not exclusively, includes: (...) (iii) claims to money, and claims to performance under contract having financial value; (...) Any change in the form of an investment does not affect its character as an investment.'	'This Tribunal accepts that Claimant's original investment consisted of the payments made to MA and Davidová between 18 April 2001 and 14 August 2001, which were transformed into an entitlement to a first secured charge in the Final Award.' (p. 77) 'Accordingly, by refusing to recognise and enforce the Final Award in its entirety, the Tribunal accepts that Respondent could be said to have affected the management, use, enjoyment, or disposal by Claimant of what remained of its original investment.' (p. 77)	– unity of investment – transformation

18 May 2010 (Award)	*ATA Construction, Industrial and Trading Company v. The Hashemite Kingdom of Jordan*	Jordan - Turkey BIT from 2 August 1993	ICSID	L. Yves Fortier, C.C., Q.C. Professor D. Ahmed Sadek El-Kosher, Professor W. Michael Reisman	'2. (a) The term "investment", in conformity with the hosting Party's laws and regulations, shall include every kind of asset in particular, but not exclusively: (...) (ii) returns reinvested, claims to money or any other rights to legitimate performance having financial value related to an investment, (...).'	'Before turning to the analysis having led to this conclusion, the Tribunal wishes to emphasize that an investment is not a single right but is, like property, correctly conceived of as a bundle of rights, some of which are inseparable from others and some of which are comparatively free-tanding.' (p. 53) 'But juridical analysis must be conducted in ways consistent with the purposes of the rules in question, with the aim of elucidating their animating policy and, of course, with respect for the manifest meaning of the rule being analyzed.' (p. 55)	– unity of investment – right to arbitrate as distinct investment

Appendix II

Date	Case	Investment Protection Mechanism	Arbitral Setup	Arbitrators	BIT Definition	Findings	Quick Reference
						'Article 25(1) of the ICSID Convention does not provide a definition of investment and, instead, simply states that "[t]he jurisdiction of the Centre shall extend to any legal dispute arising directly out of an investment". The ICSID Convention leaves the definition of the term investment open to the parties, allowing them to determine its scope and application pursuant to mutual agreement in the relevant BIT.' (p. 58) 'Article I(2)(a) of the Turkey-Jordan BIT provides that a "claim to money" or a "right to financial performance" is a	

222

discrete "investment," separate from the investment in the dispute which gave rise to it.' (p. 59)

'At this juncture, the Tribunal observes that the right to arbitration is a distinct "investment" within the meaning of the BIT because Article I(2)(a)(ii) defines an investment *inter alia* as "claims to [...] any other rights to legitimate performance having financial value related to an investment". The right to arbitration could hardly be considered as something other than a "right [...] to legitimate performance having financial value related to an investment'. (pp. 60 et seq.)

Appendix II

Date	Case	Investment Protection Mechanism	Arbitral Setup	Arbitrators	BIT Definition	Findings	Quick Reference
						'Now, measured by the standards in Saipem, the Final Award at issue in the present arbitration would be part of an "entire operation" that qualifies as an investment. Since the first legal confrontation between the parties over the Final Award occurred prior to the entry into force of the Turkey-Jordan BIT, as previously concluded, the Tribunal cannot claim jurisdiction ratione temporis over any issue concerning the annulment of the Final Award.'[1]	

1. *ATA Construction, Industrial and Trading Company v. The Hashemite Kingdom of Jordan*, note **Fehler! Textmarke nicht definiert.**, para 115.

26 November 2009 (Award)	*Romak S.A. (Switzerland) v. The Republic of Uzbekistan*	Switzerland - Uzbekistan BIT from 16 April 1993	UNCITRAL, PCA in the Hague	Fernando Mantilla-Serrano Noah Rubins Nicolas Molfessis	'(2) Le terme «investissements» englobe toutes les catégories d'avoirs et en particulier: (...) (c) les créances monétaires et droits à toute prestation ayant une valeur économique;'	'Second, such literal application of the terms of the BIT effectively ignores the second sentence of Article 31(1) of the Vienna Convention, which requires the interpreter to take into account, together with the "ordinary meaning" of the terms of the treaty, their context and the object and purpose of the treaty.' (p. 45) 'Second, the mechanical application of the categories found in Article 1(2) would create, *de facto*, a new instance of review of State court decisions concerning the enforcement of arbitral awards.' (p. 46)	– unity of investment – continuation of investment

Appendix II

Date	Case	Investment Protection Mechanism	Arbitral Setup	Arbitrators	BIT Definition	Findings	Quick Reference
						'On the basis of the allegations made and the evidence produced by the Parties in the present arbitration, the Arbitral Tribunal has come to the conclusion that the GAFTA Award is so inextricably linked to the Romak Supply Agreement that any determination as to whether Romak holds and investment under the BIT cannot be made without reference to the entire economic transaction that is the subject of these arbitral proceedings. (...) If the underlying transaction is not an investment within the	

					meaning of the BIT, the mere embodiment or crystallization of rights arising thereunder in an arbitral award cannot transform it into an investment.' (pp. 54 et seq.)	
30 June 2009 (Award)	*Saipem S.p.A. v. The People's Republic of Bangladesh*	Italy - Bangladesh BIT from 20 March 1990 note: BIT uses the word 'property' instead of 'asset'	ICSID, London	*Gabrielle Kaufmann-Kohler Christoph Schreuer Philip Otton*	'The term "investment" shall be construed to mean any kind of property invested before or after the entry into force of this Agreement by a natural or legal person being a national of one Contracting Party in the territory of the other, in conformity with the laws and regulations of the latter. Without limiting the generality of the foregoing, the term 'investment' comprises: (...)	'The Tribunal wishes to emphasize that the findings and the analysis made in the Decision on Jurisdiction are hereby incorporated by reference into the present award.' (p. 30) 'Such actions resulted in substantially depriving Saipem of the benefit of the ICC Award. This is plain in light of the decision of the Bangladeshi Supreme Court that the ICC Award is "a nullity".'	– unity of investment – crystallization – right to arbitrate may be expropriated

Appendix II

Date	Case	Investment Protection Mechanism	Arbitral Setup	Arbitrators	BIT Definition	Findings	Quick Reference
					c) credit for sums of money or any right for pledges or services having an economic value connected with investments, as well as reinvested income as defined in paragraph 5 hereafter; (...).'	Such a ruling is tantamount to a taking of the residual contractual rights arising from the investments as crystallized in the ICC Award.' (p. 40) '...the Tribunal considers that in the present case the amount awarded by the ICC Award constitutes the best evaluation of the compensation due...' (p. 59)	
1 December 2008 (Interim Award)	*Chevron Corporation and Texaco Petroleum Corporation v. The Republic of Ecuador*	USA - Ecuador BIT from 11 May 1997	UNCITRAL, PCA in The Hague	*Prof. Karl-Heinz Böckstiegel The Honorable Charles N. Brower Prof. Albert Jan van den Berg*	'(a) "investment" means every kind of investment in the territory of one Party owned or controlled directly or indirectly by nationals or companies of the other Party, such as equity, debt, and	"Taken together, the above-mentioned provisions indicate to the Tribunal that once an investment is established, the BIT intends to close any possible gaps in the	– continuation of investment – unity of investment

service and investment contracts; and includes:
(iii) a claim to money or a claim to performance having economic value, and associated with an investment;'

protection of that investment as it proceeds in time and potentially changes form. Once an investment is established, it continues to exist and be protected until its ultimate "disposal" has been completed – that is, until it has been wound up.' (p. 96)
'In the present case, the relevant language of the BIT is at least as broad in scope as the NAFTA provisions relied upon by the Mondev tribunal for its "life-span" theory of investment protection.' (p. 97)

Appendix II

Date	Case	Investment Protection Mechanism	Arbitral Setup	Arbitrators	BIT Definition	Findings	Quick Reference
21 March 2007 (Decision on Jurisdiction)	*Saipem S.p.A. v. The People's Republic of Bangladesh*	Italy - Bangladesh BIT from 20 March 1990 note: BIT uses the word 'property' instead of 'asset'	ICSID, London	*Gabrielle Kaufmann-Kohler Christoph Schreuer Philip Otton*	'The term "investment" shall be construed to mean any kind of property invested before or after the entry into force of this Agreement by a natural or legal person being a national of one Contracting Party in the territory of the other, in conformity with the laws and regulations of the latter. Without limiting the generality of the foregoing, the term 'investment' comprises: (...) c) credit for sums of money or any right for pledges or services having an economic	'...rights arising out of the ICC Award only indirectly from the investment. Indeed, the opposite view would mean that the Award itself does constitute an investment under Art. 25(1) ICSID Convention, which the Tribunal is not prepared to accept.' (p. 31) 'The ICC award crystallized the parties' rights and obligations under the original contract. It can thus be left open whether the Award itself qualifies as an investment...' (p. 35)	– unity of investment • – crystalliza-tion • – right to arbitrate may be ex-propriated

230

value connected with investments, as well as reinvested income as defined in paragraph 5 hereafter; (...).'

Bibliography

Alexander, Emily A.: Taking Account of Reality: Adopting Contextual Standards for Developing Countries in International Investment Law, in: Virginia Journal of International Law 2008, Vol. 48 No. 4, pp. 815-839.

Alvarez, José E.: Remarks, American Society of International Law and Procedure 1992, pp. 550-555.

Andreeva, Yulia: Interpreting Consent to Arbitration as a Unilateral Act of State: A Case Against Conventions, in: Arbitration International 2011, Vol. 27 No. 2, pp. 129-147.

Atik, Jeffery: Identifying Antidemocratic Outcomes: Authenticity, Self-Sacrifice, and International Trade, in: University of Pennsylvania Journal of International Economic Law 1998, Vol. 19 No. 2, pp. 229-262.

Beaulac, Stéphanie: The Social Power of Bodin's "Sovereignty" and International Law, in: Melbourne Journal of International Law 2003, Vol. 4, pp. 1-28.

Berman, George A.: The "Gateway" Problem in International Commercial Arbitration, in: The Yale Journal of International Law 2012, Vol. 37, pp. 1-50.

Bhojwani, Rashna: Deterring Global Bribery: Where Public and Private Enforcement Collide, in: Columbia Law Review 2012, Vol. 112 No. 66, pp. 66-111.

Bjorklund, Andrea K.: The Continuing Appeal of Annulment: Lessons from Amco Asia and CME, in: Todd Weiler (ed.), International Investment Law and Arbitration: Leading Cases from the ICSID, NAFTA, Bilateral Treaties and Customary International Law, London 2005, pp. 471-522.

Blackaby, Nigel: Public Interest and Investment Treaty Arbitration, in: Albert Jan van den Berg (ed.), International Commercial Arbitration: Important Contemporary Questions, ICCA Congress Series 2002, The Hague 2003, pp. 355-365.

Blackaby, Nigel/Partasides, Constantine/Redfern, Alan/Hunter, Martin: Redfern and Hunter on International Arbitration, Student Version, Oxford 2009.

Böckstiegel, Karl-Heinz: Commercial and Investment Arbitration: How Different Are They Today? The Lalive Lecture 2012, in: Arbitration International 2012, Vol. 28 No. 4, pp. 577-590.

Bodin, Jean: Six Livres de la République, 1st ed., Paris 1583.

Boone, Joshua: How Developing Countries Can Adapt Current Bilateral Investment Treaties to Provide Benefits to Their Domestic Economies, in: Global Business Law Review 2011, Vol. 1, pp. 187-202.

Bibliography

Borchard, Edwin M.: The Diplomatic Protection of Citizens Abroad or the Law of International Claims, New York 1916.
Born, Gary B.: International Commercial Arbitration, 2nd ed., The Hague 2014.
Brower, Charles N.: A Crisis of Legitimacy, in: The National Law Journal, 7 October 2007.
Brölmann, Catherine: Law-Making Treaties: Form and Function in International Law, in: Nordic Journal of International Law 2005, No. 74, pp. 1-17.
Brölmann, Catherine: Specialized Rules of Treaty Interpretation: International Organizations, in: Duncan B. Hollis (ed.), The Oxford Guide to Treaties, Oxford 2012, pp. 507-524.
Bunn-Livingstone, Sandra L.: Juricultural Pluralism vis-à-vis Treaty Law: State Practice and Attitudes, The Hague 2002.
Burke-White, William W./von Staden, Andreas: Investment Protection in Extraordinary Times: The Interpretation and Application of Non-precluded Measures Provisions in Bilateral Investment Treaties, in: Virginia Journal of International Law 2008, Vol. 48, pp. 307-410.
Burke-White, William W.: Part IV Chapter 17: The Argentine Financial Crisis: State Liability under BITs and the Legitimacy of the ICSID System, in: Michael Waibel/Asha Kaushal et al. (eds.), The Backlash Against Investment Arbitration – Perceptions and Reality, Alphen aan den Rijn 2010, pp. 407-432.
Byers, Michael: The Shifting Foundations of International Law: A Decade of Forceful Measures Against Iraq, in: European Journal of International Law 2002, Vol. 13 No. 1, pp. 21-41.
Carbone, Giulia: Interference of the Court of the Seat with International Arbitration, The Symposium, in: Journal of Dispute Resolution 2012, No. 1 Article 9, pp. 217-244.
Caron, David D.: Reputation and Reality in the ICSID Annulment Process: Understanding the Distinction Between Annulment and Appeal, in: ICSID Review, Foreign Investment Law Journal 1992, Vol. 7 No. 1, pp. 21-56.
Cheng, Tai-Heng: Power, Authority and International Investment Law, in: American University International Law Review 2005, Vol. 20 No. 3, pp. 465-520.
Cheng, Tai-Heng: Precedent and Control in Investment Treaty Arbitration, in: Fordham International Law Journal 2006, Vol. 30 No. 4, pp. 1014-1049.
Cheng, Tai-Heng: What's Reasonable Depends on Who's Asking, in: Baltic Yearbook of International Law 2008, pp. 1-28.
Clarkson, Stephen/Wood, Stephan: A Perilous Imbalance – The Globalization of Canadian Law and Governance, Vancouver 2010.
Claypoole, Charles: Recent Developments in the Jurisprudence of Investment Arbitration Tribunals, in: The European and Middle Eastern Arbitration Review 2012, pp. 22-27.
Crema, Luigi: Disappearance and New Sightings of Restrictive Interpretation(s), in: European Journal of International Law 2010, Vol. 21 No. 3, pp. 681-700.
Criddle, Evan J.: The Vienna Convention on the Law of Treaties in U.S. Treaty Interpretation, in: Virginia Journal of International Law 2004, Vol. 44 No. 2, pp. 431-500.

de Vattel, Emer: The Law of Nations, or Principles of the Law of Nature, Applied to the Conduct and Affairs of Nations of Sovereigns, 1758, in: Joseph Chitty (ed.), 2nd ed., Philadelphia 1852.

Delaume, Georges R.: Convention on the Settlement of Investment Disputes Between States and Nationals of Other States, in: International Lawyer 1966, Vol. 1 No. 1, pp. 64-80.

Delaume, Georges R.: The Finality of Arbitration Involving States: Recent Developments, in: Arbitration International 1989, Vol. 5 No. 1, pp. 21-34.

Diehl, Alexandra: The Core Standard of International Investment Protection – Fair and Equitable Treatment, The Hague 2012.

Diehl, Alexandra: Tracing a Success Story or "The Baby Boom of BITs", in: August Reinisch/Christina Knahr (eds.), International Investment Law in Context, Utrecht 2008, pp. 7-25.

Dolzer, Rudolf /Schreuer, Christoph: Principles of International Investment Law, 2nd ed., Oxford 2012.

Dolzer, Rudolf /Stevens, Margret: Bilateral Investment Treaties, The Hague 1995.

Douglas, Zachary/Pauwelyn, Joost/Viñuales, Jorge E., The Foundations of International Investment Law – Bringing Theory into Practice, Oxford 2014.

Douglas, Zachary: The International Law of Investment Claims, Cambridge 2009.

Douglas, Zachary: The Plea of Illegality in Investment Treaty Arbitration, in: ICSID Review 2014, Foreign Investment Law Journal, Vol. 29 No. 1, pp. 1-32.

Dugan, Christopher/Wallace, Don/Rubins, Noah/Sabahi, Borzu: Investor-State Arbitration, New York 2008.

Dupuy, Pierre-Marie: L'Unité de l'ordre juridique international - Cours général de droit international public, Leiden 2000.

Douzinas, Costas: Law and Justice in Postmodernism, in: Steven Connor (ed.), The Cambridge Companion to Postmodernism, Cambridge 2004, pp. 196-223.

Dyson, Lord Justice: The Eversheds Lectures: Finality in Arbitration and Adjudication, in: Arbitration 2000, Vol. 66, pp. 288-298.

El-Kady, Hamed: Revision of Model BITs: Salient Features and Global Trends, UNCTAD Training Course for Economies in Transition on a New Generation of International Investment Policies, available at http://investmentpolicyhub.unctad.org/Upload/Documents/DOWNLOAD13-UNCTAD_Revision%20of%20Model%20BITs.pdf, last accessed April 15, 2015.

Fauchald, Ole Kristian: The Legal Reasoning of ICSID Tribunals – An Empirical Analysis, in: The European Journal of International Law 2008, Vol. 19 No. 2, pp. 301-364.

Feyissa, Hailegabriel G.: The Role of Ethiopian Courts in Commercial Arbitration, in: Mizan Law Review 2010, Vol. 4 No. 2, pp. 297-333.

Fietta, Stephen/Upcher, James: Public International Law, Investment Treaties and Commercial Arbitration: An Emerging System of Complementarity?, in: Arbitration International 2013, Vol. 29 No. 2, pp. 187-221.

Fitzmaurice, Gerald: Second Report on the Law of Treaties, in: Yearbook of the International Law Commission 1957, Vol. 2, pp. 16-70.

Bibliography

Fitzmaurice, Gerald: The Law and Procedure of the International Court of Justice 1951-4, in: British Yearbook of International Law 1957, Vol. 33, pp. 203-293.

Fortier, L. Yves: Arbitrating in the Age of Investment Treaty Disputes, in: University of New South Wales Law Journal 2008, Vol. 31 No. 1, pp. 282-291.

Foster, David: Umbrella Clauses – a Retreat from the Philippines?, in: International Arbitration Law Review 2006, Vol. 100, pp. 100-108.

Foster, George K.: Recovering "Full Protection and Security": The Treaty Standard's Obscure Origins, Forgotten Meaning, and Key Current Significance, in: Vanderbilt Journal of Transnational Law 2012, Vol. 45, pp. 1095-1156.

Franck, Susan D.: Development and Outcomes of Investment Arbitration, in: Harvard International Law Journal 2009, Vol. 50, pp. 435-489.

Franck, Susan D.: The Legitimacy Crisis in Investment Treaty Arbitration: Privatizing Public International Law Through Inconsistent Decisions, in: Fordham Law Review 2005, Vol. 73, pp. 1521-1625.

Gaillard, Emmanuel/Savage, John (eds.): Fouchard Gaillard Goldman on International Commercial Arbitration, The Hague 1999.

Gal-Or, Noemi: Private Party Direct Access: A Comparison of the NAFTA and the EU Disciplines, in: Boston College International & Comparative Law Review 1998, Vol. 21 No. 1, pp. 1-41.

Gallagher, Kevin P./Shrestha, Elen: Investment Treaty Arbitration and Developing Countries: A Re-appraisal, Global Development and Environment Institute, Working Paper No. 11-01, May 2011.

Gantz, David A.: Challenges for the United States in Negotiating a BIT with China: Reconciling Reciprocal Investment Protection with Policy Concerns, Arizona Legal Studies: Discussion Paper No. 14-03, January 2014, available at http://papers.ssrn.com/sol3/papers.cfm?abstract_id=2383919 (last accessed August 7, 2014).

Garnett, Richard: National Court Intervention in Arbitration as an Investment Treaty Claim, in: International and Comparative Law Quarterly 2011, Vol. 60, pp. 485-498.

Georgiev, Dencho: Politics or Rule of Law: Deconstruction and Legitimacy in International Law, in: European Journal of International Law 1993, Vol. 4, pp. 1-14.

Ginsburg, Tom: International Substitutes for Domestic Institutions: Bilateral Treaties and Governance, Illinois Law and Economics Working Paper Series 2006, Working Paper No. LE06-027, October 2006.

Gleason, Erin E.: International Arbitral Appeals: What Are We So Afraid Of?, in: Pepperdine Dispute Resolution Law Journal 2007, Vol. 7 No. 2, pp. 269-293.

Goldhaber, Michael D.: The Rise of Arbitral Power over Domestic Courts, in: Stanford Journal of Complex Litigation 2013, Vol 1:2, pp. 373-416.

Griebel, Jörn: Die Einbeziehung von "contract claims" in internationale Investitionsstreitigkeiten über Streitbeilegungsklauseln in Investitionsabkommen, in: SchiedsVZ 2006, pp. 306-311.

Griebel, Jörn: Internationales Investitionsrecht, München 2008.

Grotius, Hugo: De Jure Belli ac Pacis, 1625, translated in *Francis W. Kelsey*, De Jure Belli ac Pacis, Oxford 1925.

Gudgeon, K. Scott: United States Bilateral Investment Treaties: Comments on Their Origin, Purposes and General Treatment Standards, in: Berkeley Journal of International Law 1986, Vol. 4 No. 1, pp. 105-135.

Guillaume, Gilbert: The Use of Precedent by International Judges and Arbitrators, in: Journal of International Dispute Settlement 2011, Vol. 2 No. 1, pp. 5-23.

Guthrie, Benjamin K.: Beyond Investment Protection: An Examination of the Potential Influence of Investment Treaties on Domestic Rule of Law, in: International Law and Politics 2013, Vol. 45, pp. 1151-1200.

Guzman, Andrew T.: Why LDCs Sign Treaties That Hurt Them: Explaining the Popularity of Bilateral Investment Treaties, in: Virginia Journal of International Law 1997, Vol. 38, pp. 639-688.

Hall, William Edward: A Treatise on International Law, 7th ed., Oxford 1917.

Halle, Mark/Peterson, Luke Erik: Investment Provisions in Free Trade Agreements and Investment Treaties – Opportunities and Threats for Developing Countries, Colombo 2005.

Hallward-Driemeier, Mary: Do Bilateral Investment Treaties Attract FDI? – Only a bit...and they could bite, World Bank Policy Research Paper 2003, No. 3121, available at http://elibrary.worldbank.org/doi/pdf/10.1596/1813-9450-3121 (last accessed September 11, 2014).

Hassan, Daud: The Rise of the Territorial State and the Treaty of Westphalia, in: Yearbook of New Zealand Jurisprudence 2006, Vol. 9, pp. 62-70.

Helmersen, Sondre Torp: Evolutive Treaty Interpretation: Legality, Semantics and Distinctions, in: European Journal of Legal Studies 2013, Vol. 6 No. 1, pp. 127-148.

Herdegen, Matthias: in: Max Planck Encyclopedia of Public International Law, Interpretation in International Law (online ed.), available at http://opil.ouplaw.com/home/EPIL (last accessed April 15, 2015).

Herdegen, Matthias: Völkerrecht, 12th ed., Munich 2013.

Homer: Iliad, translated by Samuel Butler, London/New York/Bombay, 1898.

Hunter, Martin/Silva, Gui Conde E.: Transnational Public Policy and Its Application in Investment Arbitrations, in: The Journal of World Investment 2003, Vol. 4 No. 3, pp. 367-378.

Hußlein-Stich, Gabriele: Das UNCITRAL-Modellgesetz über die internationale Handelsschiedsgerichtsbarkeit, Köln/Berlin/Bonn/München 1990.

ICSID, Possible Improvements of the Framework for ICSID Arbitration, Discussion Paper, 22 October 2004, available at https://icsid.worldbank.org/ICSID/FrontServlet?requestType = ICSIDPublicationsRH&actionVal = ViewAnnouncePDF&AnnouncementType = archive&AnnounceNo = 14_1.pdf (last accessed August 18, 2014).

ICSID, Suggested Changes to the ICSID Rules and Regulations, Working Paper of the ICSID Secretariat, 12 May 2005, available at https://icsid.worldbank.org/ICSID/FrontServlet?requestType = ICSIDPublicationsRH&actionVal = ViewAnnouncePDF&AnnouncementType = archive&AnnounceNo = 25_1.pdf (last accessed August 18, 2014).

International Commission on Intervention and State Sovereignty, The Responsibility to Protect, 2001, available at http://responsibilitytoprotect.org/ICISS%20Report.pdf (last accessed September 9, 2014).

International Law Commission, Draft Articles on the Law of Treaties with Commentaries, in: Yearbook of the International Law Commission 1966, Vol. 2, pp. 187–274.

International Law Commission, Fragmentation of International Law: Difficulties Arising from the Diversification and Expansion of International Law, 18 July 2006, available at http://www.un.org/ga/search/view_doc.asp?symbol=A/CN.4/L.702 (last accessed July 5, 2014).

International Law Commission, Guiding Principles Applicable to Unilateral Declarations of States Capable of Creating Legal Obligations, available at http://legal.un.org/ilc/texts/instruments/english/commentaries/9_9_2006.pdf (last accessed on August 14, 2014).

International Institute for Sustainable Development, Arbitrators' Role in the Recent Investment Arbitration Boom, 25 March 2013, available at http://www.iisd.org/itn/2013/03/25/arbitrators-role-in-the-recent-investment-arbitration-boom/ (last accessed on September 3, 2014).

Janis, Mark W.: Sovereignty and International Law: Hobbes and Grotius, in: Ronald St. John Macdonald (ed.), Essays in Honour of Wang Tieya, Leiden 1993, pp. 391-400.

Kaufmann-Kohler, Gabrielle: Annulment of ICSID Awards in Contract and Treaty Arbitrations: Are There Differences?, in: Emmanuel Gaillard/Yas Banifatemi (eds.), Annulment of ICSID Awards, Huntington 2004, pp. 189-222.

Kaufmann-Kohler, Gabrielle: Arbitral Precedent: Dream, Necessity or Excuse?, in: Arbitration International 2007, Vol. 23 No. 3, pp. 357-378.

Kaufmann-Kohler, Gabrielle: Commercial Arbitration Before International Court and Tribunals – Reviewing Abusive Conduct of Domestic Courts – 2011 American University Washington College of Law Annual Lecture on International Commercial Arbitration, in: Arbitration International 2013, pp. 153-173.

Kaufmann-Kohler, Gabrielle: In Search of Transparency and Consistency: ICSID Reform Proposal, in: Transnational Dispute Management 2005, Vol. 2 No. 5, pp. 1-8.

Kaufmann-Kohler, Gabrielle: Interpretive Powers of the Free Trade Commission and the Rule of Law, in: Frédéric Bachand/Emmanuel Gaillard (eds.), IAI Series on International Arbitration No. 7 – Fifteen Years of NAFTA Chapter 11 Arbitration, Huntington 2011, pp. 175-194.

Kaufmann-Kohler, Gabrielle: Non-disputing State Submissions in Investment Arbitration: Resurgence of Diplomatic Protection, in: Laurence Boisson de Chazournes/Marcelo G. Kohen/Jorge E. Viñuales (eds.), Diplomatic and Judicial Means of Dispute Settlement, Leiden 2012, pp. 307-326.

Klabbers, Jan: Virtuous Interpretation, in: Malgosia Fitzmaurice/Olufemi Elias/Panos Merkouris (eds.), Treaty Interpretation and the Vienna Convention on the Law of Treaties: 30 Years on, Leiden 2010, pp. 17-37.

Knahr, Christina: Chapter V: Investment Arbitration – Fair and Equitable Treatment and Its Relationship with Other Treatment Standards, in: Christian Klausegger/Peter Klein (eds.), Austrian Arbitration Yearbook, Vienna 2009, pp. 493-513.

Konrad, Sabine/Birch, Marcus: Non-enforcement of Arbitral Awards: Only a Pyrrhic Victory?, in: Transnational Dispute Management 2010, Vol. 1, pp. 1-9.

Kotuby Jr, Charles T./Sobotta, Luke A.: Practical Suggestions to Promote the Legitimacy and Vitality of International Investment Arbitration, in: ICSID Review 2013, Foreign Investment Law Journal, Vol. 28 No. 2, pp. 454-465.

Kreindler, Richard: Are Tribunals Setting New Limits on Access to International Jurisdiction?, in: ICSID Review 2010, Foreign Investment Law Journal, Vol. 25 No. 1, pp. 37-43.

Kreindler, Richard: Competence-Competence in the Faces of Illegality in Contracts and Arbitration Agreements, Leiden 2013.

Kryvoi, Yaruslau: Introductory Note to European Court of Human Rights: Kin-Stib & Majkic v. Serbia, in: International Legal Materials 2010, Vol. 49, pp. 1181-1194.

Kurtz, Jürgen: Australia's Rejection of Investor-State Arbitration: Causation, Omission and Implication, ICSID Review 2012, Foreign Investment Law Journal Vol. 27 No. 1, pp. 1-12.

Lafont, Sophie: L'arbitrage en Mésopotamie, in: Revue de l'arbitrage 2000, Vol. 4, pp. 557-590.

Lalive, Pierre: Concluding Remarks, in: Emmanuel Gaillard/Yas Banifatemi (eds.), Annulment of ICSID Awards, Huntington 2004, pp. 297-316.

Lalive, Pierre: On the Reasoning of International Arbitral Awards, in: Journal of International Dispute Settlement 2010, Vol. 1 No. 1, pp. 55-65.

Lalive, Pierre: The First World Bank Arbitration (Holiday Inns v. Morocco) – Some Legal Problems, in: British Yearbook of International Law 1980, Vol. 51 No. 1, pp. 123-161.

Landau QC, Toby T.: Reasons for Reasons: The Tribunal's Duty in Investor-State Arbitration, in: Albert Jan van den Berg (ed.), ICCA Congress Series Vol. 14, Alphen aan den Rijn 2009, pp. 187-205.

Lauterpacht, Elihu: Aspects of the Administration of International Justice, Cambridge 1991.

Lauterpacht, Hersch: Law of Treaties, Document A/CN.4/63, in: Yearbook of the International Law Commission 1953, Vol. II, pp. 90-162.

Lauterpacht, Hersch: The Revision of the Statute of the International Court of Justice, in: Elihu Lauterpacht (ed.), International Law – Collected Papers, Vol. 5, Disputes, War and Neutrality, 2004, pp. 112-183.

Lauterpacht, Hersch: The Development of International Law by the International Court, Cambridge 1982.

Lauterpacht, Hersch: Restrictive Interpretation and the Principle of Effectiveness of Treaties, in: British Yearbook of International Law 1949, Vol. 26, pp. 48-85.

Lenz, Carl Otto: The Role and Mechanism of the Preliminary Ruling Procedure, in: Fordham International Law Journal 1994, Vol. 18 No. 2, pp. 388-409.

Liu, Ge: UNCITRAL Model Law v. Chinese Law and Practice: A Discussion on Interim Measures of Protection, in: Albert Jan van den Berg (ed.), New Horizons in International Commercial Arbitration and Beyond, The Hague 2005, pp. 278-283.

Ludsin, Hallie: Returning Sovereignty to the People, in: Vanderbilt Journal of Transnational Law 2013, Vol. 46, pp. 97-169.

Lukits, Rainer: Die private Schiedsgerichtsbarkeit im römischen Recht und heute, in: SchiedsVZ 2013, pp. 269-274.

Mangan, Mark: Australia's Investment Treaty Program and Investor-State Arbitration, in: Luke Nottage/Richard Garnett (eds.), International Arbitration in Australia, Annandale 2010, pp. 191-218.

Maniruzzaman, A.F.M.: Modernisation of International Arbitration Law in the Age of Globalisation: A Bangladesh Perspective, in: International Company and Commercial Law Review 2004, No. 5, pp. 132-137.

McBain, Howard Lee: The Living Constitution: A Consideration of the Realities and Legends of Our Fundamental Law, New York 1927.

McLachlan, Campbell/Shore, Laurence/Weiniger, Matthew: International Investment Arbitration – Substantive Principles, Oxford 2007.

Mechlem, Kerstin: Treaty Bodies and the Interpretation of Human Rights, in: Vanderbilt Journal of Transnational Law 2009, Vol. 42, pp. 905-947.

Merlin, Philippe Antoine: Receuil Alphabétique de Question de Droit 1829, Vol. 9, Brussels 1929.

Mistelis, Loukas A.: Award as an Investment: The Value of an Arbitral Award or the Cost of Non-enforcement, in: ICSID Review 2013, Foreign Investment Law Journal, Vol. 28 No. 1, pp. 1-24.

Montt, Santiago: State Liability in Investment Treaty Arbitration, Oxford 2012.

Mortenson, Julian Davis: The Meaning of "Investment": ICSID's Travaux and the Domain of International Investment Law, in: Harvard International Law Journal 2010, Vol. 51 No. 1, pp. 257-318.

Moss, Giuditta Cordero: Commercial Arbitration and Investment Arbitration: Fertile Soil or False Friends?, in: Christina Binder/Ursula Kriebaum/August Reinisch/Stephan Wittich (eds.), International Investment Law for the 21st Century, Essays in Honour of Christoph Schreuer, Oxford 2009, pp. 782-797.

Moss, Giuditta Cordero: Full Protection and Security, in: August Reinisch (ed.), Standards of Investment Protection, Oxford 2008, pp. 131-150.

Mustill, Lord Michael: The History of International Commercial Arbitration, in: Lawrence W. Newman/Richard D. Hill (eds.), The Leading Arbitrator's Guide to International Arbitration, 3rd ed., Huntington 2014, pp. 3-32.

Nacimiento, Patricia/Lange, Sven: Case Comment – White Industries Australia Limited v. The Republic of India, in: ICSID Review 2012, Foreign Investment Law Journal, Vol. 27 No. 2, pp. 274-280.

Nagan, Winston P./Haddad, Aitza M.: Sovereignty in Theory and Practice, in: San Diego International Law Journal 2012, Vol. 13, pp. 429-520.

Newcombe, Andrew: Developments in IIA Treaty-Making, in: Armand de Mestral/Céline Lévesque (eds.), Improving International Investment Agreements, Abingdon/New York 2013, pp. 15-24.

Newcombe, Andrew/Paradell, Lluís: Law and Practice of Investment Treaties – Standards of Treatment, Alphen aan den Rijn 2009.
Nilsson, Anders/Englesson, Oscar: Inconsistent Awards in Investment Treaty Arbitration: Is An Appeals Court Needed?, in: Journal of International Arbitration 2013, Vol. 30 No. 5, pp. 561-579.
O'Connell, Daniel Patrick: International Law, London 1965.
Oppenheim, Lassa: The Science of International Law: Its Task and Method, in: American Journal of International Law 1908, Vol. 2 No. 2, pp. 313-356.
Orahelashvili, Alexander: The Recent Practice on the Principles of Treaty Interpretation, in: Alexander Orahelashvili/Sarah Williams (eds.), 40 Years of the Vienna Convention on the Law of Treaties, London 2010, pp. 117-154.
Ortino, Federico: Treaty Interpretation and the WTO Appellate Body Report in US-Gambling: A Critique, in: Journal of International Economic Law 2006, Vol. 9 No. 1, pp. 117-148.
Park, William W.: Arbitration of International Business Disputes, 2nd ed., Oxford 2012.
Park, William W.: Convention Violations and Investment Claims, in: Arbitration International 2013, Vol. 29 No. 2, pp. 175-186.
Park, William W.: Respecting the New York Convention, in: ICC International Court of Arbitration Bulletin 2007, Vol. 18 No. 2, pp. 65-77.
Paulsson, Jan: Arbitration in Three Dimensions, LSE Law, Society and Economy Working Papers 2/2010, available at http://www.lse.ac.uk/collections/law/wps/WPS2010-02_Paulsson.pdf (last accessed September 11, 2014).
Paulsson, Jan: Arbitration Without Privity, in: ICSID Review 1995, Foreign Investment Law Journal, Vol. 10 No. 2, pp. 232-257.
Paulsson, Jan: Avoiding Unintended Consequences, in: Karl P. Sauvant/Michael Chiswick-Patterson (eds.), Appeals Mechanism in International Investment Disputes, New York 2008, pp. 241-265.
Paulsson, Jan: Denial of Justice in International Law, Cambridge 2005.
Paulsson, Jan: Ethics, Elitism, Eligibility, in: Journal of International Arbitration 1997, Vol. 14 No. 4, pp. 13-21.
Paulsson, Jan: International Arbitration and the Generation of Legal Norms: Treaty Arbitration and International Law, in: Albert Jan van den Berg (ed.), International Arbitration 2006: Back to Basics?, ICCA Congress Series Vol. 13, Aalphen aan den Rijn 2006, pp. 879-889.
Paulsson, Jan: The Idea of Arbitration, Oxford 2013.
Paulsson, Jan: The Power of States to Make Meaningful Promises to Foreigners, in: Journal of International Dispute Settlement 2010, Vol. 1 No. 2, pp. 341-352.
Paulsson, Jan: Third World Participation in International Investment Arbitration, in: ICSID Review 1987, Foreign Investment Law Journal, Vol. 2 No. 1, pp. 19-65.
Penusliski, Ilija Mitrev: A Dispute Systems Design Diagnosis of ICSID, in: Michael Waibel (ed.), The Backlash Against Investment Arbitration: Perceptions and Reality, Alphen aan den Rijn 2010, pp. 507-536.
Potacs, Michael: Effet utile als Auslegungsgrundsatz, in: Zeitschrift für Europarecht 2009, Heft 4, pp. 465-487.

Poulsen, Lauge Skovgaard: The Significance of South-South BITs for the International Investment Regime: A Quantitative Analysis, in: Northwestern Journal of International Law & Business 2010, Vol. 30 No. 1, pp. 101-130.

Rajput, Aniruddha: AES Summit Generation Limited and AES-Tisza Erömü Kft v Hungary – The Scope of ad hoc Committee Review for Manifest Excess of Powers and Failure to State Reasons, in: ICSID Review 2013, Foreign Investment Law Journal, Vol. 28 No. 2, pp. 273-278.

Ralston, Jackson H.: International Arbitration from Athens to Locarno, London/Oxford 1929.

Reading, Michael R.: The Bilateral Investment Treaty in ASEAN: A Comparative Analysis, in: Duke Law Journal 1992, Vol. 42, pp. 679-705.

Redfern, Alan/Hunter, Martin/Blackaby, Nigel/Partasides, Constantine (eds.), Law and Practice of International Commercial Arbitration, 4th ed., London 2004.

Reed, Lucy/Paulsson, Jan/Blackaby, Nigel: Guide to ICSID Arbitration, Alphen aan den Rijn 2004.

Reed, Lucy: The De Facto Precedent Regime in Investment Arbitration: A Case for Proactive Case Management, in: ICSID Review 2010, Foreign Investment Law Journal, Vol. 25 No. 1, pp. 95-103.

Reinisch, August: Internationales Investitionsschutzrecht, in: Christian Tietje (ed.), Internationales Wirtschaftsrecht, Berlin 2009, pp. 346-374.

Reinisch, August: Proliferation of International Dispute Settlement Mechanisms: The Threat of Fragmentation vs. the Promise of a More Effective System – Some Reflections from the Perspective of Investment Arbitration, in: James Crawford/ Alain Pellet/Isabelle Buffard/Stephan Wittich (eds.), International Law Between Universalism and Fragmentation - Festschrift in Honour of Gerhard Hafner, Leiden 2008, pp. 107-125.

Reisman, W. Michael: Has the International Court Exceeded its Jurisdiction?, in: American Journal of International Law 1986, Vol. 80, pp. 128-134.

Reisman, W. Michael: Investment and Human Rights Tribunals as Court of Last Appeal in International Commercial Arbitration, in: Laurent Lévy/Yves Derains (eds.), Liber Amicorum en l'honneur de Serge Lazareff, 2011, pp. 521-530.

Reisman, W. Michael: Sovereignty and Human Rights in Contemporary International Law, in: The American Journal of International Law 1990, Vol. 84, pp. 866-876.

Reisman, W. Michael: The Breakdown of the Control Mechanism in ICSID Arbitration, in: Duke Law Journal 1989, No. 4, pp. 739-807.

Ris, Martin: Treaty Interpretation and ICJ Recourse to Travaux Préparatoires: Towards a Proposed Amendment of Articles 31 and 32 of the Vienna Convention on the Law of Treaties, in: Boston College International & Comparative Law Review 1991, Vol. 14 No. 1, pp. 111-136.

Rivkin, David W.: The Impact of International Arbitration on the Rule of Law – The 2012 Clayton Utz/University of Sydney International Arbitration Lecture, in: Arbitration International 2013, Vol. 29 No. 3, pp. 327-360.

Roberts, Anthea: Power and Persuasion in Investment Treaty Interpretation: The Dual Role of States, in: The American Journal of International Law 2010, Vol. 104, pp. 179-225.

Rubins, Noah: The Enforcement and Annulment of International Arbitration Awards in Indonesia, in: American University International Law Review 2005, Vol. 20 No. 2, pp. 359-401.

Rubins, Noah: The Notion of "Investment" in International Investment Arbitration, in: Norbert Horn/Stefan Kröll (eds.), Arbitrating Foreign Investment Disputes, The Hague 2004, pp. 283-324.

Ruttenberg, Valerie H.: The United States Bilateral Investment Treaty Program: Variations on the Model, in: University of Pennsylvania Journal of International Business Law 1986, Vol. 9 No. 1, pp. 121-143.

Sabahi, Borzu: Compensation and Restitution in Investor-State Arbitration – Principles and Practice, Oxford 2011.

Salacuse, Jeswald W.: The Law of Investment Treaties, Oxford 2009.

Salacuse, Jeswald W.: The Treatification of International Investment Law, in: Law and Business Review of the Americas 2007, Vol. 13, pp. 155-166.

Saldarriaga, Andrea: Investment Awards and the Rules of Interpretation of the Vienna Convention: Making Room for Improvement, in: ICSID Review 2013, Foreign Investment Law Journal, Vol. 28 No. 1, pp. 1-21.

Scalia, Antonin: Originalism: The Lesser Evil, in: University of Cincinnati Law Review Vol. 57, No. 849, 1988-1989.

Scelle, Georges: Le Pacte des Nations et sa liaison avec Le Traité de Paix, Paris 1919.

Schaffer, R.P.: Current Trends in Treaty Interpretation and the South African Approach, in: Australian Year Book of International Law 1981, Vol. 7, pp. 129-173.

Schill, Stephan W.: Enhancing International Investment Law's Legitimacy: Conceptual and Methodological Foundations of a New Public Law Approach, in: Virginia Journal of International Law 2011, Vol. 52 No. 1, pp. 57-102.

Schill, Stephan W. (ed.): International Investment Law and Comparative Public Law – An Introduction, in: International Investment Law and Comparative Public Law, Oxford 2010, pp. 3-37.

Schill, Stephan W./Kingsbury, Benedict: Investor-State Arbitration as Governance: Fair and Equitable Treatment, Proportionality and the Emerging Global Administrative Law, IILJ Working Paper 2009/6.

Schill, Stephan W.: Public or Private Dispute Settlement? Clash in Investment Treaty Arbitration and Its Impact on the Role of the Arbitrator, in: Todd Weiler/Freya Baetens (eds.), New Directions in International Economic Law: In Memoriam Thomas Wälde, Leiden 2011, pp. 23-43.

Schill, Stephan W.: The Multilateralization of International Investment Law, Cambridge 2009.

Schill, Stephan W./Jacob, Marc: Trends in International Investment Agreements, 2010/2011: The Increasing Complexity of International Investment Law, in: Karl P. Sauvant (ed.), Yearbook on International Law & Policy 2011-2012, Oxford 2013.

Schill, Stephan W.: W(h)ither Fragmentation? On the Literature and Sociology of International Investment Law, in: The European Journal of International Law 2011, Vol. 22 No. 3, pp. 875-908.

Schilling, Alexander: Gesprächskreis "Investitionsrecht und -schiedsgerichtsbarkeit" - achtes Jahrestreffen, in: Zeitschrift für Schiedsverfahren 2013, pp. 106-109.

Schmalenbach, Kirsten: Preamble, in: Oliver Dörr/Kirsten Schmalenbach (eds.), Vienna Convention on the Law of Treaties: A Commentary, Berlin/Heidelberg 2012, pp. 9-16.

Schneiderman, David: Judicial Politics and International Investment Arbitration: Seeking an Explanation for Conflicting Outcomes, in: Northwestern Journal of International Law & Business 2010, Vol. 30 No. 2, pp. 1-33.

Schöbener, Burkhard /Herbst, Jochen /Perkams, Markus: Internationales Wirtschaftsrecht, Heidelberg 2010.

Schreiber, William: Realizing the Right to Water in International Investment Law: An Interdisciplinary Approach to BIT Obligations, in: Natural Resources Journal 2008, Vol. 48, pp. 431-478.

Schreuer, Christoph: Commentary on the ICSID Convention, in: ICSID Review 1996, Foreign Investment Law Journal, Vol. 11 No. 2, pp. 316-492.

Schreuer, Christoph: Consent to Arbitration, in: Peter Muchlinski/Federico Ortino/Christoph Schreuer (eds.), The Oxford Handbook on International Investment Law, Oxford 2008, pp. 830-867.

Schreuer, Christoph: Diversity and Harmonization of Treaty Interpretation in Investment Arbitration, in: Malgosia Fitzmaurice/Olufemi Elias/Panos Merkouris (eds.), Treaty Interpretation and the Vienna Convention on the Law of Treaties: 30 Years on, Leiden 2010, pp. 129-151.

Schreuer, Christoph: Fair and Equitable Treatment in Arbitral Practice, in: The Journal of World Investment & Trade 2005, Vol. 6 No. 3, pp. 357-386.

Schreuer, Christoph: Fair and Equitable Treatment (FET): Interactions with other Standards, in: Transnational Dispute Management 2007, Vol. 4 No. 5, pp. 1-26.

Schreuer, Christoph: From ICSID Annulment to Appeal – Half Way Down the Slippery Slope, in: Eduardo Valencia-Ospina/Pierre Bodeau-Livinec (eds.), The Law and Practice of International Courts and Tribunals, Leiden 2011, pp. 211-225.

Schreuer, Christoph: Interaction of International Tribunals and Domestic Courts, in: A.W. Rovine (ed.), Contemporary Issues in International Arbitration and Mediation: The Fordham Papers, Leiden 2010, pp. 71-94.

Schreuer, Christoph: Investment Protection and International Relations, in: August Reinisch/Ursula Kriebaum (eds.), The Law of International Relations – Liber Amicorum Hanspeter Neuhold, The Hague 2007, pp. 345-358.

Schreuer, Christoph: Preliminary Rulings in Investment Arbitration, in: Karl P. Sauvant (ed.), Appeals Mechanism in International Investment Disputes, Oxford 2008, pp. 207-212.

Schreuer, Christoph: The ICSID Convention – A Commentary, 2nd ed., Cambridge 2009.

Schreuer, Christoph: The ICSID Convention: A Commentary, in: ICSID Review 1998, Foreign Investment Law Journal, Vol. 13 No. 2, pp. 507-717.

Schreuer, Christoph: Three Generations of ICSID Annulment Proceedings, in: Emmanuel Gaillard/Yas Banifatemi (eds.), Annulment of ICSID Awards, Huntington 2004, pp. 17-42.

Schultz, Thomas: Against Consistency in Investment Arbitration, in: Zachary Douglas/Joost Pauwelyn/Jorge E. Viñuales (eds.), The Foundations of International Investment Law: Bringing Theory into Practice, 2014, pp. 297-316.

Schwebel, Stephen: Anti-Suit Injunctions in: International Arbitration – An Overview, in: Emmanuel Gaillard (ed.), Anti-Suit Injunctions in International Arbitration, Huntington 2005, pp. 5-16.

Schwebel, Stephen: International Arbitration: Three Salient Problems, Cambridge 1987.

Shakalany, Amr A.: Arbitration and the Third World: A Plea for Reassessing Bias under the Scepter of Neoliberalism, in: Harvard International Law Journal 2000, Vol. 41 No. 2, pp. 419-468.

Shifman, Bette E.: Maritime International Nominees Establishment v. Government of Guinea: Effect on U.S. Jurisdiction of an Agreement by a Foreign Sovereign to Arbitrate Before the International Centre for Settlement of Investment Disputes, in: George Washington Journal of International Law and Economics 1981-1982, pp. 451-470.

Simma, Bruno: The Contribution of Alfred Verdross to the Theory of International Law, in: European Journal of International Law 1995, pp. 33-54.

Sinclair, Ian: The Vienna Convention on the Law of Treaties, 2nd ed., Manchester 1984.

Sornarajah, Muthucumaraswamy: A Coming Crisis: Expansionary Trends in Investment Treaty Arbitration in: Karl P. Sauvant (ed.), Appeals Mechanism in International Investment Disputes, Oxford 2008, pp. 39-45.

Sornarajah, Muthucumaraswamy: ICSID Involvement in Asian Foreign Investment Disputes: The AMCO and AAPL Case, in: Ko Swan Sik/J.J.G. Syatauw/M.C.W. Pinto (eds.), Asian Yearbook of International Law 1994, Vol. 4, pp. 69-98.

Sornarajah, Muthucumaraswamy: Power and Justice in Foreign Investment Arbitration, in: Journal of International Arbitration 1997, Vol. 14, pp. 103-140.

Sornarajah, Muthucumaraswamy: Power and Justice: Third World Resistance in International Law, in: Singapore Year Book of International Law 2006, pp. 19-57.

Sornarajah, Muthucumaraswamy: The Climate of International Arbitration, in: Journal of International Arbitration 1991, Vol. 8 No. 2, pp. 47-86.

Sornarajah, Muthucumaraswamy: The International Law on Foreign Investment, 3rd ed., Cambridge 2010.

Sornarajah, Muthucumaraswamy: The Retreat of Neo-Liberalism in Investment Treaty Arbitration, in: Catherine A. Rogers/Roger P. Alford (eds.), The Future of Investment Arbitration, Oxford 2009, pp. 273-296.

Sornarajah, Muthucumaraswamy: The Settlement of Foreign Investment Disputes, The Hague 2000.

South Centre, Developments in Discussions for the Improvement of the Framework for ICSID Arbitration and the Participation of Developing Countries, Analytical Note, February 2005, available at https://www.southcentre.int/wp-content/uploads/2013/07/AN_INV1_Improvement-of-the-Framework-for-ICSID_EN.pdf (last accessed September 2, 2014).

Spiermann, Ole: Individual Rights, State Interests and the Power to Waive ICSID Jurisdiction under Bilateral Investment Treaties, in: Arbitration International 2004, Vol. 20, pp. 179-212.

Stipanowich, Thomas J.: Arbitration: The "New Litigation", in: University of Illinois Law Review 2010, No. 1, pp. 1-60.

Swart, Mia: Judicial Lawmaking at the Ad Hhoc Tribunals: The Creative Use of the Sources of International Law and "Adventurous Interpretation", in: Zeitschrift für ausländisches öffentliches Recht und Völkerrecht 2010, Vol. 70 No. 3, pp. 459-486.

Tams, Christian J.: An Appealing Option? – The Debate about an ICSID Appellate Structure, in: Christian Tietje/Gerhard Kraft/Rolf Sethe (eds.), Beiträge zum Transationalen Wirtschaftsrecht 2006, Heft 57, available at http://www.economiclaw.uni-halle.de/sites/default/files/altbestand/Heft57.pdf (last accessed April 21, 2015).

Teitelbaum, Ruth: A Look at the Public Interest in Investment Arbitration: Is It Unique? What Should We Do About It?, in: Berkeley Journal of International Law 2010, Vol. 5, pp. 54-62.

Ten Cate, Irene M.: International Arbitration and the Ends of Appellate Review, in: International Law and Politics 2012, Vol. 44, pp. 1109-1204.

Ten Cate, Irene M.: The Costs of Consistency: Precedent in Investment Treaty Arbitration, in: Columbia Journal of Transnational Law 2013, Vol. 51, pp. 418-478.

Tupmann, W. Michael: Case Studies in the Jurisdiction of the International Centre for Settlement of Investment Disputes, in: International and Comparative Law Quarterly 1986, Vol. 35 No. 4, pp. 813-838.

UNCTAD, International Investment Policymaking in Transition: Challenges and Opportunities of Treaty Renewal, in: IIA Issues Note No. 4, June 2013, available at http://unctad.org/en/PublicationsLibrary/webdiaepcb2013d9_en.pdf (last accessed on September 7, 2014).

UNCTAD, Reform of the IIA Regime: Four Paths of Action and a Way Forward, in: IIA Issues Note No. 3, June 2014, p. 2, available at http://unctad.org/en/PublicationsLibrary/webdiaepcb2014d6_en.pdf (last accessed on August 14, 2014).

Vandevelde, Kenneth D.: Bilateral Investment Treaties: History, Policy and Interpretation, Oxford 2010.

Van Harten, Gus: Five Justifications for Investment Treaties: A Critical Discussion, in: Trade, Law & Development 2010, Vol. 2 No. 1, pp. 19-58.

Van Harten, Gus/Loughlin, Martin: Investment Treaty Arbitration as a Species of Global Administrative Law, in: European Journal of International Law 2006, Vol. 17 No. 1, pp. 121-150.

Van Harten, Gus: Perceived Bias in Investment Treaty Arbitration, in: Michael Waibel/Asha Kaushal et al. (eds.), The Backlash Against Investment Arbitration: Perceptions and Reality, Alphen aan den Rijn 2010, pp. 432-453.

Van Harten, Gus: The Public-Private Distinction in the International Arbitration of Individual Claims Against the State, in: International and Comparative Corporate Law Quarterly, Vol. 56 No. 2, pp. 371-394.

Van Houtte, Hans/Brunetti, Maurizio: Investment Arbitration – Ten Areas of Caution for Commercial Arbitrators, in: Arbitration International 2013, Vol. 29 No. 4, pp. 553-574.

Veeder, Van V.: The Necessary Safeguards of an Appellate System, in: Federico Ortino/Audley Sheppard/Hugo Warner (eds.), International Investment Law – Current Issues, Vol. 1, London 2006, pp. 9-11.

Verdross, Alfred: Die Sicherung von ausländischen Privatrechten aus Abkommen zur wirtschaftlichen Entwicklung mit Schiedsklauseln, in: Zeitschrift für ausländisches öffentliches Recht und Völkerrecht 1957/1958, Vol. 18, pp. 635-651.

Villiger, Mark Eugen: Commentary on the 1969 Vienna Convention on the Law of Treaties, Leiden 2009.

Waibel, Michael/Wu, Yanhui: Are Arbitrators Political?, available at https://www.researchgate.net/publication/256023521_Are_Arbitrators_Political (last accessed August 7, 2014), permission by authors obtained.

Waibel, Michael: International Investment Law and Treaty Interpretation, in: Rainer Hofmann/Christian Tams (eds.), From Clinical Isolation to Systemic Integration, Baden-Baden 2011, pp. 29-52.

Waibel, Michael: Uniformity Versus Specialisation: A Uniform Regime of Treaty Interpretation?, University of Cambridge, Legal Studies Research Paper Series, Paper No. 54/2013, available at http://papers.ssrn.com/sol3/papers.cfm?abstract_id=2353833 (last accessed September 11, 2014).

Walsh, Thomas W.: Substantive Review of ICSID Awards: Is the Desire for Accuracy Sufficient to Compromise Finality?, in: Berkeley Journal of International Law 2006, Vol. 24, pp. 444-462.

Wälde, Thomas W.: International Investment Law: An Overview of Key Concepts and Methodology, in: Transnational Dispute Management 2007 – New Aspects of International Investment Law – 2004 Research Seminar by The Hague Academy of International Law, Vol. 4 No. 4, pp. 1-86.

Wälde, Thomas W.: The Specific Nature of Investment Arbitration in: Philippe Kahn/Thomas W. Wälde (eds.), New Aspects of International Investment Law, Leiden 2007, pp. 42-120.

Weiler, Joseph H.H.: The Interpretation of Treaties – A Re-examination, in: European Journal of International Law 2010, Vol. 21 No. 3, p. 507.

Weiler, Joseph H.H.: Prolegomena to a Meso-theory of Treaty Interpretation at the Turn of the Century, in: Interpretation and Judgment in International Law, available at http://iilj.org/courses/documents/2008Colloquium.Session5.Weiler.pdf (last accessed July 5, 2014).

Weiler, Todd: The Interpretation of International Investment Law: Equality, Discrimination and Minimum Standards of Treatment in Historical Context, Leiden 2013.

Weiss, Thomas G./Hubert, Don: The Responsibility to Protect: Research, Bibliography, Background: Supplementary Volume to the Report of the International Commission on Intervention and State Sovereignty, Ottawa 2001.

Williams, Clifton: Expressio Unius Est Exclusio Alterius, in: Marquette Law Review 1931, Vol. 15 No. 4, pp. 191-196.

Wisner, Robert/Gallus, Nick: Nationality Requirements in Investor-State Arbitration, in: The Journal of World Investment and Trade 2004, Vol. 5, pp. 927-945.

Wong, Ronald: Interim Relief in Aid of International Commercial Arbitration, in: Singapore Academy of Law Journal 2012, pp. 499-532.

Wright, Quincy: Mandates under the League of Nations, Chicago 1930.

Yu, Hong-lin: A Theoretical Overview of the Foundations of International Commercial Arbitration, in: Contemporary Asia Arbitration Journal 2008, Vol. 1, pp. 255-286.

Ziegler, Andreas R.: Most-Favoured-Nation (MFN) Treatment, in: August Reinisch (ed.), Standards of Investment Protection, Oxford 2008, pp. 59-86.

Zielcke, Andreas: Sieg über das Gesetz, Süddeutsche Zeitung, 3 May 2014, available at http://www.sueddeutsche.de/politik/transatlantisches-freihandelsabkommen-ttip-sieg-ueber-das-gesetz-1.1948221 (last accessed September 3, 2014).

Zimmermann, Andreas/Tomuschat, Christian/Oellers-Frahm, Karin/Tams, Christian J. (eds.), The Statute of the International Court of Justice – A Commentary, 2nd ed., Oxford 2012.

Table of Cases

Abaclat and others v. The Argentine Republic, Decision on Jurisdiction and Admissibility, ICSID Case No. ARB/07/5, August 4, 2011, **61, 62**

AES Corporation v. The Argentine Republic, Decision on Jurisdiction, ICSID Case No. ARB/02/17, April 26, 2005, **44, 45, 85, 181, 195**

AES Summit Generation Limited and AES-Tisza Erömü Kft v. Hungary, Decision of the Ad Hoc Committee on the Application for Annulment, ICSID Case No. ARB/07/22, June 22, 2012, **185, 188**

Aguas del Tunari, S.A. v. Republic of Bolivia, Decision on Respondent's Objections to Jurisdiction, ICSID Case No. ARB/02/3, October 21, 2005, **8, 17**

Alapli Elektrik B.V. v. Republic of Turkey, Decision on Annulment, ICSID Case No. ARB/08/13, July 10, 2014, **7, 185**

Alcoa Minerals of Jamaica, Inc. v. Republic of Jamaica, Decision on Jurisdiction and Competence, ICSID Case No. ARB/74/2, July 6, 1975, **60**

Ambiente Ufficio S.p.A. v. The Argentine Republic, Decision on Jurisdiction and Admissibility, ICSID Case No. ARB/08/9, February 8, 2013, **62**

AMCO v. Republic of Indonesia, Resubmitted Case – Decision on Jurisdiction, ICSID Case No. ARB/81/1, May 10, 1988, **98, 183**

Anatolie Stati, Gabriel Stati, Ascom Group SA and Terra Raf Trans Traiding Ltd. v. Republic of Kazakhstan, Award, SCC Arbitration V (116/2010), December 19, 2013, **199**

ATA Construction, Industrial and Trading Company v. The Hashemite Kingdom of Jordan, Award, ICSID Case No. ARB/08/2, May 18, 2010, **73–77, 95, 99, 100, 106, 211, 221, 224**

Azurix Corporation v. The Republic of Argentina, Award, ICSID Case No. ARB/01/12, July 14, 2006, **48**

Bayindir Insaat Turizm Ticaret VE Sanayi A.S. v. Islamic Republic of Pakistan, Award on Jurisdiction, ICSID Case No. ARB/03/29, November 14, 2005, **63**

Bayview Irrigation District and others v. United Mexican States, Award, ICSID Case No. ARB(AF), June 19, 2007, **18**

Biloune and Marine Drive Complex Ltd. v. Ghana Investments Centre and the Government of Ghana, Award, UNCITRAL, June 30, 1990, **33**

Biwater Gauff (Tanzania) Ltd. v. United Republic of Tanzania, Award, ICSID Case No. ARB/05/22, July 24, 2008, **89**

Table of Cases

Caratube International Oil Company LLP v. Republic of Kazakhstan, Decision on the Annulment Application of Caratube International Oil Company LLP, ICSID Case No. ARB/08/12, February 21, 2014, **188**

Ceskoslovenska Obchodni Banka, A.S. v. The Slovak Republic, Decision of the Tribunal on Objections to Jurisdiction, ICSID Case No. ARB/97/4, May 24, 1999, **96, 97**

Ceskoslovenska Obchodni Banka, A.S. v. The Slovak Republic, Decision of the Tribunal on Respondent's Further and Partial Objection to Jurisdiction, ICSID Case No. ARB/97/4, December 1, 2000, **97**

Champion Trading Company, Ameritrade International, Inc., James T. Wahba, John B. Wahba, Timothy T. Wahba v. Arab Republic of Egypt, Decision on Jurisdiction, ICSID Case No. ARB/02/9, October 21, 2003, **123–124**

Chevron Corporation and Texaco Petroleum Corporation v. The Republic of Ecuador, Interim Award, UNCITRAL, December 1, 2008, **228, 229**

Chevron Corporation and Texaco Petroleum Corporation v. The Republic of Ecuador, Partial Award on the Merits, UNCITRAL, PCA Case No. 34877, March 30, 2010, **120, 121**

Churchill Mining Plc v. Republic of Indonesia, Decision on Jurisdiction, ICSID Cases Nos. ARB/12/14 and 12/40, February 24, 2014, **16, 173**

City Oriente Limited v. The Republic of Ecuador and Empresa Estatal Petróleos de Ecuador, Decision on Provisional Measures, ICSID Case No. ARB/06/21, November 19, 2007, **123**

CME Czech Republic B.V. v. The Czech Republic, Final Award, UNCITRAL, March 14, 2003, **16**

CME Czech Republic B.V. (The Netherlands) v. The Czech Republic, Separate Opinion on the Issues at the Quantum Phase of: CME v. Czech Republic by Ian Brownlie, UNCITRAL, March 14, 2003, **41, 158**

Compañía de Aguas del Aconquija S.A. and Vivendi Universal S.A. v. The Argentine Republic, Award, ICSID Case No. ARB/97/3, August 20, 2007, **32**

Compañia de Aguas Del Aconquija S.A. and Vivendi Universal v. The Argentine Republic, Decision on Annulment, ICSID Case No. ARB/97/3, July 3, 2002, **184, 185**

ConocoPhillips Petrozuata B.V., ConocoPhillips Hamaca B.V. and ConocoPhillips Gulf of Paria B.V. v. Bolivarian Republic of Venezuela, Dissenting Opinion of Georges Abi-Saab, ICSID Case No. ARB/07/30, March 10, 2014, **49, 134, 204**

Consorzio Groupement L.E.S.I.-DIPENTA v. Republic of Algeria, Award, ICSID Case No. ARB/03/08, January 10, 2005, **33, 63**

Czechoslovakia v. Radio Corporation of America, Arbitration Case, April 1, 1932, in: American Journal of International Law 1936, Vol. 30, pp. 523 et seq., **158**

David Minnotte and Robert Lewis v. Republic of Poland, Award, ICSID Case No. ARB(AF)/10/1, May 16, 2014, **106**

Desert Line Projects LLC v. The Republic of Yemen, Award, ICSID Case No. ARB/05/17, February 6, 2008, **121**

Deutsche Bank AG v. Democratic Socialist Republic of Sri Lanka, Award, ICSID Case No. ARB/09/2, October 23, 2012, **42, 62**

Duke Energy International Peru Investments No. 1, Ltd. v. Republic of Peru, Decision on Jurisdiction, ICSID Case No. ARB/03/28, February 1, 2006, **98, 99**

East Kalimantan v. PT Kaltim Prima Coal and others, Award on Jurisdiction, ICSID Case No. ARB/07/3, December 28, 2009, **85**

Eastern Sugar B.V. (Netherlands) v. The Czech Republic, Partial Award, UNCITRAL, SCC No. 088/2004, March 27, 2007, **18**

EDF International S.A., SAUR International S.A. and Leon Participaciones Argentinas S.A. v. The Argentine Republic, Award, ICSID Case No. ARB/03/23, June 11, 2012, **42**

El Paso Energy International Company v. The Argentine Republic, Decision on Jurisdiction, ICSID Case No. ARB/03/15, April 27, 2006, **40, 44, 128, 161**

Emilio Agustín Maffezini v. The Kingdom of Spain, Decision of the Tribunal on Objections to Jurisdiction, ICSID Case No. ARB/97/7, January 25, 2000, **31, 53**

Enron Corporation and Ponderosa Assets, L.P. v. The Argentine Republic, Decision on Jurisdiction, ICSID Case No. ARB/01/3, January 14, 2004, **47, 98**

Eureko B.V. v. Republic of Poland, Dissenting Opinion, UNCITRAL, August 19, 2005, **130**

Eureko B.V. v. Republic of Poland, Partial Award, UNCITRAL, August 19, 2005, **129**

Fedax N.V. v. The Republic of Venezuela, Decision of the Tribunal on Objections to Jurisdiction, ICSID Case No. ARB/96/3, July 11, 1997, **57, 61, 95**

Franck Charles Arif v. Republic of Moldova, Award, ICSID Case No. ARB/11/23, April 8, 2013, **44, 181**

Fraport AG Frankfurt Airport Services Worldwide v. The Republic of Philippines, Award, ICSID Case No. ARB/03/25, August 16, 2007, **59**

Frontier Petroleum Services Ltd. v. The Czech Republic, Final Award, UNCITRAL, November 12, 2010, **80–83, 104, 106, 210, 215, 220**

Garanti Koza LLP v. Turkmenistan, Dissenting Opinion of Laurence Boisson de Chazournes, ICSID Case No. ARB/11/20, July 3, 2013, **54, 150, 198**

GEA Group Aktiengesellschaft v. Ukraine, Award, ICSID Case No. ARB/08/16, March 31, 2011, **86–91, 94, 102, 104, 106, 109**

Generation Ukraine, Inc. v. Ukraine, Award, ICSID Case No. ARB/00/9, September 16, 2003, **59, 178**

Himpurna California Energy Ltd. (Bermuda) v. Republic of Indonesia, UNCITRAL, Interim Award, September 26, 1999, **113, 114**

Holiday Inns v. Kingdom of Morocco, Decision on Jurisdiction, May 12, 1974, **97, 98, 148**

Hrvatska Elektroprivreda D.D. v. The Republic of Slovenia, Decision on the Treaty Interpretation Issue, ICSID Case No. ARB/05/24, June 12, 2009, **138, 139**

Hulley Enterprises Limited (Cyprus) v. The Russian Federation, Final Award, PCA Case No. AA 226, July 18, 2014, **139**

Hussein Nuaman Soufraki v. United Arab Emirates, Decision of the Ad Hoc Committee on the Application for Annulment of Mr. Soufraki, ICSID Case No. ARB/02/7, June 5, 2007, **54–55, 150, 187, 198**

Industria Nacional de Alimentos S.A., and Indalsa Perú S.A. v. The Republic of Peru, Decision on Annulment, ICSID Case No. ARB/03/4, September 5, 2007, **108, 186**

Table of Cases

Iurii Bogdanov, Agurdino-Invest Ltd., Argudino-Chimia JSC v. Republic of Moldova, Award, SCC, September 22, 2005, **7, 71, 172**

Jan de Nul N.V. and Dredging International N.V. v. Arab Republic of Egypt, Award, ICSID Case No. ARB/04/13, November 6, 2008, **18**

Joseph Charles Lemire v. Ukraine, Award, ICSID Case No. ARB/06/18, March 28, 2011, **8**

Joy Mining Machinery Limited v. The Arab Republic of Egypt, Award on Jurisdiction, ICSID Case No. ARB/03/11, August 6, 2004, **40, 63, 64, 98**

Klöckner v. The Republic of Cameroon, Award, ICSID Case No. ARB/81/2, October 21, 1983, **98**

Klöckner v. The Republic of Cameroon, Decision by the Ad Hoc Committee, ICSID Case No. ARB/81/2, May 3, 1985, **183**

Lanco International Inc. v. The Argentine Republic, Preliminary Decision: Jurisdiction of the Arbitral Tribunal, ICSID Case No. ARB/97/6, December 8, 1998, **59**

Lao Holdings N.V. v. The Lao People's Democratic Republic, Decision on Jurisdiction, ICSID Case No. ARB(AF)/12/6, February 21, 2014, **157**

Liberian Eastern Timber Corp. v. Republic of Liberia, Decision on Jurisdiction, ICSID Case No. ARB/83/2, October 24, 1984, **63**

Malaysia Historical Salvors SDN, BHD v. The Government of Malaysia, Award on Jurisdiction, ICSID Case No. ARB/05/10, May 17, 2007, **59, 62, 63**

Maritime International Nominees Establishment v. Government of Guinea, Decision on the Application by Guinea for Partial Annulment, ICSID Case No. ARB/84/4, December 14, 1989, **183, 184, 186, 187**

M.C.I. Power Group L.C. and New Turbine Inc. v. Republic of Ecuador, Decision on Annulment, ICSID Case No. ARB/03/6, October 19, 2009, **185**

Methanex Corporation v. United States of America, Final Award, UNCITRAL, August 3, 2005, **49, 93, 159**

Metal-Tech Ltd. v. The Republic of Uzbekistan, Award, ICSID Case No. ARB/10/3, October 4, 2013, **16**

Mihaly International Corporation v. Democratic Socialist Republic of Sri Lanka, Award, ICSID Case No. ARB/00/2, March 15, 2002, **62**

Mondev International Ltd. v. United States of America, Award, ICSID Case No. ARB(AF)/99/2, October 11, 2002, **14, 73, 95**

MTD Equity Sdn. Bhd. and MTD Chile S.A. v. Republic of Chile, Award, ICSID Case No. ARB/01/7, May 25, 2004, **7, 34, 71, 172**

MTD Equity Sdn Bhd. & MTD Chile S.A. v. The Republic of Chile, Decision on Annulment, ICSID Case No. ARB/01/7, March 21, 2007, **185**

National Grid PLC v. The Argentine Republic, Decision on Jurisdiction, UNCITRAL, June 20, 2006, **47**

Noble Ventures, Inc. v. Romania, Award, ICSID Case No. ARB/01/11, October 12, 2005, **14, 40, 130, 138**

Nova Scotia Power Incorporated (Canada) v. Bolivian Republic of Venezuela, Award, ICSID Case No. ARB(AF)/11/1, April 30, 2014, **65, 199**

Nykomb Synergetics Technology Holding AB v. Republic of Latvia, Award, SCC, December 16, 2003, **28**

Table of Cases

Occidental Exploration and Production Company v. Republic of Ecuador, Award, LCIA Case No. UN3467, July 11, 2004, **42**

Pac Rim Cayman LLC v. The Republic of El Salvador, Decision on the Respondent's Jurisdictional Objections, ICSID Case No. ARB/09/12, June 1, 2012, **47**

Pan American Energy LLC and BP Argentina Explorations Company v. The Argentine Republic, Decision on Preliminary Objections, ICSID Case No. ARB/03/13, July 27, 2006, **123**

Pantechniki S.A. Contractors & Engineers (Greece) v. The Republic of Albania, Award, ICSID Case No. ARB/07/21, July 30, 2009, **124, 160**

Philip Morris Brands SARL, Philip Morris Products S.A. and Abal Hermanos S.A. v. Oriental Republic of Uruguay, Decision on Jurisdiction, ICSID Case No. ARB/10/7, July 2, 2013, **47**

Parkerings-Compagniet AS v. Republic of Lithuania, Award, ICSID Case No. ARB/05/8, September 11, 2007, **62**

Patrick Mitchell v. The Democratic Republic of Congo, Decision on the Application for Annulment of the Award, ICSID Case No. ARB/99/7, November 1, 2006, **88, 187–188**

Perenco Ecuador Ltd. v. The Republic of Ecuador and Empresa Estatal Petróleos de Ecuador, Decision on Provisional Matters, ICSID Case No. ARB/08/6, May 8, 2009, **123**

Phoenix Action, Ltd. v. The Czech Republic, Award, ICSID Case No. ARB/06/5, April 15, 2009, **88**

Plama Consortium Limited v. Republic of Bulgaria, Decision on Jurisdiction, ICSID Case No. ARB/03/24, February 8, 2005, **14, 31, 94, 178**

PSEG v. Republic of Turkey, Award, ICSID Case No. ARB/02/5, January 19, 2007, **98**

Quiborax S.A., Non Metallic Minerals S.A. and Allan Fosk Kaplún v. Plurinational State of Bolivia, Decision on Jurisdiction, ICSID Case No. ARB/06/2, December 27, 2012, **44, 72, 181**

Radio Corporation of America v. The National Government of the Republic of China, Decision in the Arbitration Case, April 13, 1935, in: United Nations Reports of International Arbitral Awards, Vol. 3, pp. 1621-1636, **155**

Republic of Ecuador v. United States of America, UNCITRAL, PCA Case No. 2012-5, April 24, 2012, **39**

Robert Azinian, Kenneth Davitian, & Ellen Baca v. United Mexican States, Award, ICSID Case No. ARB(AF)/97/2, November 1, 1999, **64, 110**

Romak S.A. (Switzerland) v. The Republic of Uzbekistan, Award, PCA Case No. AA280, November 26, 2009, **83–85, 88, 95, 98, 103, 105, 110, 139, 211, 225**

Salini Costruttori S.p.A. and Italstrade S.p.A. v. Kingdom of Morocco, Decision on Jurisdiction, ICSID Case No. ARB/00/4, July 31, 2001, **59, 60–62**

Saluka Investments BV v. The Czech Republic, Partial Award, PCA Case, UNCITRAL, March 17, 2006, **32**

Sempra Energy International v. The Argentine Republic, Decision on Objections to Jurisdiction, ICSID Case No. ARB/02/16, May 11, 2005, **7, 71, 172**

Siemens AG v. The Argentine Republic, Decision on Jurisdiction, ICSID Case No. ARB/02/8, August 3, 2004, **15, 46, 47, 138**

Table of Cases

SGS Société Générale de Surveillance SA v. Islamic Republic of Pakistan, Procedural Order No. 2, ICSID Case No. ARB/01/13, October 16, 2002, **122, 128**

SGS Société Générale de Surveillance S.A. v. The Republic of Paraguay, Decision on Annulment, ICSID Case No. ARB/07/29, May 19, 2014, **185**

SGS Société Générale de Surveillance SA v. Republic of the Philippines, Decision of the Tribunal on Objections to Jurisdiction, ICSID Case No. ARB/02/6, January 29, 2004, **13, 129**

Société Ouest Africaine des Bétons Industriels v. The Republic of Senegal, Jurisdictional Decision, ICSID Case No. ARB/82/1, February 25, 1988, **96**

Suez, Sociedad General de Aguas de Barcelona S.A., Vivendi Universal S.A. and AWG Group Ltd. v. The Argentine Republic, Decision on Liability, ICSID Case No. ARB/03/19, July 30, 2010, **138**

Suez, Sociedad General de Aguas de Barcelona S.A., Vivendi Universal S.A. and AWG Group Ltd. v. The Argentine Republic, Decision on Liability - Separate Opinion of Pedro Nikken, ICSID Case No. ARB/03/19, July 30, 2010, **138**

Teco Guatemala Holdings LLC v. The Republic of Guatemala, Award, ICSID Case No. ARB/10/17, December 19, 2013, **158**

The Government of Sudan v. Sudan People's Liberation Movement/Army, Final Award, PCA, July 22, 2009, **189**

Tokio Tokelés v. Ukraine, Procedural Order No. 1, ICSID Case No. ARB/02/18, July 1, 2003, **123**

Toto Costruzioni Generali S.p.A. v. The Republic of Lebanon, Decision on Jurisdiction, ICSID Case No. ARB/07/12, September 11, 2009, **123**

Victor Pey Casado and Fundación Presidente Allende v. The Republic of Chile, Decision on Provisional Matters, ICSID Case No. ARB/98/2, September 25, 2001, **122**

Waste Management, Inc. v. United Mexican States, Award, ICSID Case No. ARB/00/3, April 30, 2004, **47**

Wena Hotels Limited v. Arab Republic of Egypt, Decision on the Application by the Arab Republic of Egypt for Annulment of the Arbitral Award dated December 8, 2000, ICSID Case No. ARB/98/4, February 5, 2002, **184**

White Industries Australia Limited v. The Republic of India, Award, UNCITRAL, November 30, 2011, **64, 69–73, 84, 90, 95, 106, 109, 120, 210, 215**

World Duty Free Company Limited v. The Republic of Kenya, Award, ICSID Case No. ARB/00/7, October 4, 2006, **93**

Yukos Universal Limited (Isle of Man) v. The Russian Federation, Final Award, PCA Case No. AA 227, July 18, 2014, **42**

Index

A

Acta iure gestionis, 40
Acta iure imperii, 40
Agent theory, 66, 94
Annulment, 2, 73, 75, 76, 99, 108, 156, 182–193
Antisuit injunctions, 123
Appellate review, 190–196
Association clause, 74, 77–79, 84, 99, 100, 105, 204, 210
Autonomous theory, 66

C

Calvo-Doctrine, 34
Consistency, 45, 191, 192, 194, 196
Consuetudo, 6, 21, 174
Contractual theory, 66
Crystallization, 71, 79, 81, 82, 84, 90, 227, 230

D

De Jure Belli ac Pacis, 146
Developing states, 164–168
Diversity school, 173
Doctrine of separability, 91–94, 102, 177, 216
Double keyhole approach, 60, 88

E

Effet utile, 12
Expressio unius est exclusio alterius, 46–47

Expropriation, 26, 29, 33–35, 49, 93, 119, 127, 201, 227, 230

F

Failure to state reasons, 187–190
Fair and equitable treatment, 30, 32, 34, 48, 119, 138
Fork in the road clause, 123
Free Trade Agreement (FTA), 26, 28–29, 56
Full protection and security, 26, 32, 48

H

Hull-Formula, 34
Hybrid theory, 66

I

Internationalization clause, 35

J

Jurisdictional theory, 66

K

Kompetenz-Kompetenz, 55

L

Law-making, 5, 19–20, 55
Legitimacy, 2, 11, 18, 47–51, 54, 55, 132, 135, 141, 143, 150, 160, 164, 169, 172, 181, 182, 189, 192, 193, 200

Index

Leviathan, 145, 146

M

Manifest excess of powers, 186–187
Most favored nation clause, 26, 31, 47

O

Offer to arbitrate, 2, 39, 40, 93, 175–180
Opinio juris, 6, 21
Ordinary meaning-rule, 8–10, 15, 16, 84, 106

P

Policy space, 157–162, 168
Precedent, 17, 43–46, 102, 103, 109, 110, 130, 131, 141, 172, 180–182, 197, 209–231
Preliminary rulings, 28, 194–199, 202, 204
Privity, 50, 177
Pro-enforcement bias, 113
Pro-investor bias, 135–137, 166–167
Public interest, 40–42, 131, 141, 157–162, 168, 194
Public policy, 2, 33, 41, 93, 112, 174
Purposive interpretation, 11, 13, 137–140

R

Ratione materiae, 58
Responsibility to protect, 25, 168

Rule of law, 103, 159, 162–164, 168, 182, 199

S

Salini-test, 61–64, 73, 100, 160
Separability, 91–94, 102, 177, 216
Social Contract, 145
Sovereignty, 24, 25, 41, 144–157, 159, 166, 168, 175, 195, 204
Special-meaning rule, 15–16
Stabilization clause, 35
Stare decisis, 72, 102, 103, 161

T

Transformation clause, 82, 84, 87, 89, 90, 100–102, 104, 105, 210
Travaux préparatoires, 16–17, 46
Two Treatises of Government, 145

U

Umbrella-clause, 26, 32–33, 40, 127–131
Unilateral acts, 175–180
Unity of investment doctrine, 95–102, 104, 210
Unity school, 173

V

Vienna Convention on the Law of Treaties (VCLT), 7–17, 105–107, 172–173, 179

INTERNATIONAL ARBITRATION LAW LIBRARY

1. Moshe Hirsch, *The Arbitration Mechanism of the International Center for the Settlement of Investment Disputes*, 1993 (ISBN 07-923-1993-1).
2. Aida B. Avanessian, *Iran-United States Claims Tribunal in Action*, 1993 (ISBN 18-533-3902-4).
3. Isaak I. Dore, *The UNCITRAL Framework for Arbitration in Contemporary Perspective*, 1993 (ISBN 18-533-3573-8).
4. Vesna Lazić, *Insolvency Proceedings and Commercial Arbitration*, 1998 (ISBN 90-411-1115-8).
5. Joachim Frick, *Arbitration in Complex International Contracts*, 2001 (ISBN 90-411-1662-1).
6. Katherine Lynch, *The Forces of Economic Globalization: Challenges to the Regime of International Commercial Arbitration*, 2003 (ISBN 90-411-1994-9).
7. Christoph Liebscher, *The Healthy Award: Challenge in International Commercial Arbitration*, 2003 (ISBN 90-411-2011-4).
8. Hamid G. Gharavi, *The International Effectiveness of the Annulment of an Arbitral Award*, 2003 (ISBN 90-411-1717-2).
9. Abdulhay Sayed, *Corruption in International Trade and Commercial Arbitration*, 2004 (ISBN 90-411-2236-2).
10. Gabrielle Kaufmann-Kohler & Thomas Schultz, *Online Dispute Resolution: Challenges for Contemporary Justice*, 2004 (ISBN 90-411-2318-0).
11. Christopher R. Drahozal & Richard W. Naimark (eds), *Towards a Science of International Arbitration: Collected Empirical Research*, 2005 (ISBN 90-411-2322-9).
12. Ali Yeşilirmak, *Provisional Measures in International Commercial Arbitration*, 2005 (ISBN 90-411-2353-9).
13. Christian Bühring-Uhle, *Arbitration and Mediation in International Business*, second revised edition, 2006 (ISBN 978-9-041-12256-8).
14. Bernard Hanotiau, *Complex Arbitrations: Multiparty, Multicontract, Multiissue and Class Actions*, 2006 (ISBN 978-9-041-12442-5).
15. Loukas A. Mistelis & Julian D.M. Lew (eds), *Pervasive Problems in International Arbitration*, 2006 (ISBN 978-9-041-12450-0).
16. Julian D.M. Lew & Loukas A. Mistelis (eds), *Arbitration Insights – Twenty Years of the Annual Lecture of the School of International Arbitration, Sponsored by Freshfields Bruckhaus Deringer*, 2006 (ISBN 978-9-041-12606-1).
17. Mark Kantor, *Valuation for Arbitration: Compensation Standards, Valuation Methods and Expert Evidence*, 2008 (ISBN 978-9-041-12735-8).
18. Christoph Brunner, *Force Majeure and Hardship under General Contract Principles: Exemption for Non-Performance in International Arbitration*, 2009 (ISBN 978-90-411-2792-1).

19. Loukas A. Mistelis & Stavros L. Brekoulakis (eds), *Arbitrability: International & Comparative Perspectives,* 2009 (ISBN 978-90-411-2730-3).
20. Sam Luttrell, *Bias Challenges in International Commercial Arbitration: The Need for a 'Real Danger' Test,* 2009 (ISBN 978-90-411-3191-1).
21. Monique Sasson, *Substantive Law in Investment Treaty Arbitration: The Unsettled Relationship between International Law and Municipal Law,* 2010 (ISBN 978-90-411-3223-9).
22. Ileana M. Smeureanu, *Confidentiality in International Commercial Arbitration,* 2011 (ISBN 978-90-411-3226-0).
23. Won Kidane, *China-Africa Dispute Settlement: The Law, Economics and Culture of Arbitration,* 2011 (ISBN 978-90-411-3674-9).
24. Karel Daele, *Challenge and Disqualification of Arbitrators in International Arbitration,* 2012 (ISBN 978-90-411-3799-9).
25. Crina Baltag, *The Energy Charter Treaty: The Notion of Investor,* 2012 (ISBN 978-90-411-3428-8).
26. Alexandra Diehl, *The Core Standard of International Investment Protection: Fair and Equitable Treatment,* 2012 (ISBN 978-90-411-3869-9).
27. Manuel Indlekofer, *International Arbitration and the Permanent Court of Arbitration,* 2013 (ISBN 978-90-411-4766-0).
28. Günther J. Horvath & Stephan Wilske (eds), *Guerrilla Tactics in International Arbitration*, 2013 (ISBN 978-90-411-4002-9).
29. Albert Badia, *Piercing the Veil of State Enterprises in International Arbitration*, 2014 (ISBN 978-90-411-5162-9).
30. Nadja Erk, *Parallel Proceedings in International Arbitration: A Comparative European Perspective*, 2014 (ISBN 978-90-411-5264-0).
31. Simon Vorburger, *International Arbitration and Cross-Border Insolvency: Comparative Perspectives*, 2014 (ISBN 978-90-411-5419-4).
32. Ahmad Ali Ghouri, *Interaction and Conflict of Treaties in Investment Arbitration,* 2015 (ISBN 978-90-411-5417-0).
33. Reto Marghitola, *Document Production in International Arbitration,* 2015 (ISBN 978-90-411-5159-9).
34. Alfonso Gómez-Acebo, *Party-Appointed Arbitrators in International Commercial Arbitration,* 2016 (ISBN 978-90-411-6671-5).
35. Jonas von Goeler, *Third-Party Funding in International Arbitration and Its Impact on Procedure,* 2016 (ISBN 978-90-411-5015-8).
36. Dean Lewis, *The Interpretation and Uniformity of the UNCITRAL Model Law on International Commercial Arbitration: Focusing on Australia, Hong Kong and Singapore,* 2016 (ISBN 978-90-411-6700-2).
37. Stavros Brekoulakis, Julian D.M. Lew & Loukas Mistelis (eds), *The Evolution and Future of International Arbitration,* 2016 (ISBN 978-90-411-7004-0).
38. Rémy Gerbay, *The Functions of Arbitral Institutions*, 2016 (ISBN 978-90-411-6217-5).
39. Maximilian Clasmeier, *Arbitral Awards as Investments: Treaty Interpretation and the Dynamics of International Investment Law,* 2017 (ISBN 978-90-411-8357-6).